T0360739

Social Choice, Agency, Inclusiveness and Capabilities

The capability approach is a versatile framework rooted on issues of justice and multidimensional assessment of quality of life developed in the 1980s as an alternative approach to prevailing mainstream development ideas focused narrowly on economic development. Most closely associated with the work of Amartya Sen, it has become of great interest to development scholars from a variety of different disciplines. Much has already been done exploring the conceptual foundations of the capability approach and discussing Sen's contribution to the field, but few books have explored the links between social choice (another field with rich contributions by Sen) and human development issues. Featuring many of the world's leading experts on social choice theory and capability indicators, *Social Choice, Agency, Inclusiveness and Capabilities* combines these interrelated themes into one volume and fully explores the relevance of social choice to human development.

FLAVIO COMIM is Associate Professor of Economics and Ethics at IQS School of Management at the Ramon Llull University, Barcelona, and a research associate at the Von Hügel Institute at the University of Cambridge.

P. B. ANAND is Professor of Public Policy and Sustainable Development and Head of the Department of Peace Studies and International Development at the University of Bradford.

SHAILAJA FENNELL is Professor of Regional Transformation and Economic Security and Resilience, Department of Land Economy, and Director, Centre of South Asian Studies, at the University of Cambridge.

Social Choice, Agency, Inclusiveness and Capabilities

Edited by

FLAVIO COMIM
IQS School of Management, Ramon Llull University, and University of Cambridge

P. B. ANAND
University of Bradford

SHAILAJA FENNELL
University of Cambridge

CAMBRIDGE
UNIVERSITY PRESS

CAMBRIDGE
UNIVERSITY PRESS

Shaftesbury Road, Cambridge CB2 8EA, United Kingdom

One Liberty Plaza, 20th Floor, New York, NY 10006, USA

477 Williamstown Road, Port Melbourne, VIC 3207, Australia

314–321, 3rd Floor, Plot 3, Splendor Forum, Jasola District Centre, New Delhi – 110025, India

103 Penang Road, #05–06/07, Visioncrest Commercial, Singapore 238467

Cambridge University Press is part of Cambridge University Press & Assessment, a department of the University of Cambridge.

We share the University's mission to contribute to society through the pursuit of education, learning and research at the highest international levels of excellence.

www.cambridge.org
Information on this title: www.cambridge.org/9781009232708

DOI: 10.1017/9781009232678

© Cambridge University Press & Assessment 2024

This publication is in copyright. Subject to statutory exception and to the provisions of relevant collective licensing agreements, no reproduction of any part may take place without the written permission of Cambridge University Press & Assessment.

First published 2024

A catalogue record for this publication is available from the British Library

Library of Congress Cataloging-in-Publication Data
Names: Comim, Flavio editor. | Anand, P. B., editor. | Fennell, Shailaja, 1964– author.
Title: Social choice, agency, inclusiveness and capabilities / edited by Flavio Comim, University of Cambridge, P.B. Anand, University of Bradford, Shailaja Fennell, University of Cambridge.
Description: 1 Edition. | New York, NY : Cambridge University Press, [2024] |
Identifiers: LCCN 2023022425 | ISBN 9781009232708 (hardback) | ISBN 9781009232678 (ebook)
Subjects: LCSH: Social choice. | Capabilities approach (Social sciences) | Social psychology. | Developmental psychology.
Classification: LCC HB846.8 .S634 2024 | DDC 302/.13–dc23/enng/20230731
LC record available at https://lccn.loc.gov/2023022425

ISBN 978-1-009-23270-8 Hardback

Cambridge University Press & Assessment has no responsibility for the persistence or accuracy of URLs for external or third-party internet websites referred to in this publication and does not guarantee that any content on such websites is, or will remain, accurate or appropriate.

Contents

Part II   Inclusiveness, Social and Individual Agency

Part III   Social Choice and Capabilities in Action

Figures

Tables

Contributors

OLADELE AKOGUN is an education consultant currently working with the International Rescue Committee, New York.

RICHARD BRUNNER is a Research Associate at the Centre for Disability Research, School of Social and Political Sciences, University of Glasgow.

JOHN CAMERON is an Emeritus Associate Professor in the International Institute of Social Studies at Erasmus University Rotterdam.

ANA ESTEFANÍA CARBALLO is an Honorary Research Fellow in the School of Geography, Earth and Atmospheric Sciences at the University of Melbourne and Research and Programme Manager at Transparency International Australia.

SIAKA CISSÉ is Head of the Research Department at the National Institute of Statistics (Institut National de la Statistique: INSTAT), Bamako, Mali.

INA CONRADIE is a Research Fellow in the Institute for Social Development, University of the Western Cape, Cape Town.

REIKO GOTOH is a Professor in the Faculty of Economics and the Advanced Comprehensive Research Organization at Teikyo University, Tokyo.

JAY DRYDYK is a Professor in the Department of Philosophy at Carleton University, Ottawa.

WULF GAERTNER is a Professor Emeritus in the Department of Economics at the University of Osnabrück and in the Centre for Philosophy of Natural and Social Science at the London School of Economics and Political Science.

GAY MEEKS wrote her chapter while Senior Research Associate in the Centre of Development Studies at the University of Cambridge.

TADASHI HIRAI wrote his chapter while a research associate and Affiliated Lecturer in the Centre of Development Studies at the University of Cambridge.

HIDEYUKI KOBAYASHI is Associate Professor of Health Economics at the University of Kochi.

MOZAFFAR QIZILBASH is Honorary Professor in the Departments of Economics and Related Studies and Philosophy at the University of York.

CLAUDINE SAUVAIN-DUGERDIL is Professor Emeritus in the Institute of Demography and Socioeconomics at the University of Geneva.

JACQUES TAMIN is an Honorary Senior Lecturer in Occupational Medicine at the Centre for Occupational and Environmental Health, University of Manchester.

MICHAEL WATTS is an education consultant currently working with the Common Heritage Foundation, Abuja.

JONATHAN WARNER is a Research Fellow at the Center for Faith and Human Flourishing, LCC International University, Klaipėda, Lithuania, and a Research Associate at the Von Hugel Institute, St Edmund's College, University of Cambridge.

NICK WATSON is Chair of Disability Studies and Director of the Centre for Disability Research, School of Social and Political Studies, University of Glasgow.

NAFISA WAZIRI is an education consultant currently working with Ecorys in the United Kingdom.

Preface and Acknowledgements

This book is a result of the second and third Cambridge Capability Conferences (CCCs), held in 2017 and 2018. It is a continuation of a new phase of capability conferences in Cambridge, following the early Capability Conferences in the first half of the 2000s, which preceded the creation of the Human Development and Capability Association (HDCA). It can be seen as follow-up of a previous publication, *New Frontiers of the Capability Approach* (2018), co-edited by the same group of editors. It marks new perspectives in the way that the approach can be used to tackle a wide range of social issues related to its foundations, operationalization and applications. For the 2017 CCC we had the honour to have Professor Wulf Gaertner from the University of Osnabruck, one of the leading social choice theorists in the world, as our keynote speaker. The main objective of that conference was to examine social choice theory (SCT) as the main engine of Amartya Sen's approach. For the 2018 CCC we had the privilege of having Professor Mozaffar Qizilbash from the University of York, a distinguished capability scholar, to deliver the conference keynote speech. The main focus in this third conference was on discussing new perspectives of the capability approach, exploring concrete debates related to sustainability, poverty and inequality. We were very fortunate to have renowned capability scholars as participants of these two conferences, including the keynote speaker of our first CCC, Dr Gay Meeks. We are very grateful to all our keynote speakers for their participation. During these two conferences Professor Sen kindly accepted our invitation to come during the main break for a cup of tea and to catch up with old and new friends. We are very grateful for his time and consideration.

Putting together a small selection of papers to include in this book was an extremely hard task, given the high quality of submitted papers. We privileged the elaboration of a homogeneous narrative, selecting chapters after very rigorous scrutiny and detailed work, putting the different pieces of a complex puzzle together. We would like to thank a group of eminent capability scholars who wrote referee reports, including Bina Agarwal, Paul Anand, Izete Bagolin, Jérôme Ballet, Morten Byskov, Mario Biggeri, Mihály Borsi, Tania Burchard, Cristina Devecchi, Marc Fleurbaey, Des Gasper, Caroline Hart, Pushpam Kumar, Enrica Chiappero Martinetti, Santosh Mehrotra, Mathias Nebel, Teresa Herrera Rendon, Rosie Vaughan and Andrea Vigorito. These reports were invaluable, and we appreciate the expertise, time and attention that these scholars have dedicated to this project. We are in debt to our editor, Phil Good, who continues to believe in the value of our endeavours and has supported this second book based on our Capability Conferences.

This book should be of interest to capability scholars who wish to reflect further on themes related to Sen's work on SCT and its links to the capability approach. It can also be of interest to social choice scholars who wish to consider broader issues related to SCT, and in general to anyone interested in human development and its links to the capability approach.

1 | Introduction: social choice, agency, inclusiveness and capabilities

FLAVIO COMIM, P. B. ANAND AND
SHAILAJA FENNELL

Social choice theory (SCT) is one of the least appreciated elements of Amartya Sen's capability approach. Not that he has not alerted us many times about the importance of SCT for his work. As he put it in his Nobel Prize lecture (Sen, 2002: 66–7), 'The Royal Swedish Academy of Sciences referred to "welfare economics" as the general field of my work for which the award was given, and separated out three particular areas: social choice, distribution and poverty. While I have indeed been occupied, in various ways, with these different subjects, it is social choice theory, pioneeringly formulated in its modern form by Arrow (1951), that provides a general approach to the evaluation of, and choice over, alternative social possibilities (including, *inter alia*, the assessment of social welfare, inequality and poverty).' SCT has also figured prominently in his work throughout the years, such as *Collective Choice and Social Welfare* (Sen, 1970), *Choice, Welfare and Measurement* (1982), *Resources, Values and Development* (1984) and *Rationality and Freedom* (2002), not to mention tens of papers on the theme. His expanded edition of *Collective Choice and Social Welfare* (2017) is also testimony to the importance of SCT to his work. Moreover, two of the key influences on Sen were social choice theorists, namely the Marquis de Condorcet and Kenneth Arrow, and several of his articles interact with leading social choice theorists such as Allan Gibbard, Wulf Gaertner, Peter Hamond, Eric Maskin, Prasanta Pattanaik, Maurice Salles and Kotaro Suzumura, to mention just a few.

But social choice is not an easy field, particularly because many of its issues are solved through axioms, lemmas, proofs, theorems and the use of a mathematical language (centred on analysis and topology) that makes it harder for scholars without this specific background to engage with it. A quick look at the *Social Choice and Welfare* journal should be enough to dispel any doubts about the mathematical hurdles it is necessary to overcome in order to be able to enter this field. In addition, it is important to note that the links between Sen's own version of SCT and his 'welfare economics' are far from trivial. Sen is a thinker who has used his SCT to engage with political science, public economics and ethics, particularly theories of justice. He has pushed the boundaries of interdisciplinary work as very few have done in social sciences. His own SCT research agenda covers a wide range of issues, including variations of Arrow's theorem, such as the impossibility of the Paretian liberal, the role of rights, the use of different informational bases, equity rules, the role of different rules of aggregation on social outcomes, the importance of processes, etc. By engaging in these different aspects of social decisions with searching questions, Sen has enlarged the frontiers of social choice beyond the limits of its traditional domain. He has invited us to consider the role of individual agency, autonomy and moral sentiments in how collective choices are produced. This broader and interdisciplinary notion of social choice is the leitmotiv of this book.

Social choice is about how to arrive at a decision at the level of a collective or group of individuals when such individuals differ in how they prioritize the options available. From simple problems about two individuals who need to cooperate to solve a problem that affects both of them to problems at the level of teams, departments, neighbourhoods, communities, cities, provinces, nations and even globally, social choice situations occur everywhere. A deeper understanding of social choice helps us to appreciate the difficulties in solving coordination problems and why public and common good challenges often remain tricky, demanding or 'wicked' problems. We think social choice should be part of the core curriculum of all social sciences and policy sciences and in business schools for these powerful insights. We hope that the various chapters in this book contribute to unpacking some of this complexity and advancing our understanding of social choice.

The book is divided into three parts. The first part, titled 'Social Choice and Capabilities', sets the scene, interacting more explicitly with SCT, from its key elements towards a broader view of social choice embedded in human development. The second, called 'Inclusiveness, Social and Individual Agency', opens the black box of Sen's approach, delving into his discussions of moral and political philosophy and psychology to examine some of its key analytical categories. It includes contributions that expand the frontiers of Sen's approach. Finally, the third part, titled 'Social Choice and Capabilities in Action', shows how different empirical contexts can enlarge our understanding of social choice from a human development perspective.

Social choice is a demanding field, but Wulf Gaertner (also known for his outstanding *A Primer in Social Choice Theory*, 2009) puts us at ease and brings us to the heart of the subject in an engaging but sympathetic manner with his chapter 'The many facets of social choice theory', allowing us to understand how Sen's work fits this very complex research agenda. One can appreciate the debates about the impacts of different aggregation methods, contextualizing the links between individual rights, the concept of freedom and the choice of functioning bundles. An important, though unsettling, conclusion that emerges from this literature is that there are no ideal aggregation rules for collective choice. Gaertner also shows how SCT can be applied in the generalized game form to take into account the issue of the interdependence of actions and strategies between different individuals. More importantly, he examines a typical element of Sen's SCT related to the procedural nature of individual and social choice, discussing Sen's (1997) concepts of 'chooser dependence' and 'menu dependence'. This contribution would already be invaluable but he pushes further the boundaries of the discipline by adding an original proposal for comparing and measuring capability sets.

This chapter should be enough to convince readers that Sen's capability approach has a very specific function within SCT, namely to broaden informational spaces in normative evaluations that, as such, cannot encompass Sen's thought – a point also highlighted by Mozaffar Qizilbash and Flavio Comim in this book. Comim in his chapter, entitled 'Beyond capabilities? Sen's social choice approach and the generalizability assumption', links Sen's social choice roots to his motivational and informational pluralism and argues for the importance of explicitly acknowledging the need to work more systematically with the different informational spaces. In particular, he shows how there is a generalizability assumption behind Sen's principle of working with broad informational spaces, and puts forward a simple method to compare and conciliate different informational spaces as part of a coherent evaluation story. By doing so, it is possible to see how separated critiques of different informational spaces make an operationalization of the approach much harder, and how putting them together makes this task more manageable. The use of a method does not mean that practical judgement and contextual deliberation should be excluded from the picture; quite the opposite. It allows the informational conditions for handling them in a systematic and fair way.

Shailaja Fennell in her chapter, 'Examining the challenge of communication in diffusing innovative education programmes: an analysis drawing on public choice, social choice and capability framings', shows how SCT can be seen from both a narrow and a broader perspective, depending on whether we take the structure of preferences as given or as codetermined. She analyses an empirical case of an innovative educational policy intervention (the Activity Based Learning [ABL] programme in Tamil Nadu, India) that was not able to successfully scale up due to its particular collective choice mechanisms. This empirical illustration allows her to demonstrate how successful policy diffusion depends on how political and economic features shape social choice mechanisms. In the real world, social choice might involve different stakeholders, and their agendas and motivations play an important part in whether an intervention succeeds. In this case it included the large number of state and local officials, led by the education commissioner and supported by trained teachers, teacher training institutes, the city corporation, local schools, and education officers of UNICEF India. Context also matters. Issues of communication, consensus building, freedom and institutional change might define whether social choice can be emancipatory, as usually assumed by Sen, or oppressive. Thus, a well-designed programme might not be able to be scaled up due to particular features of the social choice mechanisms in question.

Cities can play an important role in promoting freedoms and capabilities. However, cities can also magnify and ratchet up inequalities. In the context of Sustainable Development Goal 11, P. B. Anand argues in his chapter, 'Nudging the capabilities for a sustainable city? When the libertarian paternalist meets the Paretian liberal', that framing the issues of sustainable cities to be essentially problems of social choice is fundamental. The chapter builds on the idea of the Paretian liberal and identifies six key types of injustices or impossibilities that must be addressed in the pursuit of becoming a sustainable city. Three of these are intra-generational and the other three are inter-generational. One concerns the injustices within the current boundaries of the city; another set concerns injustices caused by the city's ecological and resource footprint on regions beyond the city; and the third set of injustices concerns the transfer of impacts around the world due to global supply chains. After setting up the social choice approach to understanding these six injustices or impossibilities, Anand develops two lines of critical enquiry: one focuses on the idea of smart cities and the ethical and procedural challenges to social choice, and the second on the idea of nudges from the behavioural public policy themes influenced by the work of Richard Thaler and Cass Sunstein, who describe nudges as a part of policy interventions rooted in libertarian paternalism. Various examples of nudges are briefly discussed. Drawing from the conditions of Sen's social choice theory, the chapter calls for a multidimensional and pluralist approach, called the PULSE approach, for cities in their pursuit of becoming sustainable and to address these six injustices: P stands for the Pareto requirement that, if a citizen prefers X to Y, then the society must also prefer X to Y; U is unrestricted domain; L is liberalism; S stands for society, meaning a concern for the freedoms and well-being of other members of the society; and E is a concern for environmental ethics and a commitment of fairness to future generations.

Identity perceptions are key to social choice, as shown by Michael Watts, Nafisa Waziri and Oladele Akogun. In their chapter, 'Social choice and research capacity strengthening in Nigeria: insights from the field', they evaluate an educational project in Nigeria that provides a different context from that assessed by Fennell. The focus here is on the conditions that prevail in many developing countries: low status of the teaching profession, unqualified teachers struggling with limited incentives and poor education standards. Moreover, social choice mechanisms have been characterized by mutual intra-sectoral mistrust, little intra-sectoral collaboration and the prevalence of stereotypes. The authors show that the feeling of belonging to social groups is important for granting individuals a sense of their own social worth that is fundamental to the way that they establish individual and social priorities. Together with Fennell's contribution, they demonstrate how Arrow's distinction between tastes (individual preferences about their own good) and values (their collective choice about the social good) is more complicated than it seems on paper. In order to define their values, people go through different processes of social categorization and distinctions (for instance, between in-groups and out-groups). Social identities influence social choices through mechanisms of participation in collective decision-making processes.

The issue of inclusiveness is at the centre of this debate, and it impacts not only on the kinds of arguments that should be privileged in characterizing social choice mechanisms but also on the use of indicators for evaluating their results. The second part, entitled 'Inclusiveness, Social and Individual Agency', looks more deeply at Sen's approach, investigating his analysis of moral and political philosophy and psychology and unpicking some of its key ideas. Mozaffar Qizilbash discusses in his chapter, 'In defence of inclusiveness: on sustainable human development, capability and indicators of progress', the concept of inclusionary strategies. He argues that these strategies are important as a means to a basis of agreement between people who hold different views. He explains that a view can be inclusive either by adopting vague terms, which can be completed by different people, or by being open-ended, or by accommodating particular views under a general framework or by focusing on overlaps between different views. It seems that, in the cases reported by Fennell and Watts, Waziri and Akogun, there were elements that prevented reasoned consensus, not because of people's different views but because of the characteristics of the social mechanisms in place. Qizilbash illustrates the importance of inclusiveness for the cases of sustainability challenges and the Human Development Index (HDI), demonstrating how the capability approach incorporates some of the inclusionary strategies described by him. He also refers to 'Sen's desire to be inclusive' and to 'Sen's anti-exclusionary tendency'. This illuminates the place and the role of the capability approach within Sen's larger SCT. The debate on inclusiveness owes as much to Kenneth Arrow as it does to John Rawls. It is hard to imagine what we might be discussing today if they, together with Sen, had not participated in a joint seminar at Harvard University back in 1968/69.

Sen's desire to be inclusive is clearly manifested in his informational pluralism and in his willingness to talk about a richer picture of individuals' moral sentiments. Gay Meeks delves into the roots of Sen's pluralism in her chapter, entitled 'Exploring Sen on self-interest and commitment', by analysing one of the core conceptual distinctions in Sen's work, namely between self-interest and commitment. One might speculate whether SCT should always see individuals as grounding their actions in self-interested behaviour (even when they might consider how the welfare of others impacts on their welfare) or, rather, should allow space for them to pursue goals beyond their own welfare. Understanding this distinction is not trivial. It is worth emphasizing that the categories of commitment are important to Sen's work because acts grounded in commitment are pursued independently from the promotion of one's welfare (differently from acts grounded in sympathy or other forms of self-interest). She offers the examples of a 'dating conundrum' and of Brexit to show how these different concepts can be applied. It is clear from this discussion that individual and social choice depend on our moral sentiments and our emotions, and that the way that individuals and societies combine them is like a recipe for a complicated dish.

John Cameron argues just that in his chapter, 'Incorporating an emotional dimension in the capability approach', namely that emotions matter for our individual and collective choices and that, as such, the capability approach should acknowledge it more extensively. We can appreciate his argument both as a continuation of Meeks' analysis and Qizilbash's plea for inclusiveness. Indeed, if we were to omit the emotional dimension of our individual and collective decision making, we would get to an incomplete account of a fully human existence. Cameron explores in his chapter five views of emotions: (1) as another reality; (2) as the key to progress; (3) as an obstacle to progress; (4) as essential to being a communicating human; and (5) as key to understanding power. The importance of communicative agency cannot be overstated. Indeed, emotions are an essential aspect of human communication, essential for public reason and collective choice. In several examples discussed in this book emotions are an essential ingredient of the social choice mechanism behind certain public policies. At the very end, Cameron offers a framework to integrate an emotional dimension into the capability approach. He shows how emotional interactions may either enhance or inhibit collective decision making.

One of the key concepts in this debate is about human dignity. Several concerns raised above about informational pluralism, inclusiveness, agency, moral categories (such as commitment) and the role of emotions in our individual and social choices can be materialized when examining the concept of human dignity. Taking categories of rights into SCT, as explained by Gaertner, might be a complex conceptual issue when operationalized into criteria of basic needs or subsistence. This is no different for the issue of human dignity.

One question that illustrates this complexity is: should human dignity concentrate on the lowest ends or at the highest ends of human existence? Jay Drydyk argues in his chapter, entitled 'Sufficiency re-examined', that public reason and social choice should not be limited to the issue of what priorities are defined by different societies but at which levels they should be established. This is not a minor issue. Indeed, Drydyk suggests that standards should be optimal rather than minimal. He puts forward the concept of the 'optimum social capability' to signal the highest zones of the most valuable capabilities that can be provided by any given society, given its productive capacity. This debate about the threshold for sufficiency can provide a point of focus for the reasons that people have to support not only those below certain threshold levels but those above them. This is a key issue in a world of informational pluralism, whereby some people might be seen as being above certain thresholds (say, resources) but not others (such as rights or capabilities). This can also raise a debate about the so called 'diminution thesis', according to which, once people have enough, our reasons to support them are weaker.

The fact is that individual and social choice can be much more complex when confronted with all the peculiarities and subtleties offered by real-life contexts. This is certainly the case when some psychological aspects related to individual and social choices are taken into account. Psychology is little acknowledged by SCT, which takes it for granted that people are more often than not aware about the outcomes of their choices. However, adaptative preferences and internalization processes can bias people's judgements and their corresponding tastes and values. Tadashi Hirai in his chapter, 'Adaptive preferences versus internalization in deprivation: a conceptual comparison between the capability approach and self-determination theory', invites us to consider how people form goals according to their intrinsic or extrinsic objectives by comparing the use of subjective information in the capability approach vis-à-vis self-determination theory (SDT). He finds that there are important parallels between SDT's notions of autonomy and relatedness and Martha Nussbaum's central capabilities of practical reason and sense of affiliation. Thus, a refined concept of internalization allows us to distinguish the cases in which people's extrinsic motivation is due to their will compared to cases of compliance to external regulations. This means that the perceived locus of causality is key to characterize people's choices. Moreover, Hirai shows that people facing external deprivation can also satisfy psychological needs in their search for a eudaimonic life. It seems that inclusiveness strategies need to examine the psychological aspects of the poor and the non-poor in the processes of collective choice.

It is also important to note that social choice does not take place in a social vacuum. It depends on the particular social structures in which individuals are embedded, and, as argued by Hirai, it also depends on how individuals internalize them. However, these structural elements are normally ignored by the ethical individualism cultivated by SCT and the capability approach. Ina Conradie disputes this standard narrative in her chapter, 'Enriching agency in the capability approach through social theory contributions', advocating the use of social theory for better exploring the links between agency, moral sentiments and collective choices. She argues for an enriched view of agency (as does Meeks, although they follow different strategies), taking into account how people's objectives depend on their autonomy and personal liberty. She criticizes Sen for not conceptualizing the notion of 'interconnectedness between individuals' (a recurrent critique of the capability approach, it has to be said) and searches for alternatives in Anthony Giddens' structuration theory, Margaret Archer's morphogenesis, Pierre Bourdieu's habitus and Jürgen Habermas's communicative action. It is clear that the relational ontology of the capability approach is in tension with its SCT roots. One possible way forward is through the concept of reflexivity, which can be used to better characterize agency.

Among the most important structural factors we find those related to the economy and technological progress. As Jonathan Warner discusses in his chapter, 'Creativity and capabilities: a problem of change and uncertainty?', technological change influences the kind of productive effect that people have, and, as such, it has the potential to shape people's identities (a discussion that overlaps with the one suggested by Watts, Waziri and Akogun, and is also discussed with regard to smart cities by Anand). Together, the economy and technological change open up new perspectives about what becomes valuable in our lives. More specifically, for Warner, innovation might render some valuable kinds of lives unfeasible. As he asks, 'If redundancy, deskilling and automation make many types of work superfluous, what will a valuable and meaningful life look like?' Should artificial intelligence turn large shares of human labour into an obsolete factor of production, humanity would have to stop to discuss all over again the meaning of a productive and useful life. Warner invites us to consider a paradox, asking how human creativity (no doubt an expression of human agency) can influence technological change, which, ultimately, can undermine the types of lives that we might have reason to value, eroding agency as we know it. If current technological progress, based on advances in process automation, machine learning and deep learning, revolutionizes labour markets and the workplace in a decade, how can we resignify the meaning of autonomy and the values behind our collective choices?

Some of these questions are meant to stimulate further reflection and are not intended to produce definite answers. But they do provide a broad picture about the sorts of elements that could be considered in a broader view of SCT and the capability approach applied to the social, economic and political issues that are key for human development. Once these conceptual elements have been explored we then move on to the last part of the book, 'Social Choice and Capabilities in Action', which offers a rich discussion of emblematic cases that provide different answers to social choice challenges.

Hideyuki Kobayashi and Reiko Gotoh in their chapter, 'Measuring the independence of "dependent" persons based on the capability approach', examine the individual and social choices involved in the context of elderly people who are living in local communities or are dependent on home-caring services in Japan. The collective choice problem involved in providing social services for the elderly, taking into account ideals of equality, respect for people's existential independence and an acknowledgement of human suffering vis-à-vis the costs of diseases and disabilities, is far from trivial. This problem is not simply about efficiency but about distribution: how should these costs be distributed between individuals and society? In order to address this problem they develop a 'fractal structure of capability', together with iso-cost curves mapped against the space of sub-functionings. They show how the choices involved depend on people's utilization abilities and their corresponding capability frontiers. Kobayashi and Gotoh push the analytical boundaries of the capability approach to demonstrate what the core analytical parameters might be that could enter the arena of the public debate. How these arguments would perform would depend on how they were phrased, what concepts would be used to communicate them to the public, their cultural context, levels chosen, etc.

One context in which cultural values can be very influential in shaping collective choices is the context of some indigenous populations in the Andean region, in Latin America. Ana Estefanía Carballo in her chapter, 'Indigenous challenges to the capability approach: a relational ontology of community and sustainability', examines the case of 'buen vivir' ('good living', in Spanish), which represents a strong communal dimension in defining social values and collective decision-making. It brings to the front the concept of the good life as an ethics of sufficiency (differently from what was argued by Drydyk) and an ethics of sustainability, based on the centrality of the notion of community. She argues how our preferences and tastes (in the Arrowian sense) depend on institutions such as collective/private ownership or property rights or the characteristics of the current system of exchange of a certain society. From this perspective, there are intangible elements of social choice that belong to an imaginary collective space from which individuals can assess their development alternatives. In the case of these indigenous groups, she shows how their cosmovision and relational ontology are intensive in interconnectedness, explaining how they attach importance to values of sufficiency and sustainability. There is also a key temporal dimension whereby several key individual capabilities are the result of past collective choices that were originally produced as a balance between individuals' positions in society.

The more sceptical among us might argue that what applies to indigenous populations in Latin America might not apply to contemporary Western societies, but this case should be understood as a benchmark against which we can see the interplay of different influences that might even operate at different levels, as happens inside families. In fact, families play an important role in shaping people's individual and social priorities, as well as their capabilities and choices. For this reason, Claudine Sauvain-Dugerdil and Siaka Cissé suggest in their chapter, 'Situating the family within the capabilities framework: a collective conversion factor. The role of the household configuration in the quality of life in Mali', that we can see families as 'collective conversion factors'. Of course, this will depend on the context and on the individuals' life course stage. But how can families work as social choice mechanisms? Do they follow rules, established conventions or traditions? How do families affect the perception of individual and social needs? As the authors explain, different types of families develop distinct subsistence strategies, providing different mechanisms for people to cope with life uncertainties. Family values can be seen as meta-values, shaping one's identity (on the lines argued by Watts, Waziri and Akogun) and individual and social choices. These values can also affect the kind of agency (weak or strong) that individuals might develop with their corresponding responsibilities and commitments. They illustrate this discussion with an example from Mali, where different families chose different schooling strategies.

Another paradigmatic field of application is offered by Jacques Tamin in his chapter about disabilities, entitled 'An ethical perspective on the United Kingdom's *Improving Lives: The Future of Work, Health and Disability*'. There are evident parallels between his arguments and those offered earlier by Kobayashi and Gotoh, whereby contextual differences can highlight the essentiality of the issue of agency for human development. In this chapter Tamin examines the issue of disability and the UK government's policy of creating 1 million job opportunities for disabled people by 2027. He shows how different choice mechanisms can allow disabled people to enjoy different health capabilities – or not. Ultimately, it depends on how broad the informational scope of this policy is. In particular, it depends on how this policy can respect the agency of disabled individuals, valuing their choices in relation to the job options.

The last chapter, 'Public services as conversion factors: exploring the theory and practice', by Richard Brunner and Nick Watson, provides a rich illustration from a public service reform in Scotland. Their discussion encapsulates much of the debate on social choice and individual values, given that different mechanisms of collective choice are usually decisive for the definition of distinct public service programmes. They examine two projects: one about an anti-gang initiative, the other about a family meal scheme with a homework club. Both were motivated by a reform agenda focused on those in greatest need, and follow a collaborative governance model. The results, as they report, are very positive, increasing community capacity and allowing people to act collectively as an agent. Certain parts of the discussion overlap with Carballo's account of how a sense of interconnectedness might be conducive to more effective collective agency. Taken together, these empirical chapters illustrate how the scope of a broader notion of social choice can be relevant to a wide variety of situations.

This book invites its readers onto a long interdisciplinary journey: from an initial acknowledgement of the SCT features in Sen's work to rich analytical categories that expand the core of SCT towards new forms of social theorizing. More specifically, it includes a review of the main features of Sen's SCT and discussion of a wide range of issues related to collective choices and individual values, such as those of communication, consensus building, institutional change, identity perceptions, inclusiveness, richer notions of agency, the role of moral sentiments and emotions in shaping social choice, an ethics of sufficiency versus an ethics of optimal social capability, the influence of psychological aspects on individuals' choices, and the role of social structures, such as those given by technological change, in shaping people's social priorities. The discussion also includes some analytical proposals, such as capability models with a fractal structure, a model for comparing capability sets and a proposal for the generalizability of informational spaces, among others. It covers a wide range of empirical cases, including about the youth, the elderly, families, educational authorities, people from developing and developed countries. Taken as a whole, the book advances a proposal for a broader notion of social choice that can be richer, more interdisciplinary and more useful to human development theory and policies.

References

Arrow, K. J. (1951) *Social Choice and Individual Values*. New York: Wiley.

Gaertner, W. (2009) *A Primer in Social Choice Theory*. Oxford: Oxford University Press.

Sen, A. K. (1970) *Collective Choice and Social Welfare*. San Francisco: Holden-Day.

(1982) *Choice, Welfare and Measurement*. Oxford: Blackwell.

(1984) *Resources, Values and Development*. Oxford: Blackwell.

(1997) Maximization and the act of choice. *Econometrica*, 65 (4): 745–79.

(1999) *Development as Freedom*. Oxford: Oxford University Press.

(2002) *Rationality and Freedom*. Cambridge, MA: Harvard University Press.

(2017) *Collective Choice and Social Welfare*, expanded edn. London: Penguin.

PART I

Social Choice and Capabilities

2 | The many facets of social choice theory

WULF GAERTNER

Introduction

The theory of social choice is very rich in topics and issues that have been discussed over the last seven decades, if one takes Arrow's seminal contribution from 1951 as its starting point. The existence of social welfare functions under domain restrictions, the manipulability of voters' preferences, scoring rules of different kinds, the expansion of the informational basis away from the narrow focus on self-centred utility (which led to the formulation of so-called extended orderings and equity judgements), the consideration of capability sets as the basis for an evaluation and measurement of human well-being, the introduction of topological methods as an alternative to the consideration of sets of discrete objects, and the explicit analysis of individual rights and personal freedom are just some of the major landmarks in this area. This last sentence may look as if it has been phrased for the initiated, so that an outsider may wonder (and perhaps worry) whether all these different approaches are just expressions of academic equivocation or whether they do indeed have some practical relevance for real life. The answer to this query is – as the reader may have expected – a clear 'Yes' to the latter, and it is to be hoped that the following three examples will convince the uninitiated observer that there are various instances that, in my view, are able to substantiate this affirmation.

One of the major findings of social choice theory is the fact that different aggregation rules may lead to different social outcomes. Some of these rules are well known to the public already, as they are widely applied. The simple majority rule and the two-thirds majority rule are routinely used in many parliaments around the world. The plurality rule, which considers only the top element in each voter's ranking, is applied in French presidential elections. The Borda rule attaches ranks to positions within an individual's preference ranking; it is used in many smaller committees. The fact that different aggregation schemes may yield different social outcomes manifests itself well in the different chapters of Sen's book *Collective Choice and Social Welfare* (Sen, 1970a). I now briefly mention three cases from the more distant and the immediate past that illustrate this point.

The first one refers to the decision in Germany to move the seat of parliament and the seat of government from Bonn to Berlin, a decision that was taken in 1991. A two-stage rule made this move possible, whereas an application of the so-called Borda method would have resulted in a consolidation of the status quo (Leininger, 1993). The second case is that, for me at least, it came as a surprise that David Cameron's 2016 Brexit referendum was decided by simple majority voting. Would such a far-reaching decision not have merited a more qualified outcome, say a two-thirds majority vote, which, as we now know, would have left the United Kingdom within the European Union? Al Gore received more votes than George W. Bush in 2000, and Hillary Clinton received 2 to 3 million more votes than Donald Trump in 2016, but, due to the electoral college system that is practised in the United States, the two Republicans won the presidential elections. If, third, the assignment of delegates for each state had been carried out in proportion to the number of votes for each of the candidates in each state, the outcome would have been extremely narrow. Depending on the way rounding of non-integer numbers is handled, one can obtain a tie between Clinton and Trump, or even a slight majority of delegates in favour of Clinton (Salas Montoya, 2017).

The plan of this chapter is such that the next section looks at the different aggregation methods and properties that these rules either fulfil or violate. The following section discusses the formulation of individual rights and establishes a relationship with the concept of freedom and the choice of functioning bundles. The next section examines the procedural aspect of individual and social choice and raises the question of how this aspect can be successfully integrated into an analysis, both descriptive and formal, of different capability sets. The following section outlines ways in which capability sets can be measured and compared with each other. There are a few concluding remarks in the final section.

Properties of aggregation functions

Arrow's theorem and two escape routes

In his path-breaking work, Arrow (1951) shows that no ordinal social welfare function exists if the mapping from any profile of individual preference orderings to the set of all logically possible social orderings is to satisfy (1) unrestricted domain requirements, (2) the weak Pareto principle, (3) independence of irrelevant alternatives and (4) non-dictatorship conditions. Clearly, if any of these four conditions is 'sufficiently' weakened, Arrow's negative result of non-existence turns into existence.

Let us take just two examples. First, if the preference orderings of the individuals are restricted to being single-peaked, the simple majority rule satisfies all the properties of an Arrow social welfare function if there is an odd number of voters, while for the situation of an even number (at least) a Condorcet winner exists. Second, if the ordering property of the social relation is restricted to transitivity of the strict part of this relation, thus weakening Arrow's rationality requirement by permitting intransitivity of the indifference part, Sen's (1970b) Pareto extension rule is able to circumvent the non-existence result. However, this rule can create a lot of instances of social indifference, which may be considered as unsatisfactory. Arrow himself states that his four conditions (plus full transitivity of the social relation) are to be seen as necessary, though perhaps not sufficient, conditions to be required by any democratic aggregation procedure.

A closer look at some desirable properties

There are many other conditions that one may like to impose. In this chapter, and for the sake of brevity, I want to confine our discussion to Arrow's condition (3) from above – the property of Condorcet consistency – together with the requirement that a Condorcet loser never be chosen and the condition that the so-called 'no show paradox' should never occur.

It is easy to show that the simple majority rule satisfies the independence condition while the Borda scoring rule violates this property. For any alternatives X and Y, a simple majority rule just counts the

Table 2.1 *Condorcet winner versus Borda winner*

1	1	1	1	1	1	1
X	X	X	Y	V	Y	Z
Z	V	Y	X	Y	X	Y
V	Z	V	Z	X	V	X
Y	Y	Z	V	Z	Z	V

number of votes in favour of X and the number in favour of Y, and nothing else, while the Borda count looks at ranks and takes into consideration that, for some voters, for example, several alternatives are arranged between X and Y whereas, for others, this is not the case at all, or the number of other alternatives in between X and Y is very small. So, for the Borda rule, 'irrelevant' alternatives matter in the decision between X and Y.

The simple majority rule always picks an alternative that is at least as good as every other option in binary comparisons (so that this scheme is Condorcet-consistent) and, clearly, never chooses an alternative, the so-called Condorcet loser, which loses against every other option in binary comparisons. The following example shows that the Borda count does not necessarily pick a Condorcet winner, while Saari (1995) has shown that it never chooses a Condorcet loser.

Let there be four alternatives, X, Y, Z, and V, and seven voters. These voters are arranged in adjacent columns. Their preferences are strict, to be read from top to bottom, so that the first person on the left, for example, strictly prefers X over Z over V over Y.

Here Y is the Condorcet winner while X is the Borda winner (with 15 points against 12 for Y). Alternative Y wins against all other options with a margin of 4:3 votes; X, while losing against Y, wins against Z and V, with a 6:1 margin in each case. In the social choice community, there are mainly two fractions: the Condorcet adherents and the Borda supporters. They are divided on the issue of whether the violation of Condorcet consistency is a knock-out criterion. If it is, the Borda rule has to exit. But, when you look at all the information that Table 2.1 provides, you will see that X is a strong contestant. So the question arises as to whether the fulfilment of Condorcet consistency should have absolute priority, all things considered, or whether other

Table 2.2 *Dodgson's method*

5	3	2	5
X	Y	V	Z
Y	Z	Y	V
V	X	Z	X
Z	V	X	Y

aspects matter as well. I have called such a situation a 'wicked' problem (Gaertner, 2017).

Dodgson's method – which picks a Condorcet winner whenever it exists, or otherwise looks for the minimal number of binary inversions such that an alternative will become a Condorcet winner – fails, surprisingly, in relation to the Condorcet loser property. This was shown by Nurmi (1987) in an example of four alternatives and 15 voters who are arranged perpendicularly, as in Table 2.2 (a binary inversion is an inversion between two adjacent alternatives).

All four alternatives need three inversions in order to become a Condorcet winner. If the three voters in the second column from the left, for example, switched the positions of Z and X, alternative X would become a Condorcet winner. Therefore, all four alternatives qualify for potential choice. However, V is a Condorcet loser, so that Dodgson's procedure does not meet the requirement never to pick a Condorcet loser.

Balinski and Laraki (2007, 2010) propose an ordinal aggregation scheme that uses qualitative verdicts, from 'excellent' to 'fail', say, and require that all persons engaged in voting accept this qualitative scale as a common language. They call this rule 'majority judgement'. As examples from real life, the authors refer to wine-tasting contests or, for example, to figure skating competitions. Given a certain number of voters or judges, the median grade with respect to each and every competing alternative is determined and, finally, that alternative is selected that obtained the highest median grade. Balinski and Laraki argue that this procedure, which satisfies Arrow's independence axiom, is superior to other methods, in particular to majority voting and Borda's count. However, unfortunately, this method may not choose a clear majority winner but may even pick a Condorcet loser instead. I show this in an example with seven voters and three alternatives and ordinal

Table 2.3 *Majority judgement via grading*

	1	1	1	1	1	1	1
X	A	A	A	E	F	F	F
Y	B	B	B	D	G	G	G
Z	C	C	C	B	H	H	H

Table 2.4 *The 'no show paradox'*

42	26	21	11	10
Y	X	W	W	X
X	W	V	X	Y
Z	Z	Y	Y	W
V	Y	X	V	Z
W	V	Z	Z	V

grades increasing from A to H (see Table 2.3). Alternative Z is the majority winner with 6:1 votes; X is the Condorcet loser, by the same margin, but gets selected because of the highest median grade.

There is a very basic property that should be satisfied by any democratic voting procedure. It says that, if an individual registers a vote in favour of X (against Y, shall we say), this act should at least not weaken the position of X, and may perhaps strengthen its position in relation to the other available options. However, if this voter decides to abstain, this should not strengthen but possibly weaken X's position. The so-called 'no show paradox' says that the latter effect may occur under some otherwise quite intuitive-looking voting systems. Felsenthal and Tideman (2013) have constructed a situation with 110 voters and five alternatives that shows that Dodgson's procedure may succumb to this unpleasant feature (see Table 2.4).

The number of inversions needed for Y to become a Condorcet winner is eight, which is the smallest number among all alternatives. If the last ten voters who rank X on top decide to abstain from voting, X will indeed be picked by Dodgson's rule – a result many people feel uncomfortable with.

For brevity's sake, I just state (Gaertner, 2017) that Sen's Pareto extension rule is immune to the no show paradox and so is the Borda count, while Balinski and Laraki's majority judgement method is vulnerable to the paradox, even for the case of only two alternatives or candidates. All this shows, at least in my view, that there is no ideal aggregation procedure that is dominant in relation to *all* those properties that one may view as desirable. From this it follows that it is difficult to establish a ranking among these procedures as long as one does not possess some kind of meta-ranking. I have sincere doubts that such a ranking can ever be established without deep controversy.

An analogy between rights exercising and freedom

Individual rights: feasibility and admissibility

The literature on liberty and rights in social choice theory and welfare economics has seen two major approaches as to how to integrate individual rights and their exercise into the analysis of collective decisions. Sen's (1970a, 1970b) seminal contribution is formulated in terms of individual orderings over social states and a process that amalgamates these orderings, whereby, according to Arrow (1951), a social state is viewed as a complete description of each and every aspect of society deemed relevant. There is an immediate relationship between the exercise of individual rights, legislation, moral rights (including human rights) and 'an approach to justice that concentrates on people's capability to lead the kind of life they have reason to value – the things that they can do, or be' (Sen, 2017: 356). In Sen's approach, individuals who hold rights over particular pairs of social states are decisive in the sense that, whenever one of these persons strictly prefers state X to state Y, for example, alternative Y must get eliminated from the set of socially chosen states. Following Nozick (1974), Gärdenfors (1981) and others, Gaertner, Pattanaik and Suzumura (1992) essentially identify individual rights with the exercise of admissible actions or strategies of the individuals, and social outcomes are the result of the (simultaneous or sequential) exercise of various n-tuples of permissible strategies, where n denotes the number of persons who hold particular rights.

The following formal analysis draws heavily on Fleurbaey and Gaertner (1996). Let $N = \{1, 2,..., n\}$ be a finite set of individuals who are members of the society that we consider. We examine situations in which each individual chooses a strategy or an action from a finite set of given strategies. Let A denote a finite set of actions that are conceivable but not necessarily feasible for agent i. This agent's individually feasible strategy or action set S_i is defined as a subset of A, more formally $S_i = \{s_i, s'_i, s''_i, \ldots\} \subset A$. Given strategy set S_i, the whole society's joint strategy set S_N will be defined as $S_N = S_1 \times S_2 \times \ldots \times S_n$, where $s_N \in S_N$ constitutes an n-tuple $(s_1, s_2, \ldots, s_n)$ with $s_i \in S_i$ for all $i \in N$. For brevity's sake, I write (s_i, s_{-i}) instead of s_N when we consider a particular agent i. Given S_i for person i, the other individuals' joint strategy set will be denoted by S_{-i}, with s_{-i} being a typical element of S_{-i}.

In the sequel, I use the notion of generalized game forms (Peleg, 1998) in which the strategies or actions available to a particular person may be conditional on other persons' strategies. There are situations in which other persons' duties (in particular actions) are derived from the fact that they must render some strategy feasible for the right-holder we consider. The generalized game form allows for the possibility that not all elements from S_N are jointly feasible. I shall denote the subset of mutually feasible strategies by F. When other agents have chosen their joint strategy vector $s_{-i} \in S_{-i}$, the subset of feasible strategies for individual i, namely $F_i(s_{-i})$, is given by $\{s_i \in S_i : (s_i, s_{-i}) \in F\}$.

To illustrate the interdependence of actions or strategies, let us consider a situation in which person i has to decide whether to go to person j's house to attend a reception or stay at home, so that there are two actions ('Go'/'Not go'). Person j has the options either to invite person i or not to invite i. Three out of the four possible constellations yield feasible outcomes, as Table 2.5 shows. The 'Go'/'Not invite' combination of strategies does not lead to a feasible state, except that i intrudes into j's sphere without permission – a situation that we do not want to consider.

For each vector of mutually feasible strategies, a particular outcome is achieved. Let G denote the set of possible social outcomes. Then h: $F \rightarrow G$ is the outcome function. Note that the outcome function is defined for all co-feasible strategies. A generalized game form $\langle N, S_1,$

Table 2.5 *Feasible and non-feasible actions*

i↘j	Invite	Not invite
Go	Feasible	Not feasible
Not go	Feasible	Feasible

$S_2,...,S_n$, F, G, h> is a specification of a set N of agents or players, a set S_i of strategies or actions for each player i ∈ N, a set of mutually feasible strategies F, a set G of possible outcomes and an outcome function h.

Let T_i denote the set of admissible strategies for person i, or, more specifically, T_i (s_{-i}), since it may depend on other individuals' strategies. Person i's action to jog on j's and k's properties, for example, presupposes the permission of persons j and k to do so. If action s_i ∈ S_i means jogging and s'_i ∈ S_i stands for cycling on the lawn belonging to j and k, it is possible that s_i ∈ T_i (s_{-i}), but s'_i ∉ T_i (s_{-i}). Let T denote the set of globally admissible strategies: s_N ∈ T iff for all i ∈ N, s_i ∈ T_i (s_{-i}). Note that feasibility and admissibility are two totally distinct concepts. An action can be feasible but not admissible (such as invading the private property of one's neighbour) or admissible but not feasible (failing to purchase a seat in the concert of a well-known conductor). When s_i ∈ (F_i (s_{-i}) ∩ T_i (s_{-i})), action s_i is both feasible and admissible. I write this more succinctly as s_i ∈ TF_i (s_{-i}). We then just add one more notation. With G being the set of possible outcomes for society, let G_i = (g_i, g'_i, g''_i,...) refer to the i'th component of G in which individual i achieves alternative features or personal outcomes for him- or herself, given the strategies of the others.

We can now distinguish between different cases.

(1) The admissibility and feasibility of an action are guaranteed, and the feasibility of a particular outcome is guaranteed as well. An example is to apply for social benefits in the case of involuntary unemployment. More formally, for any i ∈ N, s_i ∈ TF_i (s_{-i}), s_{-i} ∈ $TF_{-i}(s_i)$ and $h(s_i, s_{-i})$ ∈ G.

(2) The admissibility and feasibility of an action are guaranteed, but there is no guarantee for a particular outcome. Voting in public elections is a standard example.

(3) The admissibility and feasibility of an action are guaranteed within the resource constraint of the individual considered, but there is no guarantee of a particular outcome. As an example, I may decide to donate a certain amount of money to a particular charity, but there is no guarantee that everybody else in my community will do the same, so it is totally unclear whether a particular sum of money can be reached.

(4) Admissibility is guaranteed, but there is neither a guarantee for the feasibility of an action within the resource constraint nor a

guarantee of a particular outcome. In market activities, notional demand and effective demand often go together, but this is not always the case. I may plan to get a pint of milk just before the shops close in my area of town, for example, but there is no guarantee that I will succeed.

Control over one's functioning bundle?

In a recent paper, Pattanaik and Xu (2017) argue that there is a great similarity between a consumer's ability to choose a commodity bundle and his or her ability to pick a particular functioning bundle from his or her capability set, the set of all functionings as well as combinations of functionings that a person is able to achieve. In principle, a consumer has the freedom to choose any consumption bundle that lies in his or her budget set. However, Basu (1987) has shown that, if a consumer deviates from an equilibrium allocation and tries to realize a different bundle within his or her budget set, such an action is, of course, admissible but may be infeasible due to the scarcity of available resources. This argument is closely related to point (4) above.

Pattanaik and Xu (2017) assert that there are many instances when the idea that an individual has the ability to pick any element of the set of functioning bundles available to him or her is problematic. The reason is that, 'given the scarcity of aggregate resources in the society, it is not possible to envision individuals as independently choosing functioning bundles for themselves, or ... strategic interaction among individuals makes the outcome for any given individual dependent on the actions of other individuals as well as his own action' (32). This statement is very close to what I said above about the feasibility of a particular action based on rights granted to all members of a given society.

In the second half of their paper, the authors introduce the game form concept and analyse different situations of strategic interaction between individuals. The outcomes that Pattanaik and Xu consider are n-tuples of functioning bundles with exactly one functioning bundle for each person, and they raise the question of the degree to which an individual agent has control over his or her functioning bundle.

Let us consider two different cases. In the first, farmer i is growing corn and raising cattle (s_i), and he considers to substitute cattle for pigs (s'_i). This farmer is self-supplying and lives far away from a second farmer j, who also has two alternatives – s_j and s'_j – available,

Table 2.6 *No conflict of actions*

i\j	s_j	s'_j
s_i	g_i, g_j	g_i, g'_j
s'_i	g'_i, g_j	g'_i, g'_j

Table 2.7 *Conflicting actions*

i\j	s_j	s'_j
s_i	g_i, g_j	g''_i, g'_j
s'_i	g'_i, g_j	g''_i, g'_j

which are locally confined. All this implies that there is no friction between these two when they choose their actions. Table 2.6 depicts the four possible outcomes that are all jointly feasible. Whenever farmer i picks action s_i (s'_i), he will with certainty achieve outcome g_i (g'_i) from G_i. In other words, he has complete power to determine which functioning bundle he wants to achieve. The same argument, of course, applies to farmer j.

In the second case, consider agent i, who has two possibilities for earning his living. He can either rear bees (s_i) or cultivate a special kind of tree (s'_i) on his own territory. Both actions are admissible for him. His neighbour j can either continue to cultivate his orchard (s_j) or cut down all fruit trees and open a large cleaners (s'_j), which may produce major toxic exhausts. We again assume admissibility for those two actions. If j continues to keep his orchard, agent i has two possible options that permit him to realize the functionings he desires, in particular allow for a decent living, among other amenities. In case the neighbour opens a cleaners, both actions are still admissible for agent i, but because of the externalities his functioning bundle will be heavily reduced so that the prospect of earning a decent living becomes uncertain. This means that the power and control of agent i over his functioning bundle are severely impaired. In particular, the functioning bundle connected with being an apiarist is heavily endangered.

In the situation of Table 2.7, agent i will achieve g_i only under s_i (g'_i under s'_i), when agent j chooses action s_j. If the latter picks action s'_j, agent i will no longer be able to secure either g_i or g'_i of G_i. His outcome will, against his desires, be reduced to g''_i.

This shows that, in general, the realization of a particular functioning bundle of person i, say, cannot be considered in isolation. It has to be embedded in some environment of interacting agents who may have a smaller or larger influence on the composition of person i's actual functioning bundle. An example from health care may further illustrate this assertion. The chance that I catch an infectious disease such as measles depends heavily on the precautionary measures (such as vaccination) that others in my neighbourhood take, and vice versa. My argumentation in the foregoing passages confirms the heading of this section, namely that there are parallels between the exercise of individual rights and the realization of freedom in terms of control over one's functioning bundle. Under both perspectives, the issue of feasibility is something that the person considered often cannot determine in isolation. Rather, it is a situation in which interaction of different kinds plays a major role. The action of others may be accidental or unintended but it can also be pursued on purpose.

While studying these passages, the reader may have been reminded of Coase's (1960) analysis of harmful effects on others stemming from two (or more) interacting agents. Coase was focusing on the costs arising on either side due to existing external effects. He was not arguing in terms of an impediment of agents' functionings, but the costs that he considered were a clear expression of such encroachments.

The procedural aspect

The procedural aspect, namely a focus on *how* certain states of the world come about, is largely neglected in individual and collective decision theory. It is often implicitly assumed that the processes that lead to certain economic allocations are neutral and fair to all who participate. In an Edgeworth box allocation problem, for example, it is assumed that all individuals have the possibility to articulate their 'untainted' preferences and that the market mechanism or the price system treats agents with identical preferences and identical budget sets exactly the same. However, it is rare that these procedural aspects are laid down in detail. Having said this, one should mention Sen (1997), who argues in favour of a comprehensive description of choice processes and outcomes, when the concepts of 'chooser dependence' and 'menu dependence' play a particular role. Moreover, one should not forget that, in constitutional economics and public choice, it is in particular Buchanan (1986) who emphasizes the procedural role that the market mechanism plays in the problem of economic allocations. And Sugden (1993: 1948) points out that, in the 'tradition of contractarian and libertarian thought, in which society is seen as a system of cooperation among individuals for their mutual advantage ... the primary role of the government is not to maximize the social good, but rather to maintain a framework of rules within which individuals are left free to pursue their own ends'.

Two cases come to mind when an aspect of fair and impartial treatment is explicitly stated. One, in collective choice theory, is the axiom of anonymity, which requires that all individual votes be given the same weight in an aggregation procedure. The other finds itself in the statement of Rawls' (1971) second principle of justice, in which it is claimed that social and economic inequalities are to be arranged so that they are to the greatest benefit of the least advantaged and attached to offices and positions open to all under conditions of fair equality of opportunity. The latter demand is a genuinely procedural requirement. The procedural aspect also stands out in Nozick's (1974) entitlement concept, which stresses the fundamental role that rights play in relation to the use, exchange and bequest of private property.

Sen has argued in various contributions that the game form approach to individual rights in collective decisions is mainly procedural in character, focusing on admissible strategies and not really caring about consequences. He writes in his Arrow lectures (Sen, 2002: 643) that 'all persons can then exercise their rights as they like (subject to their choices falling within permissible combinations) "irrespective" of their consequences. The *specification* of rights proceeds in this formulation without any reference to the *preferences* of the people involved, or of the *outcomes* that actually emerge' (emphasis in original). Gaertner, Pattanaik and Suzumura (1992), who, as the previous section showed, belong to the group of proponents of the game form approach to rights exercising, have never held the view that the issue of individual rights should be reduced to a purely procedural affair – in other words, that consequences should not be considered as well. However, one has to admit that an emphasis on the consideration of aspects of admissibility and feasibility in relation to individual strategies undoubtedly has a strong procedural touch.

Consider a decision problem that goes back to the economist Diamond (1967) and has been extensively discussed by the philosopher

Table 2.8 *Diamond's query*

Actions	State of nature 1	State of nature 2
I	(1,0)	(1,0)
II	(1,0)	(0,1)

Broome (1984). There are two states of nature, 1 and 2, that are equally probable; two persons, A and B, who are equally deserving; and two alternative actions, I and II, that a public official or some community might take. Table 2.8 shows the results that the alternative actions will have under the two different states of nature; the utility of person A is given first.

Which of the two actions should the public official or society take? Either action results in an unequal distribution of utilities, and, viewed ex post, the distributions are equally unequal. Expected utility maximization says that the two actions are socially equivalent, since both actions lead to an aggregate utility value of 1. Diamond argues in favour of II, but this reasoning violates the 'sure thing' principle, which is key to Harsanyi's (1955) postulate of maximizing expected utilities in order to reach maximal welfare for society.

Action I is very favourable for person A and very bad for person B, while action II treats the two agents fairly in the sense of giving each of them the same chance to be the winner. Therefore, under action II, the two persons are treated equally in a situation of chance – an aspect that the hypothesis of expected utility maximization is unable to grasp, except that this aspect is somewhere included in the utility values, which is not the case in the situation above. If these utility numbers are too abstract, the reader is asked to interpret '1' as receiving a job offer and '0' as not receiving one, or, more drastically, '1' standing for receiving life-saving treatment and '0' for the refusal of such treatment. Remember that Rawls requires in his second principle that offices and positions should be open to all under conditions of *fair equality of opportunity*. How can this procedural aspect be successfully integrated into a theory of decision making under risk or uncertainty?

Modifying an example by Sen (1988), Gaertner and Xu (2004) consider the following situation. Imagine that, in a particular country, several daily newspapers are available. Among them is one that one may view as the government's mouthpiece. It is of considerable quality, so that the agent we focus on regularly buys this paper. Let us now suppose that, for some reason or other, the government bans all papers except for the official mouthpiece. While our agent, as we just stated, has been a regular buyer of this newspaper, he or she now refuses to purchase the paper any more, so that the agent's choice set no longer contains the government's organ. The agent refuses to pick this paper and thus articulates a protest against the governmental intervention. In a variant of this situation, let us assume that all other papers had to close down due to severe financial mismanagement. In such a case, our agent would have continued to purchase the government's mouthpiece. In other words, the way a set of initially choosable objects shrinks may matter a lot.

There are quite a few other examples that shed light on the production procedure, or, differently viewed, on how a particular choice situation comes about. Are you willing to buy carpets woven by children or toys produced in prisoners' camps? Is shoe shining by children acceptable to you but gold mining by children is not? Is child labour admissible under emergency situations, such as during a severe economic crisis?

Gaertner and Xu (2004) axiomatically characterize choices under some of these situations. The authors formulate different versions of 'protest consistency' that refer to the underlying procedure. This could either be the process of production as such (an unjustified waste of scarce natural resources, say) or particular features that determine how certain objects of choice came about (ignoring basic human rights, for instance). In addition, an aspect of variety of choice was taken into consideration. In the newspaper example above, there was no variety at all after the government had issued a ban on all other papers. The authors relate their axiomatic requirements to well-known consistency conditions in standard choice theory.

In Sen's capability approach (Sen, 1985), a capability set reflects opportunities, namely the alternative combinations of functionings from which a person can choose a particular combination. Sen (2005: 153) writes that 'capabilities ... have to be supplemented by consideration of fair processes and the lack of violation of people's right to invoke and utilize them'. And he asserts that 'capability can hardly serve as the sole informational basis for the *other* considerations, related to processes, that must also be accommodated in normative social choice theory' (156, emphasis in original). How can the procedural aspect be integrated into a formal analysis of different capability sets? This appears to be an open question, but perhaps it should be tackled in a way similar to what Gaertner and Xu (2004) explicate in the case of the newspaper example.

To highlight this problem, let us discuss the following situation. Consider an individual with kidney failure who has been having a dialysis treatment several times a week. This means that a normal way of living is no longer possible. In terms of the capability concept, the opportunities that are available to the person considered are significantly curtailed. A new organ would ameliorate the situation substantially. However, organs are scarce. The waiting list for suitable organs is long, so quite a few patients die while waiting for a transplant. Various people from the fields of both medicine and economics, among them me, have provided arguments in favour of establishing a regulated and tightly controlled market for kidneys and livers in order to reduce the gap between supply and demand.

However, there is widespread and strong opposition against changing the current legislation as it exists in most civilized countries. The main objection, which comes from medicine, law, philosophy and, of course, theology (and is widely supported by politicians), is that human bodies should never become a toolbox or reservoir for others. So a strong argument exists that emphasizes the procedural aspect of the matter, and clearly dominates the counterargument that (1) mortality among those who are in the waiting line for transplantation could be reduced considerably and that (2) the opportunities of those who undergo a successful transplantation would increase significantly. The procedural argument against markets for body parts, understandably, becomes even stronger when the phenomenon of black markets is taken into consideration. The number of people who travel to China in order to receive a kidney that comes from the dead body of an executed prisoner is unknown but seems to be quite high. These persons apparently value their own survival more highly than the atrociousness with which the bodies of prisoners who were sentenced to death are treated. Are these people to be blamed for clutching at straws? Political institutions are expected to act as impartial observers. They should weigh medical urgency and individual hardship against arguments that often refer to the ruling legislation and/or ethical and religious norms. However, we should not forget that laws can be modified.

There is a dilemma that is aptly described by the earlier quotation from Sen, in which he speaks of other considerations, related to processes that must also be accommodated in normative social choice theory. The dilemma is a profound one, both practically and conceptually. The state and the general public are against the creation of markets for organs such as kidneys and liver parts, so a collective decision would come to a clear verdict, namely to prohibit organ trade. But, when the focus is on the individual members in this society, the person affected or the person whose close relative is in urgent need of an organ would often do his or her utmost to render the badly needed transplantation possible. Should this endeavour be dismissed altogether? Whose preferences are to count?

Measuring and comparing capability sets

In the preceding section I briefly referred to Sen's notion of capability (Sen, 1985), which comprises alternative combinations of valuable functionings from which a person is free to choose. How is the concept of capability to be understood, and how can it be measured and possibly compared across different persons or even nations? Is there perhaps something such as a list of (basic) functionings that should constitute each and every person's capability set? Nussbaum (2000, 2011) has proposed such a list, a rather long list indeed, which individuals should have at their disposal. Sen (2005: 158), *par contre,* is sceptical 'about fixing a cemented list of capabilities that is seen as being absolutely complete ... and totally fixed'. His main argument is 'that pure theory cannot "freeze" a list of capabilities for all societies for all time to come, irrespective of what the citizens come to understand and value' (158). He continues arguing that, even if there were a list of relevant capabilities, there would still be 'the problem of determining the relative weights and importance of the different capabilities included in the relevant list' (158). Clearly, one cannot expect that, in a comparison between different persons – or, to go one step further, between different nations – a well-ordered ranking in terms of vector dominance can be achieved that would, of course, avoid the weighting problem. This will be possible only in extreme situations in which persons or nations are very far apart in terms of opportunities they would have available (Korsgaard and Gaertner, 1993).

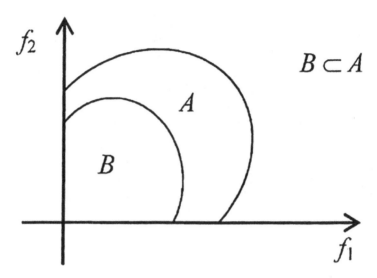

Figure 2.1 The simple case of set inclusion

Sen is also sceptical about attempts to operationalize the concept of capability and perhaps even derive 'some mechanical formula that is used, without scrutiny and assessment' (Sen, 2005: 158, fn 10). Given such a strong verdict, it is somewhat difficult and perhaps even a bit audacious to introduce and defend an approach that Gaertner and Xu (2006, 2008) put forward a few years ago.

For the moment, let us assume that the space of functionings is a subspace of the Euclidean space with dimension m ≤ n. If set B is fully contained in another set A, then for each functioning vector in B there is at least one functioning vector in A that is better because it offers a higher level of functionings (Figure 2.1). Remember that we have only valuable functionings in mind. Such a situation is rather rare, but, as mentioned above, it may be given if the opportunities of two persons or nations are very far apart. What can be said in a case when A ∩ B ≠ ϕ but B ⊂ A does not hold? If there were a preference ranking with well-defined indifference curves over the space of functionings, one could check whether the best point in A would be better than the best point in B (Figure 2.2). If this were the case, the verdict would again be uncontroversial, I think. But where do these preferences come from? Are these short-term preferences, long-term preferences, paternalistic preferences, society's preferences?

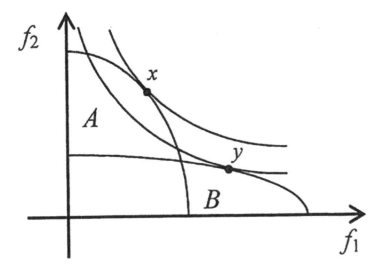

Figure 2.2 Indifference curves in the space of functionings

Gaertner and Xu have followed a different path. Their starting point is Lancaster's (1966) characteristics approach, as was Sen's in his 1985 book on 'commodities and capabilities'. Consumer goods and investment goods generate characteristics, and different combinations of consumption goods lead to different compositions of characteristics. The higher the income or the investment budget, the higher the level of combinations of characteristics that can be achieved. Due to the linear 'technology', different combinations of consumer goods (investment goods, respectively) generate different compositions of characteristics that make up convex spaces. Naturally, these combinations start from the origin of the coordinate system. The idea now is to assume linear input–output relationships in a twofold way. Consumer goods 'produce' characteristics, and these generate different functioning vectors. An investment in schooling and medical equipment, for example, promotes a higher level of literacy and a better state of health of the general public. These achievements lead to improvements in the level of functionings. Combinations of different functioning vectors generate spaces of functionings that constitute an agent's, as well as a country's, capability set. These spaces are again convex and star-shaped – that is they start from the coordinate origin.

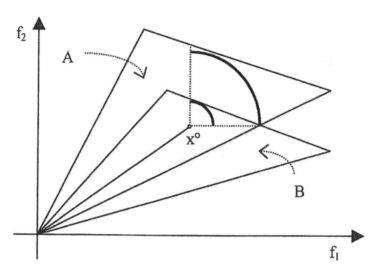

Figure 2.3 Overlapping capability sets

In order to be judged to be living a satisfactory life, a person (or a country) must have a particular vector of functionings in his or her capability set. Gaertner and Xu (2006) call it the reference functioning vector. In the case of a developing country, it could, for example, consist of a basic medical health status for each individual, elementary literacy, regular access to clean water, and other items. In order to improve upon a status quo in terms of functionings, given the uncertainty associated with a person's income situation and the development of society at large, it is not immediately clear along which direction or path an agent's or a country's functionings will grow over time. Furthermore, the reference functioning vector may – and, perhaps, should – change over time in its composition, reflecting a change of importance between its elements. Figure 2.3 shows two capability sets and a reference functioning vector x°. The two sets could represent alternative capability sets for a particular person or country, depending on the initial choice of consumption goods and investment goods, respectively.

Starting from the endpoint of reference functioning vector x°, we now consider the north-east part of a ball or circle with centre x° and extension t. It describes functioning possibilities that are better than x°. Since the path of x° over time is uncertain, as mentioned above, all

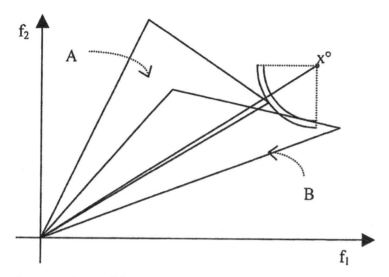

Figure 2.4 A case of deprivation

combinations north-east of x^o are equally desirable a priori. Scalar t measures the Euclidean distance between two vectors in the functioning space. We then look for the maximal radial extension of the quarter-ball north-eastwards and rank capability sets accordingly. So, in Figure 2.3, given the position of x^o, set A would provide more opportunities than set B. In Figure 2.4, where the reference vector lies outside both sets A and B, we consider the minimal distance of a quarter-ball south-westwards to either set. Gaertner and Xu (2008) call such a situation a case of deprivation. Since set B is somewhat closer to x^o than set A, B is to be preferred. The authors have formulated four axioms that characterize a complete ordering over alternative capability sets based on the quarter-ball extension. Note that this approach is quite different from the traditional way of evoking a set of well-ordered (convex) indifference curves defined over the space of functionings.

Given the model above, several generalizations are possible. First, the linear technology that we assumed may be viewed as an oversimplification. Once this assumption is relaxed, non-convexities would have to be considered. Second, one may question whether the reference vector should really be a single point. Could it perhaps be a reference surface with trade-off possibilities along its north-eastern

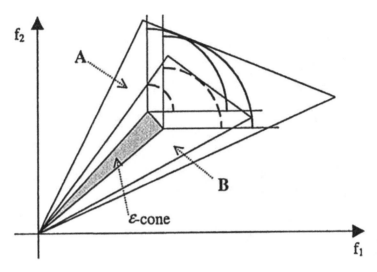

Figure 2.5 A cone and its reference surface

boundary? Third, is it justified to treat the path between the coordinate origin and reference endpoint x^o as a straight line? Would it perhaps be more convincing to conceive of this path as moving in a north-easterly direction but not necessarily on a straight line along a fixed angle from the origin?

Gaertner and Xu (2008) have tried to take care of the last two points by considering so-called ε–cones stretching north-east with the vertex at the coordinate origin. A cone with angle ε and some length λ has the property that its north-east boundary with all points of length λ away from the origin constitutes a reference surface. This surface with convex curvature looks a bit like an efficiency frontier. Its north-east boundary will extend in length the larger λ, or, in one interpretation, the higher the level of development in a country. Geometrically, λ can be interpreted as the radius of a virtual circle from the origin, where only a small segment in the north-eastern direction is considered. In a comparison between two capability sets A and B, the authors construct quarter-balls along the efficiency frontier and look for the maximal and minimal extensions north-eastwards such that the quarter-ball is still fully contained in the set that is to be evaluated. In Figure 2.5, the maximal and minimal extensions north-eastwards with respect to sets A and B, given the ε -cone, are drawn, with the result that set A is preferred to B. Gaertner and Xu again characterize their approach axiomatically.

In a companion paper, Gaertner (2012) studies cases in which the range of desirable directions north-eastwards is no longer determined by the full 90° quarter-ball, but only by some small sector of directions within this ball. Moreover, the dimensionality of the quarter-ball may decrease the higher the reference level already is. Such an argument could take care of cases of partial satiation of functionings. Imagine, for example, that, in some parts of the developing world, the problem of access to clean water has finally been solved.

Concluding remarks

My theme in this chapter has been to highlight different facets of social choice theory. The theory of collective choice is a very rich field of quite diverse topics and issues. I have been able to discuss only some of these. My emphasis was laid on issues that can be circumscribed as topics of ongoing discussion.

I started out with a brief presentation of alternative voting mechanisms and pointed to the fact that they may lead to different outcomes. For such cases, which are by no means rare, a meta-theory would be helpful, but, unfortunately, such a measuring rod does not in my opinion exist, which led me to the remark that a wicked or intricate problem remains. I then showed sizable similarities between the theory of rights in social choice and the concept of freedom and liberty. My next step was to look at the procedural aspect of choices, an aspect that is frequently mentioned but hardly ever worked out in detail. Very often in economic analysis, as well as in parts of philosophy, the focus is almost entirely on outcomes, whereas the process of how these outcomes come about is widely ignored, in spite of the fact that fair, transparent and intelligible procedures are vital for support by democratic institutions, in particular by those who are immediately affected and concerned. Finally, I suggested a method of how to compare and measure alternative capability sets. I do this without utilizing indifference curves or specific preference relations. What is needed in our approach is a direction of improvement along which monotonicity makes a lot of sense. I think that this is a minimal requirement, with which many will agree. To go beyond this is, of course, possible, but it will necessitate additional assumptions – on which opinions and arguments may diverge widely.

Acknowledgement

Comments and suggestions by the editors of this volume were very helpful. They are gratefully acknowledged.
This chapter is dedicated to the memory of my brother, Joachim.

References

Arrow, K. J. (1951) *Social Choice and Individual Values*. New York: Wiley.

Balinski, M., and Laraki, R. (2007) A theory of measuring, electing, and ranking. *Proceedings of the National Academy of Sciences*, 104 (21): 8720–5.

(2010) *Majority Judgment: Measuring, Ranking and Electing*. Cambridge, MA: MIT Press.

Basu, K. (1987) Achievements, capabilities and the concept of well-being. *Social Choice and Welfare*, 4 (1): 69–76.

Broome, J. (1984) Uncertainty and fairness. *Economic Journal*, 94: 624–32.

Buchanan, J. M. (1986) *Liberty, Market and State: Political Economy in the 1980s*. Brighton: Wheatsheaf.

Coase, R. H. (1960) The problem of social cost. *Journal of Law & Economics*, 3: 1–44.

Diamond, P. A. (1967) Cardinal welfare, individualistic ethics, and interpersonal comparisons of utility: comment. *Journal of Political Economy*, 75 (5): 765–6.

Felsenthal, D. S., and Tideman, N. (2013) Varieties of failure of monotonicity and participation under five voting methods. *Theory and Decision*, 75 (1): 59–77.

Fleurbaey, M., and Gaertner, W. (1996) Admissibility and feasibility in game forms. *Analyse & Kritik*, 18 (1): 54–66.

Gaertner, W. (2012) Evaluating sets of objects in characteristics space. *Social Choice and Welfare*, 39: 303–21.

(2017) Wickedness in social choice. *Journal of Economic Surveys*, 31 (2): 369–92.

Gaertner, W., Pattanaik, P. K., and Suzumura, K. (1992) Individual rights revisited. *Economica*, 59: 161–78.

Gaertner, W., and Xu, Y. (2004) Procedural choice. *Economic Theory*, 24: 335–49.

(2006) Capability sets as the basis of a new measure of human development. *Journal of Human Development*, 7 (3): 311–21.

(2008) A new class of measures of the standard of living based on functionings. *Economic Theory*, 35 (2): 201–15.

Gärdenfors, P. (1981) Rights, games and social choice. *Nous*, 15 (3): 341–56.

Harsanyi, J. C. (1955) Cardinal welfare, individualistic ethics, and interpersonal comparisons of utility. *Journal of Political Economy*, 63 (4): 309–21.

Korsgaard, C. M., and Gaertner, W. (1993) Commentators on Cohen and Sen. In *The Quality of Life*, Nussbaum, M. C., and Sen, A. K. (eds.): 54–66. Oxford: Clarendon Press.

Lancaster, K. (1966). A new approach to consumer theory. *Journal of Political Economy*, 74 (2): 132–57.

Leininger, W. (1993) The fatal vote: Berlin versus Bonn. *FinanzArchiv N. F.*, 50: 1–20.

Nozick, R. (1974) *Anarchy, State, and Utopia*. New York: Basic Books.

Nurmi, H. (1987) *Comparing Voting Systems*. Dordrecht: D. Reidel Publishing.

Nussbaum, M. C. (2000) *Women and Human Development: The Capabilities Approach*. Cambridge: Cambridge University Press.

   (2011) *Creating Capabilities: The Human Development Approach*. Cambridge, MA: Belknap Press.

Pattanaik, P. K., and Xu, Y. (2017) On a concept of freedom. In *Markets, Governance, and Institutions in the Process of Economic Development*, Mishra, A., and Ray, T. (eds.): 31–46. Oxford: Oxford University Press.

Peleg, B. (1998) Effectivity functions, game forms, games, and rights. *Social Choice and Welfare*, 15 (1): 67–80.

Rawls, J. (1971) *A Theory of Justice*. Cambridge, MA: Harvard University Press.

Saari, D. G. (1995) *Basic Geometry of Voting*. Berlin: Springer-Verlag.

Salas Montoya, M. F. (2017) The electoral college in theory and praxis: election inversions in the 2016 US elections. Manuscript. Humboldt University, Berlin.

Sen, A. (1970a) *Collective Choice and Social Welfare*. San Francisco: Holden-Day.

   (1970b) The impossibility of a Paretian liberal. *Journal of Political Economy*, 78 (1): 152–7.

   (1985) *Commodities and Capabilities*. Amsterdam: North-Holland.

   (1988) Freedom of choice: concept and content. *European Economic Review*, 32 (2/3): 269–94.

   (1997) Maximization and the act of choice. *Econometrica*, 65 (4): 745–79.

   (2002) Freedom and social choice: the Arrow lectures. In *Rationality and Freedom*: 581–712. Cambridge, MA: Harvard University Press.

   (2005) Human rights and capabilities. *Journal of Human Development*, 6 (2): 151–66.

   (2017) *Collective Choice and Social Welfare*, expanded edn. London: Penguin.

Sugden, R. (1993) Welfare, resources, and capabilities: a review of 'Inequality Reexamined' by Amartya Sen. *Journal of Economic Literature*, 31 (4): 1947–62.

3 | Beyond capabilities?
Sen's social choice approach and the generalizability assumption

FLAVIO COMIM

Introduction

Amartya Sen's social choice and development work is pluralist in at least four clear and well-established ways. First, it is *motivationally pluralist*, because, following Adam Smith, it considers different moral sentiments in characterizing individuals' motivations to act. This means that, for Sen, as it was for Smith, self-interest and egoism cannot explain all human behaviour. Second, it is *informationally pluralist*, because it encompasses distinct 'informational spaces' (understood here as different kinds of information that can be grouped according to a common standard) in evaluating states of affairs or people's advantage. Third, it is *intrinsically pluralist*, because some of these informational spaces are naturally pluralistic, such as the space of primary goods or capabilities (differently from the utility space, which can be homogeneous). Finally, it can be *metrically pluralist*, at the level of the particular units of measure (cardinal, ordinal, etc.) that are used to characterize its key variables. Metric pluralism is also important, because it is not always the case that options can be fully compared and that incomparabilities can be tackled in a satisfactory way.

To a certain extent, his pluralism achieves materiality from his engagement with Arrow's (1951) original formulation of the impossibility theorem and how he saw in informational pluralism a way of overcoming Arrow's challenge (Sen, 2017). It is important to note that during the mid-1970s and early 1980s Sen created several approaches that were all very similar in the pursuit of a single purpose, namely a broadening of the informational basis used in evaluating people's advantage and states of affairs. They are the 'meta-ranking approach' (Sen, 1974, 1979), the 'named goods approach' (Sen, 1979), the 'capability approach' (Sen, 1979), the 'vector view' (Sen, 1980), the 'capabilities right system' (Sen, 1982), the 'positional approach' (Sen, 1983) and the 'intersection approach' (Sen, 1986). The root of all these apparently different approaches can be found in his path-breaking *Collective Choice and Social Welfare* (Sen, 1970a) and in two other papers (Sen, 1977a, 1979), in which he further elaborates the concept of 'informational analysis' and 'informational admissibility'. The central issue here is that the capability approach is part of Sen's larger enterprise in working with broader informational spaces.

The failure to acknowledge what Sen was trying to achieve with all these approaches is responsible for two current mistakes in the capability literature. First, scholars do not recognize the key role of social choice in shaping Sen's thought (Comim, 2018). Second, they expect too much from the capability approach and do not see how the capability approach is offering only (though it is not less important for this) a way of broadening informational spaces in normative evaluations (see, for example, Garza-Vazquez and Deneulin, 2019). Thus, the capability approach is intrinsically related to Sen's informational pluralism, and other features of the approach, such as incompleteness and reasoned scrutiny, are in fact imported features from Sen's social choice approach.

Given this context, the main objective of this chapter is to show how informational pluralism can be used within Sen's social choice framework (hereafter SSC). In order to tackle this issue, two steps are necessary. First, it is important to spell out the 'generalizability' assumption behind Sen's principle of working with broad informational spaces. Second, we need to work out a method to make sense of the need to reconcile different informational spaces. By doing so, several features and issues of the capability approach can be seen as part of a systematic story. Thus, this chapter is divided into four parts. The first part explores the generalizability issue behind the capability approach. The second provides a brief characterization of Sen's social choice approach. The third demonstrates how it can be used through what can be named 'generalizability tables'. Finally, the chapter briefly concludes with some suggestions for future work.

The capability approach and the generalizability assumption

One of the puzzles in operationalizing the capability approach (hereafter CA) is that it is not enough *qua* an approach to handle complex development issues. This is not because it is an 'approach' and not a 'theory' but because its principles do not provide all the methodological elements that are necessary for normative evaluations (of people's advantage, or deprivation or states of affairs). This is not to claim that the CA should become a sociological or development theory. No; this is about the requirement that it should provide the basic elements that are necessary for what it aims to achieve. Sen has several times explained how the CA is not sufficient for certain normative evaluations. In one of his latest remarks, related to justice appraisals, he argues (Sen, 2017: 358) that 'it would be misleading to see the capability approach as standing on its own as a guide to justice, since it focuses only on some specific aspects of well-being and freedom, and there are other concerns – for example, the importance of processes and agencies – that need to be brought in to get a fuller understanding of justice than can be obtained within an exclusively "capability approach"'. This claim should not be restricted to the issue of justice but, instead, be considered in its full normative force with respect to all assessments of states of affairs and individual advantage. Sen has also argued (2009: 232) that the CA 'does not, on its own, propose any specific formula about how that information [on capabilities] may be used', in particular because it does not provide any guidance about how to solve aggregative and distributive conflicts. The message is clear: the CA should not stand on its own. It seems that the CA is about pluralism and about working with an evaluative framework that is informationally richer than current alternatives employed in assessing people's advantage and states of affairs. As a result, we should consider whether reference to the capability approach as an approach is not actually misleading and whether some difficulties faced with its operationalization are not derived from this imprecise terminology.

Sen's initial concern (1977b) with informational pluralism is with the informational admissibility of utility and non-utility information in defining moral judgments. Later (1979) he puts forward a defence of pluralism as a general principle for handling different kinds of informational spaces. Sen (1985: 176) suggests two different ways of defining pluralism: principle pluralism (in terms of the plurality of principles, which I suggested above that we could call motivational pluralism as a way of highlighting its link with Smith's theory of moral sentiments); and information pluralism (in terms of the plurality of informational variables). The CA is part of Sen's architecture of information pluralism. But Sen leaves his framework open, because his justification for introducing pluralism is a rejection of mechanical criteria and formulae for normative evaluations. His argument is that informational requirements should be played according to their contextual relevance. This is understandable. However, this comes at a cost of hiding the generalizability nature of his framework.

In a nutshell (because this issue has already been extensively discussed in the capability literature), Sen criticizes subjective well-being, resources, primary goods and other informational spaces for not being able to provide a complete characterization of one's advantage. Alternatively, we could say, as proposed here, that different informational spaces are lacking in terms of generalizability. More specifically, Sen (2008: 26) clarifies that his problem with happiness and welfarism is that 'it insists that nothing other than utilities or happiness matters'. Important informational spaces such as rights are then only instrumentally considered within utilitarianism. Sen (1999) repeats as a mantra that Rawls' primary goods are resources, and, as such, they are 'imperfect indicators' of human well-being, basically due to human diversity in conversion factors. The point is that, for Sen, it is not that resources, subjective well-being, primary goods and – for that matter – human rights are not important but that the information that they provide cannot be generalized to other informational spaces. One happy person may be resource-poor. A resource-rich person might not achieve certain primary goods if he or she lives in a restricted political regime. A sad person can live in an environment of political freedom. And so on. The point is that information pluralism is necessary. Quite often capabilities tend to provide a plausible informational basis for normative evaluations. But they also might not be generalizable. Let us talk more in detail about this requirement.

Nussbaum (1990) argues that our values are plural – that is, that they are not homogeneous. For this reason, values are often noncommensurable, and as a result we have to appeal to multidimensionality as a way of making sense of them together. Following Aristotle, she proposes that the act of choice is often characterized by a quality-based selection between goods that are plural and heterogeneous. We do not have to go that far claiming the singleness of distinct situations to see that pluralism is necessary whenever we do not have generalizability.

Before discussing generalizability it is important that we are more specific about the kinds of informational spaces that should be taken into account. In order to do so we should also introduce a distinction between informational spaces and informational categories, which are not spaces, strictly speaking. We call *informational spaces* specific kinds of information that follow a common concept and definition. In the capability literature (such as Sen, 2009, and Nussbaum, 2011) we find four main kinds of informational spaces, namely 'resources' (monetary or non-monetary), 'subjective well-being' (happiness, pleasure, etc.), 'rights' (human rights and other kinds of rights, some of them 'tradeable') and 'functionings and capabilities' (which are not equivalent but can be related). We also find reference to primary goods, but the fact is that some primary goods are rights whereas other are resources. Thus, to simplify matters, I consider here only the four big groups of informational groups as representatives of spaces. On the other hand, elements such as agency, autonomy, commitment, justice, equality, social responsibility, obligations, identity profiles and the opportunity aspect of freedom are not spaces *qua* spaces. But they are analytical categories, which make the CA relevant in comparison to other approaches that are not pluralist.

The challenge is that working within a pluralist perspective does not simply mean that we have a licence to use all types of information in normative evaluations and claim that we are using the CA (there is no problem when one is open about it; see, for example, Anand et al., 2009). It is essential to have an idea of the kinds of information that are privileged by the different perspectives and relevant to different contexts. But how can we carry out a pluralist informational analysis without a proper ex post systematization of the relevant informational spaces? To a large extent, capability lists, as put forward by Nussbaum (2006, 2011), can be seen as entry points for choosing informational spaces relevant to individuals' human development. Within Sen's CA, a great role is given to public reason as a mechanism for the identification, selection and justification of valuable capabilities. Nevertheless, public discussion and public reason are not vaccinated against false information, fake news and the other problems of asymmetric information and asymmetric power that plague democratic regimes. Here, I propose that making explicit the generalizability requirements of the CA can help to contextualize it within Sen's broader social choice framework. Moreover, it can better accommodate the role of public reason, which seems to be a panacea in Sen's normative evaluations.

Let me make explicit my suggestion: at the centre of Sen's critiques of several informational spaces is an argument about their lack of generalizability. This does not mean that they do not provide valuable informational spaces. Rather, this means that their nature and metrics should not be taken in isolation because they are not generalizable. If these informational spaces are not generalizable they produce evaluations that are not fully reliable. In this context, 'to generalize' means to use this informational space for a characterization of all the elements involved in a particular assessment. For instance, if we take into account utility as an informational space, we consider all relevant considerations in our assessment equally in terms of utility. Assume that all positive consequences are given in terms of utility. Then, generalizability would imply that we would also consider negative consequences in terms of utility. In this case, generalizability would be related to the utilitarian feature of 'welfarism', as defined by Sen (2009). Other informational spaces that have an intrinsic mechanic of generalization have been criticized by Sen precisely for their attempts at generalization, although Sen himself does not use this terminology. Indeed, he seems to avoid the issue of generalizability, advocating an ad hoc use of informational spaces in normative evaluations.

This problem can be solved by either

(1) justifying the particular use of a single informational space, given particular contexts; or
(2) generalizing the use of informational spaces on proper grounds.

But how can 'generalizing' informational spaces add value to this discussion? There are two potential benefits in looking for a generalizable format of informational spaces. First, it might assist us in thinking more logically about how different informational spaces are linked. Second, it may help us to identify and quantify different sources and kinds of inconsistencies in a pluralist approach. In order to explain more these potential benefits, it is necessary that we introduce some key elements from generalizability theory (hereafter GT).

The origin of GT goes back to Cronbach and colleagues' (1972) book on psychometrics and measurement errors, which focuses on variance procedures that assess variance components as a way of estimating the degree of reliability of several estimates (here we can think of estimates grounded on different informational spaces). The interesting point, then extended by Brennan (2001), is that information obtained from any measurement is fallible to some degree. Instead of simply contemplating the problem, he proposes that, in order to increase the precision of measurement, one can average over all pre-defined conditions of measurement, including the choice of ruler, or the persons who record the measurements, or even fix one or more conditions of measurement. There is an interesting trade-off between fixing a condition of measurement to reduce error and changing the interpretations of measurements. In the end, it depends on the conditions of measurement over which generalization is intended.

Although the context and the actual techniques put forward by GT are different from the ones faced by the CA, there is a common concern with inconsistencies and lack of reliability in informational spaces and measurement procedures. There is also a similar focus on 'universes of admissible information'. But the CA misses an important aspect of GT related to 'universes of generalization'. More formally, let us call different informational spaces 'universes of admissible information', consistent with Sen's (1977b) informational admissibility criterion. Then, generalizability analysis can lead to different 'universes of generalization'. Let us consider the following set of admissible information:

NRE = resources
NHR = human rights
NC = capabilities
NSWB = subjective well-being

The universe of admissible information will contain a condition facet and a rater facet. GT uses the word 'universe' for the conditions of measurement (which it calls prompts and raters) and the word 'population' for the objects of measurement (such as a person's education). What generalizability does is to bring together a framework in which all conditions that affect the measurement are parametrically specified. Thus, in the standard case, in which any response of any person, any prompts and any evaluations by any raters are considered admissible, the generalizability format will be a collection of a sample of n rates with p persons to t prompts – or $n \times p \times t$. (This process of putting together these combinations is known as being 'crossed with'.)

This simple insight from GT can be applied to the CA in order to produce a more systematic and informationally rich basis for normative evaluations. An example might be helpful. Assume that one person has a resource in the format of a book (r), and that this person has a certain literary skill to read the book (*c*) that produces a corresponding satisfaction with his or her reading (*s*). Specifying the conditions of use in the original generalizability theory for the impact of a certain resource on capabilities and subjective well-being will produce a 'crossed with' of $r \times c \times s$.

The CA can benefit from this simple insight from GT. It allows researchers or policy makers to identify and quantify the sources of inconsistencies in observed scores that arise, or could arise, over replications of a measurement procedure. Because context matters in the CA and no mechanical algorithm should be used, it is important that any informational analysis is shaped by the following five steps.

(1) Characterization of the facets of measurement that are of interest: it is here that context *prima facie* shapes the analysis. The choices of these facts, events, affairs are partially technical *and* partially normative (and this should be explicitly acknowledged), given that they depend on the 'moral salience' (as defined by Herman, 2007) of the situations being analysed. For instance, the same beggar can be perceived with indifference by a socially unconcerned person but can provoke a strong emotion on the part of someone shocked with his or her deprivation of basic capabilities.

(2) Once the facets have been specified, the different relevant informational spaces and universes of admissible observations should be chosen. Then, generalizability analyses can lead to different universes of generalization. This is not simply about the choice of relevant informational spaces but about an assessment of their 'generalization power' – that is, their potential for providing an inclusive informational basis.

(3) Admissible observations: Xre, Xhr, Xswb, Xc (namely 'resources', 'human rights', 'subjective well-being' and 'functionings and capabilities').

(4) 'Crossed with': Xre, Xhr, Xswb, Xc.

(5) Any observable measurement can be represented by some possible combinations of the different informational spaces that might be considered relevant to the situation:

$$\text{Advantage} = \text{Xre} + \text{Xhr} + \text{Xswb} + \text{Xc} + \text{Xre.hr} + \text{Xre.swb} + \text{Xre.c} + \text{Xhr.swb} + \text{Xhr.c} + \text{Xswb.c}.$$

This last step is important, because generalizability is not simply about a collection of individuals with '*re*' resources, entitled to '*hr*' human rights, enjoying a certain level '*swb*' of subjective well being and with the potential for '*c*' functionings and capabilities. In fact, generalizability is about the possibility of identifying and assessing the sources and degrees of inconsistencies in observed informational spaces, as represented by step (5).

It is important to note that generalizability goes beyond the solutions offered by Alkire, Qizilbash and Comim (2008) in classifying the CA into a narrow and a broad version. According to them, there is a narrow interpretation of the CA, which sees it as chiefly identifying capabilities and functionings as the primary informational space for certain normative exercises, contrasted against a broad interpretation, which allows a more extensive framework that could include, for instance, human rights or other values such as equity or responsibility. In the first interpretation, the CA would not be informationally pluralist, which does not seem very coherent with Sen's social choice framework, as discussed below. In the second interpretation, there is no organized way of handling plurality and richer informational spaces without an explicit recognition of the need to cross within the relevant spaces and variables. In order to examine a possible conceptual structure for generalizing different informational spaces within the CA, it is essential to contextualize it within SSC. In a nutshell: arguing that there is a narrow and a broad version of the CA is not sufficient for tackling the generalizability issue. For that, we should articulate it to Sen's SSC.

Sen's social choice approach

Apart from Sen himself (for example, 2002, 2009, 2017), only a few, such as Qizilbash (2007), have recognized the links between the CA and SSC (but see also Gaertner in this book). This might be due to the fact that the whole literature on social choice theory is very mathematical in its nature, and it might be harder for philosophers, social scientists and development economists (among others) to engage with it (Sen, 2009: 94–5). In addition, formal social choice theory has tended to concentrate on theoretical analyses that are remote from instant application (Sen, 2017: xii). However, this understandable difficulty is not sufficient to justify a lack of engagement with Sen's social choice analytical structure. Without repeating the arguments developed in Comim (2018), it is possible to introduce SSC with Figure 3.1.

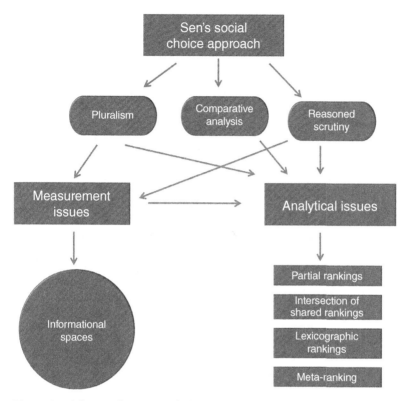

Figure 3.1 Scheme of Sen's social choice framework

This framework suggests that Sen's social choice approach has three pillars, namely pluralism, comparative analysis and reasoned scrutiny. It is within pluralism and the measurement issues that we find the issue of informational spaces. It is here that the CA has a role to play. But Sen's framework is much broader than the one offered by the CA, because it also comprises the pillars of comparative analysis and reasoned scrutiny. Very briefly, pluralism is the characteristic that demands an informationally rich account of state of affairs and the confrontation of different informational spaces. I consider it here represented by four main informational spaces (resources, rights, subjective well-being and capabilities), as represented by Figure 3.2, but it is in fact more complex, because other information categories could be added. For instance, the introduction of individual rights by Sen (1970b) in his article 'The impossibility of a Paretian liberal' has

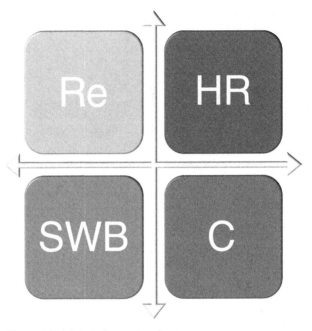

Figure 3.2 Main informational spaces

allowed the introduction of other features within his general framework, such as non-consequentialism.

Comparative analysis is the feature that motivated Sen's (2009) criticism of Rawls' transcendental institutionalism. It defies the usefulness of complete metrics or ideal standards for normative evaluations. It argues that assessments should be carried out within the limits of the possibilities of what is available and what it is possible to compare rather than between optimal options. One can also see this feature of SSC in Sen's (2002) distinction between optimization (choosing the best alternative) and maximization (choosing an alternative that is not worse than others). Comparative analysis is operationalized in SSC through the concepts of 'partiality' and 'incomplete rankings'. Thus, comparative analysis in SSC is intrinsically related to an analysis of situations that do not demand full comparability.

In its turn, reasoned scrutiny is the less visible pillar of SSC. It appears as a necessity for individual, public scrutiny and open impartiality (Sen, 1993). Outside Sen's SSC, too much is asked of reasoned scrutiny. But, as part of Sen's SSC, it is not a panacea, a way in which

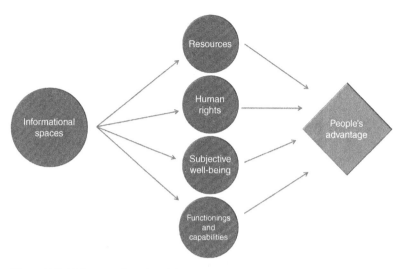

Figure 3.3 'Advantage' as the ultimate category

Sen can solve the issue of the identification and selection of dimensions and weights, as one would assume in a formal normative evaluation. Rather, it is an element in which positional objectivity can be overcome and impartiality can be achieved – an essential ingredient in any theory (or idea) of justice. Reasoned scrutiny comes with a strong argument against mechanical arguments. It is where context plays a role in SSC. Other information categories, such as 'consequence-sensitive' or 'comprehensive' outcomes, are derived from reasoned scrutiny.

Together, these three pillars constitute the foundation and analytical structure of SSC. They are clearly influenced by Sen's reaction to Arrow's impossibility theorem and provide a wider framework than the CA (Sen, 1986). This acknowledgement allows a proper focus on the contribution of the CA and its informational nature. In particular, it allows us to focus on how we can think logically about how different informational spaces are linked and how different methods may allow us to identify the main tenets of the CA in less arbitrary ways than those suggested by capability lists or by direct appeals to public reason.

For an illustration, we can return to the four key informational spaces discussed above, namely resources, human rights, subjective well-being and functionings and capabilities. Together, they can represent what Sen calls 'people's advantage' (Figure 3.3). This is an important concept. Although it is largely accepted that 'welfare' or 'well-being' do not represent an ultimate category for Sen, because, for instance, he highlights the importance of people's agency or autonomy (Sen, 1985), it is usually ignored that what he calls 'advantage' is actually employed by him as the most encompassing concept about one's life. However, this does not mean that 'advantage' is a homogeneous denominator. Rather, 'advantage' is plural and includes several different qualities and informational spaces, as illustrated below. Assuming otherwise would be a contradiction in Sen's thought, given that he is critical of the role of welfarism in normative evaluations (Sen, 1985, 2009).

A generalized approach: the generalizability tables

A generalized view of the CA allows a more systematic understanding of how these different spaces are related. If we start with resources, it is worth repeating that Sen's main critique is that 'resources are imperfect indicators of human well-being' (Sen, 1999: 80). It is important to note that he does not claim that resources provide no indication or reference of human well-being. Instead, he argues only that these resource indicators are 'imperfect'. This happens because, for Sen, individuals are diverse and heterogeneous in their characteristics and in their ability to convert resources into actual achievements. For this reason, the informational space of resources is not sufficient for a complete description of a person's advantage. On the other hand, it would be a mistake to ignore resources as an important informational space in assessing one's advantage.

Similarly, subjective well-being, or happiness, should not be fully ignored by normative assessments, despite its shortcomings. Indeed, Sen (2008) argues that it can provide an 'evidential role' in welfare evaluations. It is true that utility information can present several biases and distortions such as 'adaptive preferences'. But it should also not be ignored that subjective well-being can be an important functioning in itself and that, despite its biases, it accounts for an important category of information related to human flourishing.

In their turn, rights and liberties are extremely relevant for justice and policy making. At the same time, they should not be seen as absolute or lexicographic imperatives, because they must be considered alongside other concerns (Sen, 2009: 59). Rights could be formally granted without the guarantee of their actualization. In fact, there are

Table 3.1 *A 'generalizability table'*

Cases	Resources	Rights	SWB	Capabilities	Advantage
1	T	T	T	T	Full advantage
2	F	F	T	F	Adaptive preferences
3	T	F	T	F	Impossibility of a Paretian liberal
4	T	F	F	F	Conversion issues/ resourcist
5	F	T	F	F	Empty rights
6	F	F	F	T	Resilience

many international treaties and conventions that have been celebrated when agreed upon and signed without being implemented as planned.

A natural way of crossing all these different informational spaces is by using a 'generalizability table'. In its essence, this table is a way of systematically approaching different informational spaces. There is no particular order in which the different spaces can be listed. The important element is in checking the consistency and generalizability of the different spaces and in making an overall judgement under the rubric of 'advantage' (understood here as the most encompassing and comprehensive category of human flourishing in Sen's work). This analysis might be particularly relevant in conditions of 'unresolved conflict', as described by Levi (1986). There is no scope here to consider this issue with the detail that it deserves. It is enough to note that often evaluations hide moral struggles that are the essence of the problem at hand.

For simplicity's sake, it is suggested that, when positive outcomes of a particular informational space apply, they are considered 'true' (T) and, when they are negative, they are considered 'false' (F). Table 3.1 provides an abstract illustration of a generalizability table for six logically possible cases. Other combinations are possible, but these six cases represent an attempt to provide a logical structure within informational spaces, as explained in what follows.

Case (1) refers to a situation in which an individual (or a group of individuals, or a country) has enough resources to be in a favourable position. This could be an individual above a country's poverty line, or someone among the 10 per cent of the richest individuals in a nation, or a country classified as 'developed' according to its gross domestic product (GDP), etc. The point here is not the particular chosen measure but about someone being classified as 'fine' from a perspective that considers only resources as evaluation criteria. It might also be the case that this person enjoys certain rights (no matter which ones we have in mind) and that, according to this informational perspective, we also classify him or her as belonging to a favourable group. When asked, this same person (or national survey, in the case of countries) might be happy or not with his or her situation. Let us assume here that the person is very happy with whatever is the issue at stake. Moreover, if objective valuable functionings and capabilities can be verified, then we might also logically conclude that the person has a positive advantage. In other words, in this quite ideal case, all informational spaces would provide the same evidence of a person's or country's advantage. This could be the case for a person who has a health insurance plan, regulated by government legislation (granting certain rights), who not only is very happy with the treatment that he or she receives but who also enjoys good health. In this case, we will have to conclude that, either from a resources, or a rights, or a subjective or a capabilities perspective, this person is in a favourable advantage position.

Case (2) provides a more interesting possible circumstance. It reflects the situation when someone does not score well in terms of resources, rights or capabilities but subjectively considers him- or herself well or happy. When this happens, in this pure form, it provides a picture of the problem of adaptive preferences (when one adapts to a bad situation in order to survive in psychological terms). Happiness studies assume that subjective information can be generalized as an indicator of people's advantage. The problem is that this is an issue difficult to settle a priori in conceptual terms, and that it is better left as an empirical issue that might or might not be the case. Be it as it may, a generalizability table provides a simple way to visualize this issue.

Case (3) addresses a more complex situation, when resources and subjective informational measures suggest that a person is well but that his or her rights are not respected, with a corresponding deprivation of valued capabilities. This seems to be an extension of the case previously described by Sen (1970b) as the impossibility of a Paretian liberal, when subjective evaluations (in Sen's article, expressed by people's majority vote) end up violating the minimal liberty rights of a minority. This could be the case of a person with resources and happy with his or her life but who lives without political liberties or basic labour rights and who, as a result, cannot achieve certain freedoms (that is, certain potential functionings are not available to him or her, such as being able to freely express his or her political views).

Case (4) provides a characterization of the conversion problem, in which resources are imperfect indicators of people's advantage. This might be the case for someone who is affluent but who is nonetheless unhappy with his or her life and is deprived of rights and valued capabilities. Because people are diverse, they use resources differently according to their own possibilities. This means that someone might have a resource (for instance, a book), but might have it not because he or she has a right to have a book (or, worse, the book might be given to the person as the counterpart of a violation of his or her right). In addition, there is no necessity that this person is happy about having a book if it is about something in which the person is not interested. And, finally, he or she might not even open the book to read (not achieving a functioning or capability), because he or she does not value doing so, or because he or she simply cannot do so (in the event that the person is illiterate).

Case (5) is about empty rights, when one is formally entitled by rights granted by laws that are not translated into corresponding resources, subjective satisfaction or capabilities. This is often the case in many developing countries, where parliaments enact simplistic laws that are expected, on their own, to solve complex situations. In its simplest form, laws might not be implemented for lack of resources. As a result, ordinary people might not have their freedoms and capabilities expanded and might become very cynical about the existence of these rights on paper only. For instance, a country can pass a law to protect women from male violence, but, if insufficient resources are dedicated to implement the law and if other factors (such as male values) are not addressed, the enacted rights are empty.

Finally, case (6) considers the possibility that a person does not have enough resources to achieve a certain function or capability, is unhappy about it and does not have any rights on the matter, but, despite all that, he or she manages to achieve a valuable functioning or capability. This might happen when a child does not have certain constitutional rights in terms of being protected, lives a tough life (without the necessary resources, such as not having enough food) and is unhappy about his or her life, but somehow struggles through and manages to finish his or her education and accomplish a successful career. Another example would be a poor country that manages lower infant mortality rates despite unfavourable economic conditions, suffers from human rights violations and has a population that does not see it as a valuable achievement, because it values other things. There is no label in the CA literature for this kind of situation, but we can call it 'resilience' as a way of illustrating an unlikely positive outcome (in terms of functionings and capabilities) given the other negative circumstances.

Altogether, these six cases are not meant to be comprehensive, because other informational spaces and other combinations can be tried, but they provide a systematic way in which we can look from an integrated perspective at different informational spaces. This perspective does not assume that informational spaces are fully generalized, as is assumed by some approaches, such as the SWB or the narrow view of the CA, which advocates that everything should be portrayed in terms of capabilities. The use of generalizability tables has the potential to transform empty and unfruitful philosophical debates into concrete and practical empirical exercises in which different informational spaces are used in order to characterize the advantage position of a person, a group or a country.

But how can a generalizability table be seen as an instance of operationalization of Sen's social choice approach? First, it is quintessentially pluralist, because it combines several informational spaces, transforming their conceptual claims about generalizability into empirical and verifiable arguments. One cannot advocate Sen's pluralism and pursue an informational analysis based on a single information space (even if we are talking about the capability informational space). Second, its display is comparative, facilitating an internal comparison (between the different informational spaces used to assess people's advantage) independently from the outcomes of external comparisons (between the final advantages of different individuals or countries). Finally, the generalizability tables are not mechanical. They need to be interpreted according to the situations that they reflect. This means that scrutiny needs to be reasoned and justified. However, rather than starting with a *tabula rasa*, it provides an easier engagement with the approach.

Concluding remarks

Pluralism has always been an admired feature of the CA. But it has also been a hurdle for its operationalization, allowing ad hoc uses of the approach and a lack of rigour in its empirical applications. Pluralism should not do whatever one wishes it to do. Informational pluralism should not be about using whatever informational space that seems more convenient without any form of justification (often only because of data constraints). It should be about actually using different informational spaces. Moreover, it seems that viewing the CA *qua* an approach provides a misleading picture about the real nature of Sen's social choice approach, which is in fact much broader than what is suggested by the CA.

With this in mind, this chapter offers a possible simple way forward to handle pluralism, comparative analysis and reasoned scrutiny (the three key ingredients of the SSC approach) through the conceptualization of a generalizability table. Its formulation is inspired by Brennan's (2001) generalizability theory, expressing a way of producing 'crossed with' different informational spaces. In doing so, it avoids the two most common attitudes towards the issue of pluralism:

(1) total dismissal of the problem, by choosing a single informational space (often informational spaces that have been extensively criticized by the CA); or
(2) the use of composite indices that assume full commensurability and comparability between different elements (whether or not they come from different informational spaces).

It also faces the issue of reasoned scrutiny without overloading it, given that it provides a starting point, a concrete way of thinking about conflicting claims emerging from the different informational spaces without having to start from scratch. For this structure, it uses some CA analytical categories (it should be noted here that not much has been said by the CA literature about the issue of resilience). This point deserves full consideration, because the usual claims made by alternative informational approaches tend to fully or partially dismiss other informational spaces, which does not seem very reasonable. At the same time, Sen's claim for informational pluralism *cum* reasoned scrutiny cannot be a panacea for handling different (and sometimes conflicting) informational spaces in normative evaluations.

There is an empirical agenda for future research based on the use of generalizability tables. This work can be directed either towards characterizing some of the issues that have been mentioned, such as adaptive preferences or conversion problems, or towards making more explicit trade-offs and reconciling conflicting stances between different informational spaces.

References

Alkire, S., Qizilbash, M., and Comim, F. (2008) Introduction. In *The Capability Approach: Concepts, Measures and Applications*, Comim, F., Qizilbash, M., and Alkire, S. (eds.): 1–25. Cambridge: Cambridge University Press.

Anand, P., Hunter, G., Carter, I., Dowding, K., Guala, F., and Van Hees, M. (2009) The development of capability indicators. *Journal of Human Development and Capabilities*, 10 (1): 125–52.

Arrow, K. J. (1951) *Social Choice and Individual Values*. New York: Wiley.

Brennan, R. L. (2001) *Generalizability Theory*. New York: Springer.

Comim, F. (2018) Sen's capability approach, social choice theory and the use of rankings. In *New Frontiers of the Capability Approach*, Comim, F., Fennell, S., and Anand, P. B. (eds.): 179–97. Cambridge: Cambridge University Press.

Cronbach, L., Gleser, G., Nanda, H., and Rajaratnam, N. (1972) *The Dependability of Behavioral Measurements: Theory of Generalizability for Scores and Profiles*. New York: Wiley.

Garza-Vazquez, O., and Deneulin, S. (2019) The capability approach: ethics and socio-economic development. In *Routledge Handbook of Development Ethics*, Drydyk, J., and Keleher, L. (eds.): 68–83. Abingdon: Routledge.

Herman, B. (2007) *Moral Literacy*. Cambridge, MA: Harvard University Press.

Levi, I. (1986) *Hard Choices: Decision Making under Unresolved Conflict*. Cambridge: Cambridge University Press.

Nussbaum, M. C. (1990) *Love's Knowledge: Essays on Philosophy and Literature*. Oxford: Oxford University Press.

 (2006) *Frontiers of Justice: Disability, Nationality, Species Membership*. Cambridge, MA: Belknap Press.

 (2011) *Creating Capabilities: The Human Development Approach*. Cambridge, MA: Belknap Press.

Qizilbash, M. (2007) Social choice and individual capabilities. *Politics, Philosophy and Economics*, 6 (2): 169–92.

Sen, A. (1970a) *Collective Choice and Social Welfare*. San Francisco: Holden-Day.

 (1970b) The impossibility of a Paretian liberal. *Journal of Political Economy*, 78 (1): 152–7.

 (1974) Choice, orderings and morality. In *Practical Reason*, Körner, S. (ed.): 54–67. Oxford: Blackwell.

 (1977a) Rational fools: a critique of the behavioural foundations of economic theory. *Philosophy & Public Affairs*, 6 (4): 317–44.

(1977b) On weights and measures: informational constraints in social welfare analysis. *Econometrica*, 45 (7): 1539–72.

(1979) Informational analysis of moral principles. In *Rational Action: Studies in Philosophy and Social Science*, Harrison, R. (ed.): 115–32. Cambridge: Cambridge University Press.

(1980) Plural utility. *Proceedings of the Aristotelian Society*, 81: 193–215.

(1982) Rights and agency. *Philosophy & Public Affairs*, 11 (1): 3–39.

(1983) Evaluator relativity and consequential evaluation. *Philosophy & Public Affairs*, 12 (2): 113–32.

(1985) Well-being, agency and freedom: the Dewey lectures 1984. *Journal of Philosophy*, 82 (4): 169–221.

(1986) Foundations of social choice theory: an epilogue. In *Foundations of Social Choice Theory*, Elster, J., and Hylland, A. (eds.): 213–47. Cambridge: Cambridge University Press.

(1993) Positional objectivity. *Philosophy & Public Affairs*, 22 (2): 126–45.

(1999) *Development as Freedom*. Oxford: Oxford University Press.

(2002) *Rationality and Freedom*. Cambridge, MA: Harvard University Press.

(2008) The economics of happiness and capability. In *Capabilities and Happiness*, Bruni, L., Comim, F., and Pugno, M. (eds.): 16–27. Oxford: Oxford University Press.

(2009) *The Idea of Justice*. London: Penguin.

(2017) *Collective Choice and Social Welfare*, expanded edn. London: Penguin.

4 | Examining the challenge of communication in diffusing innovative education programmes
An analysis drawing on public choice, social choice and capability framings

SHAILAJA FENNELL

The sustained engagement between development policy and the capability approach (Sen, 1999) has resulted in a deeper treatment of the relationship between educational outcomes and individual flourishing (Hart, 2018; Unterhalter, 2017). There has also been a sustained engagement in political analysis with social choice theory to examine democratic outcomes, particularly through the theory of elections (Roemer, 1993; Elster, 1993) but there has been less direct interaction between development policy, in particular educational provision, and social choice theory.

There is a set of theoretical propositions that makes the case that education policy taking explicit account of the tenets of the capability approach can provide young people the opportunity to live a better future (Walker, 2005). There is also a powerful intellectual link between the capability approach and social choice theory, which regards the relationship between the policy making and human welfare as being mediated by a clear set of principles and ranking (Comim, 2018).

There is a distinctly different set of arguments, associated with a public choice perspective, that implies that public policy is not going to be an effective way of improving individual welfare, on account of adverse political and economic agendas. An associated problem is that innovation in educational policy sees challenges in scaling up, on account of adversarial relations between educational experts and government policy makers (Fennell, 2007).

Additionally, positions vary in the field of public policy making regarding how individual preferences are reflected in collective decision making. The narrow (positive) view is that it is the aggregation of individual preferences that determines collective decision making, while a broader (normative) approach requires the dissemination of public information as a necessary feature for making democratic decisions regarding social choices (List, 2018). The difference between the narrow and broader understandings of social choice theory (SCT) is that there is a focus on the structure of preferences by the former, while the latter regards the content of preferences as the central feature in understanding what ensures that individual preferences are deliberated on to form decisions at the collective level (Aldred, 2004).

This chapter addresses the questions of how policy choices to improve education might be addressed by looking across social choice theory, public choice theory and capability approaches. The intention is to try and understand how to evaluate innovative programmes that are set up to improve the chances of the most disadvantaged children, and why these well-intentioned programmes continue to face challenges in terms of ensuring a scaling-up procedure. The chapter draws on an evaluative study undertaken in 2014 and 2015 to examine the phenomenon of disseminating and scaling up the educationally innovative Activity Based Learning (ABL) programme.[1] The ABL programme was originally devised in the Indian state of Tamil Nadu, to improve the retention rates and learning outcomes of children from families living in challenging socio-economic circumstances. Our study was devised so that it could compare the manner in which the ABL programme was devised and implemented within the state of Tamil Nadu with the conceptual and operational methods for rolling out ABL in other locations, both within the nation and in other national educational environments. The intention was to understand why and how the transplanting of the original ABL innovation from its primary location and political economy had been undertaken in new sites/nations to which the ABL has been transported, and the extent to which it proved successful.

The expected outcome of this study was to distil the lessons of opportunities and challenges that are encountered in the process of moving successfully from pilot study to system-wide educational

---

[1] The evaluation, comprising four individual studies, was funded by the United Kingdom's former Department for International Development (DFID). The grant was awarded to Dr Shailaja Fennell at the University of Cambridge and the studies were undertaken by a group of researchers at the University of Cambridge, Institute of Education, University of London and Indian Institute of Technology, Madras.

reform. However, it became clear that both the pitfalls and the possibilities of creating a sustainable public policy regime so that an administration can ensure the functionality of its programmes have to be explored in order to understand the likelihood of an innovative education policy being scaled up through a diffusion of the original innovation. The contradictions that are uncovered in this exercise to reveal what ails the efforts to ensure the sustainability of programmes is, accordingly, reflected on by returning to the tenets of public choice and social choice theory.

The Paretian liberal and innovative educational programmes

The impossibility that faces a Paretian liberal arises from the difficulty of having to make a decision about the kind of policy approach to take with regard to the provision of goods and services when it is extremely likely that there are going to be more than two alternatives that relate to any choice made (Sen, 1970). The conundrum of the Paretian liberal continues to fascinate policy makers, and in the past decade there has been a growing interest in analysing the role that SCT plays in explaining choices undertaken by government with regard to public policy directives. One primary consideration is that of aggregation, and of how to group multiple factors so that we can compare each alternative, and this is a problem that is at the core of public policy making (Patty and Penn, 2014).

The example mirrors the case set out in Rawls (1971) concerning the aggregation of two principles – the first that of guaranteeing basic liberties, and the second that of equality of access to primary goods – and this raises the need to aggregate to make a decision as to which of the two states is more just. Beattie (1978) directs us to think of the consequences of the particular example of education: given the first principle being, of guaranteeing equality, and the second, of ensuring economic and social benefits, then providing basic education must be at the core of guaranteeing equality, and inequalities in education must be addressed by ensuring the most disadvantaged are best served. This logical extension makes the case that educational policy making should follow the principle of distributional justice.

Using this challenge of aggregation, let us consider an alternative A, when parents choose to send their children to school, and alternative B, the use of a teaching method that allows children to direct their own learning by choosing the pace of undertaking exercises. In understanding the freedom that children are able to experience through accessing education, there would be the distinct features of the opportunity aspect and the process aspect (Sen, 2005). Policy evaluations of educational innovations would need to examine whether the intervention was capable of ensuring that children are able to experience both features, and we need to consider what happens when only one aspect is available to children.

It is also important to consider the wider problem of how educational policy makers view the implications of the alternative forms of educational provision under consideration with regard to ensuring distributional justice. This would mean that in the case of alternative B – the use of a new teaching method being decided upon by an educational authority, or a state government within a federal system – there would also be a need to address the question of whether to use a process based on a narrow understanding of social choice, as an aggregation of individual preferences, or whether it should have a broader interpretation, with public information about the intervention widely disseminated.

A case study in innovative educational policy

Studying the pedagogic design, learning outcome, political economy and scaling up of the educationally innovative Activity Based Learning programme, originally devised in Tamil Nadu between 2014 and 2016, raised the puzzle as to why a programme that was widely acclaimed did not continue to flourish.[2] Innovations in education have been an important form of intervention, and they have focused on improving both the cognitive outcome at individual level and the experience of education in the country as a whole.

The state of Tamil Nadu is located in the southern part of India, with 32 districts, and it is ranked sixth in the country in relation to the Human Development Index and has a literacy rate of 80 per cent, according to the latest census figures (see www.censusindia.info/

[2] The DFID funded this evaluation study of the ABL programme as it was regarded as an important opportunity to understand how innovative educational programmes might be more fully analysed with regard to pedagogic methods and learning outcomes, as well as the political economy context and the innovative dissemination and scaling up of the programme.

tamilnadu.html). The ABL approach was initially introduced into 13 schools in the state capital, Chennai, in 2003, followed by a phased rollout across the entire state for all children studying in grades 1 to 4 in all government and aided schools by 2007/8 (World Bank, 2008). There was a subsequent rollout of ABL in the neighbouring union territory of Puducherry, which took place between 2009 and 2011. The dissemination to other states in India began with visits to the ABL schools in Tamil Nadu in 2008, and international interest in the innovation, and visits to ABL schools, sharply increased after the DFID education advisors' meeting in Chennai in 2009.

The focus of my own study within the larger project was to understand (1) how innovation spread through the educational sphere, in relation to the rationale for and the nature of the engagement displayed by the agents who adopted the innovation, and (2) the manner in which these agents further promoted the innovation to become a widespread system-level programme. My study undertook an institutional analysis of the process by which development pilots expanded into a programme across the whole state, and the particular form of dissemination that was adopted.

It was clear that, just because an innovative programme has been successfully piloted in a small geographical location, this does not mean that it no longer faces a major challenge in the transmission and adoption of the programme across the entire region/country. An early attempt to conceptualize the processes required for conscious communication is Rogers (1962), which maps out the diffusion process, stressing that, in most cases, an initial farsighted few are open to the new idea and adopt its use. As these early innovators 'spread the word' further, it is this communication that results in more people becoming open to adopting this idea. It is the ability of this early group to provide information and show aspects depicting the value of the innovation that is crucial in winning over the large remaining majority. In situations in which this process of diffusion gathers pace it leads to the development of a critical mass. Over time the innovative idea or product becomes diffused among the population, until a saturation point is reached. The progression of adoption is identified through five categories with regard to the adoption of an innovation: innovators, early adopters, early majority, late majority and laggards (Rogers, 1962).

Kaminski (2011) develops this line of thinking further, by focusing on the movement from innovator to laggards as representing a process of innovation. She argues that achieving a critical mass to ensure success depends on the ability of the innovators and early adopters to ignite the initial 'take-off' of the innovation adoption process, through their ability to generate favourable opinions of the results of the original innovation. Kaminski regards these opinion leaders as the integral change agents who influence their peers in the system, through (1) peer to peer communication, (2) role modelling and (3) networking.

There is also new thinking on how the relationship between innovators and adopters of innovative design can be examined in the case of educational innovations deployed in schools in the United States (Cohen and Ball, 2007). An important feature seems to be the relationship between the adopters and the designers. It appears that, in successful cases, it is important to distinguish between features of 'elaboration', which deal with the detail with which a reform is developed, and of 'scaffolding', which deal with the degree to which the innovation incorporates a strategy by which learning is carried out (Cohen and Ball, 2007).

The case of the educational sphere in Tamil Nadu was a valuable study of innovative education practice, undertaken by the state's Education Department as an equal partner with the national educational programme, known as the Sarva Shikha Abhiyan (SSA). The educational reform undertaken by the government of Tamil Nadu was based on a commitment for reform within the educational institutions of the state government, and has been identified as part of the growing acceptance of the need for public–private partnerships in education (Gopalan, 2013: 33). Previous evaluations had indicated that the completion of the rollout of ABL across all districts of Tamil Nadu was a success and that this boded well for the adoption of a national-level programme across other Indian states. The ABL programme came to be regarded as a model for a system-wide high-quality reform that other Indian states might like to observe in action and to consider as a blueprint for their own reform of primary education (Geetha Rani and Kannappan, 2011).

Sampling criteria

The study was conducted in the state of Tamil Nadu, where ABL was originally devised, and also the neighbouring administrative unit, the union territory of Puducherry. The rationale for this sample selection was that the schools in the Kanchipuram district of Tamil Nadu were part of the rapid rollout of the state-wide ABL programme between 2006 and 2008 (see Mohapatra, Baker and Sahoo, 2008), while with Puducherry it was the case of a late adopter through a process of political engagement. The research tools adopted in the study were focus group discussions and interviews with teachers and headteachers. Interviews were also conducted with the key educational stakeholders at the state and federal levels.

Rationale for educational innovation

The original identification of the problems in successful educational provision in Tamil Nadu was with regard to children in difficult environments, particularly those whose families were in bonded labour. It was this challenge that instigated the push for an innovative design and the preparation of content that had the ability to retain child labourers in the school system. The formal process began with the signing of a memorandum of understanding between the city corporation and a teacher-training institute, which resulted in about 100 teachers from 13 schools of the city corporation undertaking the training programme and forming the innovator group.

The dedication of the teachers, who were the early adopters of the idea of ABL, and their sense of professionalism and personal importance was paramount for the creation of a volunteer group throughout 2003/4. It was largely a consequence of the unflagging effort and commitment of this group that a new set of teaching and learning materials was designed and was made available for use in corporation schools by April 2004. The full set of feedback and improved cards were subsequently developed on the basis of the prototypes and printed for incorporation into teacher resource packs (Pillay and Ramaswami, 2009).

There was also active and regular interaction between the bureaucrats, teachers and educational institutions in Tamil Nadu, which become a hallmark of the early stage of innovation work in the ABL programme. This collaboration, and the attention to detail that went into the design and production of materials, indicate that careful regard was paid to both the elaboration and scaffolding aspects of the original design of the educational innovation, both of which were key aspects of the Cohen and Ball (2007) analysis.

All the teachers in the Chennai Corporation were informed about the persistent problem of children in difficult environments not staying on at school, so as to make them fully aware of the problem. This was followed by bringing on board the district-level officers with an invitation to be part of the process. This peer-to-peer engagement and the role model effect of the personal and professional actions played a fundamental role in bringing about a powerful form of opinion leadership. The resultant sharing of a common information set to assist in the creation of a collective consensus as to the value of this educational intervention was crucial in ensuring a motivated and active set of early adopters.

The commissioner of Chennai Corporation and the education secretary were also able to gain traction at the national level, and had the full support of the federal joint secretary to get support for a state-wide pilot with ten schools in each of the development blocks in the state. The commissioner was also able to enlist the support of key institutional figures in the educational establishment, and UNICEF helped fund a state-wide ABL pilot in Tamil Nadu. All education officers in UNICEF India were able to participate in a week-long innovator training programme in 2005 (UNICEF, 2011). In contrast, the lowest level of administrative unit, the block training institutions, and their established teacher trainers were not invited to be part of the project. This choice of working with external facilitators at the pilot stage seemed to keep the focus on how to create an innovation attractive enough to teachers to ensure that they would choose to be the change agents, through designing teaching and learning tools. The omission of the existing training providers fits in with the notion that this was not a programme to replace the existing system of education provision but to guarantee the introduction of a specific programme to ensure that the most marginalized students might be retained in the schooling system.

At the juncture where the pilot project was being converted into a full-scale state-wide reform the ABL initiative benefited tremendously from explicit encouragement and approval from national government officials and international donors. The biggest draw of the ABL initiative, for these stakeholders, was that the programme was built around child-centred activities. It was this primary set of features, and the manner in which it was developed, namely directed and driven by the teachers themselves, that made the initial diffusion of the innovation and the quantitative scaling up so successful. The subsequent stages of scaling up – those of functional improvements, such as the revising of cards, and congruence between cards and books – required a feedback mechanism between the larger teacher body and the SSA office. The ability to ensure functional improvements proved to be the difference between success and failure in transferring the ABL programme from Tamil Nadu to Pondicherry. Furthermore, the lack of will to work through the conditions for political scaling up in Pondicherry meant that the organizational scaling up in this neighbouring union territory did not eventuate. The energy generated by the innovator/early adopter nexus was at the very core of creative and innovative design, but this was not transferred to the recognition of individual teachers in every single school once the programme had been rolled out across the entire state.

These policy features corroborate the findings of other research that show that success in scaling up requires an effective assignment of functions to specific actors at different levels by the agent(s) of change. Clear instructions as to what, and how, actions should be taken and what tools should be used employing field-tested operational manuals are emphasized (Binswanger and Aiyar, 2003). However, the results of scaling up should not be presumed to emerge quickly or readily in a process of educational innovations. As the educational reform requires an institutional response to ensure that it becomes embedded in the environment, it takes time. In the case of the ABL programme, the available resources, both financial and human, were expended on the creation of the core team of early adopter teachers at the pilot stage. In the next stage of rolling out the programme across Tamil Nadu the consensus of the teachers, who formed Rogers' 'early majority' group, was achieved by active information exchange between teachers in the state education system. This channel of communication was less readily available when the ABL programme was subsequently offered to other states in the country, due to both a shortfall of financial support and challenges arising from a lack of capacity to undertake workshops for the rapid translation of teaching and learning materials into other regional languages (Sarangapani et al., 2013).

The key messages and the findings of the DFID study (Singal et al., 2016; Aslam et al., 2016; Bedi and Kingdon, 2016; Fennell, Duraisamy and Shanmugam, 2016) indicate that the power of experiencing the ABL pedagogy was the key lever that persuaded teachers of the value of a child-led learning process. The importance of an innovation design that permitted internal agents – the teachers in the corporation schools – to work with the innovator trainers created a strong sense of motivation. The education professionals who had the opportunity to observe the ABL pedagogy successfully used peer-to-peer methods and networking to provide an effective and supportive platform to raise the visibility of ABL (Westbrook et al., 2013). The leverage of these processes seemed to emerge from the ability to ensure that the various dimensions of Uvin's (1995) scaling-up process – the quantitative, functional, political and organizational – were taken into account. The pilot was successfully transformed into a state-level programme for government schools, and the skills needed to generate an ABL programme were transferred to make sure that the functional aspects were in place, there was buy-in from state level and federal officials for political approval, and district-level institutions as well as other state educational institutions were brought into the process to ensure institutional involvement.

It also seemed to meet the features of Kaminski's (2011) diffusion criteria – peer-to-peer learning, role models and networking – within the state of Tamil Nadu. With the support of key institutional figures in the educational establishment, and a core team of 100 volunteers, it would appear that they did have considerable opportunity to learn and network. In contrast, it was also evident that in new environments, such as the neighbouring union territory of Puducherry, which had previously run a different teaching curriculum; or in poorer communities with pastoral backgrounds, resulting in high absentee rates or multi-grade classrooms that created more challenging environments, there was a lower level of success in rolling out ABL-type programmes. This seemed to indicate that it was the weaker political will in other states or the economic challenges of working in poor communities that resulted in a low success rate for the transference of the programme.

However, it might also have been that analysis of the diffusion process required the inclusion of criteria that had elements of choice that had been missing in the earlier exercise. More recent frameworks in the social sciences indicate that there is a need to concentrate more explicitly on the freedom available to late adopters to take up or refuse a new innovation. The consensus building that was a central feature for convincing the early majority was the result of deliberative decision making among teachers in Tamil Nadu. This was the result of a clear strategy of communication that was an explicit part of the procedures set up at the within-state stage of the rollout of the programme.

It is key to note that the methods of communication adopted were based on equality of treatment for teachers and mutual respect for the design and teaching skills of each member of the early adopters and early majority groups.

There remain challenges about how to evaluate choices made between programmes of education provision. It is clear that, in the case of the ABL, there was little attempt made by the original team to aggregate the various criteria for the selection of participants; nor was there a specification of within-programme goals, and the sole focus was on the rollout at the state level. The result of this shortcoming was that it was not possible to undertake a comparison of the objectives, uptake and outcome of the ABL programme in relation to other, alternative interventions.[3] To put it in another way, our 'alternative B' was inadequately defined and communicated. This also meant that no index was established by which to examine the aggregation of choices, by teachers, schools or states, and evaluate the learning outcomes (Patty and Penn, 2015).

The continued challenge of policy diffusion

A model by Shipan and Volden (2008) identifies four mechanisms of policy diffusion: learning from earlier adopters, economic competition, imitation and coercion. By bringing in the importance of economic features such as competition and coercion, they go beyond the broad-brush category of the political environment set out by Uvin, and indicate that it is important to look at the reasons for adoption. In particular, this facilitates the realization that learning in schools is part of the larger democratic exercising of choice (Shipan and Volden, 2008)

This additional set of criteria makes it possible to instigate an explicit review, allowing us to look at the relationship between early and later adopters in greater depth than purely the form of engagement focused on by Kaminski, to the political and economic reasons

---

[3] In the report submitted to the DFID, there was a review of other innovative education programmes in India that were running at the time. It remains the case that there has been no evaluation of the variation in the level of collective consensus that was generated by these programmes. This is an unfortunate state of affairs, as there is a plethora of innovative practice that could benefit from an examination through the creation of a complex index to generate a fuller understanding of educational outcomes.

as to why policy makers take on or reject policy innovations that are offered by other jurisdictions. The second feature, competition, is introduced to take up the matter of economic spillovers: that it is only when there are economic benefits from adoption that late adopters are likely to be amenable to adoption. The third criterion, imitation, makes a more explicitly political point, by making the case that adoption will be more attractive where there is value in emulation, and, specifically, in looking and behaving like the early adopters. In contrast, Cohen and Ball (2007) presume that early and late adopters share the same preferences as they are all teachers. This assumption is replaced by the possibility that there might be a difference in explicit objective function between the early adopter government and later adopter governments. The final mechanism, that of coercion, brings to the fore the possibility that the decision to become a late adopter might not be the result of choice but an imposition due to overt political pressure.

The introduction of an explicit choice dimension helps us understand more fully the process of diffusion for innovative policies, and also makes it logical to bring in institutional analysis, such as that of Streeck and Thelen (2005), which identifies the types of institutional change that take place when new policies are adopted. Their model identifies five different types of change: displacement, layering, drift, conversion and exhaustion. The first of these, displacement, is a form of institutional change brought in because the existing/traditional policy is not regarded as fit for purpose, or the nature of the problem that it is addressing has been reconceptualized or there has been a reconsideration of an alternative route to overcome the problem. The second change, that of layering, is when modifications are made to existing institutions with the intention of changing the dynamics of the organization. The third, drift, is, in contrast, a process of change that is not purposive but comes about due to erosion and gaps in the existing system of rules in the institution. The fourth, conversion, is far more political – an active desire to change goals and functions – and can be the result of contestation within the institution. The final type of change, exhaustion, occurs when there is clear breakdown in the institution.

The explicit use of the economic and political features of making choices for future social policy, and the implications for the successful diffusion of that policy, are set out in Table 4.1.

Table 4.1 *Diffusion of innovation and institutional change*

Uvin (1995)	Shipan and Volden (2008)	Streeck and Thelen (2005)
Quantitative	Learning	Displacement
Functional	Economic competition	Layering
Political	Imitation	Drift
Organizational	Coercion	Conversion
		Exhaustion

Source: Author's own.

Placing these categories against the original proposition set out by Rogers (1962), on using communication as a form by which the diffusion of innovation can be ensured, shows that there is a need to examine the political and economic features of the underlying choice. The original proposition focuses on the power of communication, and the effectiveness of the spread of the message. The message was seen as sufficient to bring about change.

The explicit treatment of the dissemination of ideas with the logic of how the preferences of policy makers might affect the success that early adopters have of gaining the support of late adopters can be understood by making explicit the nature of economic and political consequences. While Uvin's model regards the 'political' as the ability to get across the message as set out by Rogers (1962), the Shipan and Volden model points out that the information is reviewed in the light of the economic (competition and spillover) and political (imitation) gains that can be achieved by adoption, and the Steeck and Thelen model indicates that these can come in the context of a range of conditions in existing institutions, with some choices being that of replacing existing policies and others of additional value being added to existing policy.

There is also the possibility that the early adopters were placing explicit political demands on the late adopters – coercion in the Shipan and Volden model and conversion in the Steeck and Thelen model. These ideas of domination were absent in the Kaminski extension of the Rogers model, as it was presumed that there was freedom of choice, that a late adopter would not take on board a new policy change if it was not superior to the previous model in achieving their objective function. Kaminski (2011) emphasizes that, when the innovator is an external actor, the ability to attract early and late adopters is dependent on the power of communication. Power is understood as the successful ability to convey the key ideas of the innovation to a new audience, and promote public deliberation among the members of the audience. In the case when the adopters of the original innovation are themselves the designers, and therefore internal agents, of the method of adoption – as in the case of the adoption of educational innovations in US schools (Cohen and Ball, 2007) – it becomes important to identify whether the method of engagement between early and late adopters has been one of 'elaboration', dealing with the detail with which a reform is developed. The second is 'scaffolding', which deals with the degree to which the innovation incorporates a strategy, and means of learning, for carrying it out. Some innovations contain detailed elaboration, such as a curriculum, examples of learning outcomes and testing of outcomes. This type of elaboration provides adopters with an important starting point, and is a useful enabling feature. It could be argued that, in contrast, when there are limited instructions in terms of design, scaling up may well result in weak and variable implementation. An elaborate design may also push away adopters who feel obliged to go through a detailed process of implementation in order to realize the innovators' design. The second feature of innovation, that of scaffolding, has to do with the provision of materials and social processes to support the learning process (the 'scaffold'). Any innovation needs to provide guidance on new practices, such as the use of new published or video materials for teaching lessons. Scaffolding provides the process of teaching and learning, while elaboration provides the objectives of learning (Cohen and Ball, 2007).

Considering the rollout of the ABL programme, it appears that the early majority teacher group (in Kanchipuram) was exposed to a form of diffusion that incorporated elements of elaboration as well as scaffolding. In contrast, the later majority (those in the neighbouring union territory of Puducherry) had a disproportionately large element of elaboration and inadequate incorporation of aspects of scaffolding.

This resulted in a lower level of collective consensus in the latter territory, and the results indicate that these component parts of an innovative educational programme need to be explicitly evaluated in order to ensure sufficient financial and human resources for a successful rollout.

This logic of choosing between educational programmes by the local authority of a state was a matter that was addressed by Arrow (1951: 3) with regard to considerations of how to fund public education. In these considerations of social choice. It is clear that, when there is a need to ensure the creation and support of collective choices, it becomes important to explicitly take account of the ordering of values (Arrow, 1951: 18). In this regard, the evaluation of the ABL programme would require taking explicit account not just of individual tastes but also of individual values. Thinking in relation to our 'alternative B', a fuller description would require not only a description of the intention of the innovation but an additional explanation of how teachers and schools can choose to participate, and the procedures in place to provide information that would facilitate deliberate decision making. Using this type of more comprehensive framing of public choice in the field of diffusion of innovations in the sphere of educational programmes would be in keeping with a broader view of social choice that emphasizes the important of deliberative outcomes.

Innovation and educational choice

The central conceptual proposition set out by the Shipan and Volden and Streeck and Thelen expanded frameworks on policy innovation and adoption emphasize that, while studying how change makers (both innovators and early adopters) seek to influence later adopters, it must be situated within a larger context of economic and political consequences. These can be evaluated through a separate exercise of the benefits and costs of adoption for the late adopters.

Successful implementation in terms of the dissemination and scaling up of innovative programmes requires more than an examination of how change makers influence political opinion makers (the Uvin model: column 1 of Table 4.1). It is also important to consider whether this was the consequence of coercion (column 2, row 4) or conversion (column 3, row 4), which would indicate that, rather than being enthused by a process of bureaucratic activism, the late adopters were driven by considerations of the political limitations of their own state institutions. The explication of the political in these models allows a fuller understanding of the aspects of public choice thinking, and needs to be explicitly addressed as part of the innovative education programme design and plans for diffusion of the innovation.

Let us revisit the approach adopted by my previous study of ABL in Tamil Nadu, when the model had led us to regard the programme as successful as it had a combined critical mass of the innovator and early adopters, and include the new consideration of the reasons why the adopters from other jurisdictions – other Indian states and international players alike – were keen to adopt the programme. Both sets of players were keen to adopt the programme because of the explicit elements of elaboration and scaffolding, which caught the attention of teachers in these other jurisdictions. This keenness needs to be examined through the lens of the Streeck and Thelen model to identify how the desire for institutional change might have been due to either drift or exhaustion (column 3, rows 3 and 5) in their own jurisdictions. The choices made cannot be fully comprehended without a fuller examination of the conditions in the educational institutions in their own countries. It might even be that there was a behavioural nudge that was inappropriately introduced, more akin to that of 'libertarian paternalism', as identified by Thaler and Sunstein (2008).

It is important to consider what it is that innovative educational programmes set out to achieve, and where they fall foul of the principles of successful scaling up of programmes on account of inadequate consideration of principles of choice, in particular with regard to the differences between individual tastes and values, in policy making. Recognizing that the core feature in policy making is to ensure basic liberties and access to primary goods for the most disadvantaged, as set out by Rawls, then it is important to ask whether the ABL programme, or any other innovative educational programme, was able to ensure that child-centred pedagogy was able to operate in all jurisdictions.

From the perspective of the educational institutions that were looking to adopt these programmes, the rationale for adoption needs to be investigated more thoroughly. If the intention of the administrative jurisdiction is to improve the freedom of opportunity and process aspect of freedom for the most disadvantaged children, then we can see how social choice theory does lead directly into the capability space (Comim, 2018). The teacher is then able to fully support the decision of an individual child being free to choose which puzzle he or she wants to take down from the shelf to test his or her linguistic or numerical skills.

However, if an institution is making the decision to adopt not on the basis of the simple political buy-in based on the informational content regarding the innovation (Uvin's model) but on its own political logic related to the current state of its institutional capacity, then there is a lower likelihood that the adoption of the innovation will result in successful delivery of an improved educational delivery. It is only situations that correspond to the first two rows in each of the three columns – Uvin, Shipan and Volden, Streeck and Thelen: quantitative and functional diffusion, learning and competition, and replacement or layering, respectively – that will result in improved delivery.

If, instead, the adoption is based on political manoeuvring on the parts of both early and late adopters, whether more or less skilfully, corresponding to imitation or conversion due to the conviction of the early adopters in the former situation, or due to coercion or exhaustion due to lack of resources among late adopters in the latter situation, it would appear that we are no longer in a world where the principles of individual choice are paramount. This would hold even in a situation of a policy change based on public announcements that its entire purpose is to improve the choices of the most disadvantaged child, as it is now driven by the political considerations of the institution itself.

Increasing people's functioning capabilities will certainly involve improving their functioning prospects, Nussbaum and Sen (1993) suppose, so that focusing on capability does not involve neglecting prospects. But there are other ways of improving functioning prospects apart from increasing functioning capabilities, and the position they adopt is that capability is the only route to functioning that we can wholeheartedly embrace. Although they do not address the matter in these terms, they may think that capability is lexically prior to prospects, in the sense that, although it is better to have higher rather than lower prospects, capabilities should never, or perhaps never in ordinary circumstances, be sacrificed for the sake of improving prospects (Pettit, 2001).

In general, informational broadening, in one form or another, is an effective way of overcoming social choice pessimism and of avoiding impossibilities, and it leads directly to constructive approaches with viability and reach. Formal reasoning about postulated axioms (including their compatibility and coherence), as well as informal understanding of values and norms (including their relevance and plausibility), both point in that productive direction. Indeed, the deep complementarity between formal and informal reasoning – so central to the social sciences – is well illustrated by developments in modern social choice theory (Sen, 1999).

If the means of securing for the most disadvantaged children the right to schooling through their ability to choose their preferred pace of learning are not put in place at the outset of an innovative educational programme, then any subsequent discussion of the 'means' that are argued to achieve an 'end' cannot be adequate from the point of view of social justice.

Conclusion

The implication for educational policy making is that ensuring a move away from a welfarist approach to one in which the focus is on an equitable society must concentrate on equality of opportunity and the process aspect of freedom (Ferreira and Peragine, 2016). It is not enough that the educational innovation has an innovative design in relation to elaboration and scaffolding (Cohen and Ball, 2007), for, although these will work for the layering of institutional change and fostering imitation among late adopters, these institutional changes can fall foul both of the impossibility faced by the Paretian liberal and of ensuring the conditions needed to bring into play the nudge of the 'libertarian paternalist'. This situation arises because of principle A – that all parents have the ability to choose schooling for their children – and principle B: that the innovative design introduced in schools to allow the most disadvantaged children to choose their pace of learning can work only in tandem, when there is an egalitarian view of educational provision. It is impossible to achieve this in a world of explicit political considerations in educational institutions, as the logic of choice is no longer exclusively that of the child but is weighted in favour of the needs of the institution.

This is not to disregard the importance of the resource requirements of educational institutions or of pressures that force them to operate through logics of coercion or conversion. The central point to make is that the study of innovative educational design through the diffusion process cannot be understood via a model that adopts a simple logic of communication; it needs a richer information base to be able to analyse the interactions between the early adopters and late adopters within the explicit context of the educational institutional framework of different jurisdictions.

The need for innovative educational programmes is strongly felt precisely because of the difficulties faced by the most disadvantaged children in trying to succeed in the schooling system. To guarantee a just educational system it is necessary to ensure that the families in these most disadvantaged circumstances have the surety that their children will be able to gain from accessing education – and this will require both opportunity of freedom of choice and the process of freedom of choice.

An aspect of this feature of a just educational system, from the perspective of the philosophy of education that has been recently been discussed, is that educational policy should enable children to be self-supporting in the future (Hart and Brando, 2018). The implication of this position is that young adults should be able to manage their way through different avenues of life, be they as minimal as being aware of their rights to vote. There is an aspect here that links to Sen's own differentiation between the opportunity aspect of freedom and the process aspect of freedom in living one's life. It could be argued that these are learnt in school.

The consequences of this proposition for the principles are as I set out at the start of the chapter: for alternative A, that parents should be able to choose education for their children they would need to agree that there was some value that results from education; and, for alternative B, that children should be able to choose a method of solving problems that is best suited to their learning. The ABL, and every other innovative education programme that sets out to ensure that a child does have better access to education, should be based on meeting the objectives of the opportunity and process aspects of freedom alike: that children can access the new methodology and that they can benefit from the experience. The upshot is that any innovative education programme, set up as a result of a set of change makers, must be evaluated not only through its ability to move from early to late adopters; it must also be assessed with regard to the economic and political contexts within which the late adopter institutions took to the new programme. In those contexts in which there were challenging resource constraints, or poor monitoring of educational outcomes or limited ability to communicate the need for a richer information base so as to make fully informed choices, it becomes very possible that a well-designed programme will not be able to sustain itself through the scaling-up process.

The value of innovative education programmes becomes nullified in a political and economic environment in which there is an institutional push to transfer a successful educational programme from one jurisdiction to another without a full review of the resource availability and institutional capacity of existing educational institutions. Although educational innovation is more necessary than ever in social situations in which there is rise in inequality, which increases the likelihood of forms of disadvantage, the perverse operation of political and economic constraints could result in an outcome that aligns more closely with the prognosis associated with public choice rather than social choice theory (Mueller, 2015).

The capability approach makes the argument that policy making can be emancipatory when it is based on participation and public reasoning (Sen, 1999), paving the way for a clear case that the outcome will be one of greater ability on the part of young adults to experience both freedom of opportunity and the process element of opportunity. The challenge is that, when educational policy is plagued by inadequate resources and there is the perverse condition that educational administrations need to resort to political opportunism – or, worse still, are forced into conditions of coercion or conversion of late adopter institutions – it is clear that the situation is one in which public policy has moved from the benefits of meeting the principles of social choice theory to the challenges of dealing with public choice conundrums.

In this flip-flop scenario, in which policy making can shift across conceptual frameworks, it becomes clear that the original design of the innovative educational programme would cease to be egalitarian, one that has been undertaken to support the most disadvantaged youth. It would become regarded as one that can be opportunistically used to shift from an egalitarian solution to one that is hijacked to overcome the economic and political constraints of other jurisdictions. There is a further danger: that there could be a move away from ensuring that the principles of social choice theory are met, to be replaced by a policy-making agenda that regards it as necessary to adopt education policies based on what is needed to direct the most disadvantaged to make the better choice, taking one into a scenario that is a version of the currently preferred policy of the 'nudge'. This is a world in which 'libertarian paternalism' rules.

The case of innovative educational programmes makes it clear that it is a challenge to understand why these well-intentioned programmes do not easily transition into sustainable systems that improve the life chances of individuals. Indeed, what this case study shows is that application of the principles of social choice and public choice to an innovative education programme in India, with implications for similar programmes in other countries, remains a difficult proposition. It opens up the uncomfortable position of recognizing that a consequence of the operation of the new educational innovation is that there must be a much more rigorous analysis of the principles of welfare, and a willingness to examine the kinds of political and economic contexts that are in place. Without this additional evaluation of the principles of institutional functioning, and how the interactions between early adopters and later adopters can further or thwart the advancement of human lives, there will continue to be unpleasant discoveries to the effect that good intentions do not ensure social justice.

References

Aldred, J. (2004) Theory and deliberative democracy: a comment. *British Journal of Political Science*, 34 (4): 1747–52.

Arrow, K. J. (1951) *Social Choice and Individual Values*. New York: Wiley.

Aslam, N., Rawal, S., Vignoles, A., Duraisamy, M., and Shanmugam, M. (2016) The trajectory of learning: the ABL story in Tamil Nadu, India. London: DFID.

Beattie, N. (1978) Formalized parent participation in education: a comparative perspective (France, German Federal Republic, England and Wales). *Comparative Education*, 14 (1): 41–8.

Bedi, J., and Kingdon, G. (2016) The political economy of the scale-up of the ABL programme in Tamil Nadu. London: DFID.

Binswanger, H. P., and Aiyar, S. S. (2003) Scaling up community-driven development: theoretical underpinnings and program design implications, Policy Research Working Paper 3039. Washington, DC: World Bank.

Cohen, D. K., and Ball, D. L. (2007) Educational innovation and the problem of scale up. In *Scale-Up in Education*, vol. 1, *Ideas in Principle*, Schneider, B., and MacDonald, S.-K. (eds.): 19–36. Lanham, MD: Rowman & Littlefield Publishers.

Comim, F. (2018) Sen's capability approach, social choice theory and the use of rankings. In *New Frontiers of the Capability Approach*, Comim, F., Fennell, S., and Anand, P. B. (eds.): 179–97. Cambridge: Cambridge University Press.

Elster, J. (1993) Some unresolved problems in the theory of rational choice. *Acta Sociologica*, 36 (3): 179–90.

Fennell, S. (2007) Tilting at windmills: public–private partnerships in Indian education today. *Contemporary Education Dialogue*, 4 (2): 193–216.

Fennell, S., Duraisamy, M., and Shanmugam, M. (2016) Dissemination and scaling up of the Activity Based Learning programme. London: DFID.

Ferreira, F. H. G., and Peragine, V. (2016) Individual responsibility and equality of opportunity. In *The Oxford Handbook of Well-Being and Public Policy*, Adler, M. D., and Fleurbaey, M. (eds.): 746–84. Oxford: Oxford University Press.

Geetha Rani, P., and Kannappan, S. (2011) Provision of quality elementary education for all under Sarva Shikha Abhiyan at an affordable cost in Tamil Nadu. In *Millennium Development Goals and India: Cases Assessing Performance, Prospects and Challenges*, Mishra, R. K., and Raveendran, J. (eds.): 95–104. New Delhi: Allied Publishers.

Geetha Rani, D. S., and Tideman, N. (2013) Varieties of failure of monotonicity and participation under five voting methods. *Theory and Decision*, 75 (1): 59–77.

Gopalan, P. (2013) *PPP Paradox: Promise and Perils of Public–Private Partnership in Education*. New Delhi: Sage.

Hart, C. S., and Brando, N. (2018) A capability approach to children's well-being, agency and participatory rights in education. *European Journal of Education*, 53 (3): 293–309.

Hart, S. (2018) Education, inequality and social justice: a critical analysis applying the Sen–Bourdieu analytical framework. *Policy Futures in Education*, 17 (5): 582–98.

Kaminski, J. (2011) Diffusion of innovation theory. *Canadian Journal of Nursing Informatics*, 6 (2): http://cjni.net/journal/?p=1444.

List, C. (2018) Democratic deliberation and social choice: a review. In *The Oxford Handbook of Deliberative Democracy*, Bächtiger, A., Dryzek, J. S., Mansbridge, J., and Warren, M. (eds.): 463–89. Oxford: Oxford University Press.

Mohapatra, A., Baker, K. L., and Sahoo, R. N. (2008) *Activity Based Learning: Effectiveness of ABL under SSA*. Chennai: SchoolScape.

Mueller, D. (2015) Public choice, social choice, and political economy. *Public Choice*, 163 (3): 379–87.

Nussbaum, M. C., and Sen, A. K. (eds.) (1993) *The Quality of Life*. Oxford: Clarendon Press.

Patty, J., and Penn, E. (2014) *Social Choice and Legitimacy: The Possibilities of Impossibilities*. Cambridge: Cambridge University Press.

Patty, J., and Penn, E. (2015) Aggregation, evaluation, and social choice theory. *The Good Society*, 24 (1): 49–72.

Pettit, P. (2001) Capability and freedom: a defence of Sen. *Economics and Philosophy*, 17 (1): 1–20.

Pillay, M., and Ramaswamy, R. (2009) Qualitative studies of selected educational initiatives in south Indian states (Karnataka, Tamil Nadu and Andhra Pradesh): revisiting education for all. 158143834.

Rawls, J. (1971) *A Theory of Justice*. Cambridge, MA: Harvard University Press.

Roemer, J. (1993) A pragmatic theory of responsibility for the egalitarian planner. *Philosophy & Public Affairs*, 22 (2): 146–66.

Rogers, E. M. (1962) *Diffusion of Innovations*. New York: Free Press.

Sarangapani, P. M., Jain, M, Mukhopadhyay, R., and Winch, C. (2013) *Baseline Survey of the School Scenario in Some States in the Context of RTE: Study of Educational Quality, School Management, and Teachers: Andhra Pradesh, Delhi and West Bengal*. Mumbai: Tata Institute of Social Sciences.

Sen, A. (1970) The impossibility of a Paretian liberal. *Journal of Political Economy*, 78 (1): 152–7.

(1999) The possibility of social choice. *American Economic Review*, 89 (3): 349–78.

(2005) Human rights and capabilities. *Journal of Human Development*, 6 (2): 151–66.

Shipan, C., and Volden, C. (2008) The mechanisms of policy diffusion. *American Journal of Political Science*, 52 (4): 840–57.

Singal, N., Pedder, D., Duraisamy, M., Manickavasagam, S., Shanmugam, M., and Govdinrajan, M. (2016) ABL pedagogy in schools and classrooms in two districts in Tamil Nadu. London: DFID.

Streeck, W., and Thelen, K. (2005) *Beyond Continuity: Institutional Change in Advanced Political Economies*. Oxford: Oxford University Press.

Thaler, R., and Sunstein, C. (2008) *Nudge: Improving Decisions about Health, Wealth and Happiness*. London: Penguin.

UNICEF (2011) *Evaluation of UNICEF's Position in India: Final Evaluation Report*. New York: UNICEF.

Uvin, P. (1995) Fighting hunger at the grassroots: paths to scaling up. *World Development*, 23 (6): 927–39.

Unterhalter, E. (2017) A review of public private partnerships around girls' education in developing countries: flicking gender equality on and off. *Journal of International and Comparative Social Policy*, 33 (2): 181–99.

Walker, M. (2005) Amartya Sen's capability approach and education. *Educational Action Research*, 13 (1): 103–10.

Westbrook, J., Durrani, N., Brown, R., Orr, D., Pryor, J., Boddy, J., and Salvi, F. (2013) *Pedagogy, Curriculum, Teaching Practices and Teacher Education in Developing Countries*. Brighton: Centre for International Education, University of Sussex.

World Bank (2008) Field visit to Sarva Shiksha Abhiyan. Washington, DC: World Bank.

5 | Nudging the capabilities for a sustainable city?
When the libertarian paternalist meets the Paretian liberal

P. B. ANAND

Introduction

Cities offer choices; in general, the larger the city, the greater the range of choices. Thus, in principle, urbanization (i.e. the increase in the share of the population living in urban areas) and the process of expanding substantive freedoms must go hand in hand. The visionary development economist Sir W. Arthur Lewis (1955) foresaw a central role for urban economies in the transformation of societies and in significantly boosting productivity-enhancing jobs. However, this is not universal. For example, we know that, as some countries urbanized, their urban poverty also increased significantly, and some countries urbanized without any change in life expectancy at birth of the urban population (Anand, 2018).

The UN Sustainable Development Goal 11 (SDG11) focuses on sustainable cities and communities. All SDGs are interconnected, and cities cannot become sustainable unless they become inclusive and equitable, especially by taking urgent steps to address gender inequalities (SDG5) and all forms of inequalities (SDG10), conserve water and energy (SDGs 6 and 7) and promote innovation for responsible production and consumption (SDG12). Cities have a complex and three-sided relationship with climate change: as significant contributors of greenhouse gases, and thus complicit in causing climate change; as important victims of the effects of climate change; and as a source of innovation and public action, and therefore able to help mobilize global, national and local actions to mitigate climate change. In many cities, the poorest and most disadvantaged people within the cities are the ones who are most vulnerable to climate change impacts, although it is difficult to be precise, as vulnerability is contextual and poverty is multidimensional. (For some early estimates on the link between urban poverty and climate change, see Satterthwaite et al., 2007.) Islam and Winkel (2017: 5) examine the links between climate change and social inequality within countries using a conceptual framework that connects multidimensional inequality to three pathways of climate change effects, namely 'greater exposure to climate hazards', 'greater susceptibility to damages caused by climate hazards' and 'less ability to cope with and recover from the damages caused by climate hazards'.

Cities can be great liberators and play an important role in promoting awareness of freedoms, liberty and human rights. The images of Martin Luther King Junior addressing the crowds in Washington, DC, in August 1963, or the narrative description of the thousands of people who thronged the streets of Cape Town on 11 February 1990 to greet Nelson Mandela at the City Hall (Mandela, 1994: 563), are unforgettable examples of the intimate connection of cities and freedoms. However, these images of cities as cradles of freedom are also contrasted with cities as the theatres of rape, oppression, corruption and obscene wealth inequalities. Inequality in access to education and health entrench existing social inequalities and make them generational inequality traps. Escaping from such a trap is difficult and rare, and involves opportunism, cleverness and sheer luck. From Charlie Chaplin's *City Lights* to Raj Kapoor's *Sri 420* to Danny Boyle's *Slumdog Millionaire*, numerous Hollywood and Bollywood films portray such social mobility to be entwined with significant moral dilemmas.

A freedom-centred perspective on cities is about the inherent plurality of the citizens. Different people in the city have different preferences and priorities. Allocating the scarce resources of the city to improve infrastructure and public services requires careful attention to the distributional equity and social justice considerations. Therefore, all urban public policy questions require multidimensional evaluations and involve some degree of aggregation of preferences. The capability approach helps urban policy analysts to expand the informational space and develop multidimensional evaluations. Social choice theory (SCT) can help in understanding the dilemmas and impossibilities of aggregating individual preferences to arrive at socially preferred rankings of alternative projects for public services.

This chapter aims to examine some of the challenges and opportunities in applying SCT and the capability approach for urban public policy analysis. Few studies exist on applying social choice theory and the capability approach to urban sustainability issues. In the conclusion of an extensive review of Arrow's impossibility theorem for planning process, Sager (1998: 136) recommends that 'further theoretical knowledge of the functions of planning might be drawn from a similar analysis based on Amartya Sen's paradox of the Paretian liberal and other impossibility theorems'. This chapter aims to contribute towards bridging this gap, but with a greater focus on practical applications. In particular, I want to focus on behavioural dimensions of public policy and critically examine the extent to which nudges can be used in making cities sustainable, and what some of the procedural and moral dilemmas are in this context. I take case studies of specific urban challenges and highlight these issues.

The elusive quest for an inclusive city: social choice and the Paretian liberal in the city

Making a city truly inclusive requires many institutional and policy interventions. Although all cities utter the language of participation and inclusion, in reality few cities transform themselves to become 'cities that listen'. Majoritarian rule is an easy (and, one might say, lazy) solution, and a form of local democracy is (incorrectly) considered a pathway to making cities inclusive. There is some confusion here. Drawing from the principles of justice enunciated by John Rawls (1971), it is possible to set up institutional arrangements to deliver equality of opportunity for everyone to participate in decisions concerning the allocation of public resources. However, as both Rawls and Amartya Sen (2009) have emphasized, equality of opportunity is a necessary element of inclusive institutions, but it is not sufficient in itself to guarantee inclusiveness. The fact that there are so few professors of black and minority ethnicity in the higher education institutions in the United Kingdom is a good reminder that equality of opportunity does not translate into equality of outcomes.

In 'The impossibility of a Paretian liberal', Sen (1970) highlights important dilemmas of social decisions. Suppose that there are at least two different individuals (say, 1 and 2) in a city and that they have preferences over some social arrangements such as transport (say, x = public transport and y = private vehicle). The condition of unrestricted domain (U) requires that 'every logically possible individual ordering is included in the domain of collective choice rule'. Condition P (Pareto principle) requires that, if everyone prefers x to y, then that society as a whole should also prefer x to y. Condition L (liberalism) requires that, for each individual citizen, there is at least one preference ordering that the society should accept. (Condition I is about the independence of irrelevant alternatives – that is, all relevant alternatives are included in the choice sets. In the rest of the chapter, it is assumed that only options that meet this criterion are included in the social choice formulation.)

The impossibility theorem suggests that, in a democratic setting, there is no social decision function that meets all three of these conditions simultaneously. In the context of cities, there are numerous situations of social decisions, all of which present impossibility. Suppose individual 1 prefers public transport (x) to private vehicle (y) but individual 2 prefers private vehicle (y) over public transport (x). Similar kinds of social ordering issues can be raised with publicly funded schools versus private schooling; publicly funded hospitals versus private hospitals; and so on. In the case of unrestricted resources, there is no conflict, and it would appear that we can grant both of these choices to the two individuals according to their preference. Let us call this a 'win-win' social choice situation. However, in many cases, the allocation of more resources to meeting one citizen's preferences would entail cutting the budget for other projects that are a priority for another citizen. We can call them 'zero-sum' (or 'nosey') social choice situations. Many allocation problems faced by cities are indeed 'zero-sum' social choice situations, and meeting the liberties of one person (or one group) will entail sacrifices of the minimal liberties of another person (or other groups).

Let us take a few more examples. Suppose 1 likes to go walking every day and finds that the city's roads do not have proper pavements or walkable infrastructure for pedestrians (highlighted in Anand, 2018). Citizen 1 would like the city government to invest in pedestrian facilities (x), creating more parks in each neighbourhood (y) and widening the streets (z). However, the committed driver who is citizen 2 would prefer the money to be spent on road widening, then perhaps better parks (to which he or she could drive), and thus is not the least bit concerned about pedestrian facilities (z > y > x). Under budget constraints, these choices become 'nosey' and the social choice situation becomes an impossibility.

Another example within the domain of education: suppose citizen 1 is an adult who did not have a chance to go to high school but now has reached a station in life that her curiosity has been triggered, and she wants to go to evening school. She would prefer the city government to spend on adult education/evening classes (x), while she also would like better schools for her own children (y). She has little preference for spending on high level scientific research in the university (z). Citizen 2 is a middle-class professional and already sends his children to a good-quality private school. He would like the local university to maintain its position in the rankings of universities, and thus prefers more research funding (z), with perhaps the remaining money going to evening classes (x), so that there is less competition for his own children from other children attending the ill-equipped local schools (y).

A third example is relevant to discussions on the role of the city in culture. A group of people (say, maybe those athletically inclined) would prefer that the city spends the resources to upgrade training facilities and running tracks (x), and invest in community gyms and swimming pools (y), rather than the city spend on repairing the major venue for cultural events (z). Another set of citizens who are afficionados of classical music and opera prefer the city to invest in theatre (z) than in running tracks or gyms. Investing in a theatre might itself privilege certain forms of cultural activities and not others (such as Bollywood dance classes or laughter clubs).

These social choice dilemmas highlight the fact that, by nature, a city is a battlefield of conflicts of different interests and preferences. Inclusivity here means that the city gives equal value to all freedoms of all individuals, but uses a transparent and consistent approach in imposing restrictions on freedoms when this is justified by the ends. The quest for an inclusive city is elusive for the very reason that such a process of sorting social choices from individual freedoms has to be gone through again and again for every important issue that concerns citizens. By improving the institutions and transparency processes for social choices and their evaluation, the city can strive to become inclusive.

An enigma of a sustainable city

The United Nations (2018) has estimated that in 1950, out of just under 3 billion inhabitants on the Earth, two-thirds were in rural areas and the remaining third lived in urban areas. By 2018 there were 4.2 billion people living in urban areas (while 3.4 billion people lived in rural areas). It also estimated that, between 2018 and 2050, the world's urban population will increase by a further 2.5 billion people, with nearly a half of this accounted for by just eight countries, namely India, China, Nigeria, the Democratic Republic of the Congo, Pakistan, Indonesia, the United States and Bangladesh. Thus, as the urban population has grown, the recognition that cities are central to realizing sustainable development has also grown.

The expression 'sustainable cities' has been quite popular (albeit a bit less popular than 'green cities') for over two decades, although since 2014 the expression 'smart cities' has become a lot more popular (see Figure 5.1).

For a city to become a sustainable city, the needs of the present generation should be met without placing an ecological imposition on other communities or compromising the ability of future generations to meet their needs. However, cities do consume a lot of water, energy and other material resources and produce large quantities of waste.

For many cities, the fundamental aspect of sustainability concerns water and food security. Water scarcity is a complex issue, and many cities, especially in the Global South, face chronic shortages of water. In previous publications (Anand, 2007), I have explored in great detail water consumption patterns globally and through various cross-national relationships. I find that, even within a city, there are huge variations in the amount of water consumed per person. An entitlements analysis suggests that the urban poor households, typically those living in slums and peri-urban locations, tend to have more limited entitlements to water, and thus have a precarious command over their access to water. This is an example of intragenerational inequality that is highlighted by Solow (1993) and Anand and Sen (2000). A campaign urging citizens to save water or reduce their water consumption has no relevance to the urban poor households that already have a very limited amount of water. A human right to water is an attractive proposition, and many countries have endorsed the UN General Assembly resolution 64/292 of 2010. However, a proclamation of access to water (and sanitation) as a human right does not automatically translate into improved access to water, especially for the urban poor households and marginalized individuals (see Anand, 2007). As Sen (2017: 347) notes, a libertarian approach to justice might accord

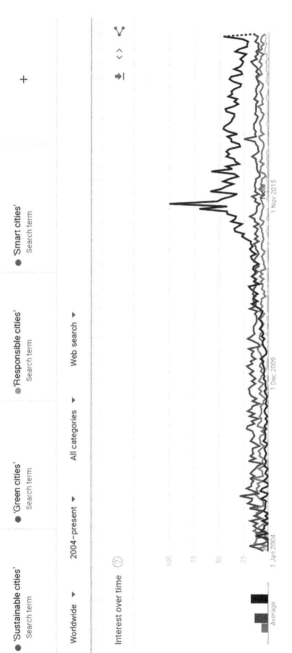

Figure 5.1 Popularity of 'sustainable cities' in Google searches, January 2004–April 2021

high priority to rights and liberties, but 'even large famines can occur without anyone's libertarian rights being violated'.

Data from the Aquastat data portal of the Food and Agriculture Organization (FAO) suggest that, between 2013 and 2017, 183 countries (for which data are available) jointly consumed 475 cubic kilometres (or billion cubic metres) of water for municipal purposes. This works out to approximately 68 cubic metres per person per year or 186 litres of water per capita per day for every one of us on this planet. However, we know that there are huge inequalities in access to freshwater resources. People with municipal access in better-organized cities tend to consume more water every day than people who have to fetch water from communal water points or depend on private water vendors. Thus, power asymmetries impact on social choice. Cities consume large quantities of water, often by transfer from distant sources such as rivers, lakes and aquifers. This can raise intragenerational fairness issues, let alone intergenerational issues. For example, Chennai in the Indian state of Tamil Nadu has been facing water scarcity for more than five decades. Arrangements have been made over the years to transfer water from the river Krishna with an inter-state agreement, and also from Veeranam Lake, and so on. Similarly, the Municipal Corporation of Greater Mumbai procures water from various sources, including from dams and lakes in the Nasik, Thane and Palghar districts. During the summer months local wells in the villages near Palghar can run dry, while water flows without interruption to the distant Mumbai. Similarly, water is transported to Delhi from the distant Tehri dam.

The website of the C40 Cities network estimates on its webpage (www.c40.org) that cities 'consume over two-thirds of the world's energy and account for more than 70% of global CO_2 emissions'. The United Nations estimated a decade ago (UN Habitat 2012) that cities consumed over 70 per cent of primary energy. The relationship between economic growth in gross national income per capita, urbanization and energy use per capita is rather complex but it appears that the pursuit of economic growth can lock in countries to higher energy intensity unless specific steps are taken to decarbonize urbanization. This requires huge investment in renewable energy and a clear urban energy strategy. Some cities have committed themselves to become net-zero carbon entities. For example, seven cities – Bistrita, Frankfurt, Manchester, Modena, Tartu, Vilvoorde and Zadar – have formed a network to become net-zero cities by 2050. Another group of cities have formed a network called the Carbon Neutral Cities Alliance and aim to become carbon-neutral in the next ten to 20 years. However, it is not easy to compute a city's CO_2 emissions. There are direct emissions from the city (scope 1), due to energy use by household energy consumption (for heating or cooling, and domestic energy use for cooking), the transportation of passengers and goods, and industry and commercial activities. Then (scope 2), there are emissions attributable to the city for the electricity it consumes no matter where that electricity was generated. There are also indirect emissions (scope 3), attributable to the consumption in the city even though such emissions occur outside the boundary of the city (whether within the same country or far away in another part of the world). If a city imports meat that is produced in faraway Brazil or New Zealand, should we count the CO_2 in the production of that meat as belonging to those countries or should it be accounted for at the city where it is being consumed? What about the emissions during the transport of such goods?

To become truly carbon-neutral, cities will have to reduce their energy use significantly, switch from fossil fuels to renewables (and export surplus energy), reduce their water and waste footprints significantly, increase their recycling rates significantly and – as far as possible – encourage the consumption of locally grown produce to reduce emissions in transport. However, global cities are part of international loops, and the livelihoods of many poor people in faraway locations who are part of such loops rely on the consumption patterns of cities. If all cities switched overnight to local-level looping and started sourcing all their materials from local producers, the consequences could be catastrophic for many millions of people producing food and various commodities in many different countries. In the pursuit of carbon neutrality, it should not be forgotten that people living in slums already have very little ecological footprint. In fact, the average level of CO_2 emissions for cities with slums would appear to be lower than those for comparable cities without slums, and such average emission figures hide the considerable inequality within the city (McGee et al., 2017).

Calcott and Bull (2007) use the ecological footprint methodology to estimate the footprints of 60 cities, and find that citizens in the United Kingdom have a footprint that ranges from 2.78 global hectares (gha) per capita in Newport and Plymouth to 3.62 gha per capita in Winchester. Kennedy et al. (2015) estimate that the 27 largest cities in the world (the mega-cities, each with a population greater than 10 million inhabitants) together accounted for over 9 per cent of global electricity consumption, 10 per cent of gasoline and 13 per cent of solid waste. A World Bank study (Kaza et al., 2018) estimates that 2.01 billion tonnes of municipal solid wastes were generated in 2016 and that per capita waste generation rates were on average about 0.74 kilograms (kg) per person per day, but this varied over a wide range, from 0.11 kg to 4.54 kg per person. Typically, citizens in high-income countries tend to generate a lot more waste per capita than their counterparts in least developed countries. The United Nations (2010) estimates that 2 million tonnes of human wastes are disposed of in water courses.

Thus, as the world urban population continues to grow, the various environmental impacts of cities will significantly increase in two ways: first, there will be more urban residents each contributing to the water, energy and material demands; second, the hypothesis of the environmental Kuznets curve (EKC) suggests that, as economic prosperity grows, the per capita energy and resource consumption rates are likely to increase significantly. Without serious efforts to reduce the environmental and resource impacts of cities, the possibility of making cities sustainable remains a mirage.

However, at first sight, imposing restrictions on citizens and curtailing their freedoms appears to go against the idea of minimal liberties. It appears that to tell people to spend less time in the shower or to leave their car at home or to use a bit less of their central heating or air-conditioning is akin to preventing someone from painting his or her house pink while everyone else prefers the house to be painted white (an example used in Sen, 1970). Anand and Sen (2000: 2030) remind us:

We cannot abuse and plunder our common stock of natural assets and resources leaving the future generations unable to enjoy the opportunities we take for granted today. We cannot use up, contaminate, our environment as we wish, violating the rights and the interests of future generations. The demand of 'sustainability' is, in fact, a particular reflection of universality of claims – applied to the future generations vis-à-vis us.

Later in that paper, Anand and Sen ask the question 'sustaining what?' and emphasize that what needs to be sustained is the 'nature of lives that people can lead'. They further remind us that 'the fact that in that sustaining, human agency would be pivotal, does not reduce in any way the significance of human life as an end' (2040).

Table 5.1 *Six types of injustices or inequalities caused by cities*

	Present generation	Future generations
Within the city	Type A: present inequalities within the city	Type D: effects of present citizens on future citizens of the city
Beyond the city – but through direct footprints	Type B: present injustices due to direct impacts on distant communities due to extraction of water, resources and transfer of wastes	Type E: intergenerational injustices on indigenous people, deforestation effects
Nationally or globally through extended and indirect footprints	Type C: present injustices due to indirect impacts and global supply chain effects	Type F: climate change effects, long-term effects due to transfer of hazardous wastes

Source: Author's construction.

A central emphasis of the sustainable human development approach is to empower citizens to make choices that recognize this universalism of claims of present and future generations. Deliberative public reasoning may be one of the ways through which important decisions on responsible consumption may be made. I have discussed some criticisms of applying the capability approach to sustainable development and how these criticisms can be overcome in Anand (2014). The main criticisms are that the capability approach is not a dynamic concept; that it may be individual-centred, and therefore it may be difficult to connect an analysis based on capabilities with systemic level of sustainability constraints; and that, although the capability approach helps us in recognizing the multidimensional nature of well-being, it may not be useful in explaining decision pro-cesses. These are surmountable. Building institutions that empower citizens to exercise their full agency can help to overcome most of these criticisms.

The pursuit of sustainability involves moving from less just to more just situations (more just for the future generations or communities impacted by the ecological footprint of cities). However, due to the magnitude of their impacts, cities pose six types of distributional jus-tice or equity issues (see Table 5.1). Of these, three (types A, B and C) are within the present generation (hence intragenerational equity issues), while another three (D, E and F) are intergenerational issues.

To some extent, type A inequalities (present-day inequalities within the city) can be handled through city-wide municipal bodies and planning processes. However, this is not as simple as that. For example, the work of Sir Michael Marmot (2010) has shown that, within cities, there can be significant differences in the life expectancy. This has come to be known as the 'social gradient'. I have shown from 2014 data that, within the Bradford district, there was a life expectancy gap of nearly 14 years between the residents of inner-city wards such as Manningham compared with rural Keighley or Ilkley (Anand, 2018). Health inequality reflects the underlying social inequality (see Institute of Health Equity, 2020, and Bambra 2016). Social gradients are difficult to estimate for cities in the Global South due to the difficulty in getting appropriate data, as well as the fact that, in many cities, the urban poor households are a majority and they live in all locations in the city (with the exception of enclaves of high-income neighbourhoods). However, results from Mberu et al. (2016), which compare the health outcomes and indicators of slum residents with rural and urban (non-slum) residents in Bangladesh, Egypt, India and Kenya, indicate that, for almost all health indicators, slum residents fare worse than non-slum urban residents.

Type B inequalities (present-day injustices due to direct impacts on distant communities) may not be brought to light because of the collective action challenges of distant hinterland communities. Think of the difficulty of organizing a protest by small farmers in rural Palghar to have their voice heard in Mumbai, or of the farmers of distant Tehri to be heard in Delhi.

It is even more difficult to restore injustices of type C (present-day injustices due to indirect impacts), which are difficult to trace precisely because they are indirect. Those who cannot be seen cannot be heard. 'Nimbyism' (where 'nimby' stands for 'not in my backyard') contributes to exporting problems to distant locations. A simple example is that of the thousands of consumers in the United Kingdom and the European Union buying cheap clothes made by workers in risky garment factories in places such as Bangladesh. The Rana Plaza fire disaster in April 2013 brought to light the moral dilemmas of consumption decisions that involve global supply chains. That incident has triggered increased attention to corporate social responsibility (CSR), but the problem is not yet fully resolved given that it is difficult to distinguish between real CSR, which transforms the core values of a company, and so-called CSR projects that are mere greenwash. Another example of a type C dilemma can be petroleum that is sourced from conflict locations such as Angola or Libya and used to produce automotive fuels used by consumers in North America or Europe (see Wenar, 2008). Another example concerns plastic wastes. With increased awareness about plastic wastes and their impacts on marine ecosystems, many nations are beginning to take stricter actions aimed at curbing single-use plastics and restricting plastic waste imports. In January 2020 Malaysia returned 42 containers of illegal plastic waste to the United Kingdom. As more and more consumers care about the environmental impact of their consumption decisions, consumer goods companies such as Unilever are pledging to halve their use of virgin plastic by 2025 and increase the content of post-consumer recycled plastic in their products. Some countries, such as Kenya, have been early to act by banning single-use plastic bags.

An example of a type D injustice (effects of present citizens on future citizens) is increased groundwater pumping by today's citizens. Years of such pumping can result in a significant fall in the groundwater levels, and in some coastal cities this can also lead to saline water ingress. Thus, the overconsumption of groundwater by present citizens can significantly limit the availability of groundwater for future citizens.

An example of a type E injustice (intergenerational injustices on indigenous people and deforestation) is the long-term effect of leaching action from solid waste disposal, especially through landfill. Wastes exported from consumers in a large city today to landfill locations in the outskirts may continue to leach and affect groundwater, and in turn the flora and fauna in the area. For example, there is an infamous waste landfill station near Ghazipur, north of Delhi. Alam, Sharholy and Ahmad (2020) note that, due to leachate from the waste site, groundwater in the vicinity of the site is not suitable for domestic or commercial consumption. The World Health Organization (WHO, 2015) notes that health impacts of landfill sites can include an increased incidence of cancer, birth defects and respiratory diseases. Tomita et al. (2020) note that, in South Africa, living within 5 km of a waste site was significantly correlated with asthma, tuberculosis, diabetes and depression.

Type F impacts (climate change effects) do not really need elaboration. Current fossil fuel consumption in cities contributes to greenhouse gas emissions and thus increases the risks of climate change effects on future citizens everywhere. Certain climate change impacts are already occurring, and in this case they can be included under type C (present-day injustices due to indirect effects) in this model.

To be truly sustainable, every city must act on all six of these injustices. However, localism tends to prioritize cities on issues of types A and B; and short-termism limits actions on D, E and F. Collective action is essential for some of the issues to be heard and considered in policy discussions. Many relevant stakeholders, especially for injustices of types B, C, D, E and F, tend to have limited opportunities to participate in city-level deliberations. Each of these six types of challenges to justice raises concerns for the Paretian liberal. Pure liberalism of unfettered freedoms clashes with universalism and the responsibility to protect the lives of others, both in present and future generations. The Covid-19 pandemic required governments, including those of liberal social orders, to impose lockdowns and social-distancing measures in order to save lives. The Covid-19 lockdown issues require an in-depth analysis of their own – something for further research by readers of this volume. However, this experience shows that there is no real conflict or inconsistency to liberalism when there is clear reasoning that such restrictions are to save lives. Another similar event is when emergency services ask residents to evacuate their homes due to an impending hazard such as a flood or a volcanic eruption. A commitment to become a sustainable city would require careful consideration of the various injustices and then the taking of the necessary steps to remove them. The scheme of deliberative public reasoning can help to set reasonable limits and guide social choice.

Nudging towards sustainability

Although behavioural public policy has existed for a long time, Thaler and Sunstein (2008) propelled it to the mainstream of public policy with their influential book *Nudge*. This is based on the irrationality of our preferences and flaws in the process of choice. Thaler and Sunstein suggest that intervening in the decision-making process to guide the citizen to choose pro-social choices is paternalism, but, since individual freedoms are not violated, it amounts to libertarian paternalism.

Sen (1977) highlights the shortcomings of the rational choice models and the theory of revealed preference. If we are observed choosing x when both x and y are available, the revealed preference theorist concludes that we prefer x to y. However, Sen reminds us that there is nothing wrong with inconsistencies in preferences reflected by choosing x over y on one occasion and choosing y over x on another occasion. In fact, we can picture in our minds a twinkle in the eye of Professor Amartya Sen (1977: 323) as he suggests that 'you can frustrate the revealed preference theorist through more sophisticated inconsistencies as well'.

Thaler and Sunstein (2008) suggest that, by rearranging the sequence in which options are presented, the choice architect can influence the decision process. Profit-oriented firms have been doing this for decades, such as by keeping high-calorie sweets and crisps within easy reach near checkout queues in supermarkets and petrol stations. For example, Marcano-Olivier et al. (2019) report a randomized control study of four primary schools to study the impact of a low-cost nudge, namely improved positioning of fruit and better and attractive labelling. They observed a significant increase in fruit consumption by children in the intervention schools. Upton, Upton and Taylor (2013), in an earlier study of the so-called 'Food Dudes' programme, attempted to study a similar intervention in six schools compared with seven schools without the intervention. Their study shows increased intake of fruit and vegetables three months after the intervention, but finds no difference 12 months after the intervention. Perhaps children were indeed following Professor Sen's advice to frustrate the randomistas. Bauer et al. (2021) examined three nudges in connection with the consumption of fruits and vegetables in the cafeteria of a medium-sized company in Germany. One intervention is an email that employees received before lunchtime reminding them about the Green Line (a section of the cafeteria with a salad bar). A second intervention was to close one of the tills ('under maintenance') for the all-inclusive section, thereby increasing the queuing time there while the Green Line remained unchanged. A third intervention was to paint green footprints on the cafeteria floor to gently draw people towards the Green Line. The strongest increase in Green Line was observed in study 2 but the authors recognize that, of the three interventions, this was a natural experiment and was less transparent and less directly related to the goal of increasing vegetable and fruit consumption. Schubert et al. (2021) report that both graphic general health warnings (without mentioning any specific disease) and specific health warnings about diabetes can help reduce the consumption of sugar-sweetened beverages. Giacherini et al. (2021), in a study of over 23,000 consumers in 14 restaurants, show that 'norm' nudging by offering a doggy bag to pack away food left over by a consumer can help overcome the shyness and sense of shame and significantly reduce food waste in restaurants.

In another study, Hoxby and Turner (2012) show that a low-cost nudge can significantly increase the proportion of low-income high-achieving school students applying to selective colleges.

In a study of the adoption of smart meters for energy consumption by European consumers, Giest (2020) notes that nudges are context-dependent, and various other factors including regulation affect whether a nudge works. Drews, Exadaktylos and van den Bergh (2020) note that nudges and incentives have to be used carefully in a policy mix. They study energy use and note that, although many studies individually study either nudges or incentives, when using both of these, policy makers need to be cautious as there can be crowding out effects (meaning we should not assume that the effectiveness of a policy instrument when used on its own may be greater than when it is used in combination with other instruments).

In transport, nudges can help in improving driver behaviour and reduce pollution and accidents. Rubaltelli et al. (2021) examined the driving behaviour of a group of college students on a simulator, and they tested whether the so called 'left-digit' nudge had any effect on the speed of driving. Thus, in the experiment, road signs were modified to show 49 miles per hour instead of 50 miles per hour. Their study shows that the average speed in the experiment group was consistently lower than in the control group, for whom no such change was presented.

Nudges can help in reducing waste and improving recycling rates. Akbulut-Yuksel and Boulatoff (2021) examined the effect of a green nudge, the transparent bag policy in Halifax, Nova Scotia, Canada, on the overall recycling rate and municipal solid waste generation; they note that such a policy contributed to improved recycling and reduction in the total amount of waste generated. Wensing et al. (2020) report that nudges such as pictures, as well as detailed information for reflection about environmental impacts, can influence consumer willingness to pay for bio-based plastic packaging.

In an extensive review of 95 studies of environmental policy interventions, Grilli and Curtis (2021) identify five types of interventions: education and awareness; outreach and relationship building; social influence; nudges and behavioural change instruments; and incentives. They find that all these approaches include successes and failures and that there is no single approach that is better than the others. They suggest that environmental policy makers should choose appropriate strategies carefully.

Nudges have become an important tool for policy intervention. Beshears and Kosowsky (2020) provide an extensive review of the literature on nudging, analysing 174 papers including successful and unsuccessful attempts; they note that many nudges have only a moderate effect, and that 'nudges that automate some aspect of the decision-making process have an average effect ... larger than other nudges'. Lehner, Mont and Heiskanen (2016) review nudges in residential energy use and the food and transport sectors, and note (174) that, 'across all policy domains, the greatest opportunities appear to be the use of nudges as a part of a package of policy instruments'. They caution that nudges should be used carefully and only when there is a role for government to adapt libertarian paternalism. Hummel and Meadche (2019) conducted a systematic review of 100 studies on nudging. They find that these 100 papers reported 317 results, of which 308 were significant, and 190 effects were statistically significant: overall, nudges had a median effect size of 21 per cent. These reviews suggest that there has been considerable growth in the use of nudges, especially in the fields of health, food choice, energy and transport decisions.

Smart cities and smarter citizens

Although there has been considerable growth in the use of the term 'smart cities', there is a fundamental paradox. On the one hand, the definitions of what constitutes a smart city are ambitious and multidimensional and emphasize the importance of including all stakeholders (see Anand, 2020, for a critical review). However, most of the smart city projects have tended to reflect centralization of command and control, intrusive surveillance and limited transparency (violating the requirement of minimal liberty in the social choice theory as formulated by Sen). For example, Shamsuzzoha et al. (2021: 11), from a study of smart city projects in Helsinki, London and Singapore, note:

For a large part the smart city is seen only as a technology exercise, where the latest ICT innovations are expected to solve problems especially in city governance, planning, transportation and mobility, citizen engagement and participation, sustainability, economy and safety. However, the solutions to many of these problems would require a human viewpoint and more holistic evaluation, which are still largely missing from the smart city evaluation.

Although smart cities proclaim a vision of efficiency and a low-carbon future, we do not yet have enough information to evaluate whether smart cities are indeed sustainable. Of course, smart cities can contribute to improved efficiency in the use of certain infrastructure, and any efficiency savings definitely contribute towards sustainability. Thus, if a smart city project helps in smoothing of traffic or a reduction in congestion, which in turn saves some fuel and reduces emissions, that is certainly a positive outcome. However, as of now, we do not yet have such information on the specific effect of smart city projects on emissions or fuel use. An important research question for future research on smart cities is to generate and provide evidence on specific impacts of smart city projects on environmental quality, health benefits and – through longitudinal studies – the real impact on life expectancy. For example, if cities need to switch to 100 per cent renewable energy by 2050, this would require the development of an appropriate energy strategy for the city and a holistic plan with great transparency at each step (see, for example, Thellufsen et al., 2020, for the case of Aalborg). Further, Wang and Moriarty (2019) note that, although smart cities have great potential to reduce energy use, in realizing this potential caution is needed with regard to the privacy of information from consumers.

There are numerous governance challenges for smart cities (see Anand and Navio, 2018). At present many cities worldwide are pursuing smart city projects. In most cases, the foremost investment is made in developing a command-and-control centre (CAC), with a large wall of television screens. In many cases, as part of a smart city project, CCTV cameras are installed in public places, and these provide live TV feeds to the CAC. However, there is as yet limited information to understand how the market for smart cities is actually working. While the demand for smart city projects comes from mayors and city authorities wanting better tools for managing the city, the supply of smart city projects is dominated by large digital corporations or management consulting companies. In the absence of full transparency about the product specifications and pricing, it is extremely difficult for market intelligence to emerge. If you are a mayor of a small city looking to procure a smart city infrastructure platform for your city, there is currently very little information that you can use to make decisions on how best to spend your budget (and how much to budget in the first place). As a result, the market appears to be one of oligopolistic competition by a few well-known firms and many new start-ups that have never had anything to do with cities. There is a danger of the knowledge of municipal experts being ignored or downgraded in favour of experts in digital technologies. There are few mechanisms for using market competition as a way to keep the cost of smart city projects down. There are huge information asymmetries, and the risks are disproportionately borne by the cities and their municipalities. There is no insurance market emerging for smart cities. This means that the process of social choice can be biased due to oligopolies, and cities that sign up to be smart cities bear all the risks.

Many smart cities recognize that there is a need to move from top-down and one-directional information flows to two-directional information flows that close the feedback loops. Some smart cities develop smart phone applications or other such platforms. However, there is a lot of naivety and rather limited understanding of the complexity of the relationship between city and citizens, especially within the political economy context of power and its distribution. Prior to smart city development, many cities promoted a single point of contact for reporting problems such as power outages, problems with roads or drainage, nuisance or fly tipping, and so on. Smart city projects have helped to digitalize such reporting mechanisms. However, given that there can be significant 'digital divides' in many cities, merely creating such platforms should not be considered as a solution to resolving urban consumer issues. Kontokosta and Hong (2021) analysed data from the 311 phone line (a one-point number for citizens to report any problems) from Kansas City, and find that such data may be biased because low-income and minority residents tend to under-report problems, reporting only major issues, whereas high-income residents may be over-reporting.

Guimaraes et al. (2020), in a study of a smart city project in Natal in north-eastern Brazil, conducted a survey of 829 citizens on aspects of transparency, collaboration, participation and partnership, communication and accountability and the importance of each of these attributes for quality of life; they note that all these attributes of smart governance have a strong and positive effect on quality of life. Butot et al. (2020: 8) used three vignettes to depict smart urban safety and used qualitative research of interviews with 32 residents of Rotterdam in the Netherlands. Based on their analysis, they argue that 'the tendency to research citizen perspectives on smart urban safety foremost in terms of technology acceptance risks obscuring the variability and complexity of multiple interacting arguments'.

The most important challenge for smart cities concerns the ethics of the concept of the person, of information governance and of data privacy. The computational models of smart cities are based on rational choice paradigms of observed choices. As such, all the criticisms of rational choice models indeed apply equally to these models too. Urban science and big data analysis of urban data trends approach such data without an a priori theory or conceptual model of urban economy or urban sociology. Algorithms can be biased (Hedden, 2021), and repeated use of machine learning can generate models and results that are distanced from human oversight or responsibility. As Kitchin (2016: 4) notes, '[S]uch a framing led to initial spatial and urban science to be roundly criticised within the social sciences for being too closely aligned with positivist thinking, being reductionist, mechanistic, atomizing, essentialist, deterministic and parochial, collapsing diverse individuals and complex multidimensional social structures and relationships to abstract data points and universal formulae and laws.'

Smart cities collect and store vast amounts of data about individual citizens. Data security and privacy are fundamental issues, but there are several other related ethical concerns also. With regard to privacy, Kitchin (2016: 5) identifies various dimensions of privacy, including 'identity privacy, bodily privacy, territorial privacy, locational and movement privacy, communications privacy and transactions privacy'. Many smart cities are silent on what safeguards they have in place to ensure data security and preventing abuse. They may have appropriate cyber-security safeguards and data back-up infrastructure to protect their own data, but whether they treat data from citizens to be equally worthy of such protections is a moot point.

Smart cities focus on technology and infrastructure services such as energy use and access to cloud and broadband or internet connections, or provide regular updates on energy use by consumers through smart meters. Although these are all useful services and can contribute to improving the quality of life of some citizens, they cannot be prioritized at the cost of providing urgent services to many poor and low-income householders who lack access to clean energy, may live in damp and squalid housing and suffer significantly from air pollution. So, one ethical issue is about how to ensure that policy priorities reflect the needs of all citizens and not merely some of the citizens, and use deliberative processes to recognize and arrive at trade-offs or restrictions on certain choices for the collective interest. This is the foundational issue of social choice theory as developed by Sen (1970, 2017). Reflecting the needs of all citizens requires smart cities in order to conduct multidimensional analysis. Here, smart cities can benefit significantly from adapting the capability approach for the evaluation of what matters to the citizens. Smart tools can make it easier to conduct deliberative public reasoning. However, smart cities need to ensure that the 'hackathon' approach, which can be quite popular and promote the participation of certain sections of the population, may not be appropriate for other citizens, such as elderly residents or those who cannot afford to spend several hours in the city hall due to care responsibilities.

Most importantly, smart cities need to ensure that there is greater transparency and ethics oversight for continuous ethical monitoring. Because smart technologies are intrusive and smart cities rely on surveillance on a very large scale, embedding an ethical oversight mechanism as an integral part of the decision process rather than obtaining an ethical clearance at the beginning of the project is essential.

From the capability approach and social choice theories, we can recognize some important policy measures. First, a citizen jury or citizen-led ethics advisory board should be constituted for every smart city, and this should have real authority so as to be able to enquire into and make recommendations for changing policy directions or investment decisions. Second, due to the technological determinism inherent in smart cities, they are likely to be gender-blind, and may in fact discriminate against women. Therefore, every smart city should also constitute a high-level gender equality panel to advise on and have an oversight of its operations and strategies for gender equality impacts. Third, there is no point to smartness if such technologies do not facilitate the greater use of democracy and democratic mechanisms, to give agency to people whose voices may not otherwise be heard in public policy making. Fourth, there is nothing smart if technologies cannot help to close the gap and reduce inequalities, especially in health, education and well-being. Therefore, important policy decisions should be put to a greater level of consultation in a meaningful manner, and the goal of making the city more equal and just must override smartness. Smart cities need to try harder to use both digital and non-digital means of genuine consultation and participation by the public. We shall be impressed more by the genuineness of their consultative and participatory ethos than by the cleverness of their algorithms. Citizens or mayors of cities pursuing smart city projects should consider joining international networks, such as the Human Rights Cities Network, to publicly proclaim their commitment to advancing human rights. The transition of Barcelona from a techno-centric view of smart cities to a citizen-centred stance seems to exemplify how such a commitment can prioritize citizens over technology (see Charnock, March and Ribera-Fumaz, 2021).

The smart sustainable city: where the libertarian paternalist meets the Paretian liberal?

This chapter has sought to draw upon the social choice theory and the capability approach to advance our understanding of key policy issues for sustainable cities. In their transition to be sustainable cities, cities need to address the six types of injustices outlined above, and for this they will need to use the full range of policy instruments available, including appropriate pledges and public proclamations of commitment to sustainability and reducing environmental footprints; a commitment to embedding sustainability in all aspects of the city; the identification of rights and clear designations of duty-bearer institutions; and appropriate financial incentives and subsidies to help the transition to low-energy and low-carbon buildings and electric vehicles. Smart technologies can be a means to achieving some of these instruments. At present, smart cities attract the criticism that they treat all cities and their urban problems as similar, without regard to the historical, political, social and cultural uniqueness of each city. Thus, the core ideas of smart cities remain the same while a superficial attempt is made to identify with the city only in the appearance or naming of the smart city platforms. Naming an app 'Our Chennai' or 'Our Kumasi' is a good starting point, but this alone does not create genuine ownership by local people. In addition, many urban problems, such as transport, involve structural factors that have lock-in mechanisms and path dependence. The capability approach highlights how a disabled person faces social and environmental conversion factors in order to achieve a basic functioning of mobility (Sen, 1999: 88). The United Nations (2019: 38), in its global report on disability and development, notes that extra costs due to disability can range from 12 per cent of income in Vietnam to 70 per cent in Spain. The report also notes that in eight developing countries included in its survey, namely Cameroon, Chile, Sri Lanka, Lesotho, Nepal, Mozambique, Malawi and South Africa, on average 36 per cent of people with disabilities considered transportation to be not accessible (226). In the absence of inclusive public transport, such individuals are locked in to using a car (if they can afford one) or not moving at all. A mere sprinkling of smart technologies without addressing these core structural factors will amount to 'smart-washing'.

In the portfolio of instruments available for realizing smart sustainable cities, nudges can play an important role. Nudges require careful and sensitive design and should be used only when it is appropriate. In a context of acute water scarcity, for example, nudges to reducing water consumption are pointless. Nudges work best when there are some shared and common minimum standards of acceptable behaviours. In the context of a heterogeneity of views and perspectives, nudges may not be effective. The impossibility theorems remind us that in non-dictatorial settings, in certain cases (assuming that the independence of irrelevant alternatives criterion is already met), it is difficult to produce a social choice that meets the three requirements of unrestricted domain (U), the Pareto principle (P) and liberalism (L). However, some limits on liberalism and freedoms are essential when these are to protect the lives or freedoms of other members of the society (S) or the environment for future generations (E). Combining these, we can generate the requirement that a smart sustainable city should always check the PULSE, and use this to address the six types of injustices that need to be overcome. Thus, a genuinely consultative and participatory approach can help cities to advance their progress towards SDG11 and beyond – towards becoming net-zero-carbon cities without compromising the needs of those who are poor and marginalized and do not have a voice.

Acknowledgements

The chapter builds on my research made possible by the British Academy grant IPM 15008 and my presentations at the three Cambridge Capability Conferences. I have learnt much from the comments and questions by the fellow participants and keynote speakers at these conferences. I have also presented some of the ideas on nudging as well as those on smart cities at different fora, including at the annual conferences of the Development Studies Association in Oxford, Bradford, Manchester and Milton Keynes; at the Jindal Global University conference at Universitas Mohammadiya Yogyakarta; at the Edinburgh–Kobe conference on economic development in south Asia; and at a seminar at the Centre for Policy Studies of the Indian Institute of Technology, Mumbai. I am grateful to Anita Patil-Deshmukh, Shrutika, Kiran, Bali and Nizam – my sources of inspiration at Partnership for Urban Knowledge and Action Research (PUKAR), Mumbai. I am also grateful to the entire team in Bhubaneshwar Smart City, and also to Prof Haider Khan, Prof R. Sudarshan, Prof Sudhir Chella Rajan, Sir Richard Jolly, Dr B. Chandramohan and S. Narayanan. I am also grateful to Eko Priyo Purnomo, Dionysius, Tiwi and Agus at Jogja for hosting me and facilitating my research on Jogja Smart City. However, I alone remain responsible for the contents of this chapter and all the flaws that are here.

References

Akbulut-Yuksel, M., and Boulatoff, C. (2021) The effects of a green nudge on municipal solid waste: evidence from a clear bag policy. *Journal of Environmental Economics and Management*, 106 (C): DOI 10.1016/j.jeem.2020.102404.

Alam, P., Sharholy, M., and Ahmad, K. (2020) A study on the landfill leachate and its impact on groundwater quality of Ghazipur area, New Delhi, India. In *Recent Developments in Waste Management: Select Proceedings of Recycle 2018*, Kalamdhad, A. S. (ed.): 345–58. Singapore: Springer Nature.

Anand, P. B. (2007) *Scarcity, Entitlements and the Economics of Water in Developing Countries*. Cheltenham: Edward Elgar.

(2014) Sustainability and the capability approach: from theory to action? In *The Capability Approach: From Theory to Practice*, Ibrahim, S., and Tiwary, M. (eds.): 118–47. Basingstoke: Palgrave Macmillan.

(2018) Cities and the capability approach. In *New Frontiers of the Capability Approach*, Comim, F., Fennell, S., and Anand, P. B. (eds.): 519–47. Cambridge: Cambridge University Press.

(2020) Assessing smart city projects and their public policy implications in the Global South. *Contemporary Social Science*, 16 (2): 199–212.

Anand, P. B., and Navio, J. (2018) Governance and economics of smart cities: opportunities and challenges. *Telecommunications Policy*, 42 (10): 795–9.

Anand, S., and Sen, A. K. (2000) Human development and economic sustainability. *World Development*, 28 (12): 2029–49.

Bambra, C. (2016) *Health Divides: Where You Live Can Kill You*. Bristol: Policy Press.

Bauer, J., Bietz, S., Rauber, J., and Reisch, L. (2021) Nudging healthier food choices in a cafeteria setting: a sequential multi-intervention field study. *Appetite*, 160: DOI 10.1016/j.appet.2021.105106.

Beshears, J., and Kosowsky, H. (2020) Nudging: progress to date and future directions. *Organizational Behaviour and Human Decision Processes*, 161 (Supp.): 3–19.

Butot, V., Bayerl, P., Jacobs, G., and de Haan, F. (2020) Citizen repertoires of smart urban safety: perspectives from Rotterdam, the Netherlands. *Technological Forecasting & Social Change*, 158 (2020): DOI 10.1016/j.techfore.2020.120164.

Calcott, A., and Bull, J. (2007) *Ecological Footprint of British City Residents*. London: Worldwide Fund for Nature.

Charnock, G., March, H., and Ribera-Fumaz, R. (2021) From smart to rebel city? Worlding, provincializing and the Barcelona model. *Urban Studies*, 58 (3): 581–600.

Drews, S., Exadaktylos, F., and van den Bergh, J. (2020) Assessing synergy of incentives and nudges in the energy policy mix. *Energy Policy*, 144: DOI 10.1016/j.enpol.2020.111605.

Giacherini, M., Gilli, M., Mancinelli, S., and Zoli, M. (2021) Nudging food waste decisions at restaurants. *European Economic Review*, 135 (C): DOI 10.1016/j.euroecorev.2021.103722.

Giest, S. (2020) Do nudgers need budging? A comparative analysis of European smart meter implementation. *Government Information Quarterly*, 37 (4): DOI 10.1016/j.giq.2020.101498.

Grilli, G., and Curtis, J. (2021) Encouraging pro-environmental behaviours: a review of methods and approaches. *Renewable and Sustainable Energy Reviews*, 135: DOI 10.1016/j.rser.2020.110039.

Guimaraes, J., Severo, E., Felix Júnior, L., Preston, W., Da Costa, L., and Salmoria, F. (2020) Governance and quality of life in smart cities: towards sustainable development goals. *Journal of Cleaner Production*, 253: DOI 10.1016/j.jclepro.2019.119926.

Hedden, B. (2021) On statistical criteria of algorithmic fairness. *Philosophy & Public Affairs*, 49 (2): 209–31.

Hoxby, C., and Turner, S. (2012) Expanding college opportunities for high-achieving, low income students, Discussion Paper 12-014. Palo Alto, CA: Stanford Institute for Economic Policy Research, Stanford University.

Hummel, D., and Meadche, A. (2019) How effective is nudging? A quantitative review on the effect sizes and limits of empirical nudging studies. *Journal of Behavioural and Experimental Economics*, 80: 47–58.

Institute of Health Equity (2020) *Marmot Review: Ten Years On*. London: Institute of Health Equity, University College London.

Islam, S., and Winkel, J. (2017) Climate change and social inequality, Department of Economic and Social Affairs Working Paper 152. New York: United Nations.

Kaza, S., Yao, L., Bhada-Tata, P., and Van Woerden, F. (2018) *What a Waste 2.0: A Global Snapshot of Solid Waste Management to 2050*. Washington, DC: World Bank.

Kennedy, C., Stewart, I., Facchini, A., Cersosimo, I., Mele, R., Chen, B., Uda, M., Kansal, A., Chiu, A., Kim, K., Debeux, C., Rovere, E., Cunha, B., Pincetl, S., Keirstead, J., Barles, S., Pusaka, S., Gunawan, J., Adegbile, M., Nazariha, M., Hoque, S., Marcotullio, P., Otharan, F., Ganena, T., Ibrahim, N., Farooqui, R., Cervantes, G., and Sahin, A. (2015) Energy and material flows of megacities. *Proceedings of the National Academy of Sciences*, 112 (19): 5985–90.

Kitchin, R. (2016) The ethics of smart cities and urban science. *Philosophical Transactions of the Royal Society A*, 374: DOI 10.1098/rsta.2016.0115.

Kontokosta, C., and Hong, B. (2021) Bias in smart city governance: how socio-spatial disparities in 311 complaint behaviour impact the fairness of data-driven decisions. *Sustainable Cities and Society*, 64: DOI 10.1016/j.scs.2020.102503.

Lehner, M., Mont, O., and Heiskanen, E. (2016) Nudging: a promising tool for sustainable consumption behaviour? *Journal of Cleaner Production*, 134 (Part A): 166–77.

Lewis, W. A. (1955) *The Theory of Economic Growth*. London: Allen & Unwin.

McGee, J., Ergas, C., Greiner, P., and Clement, M. (2017) How do slums change the relationship between urbanization and the carbon intensity of well-being? *PLoS ONE*, 12 (12): DOI 10.1371/journal.pone.0189024.

Mandela, N. (1994) *Long Walk to Freedom*. London: Little, Brown.

Marcano-Olivier, M., Pearson, R., Ruparell, A., Horne, P., and Viktor, S. (2019) A low-cost behavioural nudge and choice architecture intervention targeting school lunches increases children's consumption of fruit: a cluster randomised trial. *International Journal of Behavioural Nutrition and Physical Activity*, 16 (1): DOI 10.1186/s12966-019-0773-x.

Marmot, M. (2010) *Fair Society, Healthy Lives: The Marmot Review*. London: Institute of Health Equity, University College London.

Mberu, B., Haregu, T., Kyobutungi, C., and Ezeh, A. (2016) Health and health-related indicators in slum, rural, and urban communities: a comparative analysis. *Global Health Action*, 9: DOI 10.3402/gha .v9.33163.

Rawls, J. (1971) *A Theory of Justice*. Cambridge, MA: Harvard University Press.

Rubaltelli, E., Manicardi, D., Orsini, F., Mulatti, C., and Lotto, L. (2021) How to nudge drivers to reduce speed: the case of left-digit effect. *Transportation Research Part F: Traffic Psychology and Behaviour*, 78: 259–66.

Sager, T. (1998) Arrow's impossibility theorem and planning process. *Progress in Planning*, 50 (2): 75–140.

Satterthwaite, D., Huq, S., Pelling, M., Reid, H., and Lankao, P. (2007) Adapting to climate change in urban areas: the possibilities and constraints in low- and middle-income nations, Human Settlements Discussion Paper 1. London: International Institute for Environment and Development.

Schubert, E., Smith, E., Brydevall, M., Lynch, C., Ringin, E., Dixon, H., Kashima, Y., Wakefield, M., and Bode, S. (2021) General and specific graphic health warning labels reduce willingness to consume sugar-sweetened beverages. *Appetite*, 161: DOI 10.1016/j .appet.2021.105141.

Sen, A. K. (1970) The impossibility of a Paretian liberal. *Journal of Political Economy*, 78 (1): 152–7.

(1977) Rational fools: a critique of the behavioural foundations of economic theory. *Philosophy & Public Affairs*, 6 (4): 317–44.

(1999) *Development as Freedom*. Oxford: Oxford University Press.

(2009) *The Idea of Justice*. London: Penguin.

(2017) *Collective Choice and Social Welfare*, expanded edn. London: Penguin.

Shamsuzzoha, A., Nieminen, J., Piya, S., and Rutledge, K. (2021) Smart city for sustainable environment: a comparison of participatory strategies from Helsinki, Singapore and London. *Cities*, 114: DOI 10.1016/j .cities.2021.103194.

Solow, R. (1993) *An Almost Practical Step toward Sustainability*. Washington, DC: Resources for the Future.

Thaler, R., and Sunstein, C. (2008) *Nudge: Improving Decisions about Health, Wealth and Happiness*. London: Penguin.

Thellufsen, J., Lund, H., Sorknaes, P., Oostergard, P., Chang, M., Drysdale, D., Nielsen, S., Djorup, S., and Sperling, K. (2020) Smart energy cities in a 100% renewable energy context. *Renewable and Sustainable Energy Reviews*, 129: DOI 10.1016/j.rser.2020.109922.

Tomita, A., Cuadros, D., Burns, J., Tanser, F., and Slotow, R. (2020) Exposure to waste sites and their impact on health: a panel and geospatial analysis of nationally representative data from South Africa, 2008–2015. *Lancet Planetary Health*, 4 (6): e223–34.

United Nations (2010) Water and cities: facts and figures. New York: United Nations.

(2018) World urbanization prospects 2018: highlights. New York: United Nations.

(2019) *Disability and Development: Realising the Sustainable Development Goals by, for and with Persons with Disabilities, 2018*. New York: United Nations.

United Nations HABITAT (2012) *Sustainable Urban Energy: A Sourcebook for Asia*. Nairobi: UN Human Settlements Programme (HABITAT).

Upton, D., Upton, P., and Taylor, C. (2013) Increasing children's lunchtime consumption of fruit and vegetables: an evaluation of the Food Dudes programme. *Public Health Nutrition*, 16 (6): 1066–72.

Wang, J., and Moriarty, P. (2019) Energy savings from smart cities: a critical analysis. *Energy Procedia*, 158: 3271–6.

Wenar, L. (2008) Property rights and the resource curse. *Philosophy & Public Affairs*, 36 (1): 2–32.

Wensing, J., Caputo, V., Carraresi, L., and Broring, S. (2020) The effects of green nudges on consumer valuation of bio-based plastic packaging. *Ecological Economics*, 178: DOI 10.1016/j.ecolecon.2020.106783.

WHO (2015) Waste and human health: evidence and needs, meeting report. Copenhagen: WHO Regional Office for Europe.

6 | Social choice and research capacity strengthening in Nigeria
Insights from the field

MICHAEL WATTS, NAFISA WAZIRI AND
OLADELE AKOGUN

Introduction

This chapter considers how membership of social groups is influenced by the perceptions individuals have of themselves and of others and how those perceptions influence collective decision-making processes. It is based on the qualitative evaluation of a two-year educational research project in northern Nigeria conducted by EDOREN (Education Data, Research and Evaluation in Nigeria: www.opml.co.uk/projects/education-data-research-evaluation-nigeria-edoren). The innovative project we were evaluating involved bringing practitioners (acting as proxies for policy makers) and academics together in state-based research teams to generate evidence-based policy recommendations intended to improve the quality of primary education. The researchers were representative of their wider educational subsectors, certainly in the early stages of the project, in two key respects. First, their effective collaboration was initially inhibited by long-standing intra-sectoral mistrust, which influenced the substantive freedoms of the researchers to work together towards a common aim. Second, although most of the researchers wanted to work together, their opportunities to do so were delimited by their resources (i.e. their experiences and skills) and, more importantly, by the willingness of their colleagues to recognize these resources as being of value. By tracing the processes of collaboration here, we call attention to the influence of social identity on social choice, and therefore on the professional capabilities (Devecchi and Watts, 2018) of individuals to fulfil their potential in contributing to the well-being of others.

To provide the context for these choices, the chapter begins with a summary of the crisis in primary education in northern Nigeria and the response of EDOREN to it through, *inter alia*, its Research Capacity Strengthening Strategy (RCSS). The capacity development of the researchers and their collaborative efforts to improve teacher recruitment is described and examined through the lenses of social identity theory, social choice theory and capability. The chapter closes with a series of conclusions indicating how the findings of this highly focused study are relevant beyond northern Nigeria.

Education in northern Nigeria

Appropriate and effective education policy can be usefully informed by appropriate and effective education research. However, policy makers often fail to make use of research produced by academics, and academics often fail to make their research accessible to policy makers (Bridges and Watts, 2008; Watts, 2010; Watts and Agokun, 2017). In northern Nigeria, and elsewhere, it significantly weakens opportunities to improve the education sector in general and the primary education sector in particular.

The RCSS was designed within the context of an educational crisis in the quality and overall effectiveness of the primary school teaching force in northern Nigeria. Classrooms are overcrowded and under-resourced (Bennell, Anyawu and Dodo, 2014; Kontagora, Watts and Allsop, 2018) and dismal results from various assessments in the two states targeted in the first year of this study – Kaduna and Kano – had shown that many teachers were unqualified (Education Sector Support Programme in Nigeria [ESSPIN], 2013). With limited incentives to pursue a career in the teaching profession, the quality of applicants was generally low, and this was consequently reflected in the low selectivity of teacher-training institutes. Moreover, the official processes and procedures set up to guide the recruitment and management of teachers were heavily influenced by political interference (Bennell, Anyawu and Dodo, 2014; Allsop and Watts, 2017; Kontagora, Watts and Allsop, 2018). As a result, despite the government's considerable efforts to address the significant challenges around enrolment and equity issues, these investments were undermined by the poor quality of education provided to children who had managed to gain access to schooling.

In the two states, there had been efforts to develop and implement strategies to address the significant deficit of competent and qualified primary school teachers. Special attention was paid to raising the status of the teaching profession and to improving systems of recruitment, management and professional development. The Kaduna state government adopted a 'carrot and stick' approach to the problems, simultaneously carrying out proficiency and competency tests on primary school teachers to filter out unqualified teachers while also introducing a new salary scale in a bid to retain experienced teachers and attract more applicants to the profession. Kano state had also made similar efforts, most notably supporting a Teaching Skills Programme to upgrade the qualifications of in-service primary school teachers. The authorities were also enforcing tighter regulations on schools to meet legal requirements, albeit with mixed results. Nonetheless, the problem of recruiting and retaining good teachers remained daunting.

EDOREN initiated the project 'Identifying, Recruiting and Deploying Effective Teachers in Kano and Kaduna States' in 2016, and extended it to include Jigawa, Katsina and Zamfara states in 2017. Our concern here is with the first year of the project. The first phase of the first year involved the identification of the context-specific characteristics of effective primary school teachers in Kaduna and Kano states. Although the characteristics of effective teachers are generally well known in the education sector (Akogun et al., 2017; Allsop and Watts, 2017, 2018), they are not necessarily realistic in the typically overcrowded and under-resourced classrooms of Kaduna and Kano, where, for example, up to 300 pupils in a single class may be using bottle tops or stones to practise their mathematics. The personal and professional characteristics of effective teachers working under such conditions therefore needed to be documented. The second phase required the researchers to make use of the evidence from phase one to design a series of policy recommendations that were then subject to a validation process involving key stakeholders – from senior bureaucrats to student teachers – in the two states.

The RCSS was integrated into the 'Effective Teachers Study'. The 'Effective Teachers Study' was important, but our concern here in this chapter is to examine the RCSS to consider the links between social identity, social choice and capability.

EDOREN and the RCSS

EDOREN was a five-year initiative, running from 2013 to 2018, funded by the United Kingdom's former Department for International

Development (DFID) to generate new evidence and understanding of how best to support equitable access and improved learning outcomes for all Nigerian children. To help achieve this aim, it designed the RCSS, which required practitioners (acting as proxies for policy makers) to collaborate with and work alongside academics in designing and delivering rigorous policy-focused research. The strategy was based on models used in the health sector (Ogundahunsi et al., 2015).

The RCSS had five key components, listed below together with the hypotheses justifying them. Each component had the potential to enhance the professional capabilities of the researchers. Here, such freedoms progress from simply doing a job to making it personally meaningful and satisfying (Alkire, 2002; Watts and Bridges, 2006) by potentially enhancing the well-being of others (Devecchi and Watts, 2018) and so being able to appear in public without shame (Sen, 1999; Alkire, 2002) by doing that job properly.

Engagement in policy-driven research

Practitioners taken out of their daily routine would be able to directly engage in extensive policy assessments through the research process. This was envisaged as enabling an improvement in their ability to understand and make use of evidence. The ability of the academics, on the other hand, would improve when engaged in policy-driven research.

Partnership

The interaction between practitioners and academics was aimed at fostering the closer interaction and understanding necessary for strengthening capacity for the demand, supply and use of evidence in policy making. The design deliberately encouraged (1) partnerships between state Ministries of Education and state Universal Basic Education Boards; (2) academic collaboration between different academic institutions and departments; and, most importantly, (3) intra-sectoral collaboration between practitioners and academics at the individual level. The partnerships were intended to provide a method of peer learning that was likely to provide capacity strengthening across both technical and political dimensions. This, in turn, was intended to improve (4) the policy makers' ability to find reliable assistance in solving future policy challenges; and (5) the academics' ability to better understand the policy priorities of policy makers, thus allowing them to produce more relevant research and attach greater importance to solving policy challenges.

Mentoring

The organizational habits that the process was trying to affect (i.e. improving the production and use of evidence in education decision making) are passed down between senior and junior members. By asking members to operate in a different manner, senior members could provide a good example, and even a mentoring role, to more junior members of their organizations. This would, in turn, spread the capacity-strengthening benefits to a wider audience and provide more internal pressure to shift organizational behaviours. It could also provide a better way to deliver the research, as it was expected to combine senior officers with more authority (vital for policy impact) and junior members with more technical skills (vital for research outcome). Both should therefore have been able to learn from each other.

Repeated policy feedback

This was intended to provide external pressure to utilize evidence for policy and effectively demonstrate how best to communicate research findings to a policy audience.

Providing hands-on technical support

The provision of hands-on technical skills for data gathering, processing, interpretation and packaging for policy use was expected to be an important input into the study design.

Research teams comprising senior and junior practitioners and academics were formed in Kaduna and Kano states and tasked with generating policy-focused research, which was then used to inform a series of appropriate policy recommendations. By the end of the first year of the project these recommendations had been broadly accepted by the education secretaries from the two states, and there was evidence of some recommendations being implemented at the local government authority (LGA) level.

However, the RCSS was subject to three key issues (Watts and Akogun, 2017), which also influenced the substantive opportunities of the researchers to contribute to the design and conduct of the research.

The researchers – both the academics and the practitioners – initially saw the main study as a chiefly academic exercise. This disrupted the fundamental principle of academics and practitioners collaborating as co-researchers with equal status and equally important contributions to make. It was mostly resolved as the main study progressed and as the practitioners demonstrated the value of their knowledge and skills.

The study highlighted considerable deeply embedded intra-sectoral mistrust. It was disguised by the rhetoric of collaboration but its origins could be traced to the belief that neither sector respected the potential contributions to education policy and practice of the other. The extent of this mistrust inevitably varied between individuals but it presented significant barriers to successful intra-sectoral collaboration, particularly in the early stages of the project. It too was mostly negotiated as researchers from both sectors acknowledged and accepted the value of what their colleagues from the other sector contributed to the main study.

A third party was needed to help the researchers from both sectors negotiate this mistrust. EDOREN provided necessary technical support to the state-based research teams. This enabled the provision of the brokerage that allowed most of the researchers – the practitioners and the academics alike – to negotiate the intra-sectoral mistrust and to acknowledge and appreciate what their colleagues contributed to the main study. This in turn enabled most of them to become and to be recognized as members of the research-focused social group making collective decisions to progress the research.

The evaluation design

A major element of the RCSS was to develop linkages between the demand and supply for policy-relevant research and information and to build capacity through training and organizational development support (Steenbergen, 2016). To meet these objectives, two state research teams (one for each state) were constituted in the project's first year, with team members drawn from a pool of two major stakeholder groups: policy makers (with practitioners acting as their proxies) and academics.

This approach has some important benefits that articulate with Sen's concern to develop policies that enhance human well-being (1999). First, in actively engaging stakeholders from the two sectors in the research process, it ensured that the study was both relevant and applicable to the local contexts. It also improved the likelihood that the policy recommendations could be adopted by the states upon completion of the study. Second, in an environment highly influenced by the political economy and underlying cynicism, this approach fostered a process of close collaboration on multiple levels, both within and across key groups in the sector. Third, it equipped the researchers with technical skills and a greater understanding of how to better target research questions and offer specific solutions tailored to their state's needs. The approach also articulated with Sen's concern that choices are properly informed.

The starting point was to establish a baseline of the current conditions surrounding policy makers' use of evidence in education policy making, their research capacity skills and existing collaborations between policy makers and academics, if any. On the academics' side, it also sought to establish whether they had engaged in research that was policy-oriented. To initiate this process, EDOREN organized a launch event inviting government officials and members of academic institutions from Kano and Kaduna to prepare and submit letters of interest. Potential members of the research teams participated in group discussions on the study and then had to form teams based on requirements (pertaining to gender, experience, expertise and time commitment to the deliverables) set out by EDOREN. Five proposals were submitted (two from Kaduna and three from Kano), and the strongest team from each state (based on a review of the team structure, quality of the pairings, policy impact potential and content of the proposals submitted) was contracted to carry out the study.

It was intended that there would be eight members in each team – two senior and two junior academics and two senior and two junior practitioners. However, the Kano team lost one of its senior practitioners to a promotion at the outset of the project, and he was not replaced (there was no evidence to suggest that this slight imbalance influenced the team relationships considered here). Both team leaders were academics and both deputy team leaders were practitioners, in keeping with the requirement for these positions to be shared across the two subsectors.

The evaluation of the RCSS was contemporaneous and continuous. Periodic workshops were organized at which EDOREN facilitators provided guidance and quality reviews of the products. The workshops were closely observed and records were kept of how the researchers engaged with their colleagues and what was said by whom. Records were also kept of data generated by informal interviews conducted during these workshops.

All members of the research teams were formally interviewed during these workshops to generate data from the baseline, mid-point and end-line stages of the project. The researchers were asked to describe their professional backgrounds, including any previous experiences of intra-sectoral collaboration, their expectations of the study, their engagement with the Strategy's five components and any issues of particular concern to them. All formal interviews were recorded and transcribed to ensure the accuracy of the data.

These two approaches generated rich datasets and enabled the triangulation of data, thereby reducing biases (for example, the risk of researchers saying what they believed might be expected of them during the formal interviews).

The data were analysed iteratively and based on the five main themes and emerging categories. Data from individuals and their teams were examined and compared at the three stages, and individual and team engagement was traced across the year-long project. This engagement was considered in the wider contexts of the two subsectors to which the researchers belonged and their seniority. The nature of the evaluation required subtle analyses that not only took account of what was said and done but what was not said and not done.

Qualitative studies such as this are concerned with the particularity rather than the typicality of actions and preferences. They are intended to be subjective and seek to generate understanding from individual perspectives. They can therefore usefully inform capability assessments by identifying the 'doings and beings' individuals value and have reason to value and the factors influencing the individual's substantive freedoms to achieve them (Watts and Ridley, 2007; Watts, 2008, 2009).

These datasets provided insights into many of the social identity processes, and their impacts on choice and capability were brought to light in this way. The full account of the evaluation is reported elsewhere (Watts and Akogun, 2017). What follows is a summary of the interactions between the two sectors and a reflection on how the intra-sectoral mistrust influenced the substantive freedoms of the researchers – both academics and practitioners – to develop the professional capabilities needed to contribute to the improvement of primary education in northern Nigeria.

The RCSS in practice

The main study was divided into two phases. Phase one entailed the production of research plans and the start of fieldwork by the state research teams. The objective was to identify the characteristics and practices of effective primary school teachers. For the fieldwork, researchers were required to collaborate closely to conduct interviews with teachers, discuss and develop a 'profile of effective teachers' and report on their findings.

The second phase began with the research teams using their evidence to develop a series of policy recommendations concerning teacher recruitment. These were then trialled through a series of meetings with key stakeholders in the two states. The draft policy recommendations were reviewed and revised following this initial validation phase and presented to LGA education officials. They received considerable support from those officials. This ended the first year of the main study.

At the beginning of phase one the researchers participated in a workshop designed to develop their research skills and to design their research. It was essential that the research designs were adapted to each state's specific context, and it was anticipated that the practitioners would share their knowledge and experiences to facilitate the likelihood of long-term policy impact and follow-up plans. However, the academics tended to dominate this early stage of the project, and the practitioners were typically willing to let them. This limited the practitioners' input and so limited the research teams' ability to make informed decisions about the conduct of the research.

Led by the academics, the teams' preferred methodologies for the research had included large-scale surveys that were financially and practically unfeasible and that were not properly focused on the generation of policy-relevant data. The EDOREN facilitators explained that they were inappropriate to the objectives of the main study and guided the researchers towards more suitable approaches to their research. This included giving greater encouragement to the practitioners to share their experiences and perspectives. This led to some tensions between the researchers, with two of the academics protesting that their expertise was being ignored.

When going into schools to conduct the subsequently agreed smaller-scale research, the researchers typically worked in pairs – practitioners and academics, as well as senior and junior partnerships – to conduct the fieldwork. Despite the school-based experiences of the practitioners, the interviews were led by the academics, with the practitioners using the opportunities to learn from them. Analyses of the collected data were led by the academics with some contributions from the practitioners. However, most of the academics acknowledged the contributions of the practitioners to the data collection and analyses.

The second phase saw a shift in the team dynamics. Again, there were some protests from some academics as the facilitators overruled their argument that the data should be theorized (and here we should pause briefly to acknowledge the irony in subsequently theorizing their protests). However, most of the academics were keen to learn from the practitioners as they explained what would be acceptable to the policy makers. The practitioners were also able to facilitate many of the meetings with the stakeholders, including those at government level.

The final presentations to government stakeholders were jointly led by the academics and practitioners. This had a practical benefit, as some of the government officials had informally expressed concerns that the presentations would be another academic exercise in undermining their work. However, there was also a symbolic element: as the first year of the project ended, most of the researchers had acknowledged the contributions of their colleagues from the other subsector, and this had allowed them to negotiate the barriers that had initially limited their collaboration.

Most of the researchers had initially viewed the main study as an academic exercise. This was understandable, as both team leaders were academics and phase one of the main study was more like the research undertaken by the academics. The researchers were familiar with the project's design and, during the initial interviews for the evaluation of the RCSS, had spoken about the importance of intra-sectoral collaboration. However, as these interviews progressed, the researchers focused more on the sharing and acquisition of academic research skills rather than engagement with education policies and practices. Moreover, the rhetoric of collaboration was undermined by observational data clearly indicating the dominance of the academics in the planning of the fieldwork, and all but two of the practitioners required the intervention of the facilitators to make their contributions.

These intra-sectoral relationships were also informed by what was characterized as mutual mistrust (Watts and Akogun, 2017). Members of each subsector typically asserted that the other subsector did not take them or their work seriously. This was evident from the extensive literature review informing the evaluation and articulated by the researchers themselves. The interview data made it clear that very few of the researchers had any previous experience of working with members of the other subsector, but they were nevertheless disparaging about them. The practitioners typically described the academics as being focused on theory and with no interest in the practical implications of the research they conducted. The academics typically described the practitioners and policy makers as being unwilling or unable to understand their work. Data from informal interviews conducted during the observations emphasized these viewpoints.

However, as the project entered the second phase – that of using the research findings to inform policies – the teams began to appreciate the specific skills and experiences of the practitioners. Interview and observational data showed them providing greater input and most of the academics asking for and listening to their guidance. Despite this policy focus being central to the project, though, two of the academics continued to complain that the findings should be theorized and complained further when the facilitators overruled them. It was clear from the observational data that they engaged less with their teams, and during the final interviews they both complained that the practitioners should not have been involved in the project except as interviewees. However, the other team members described the benefits of having worked with their colleagues from the other subsector.

As indicated above, the resolution of these issues required the intervention of the EDOREN facilitators. However, the need for these interventions declined as the project progressed.

The RCSS and social identity

The mutual intra-sectoral mistrust identified in the study was widespread and long-standing but not always obvious. All the researchers enthused about the opportunity to collaborate with their colleagues from the other sector. This rhetoric was not particularly surprising, given that intra-sectoral collaboration was a central element of the project, but most were able to specify what they might learn from it.

However, the potential for learning was undermined by this mistrust, with some researchers unwilling to acknowledge the skills, knowledge and experience of their colleagues. Most of the researchers were able to negotiate it, but for some – particularly some of the academics – it lingered throughout the project. It was evident in their unwillingness to acknowledge the contributions of their practitioner colleagues and the value of their status as co-researchers, and it occasionally erupted in squabbling. As discussed below, it also inhibited the practitioners' ability to fully contribute to the project.

When discussing the potential for collaboration, the practitioners typically described the academics as theory-focused 'eggheads' with no appreciation of the realities of educational policy and practice, while the academics described the policy makers (represented here by the practitioners) as unable and unwilling to understand and accept the findings of their research. These perceptions were typically not based on personal experience, as most of the researchers had little, if any, previous experience of intra-sectoral collaboration. The assumptions they had about their colleagues were therefore based on stereotypes. Social identity theory (Tajfel, 1978; Tajfel and Turner, 1979; Turner, 1987, 1999) helps explain the formation of such stereotypes, and the experiences of these researchers usefully illustrate their potential consequences.

Social identity theory rests on the understanding that the individual's sense of who he or she is depends on the groups with which he or she identifies. These social groups allow individuals to make sense of the social world they inhabit and typically foster a sense of self-worth. This sense of the 'self' is enhanced by emphasizing the value of the group(s) to which the individual belongs and by devaluing other groups. The cognitive processes of identification simplify complex social arrangements through this grouping and lead to the exaggeration of the similarities and differences that divide the social world into the categories of 'us' and 'them.'

Tajfel and Turner (1979) identify three stages: (1) social categorization; (2) social identification; and (3) social comparison. The mental process of categorization helps the individual make sense of the social world by sorting the actions of others into simplified group-based activities and beliefs. Individuals categorize their social worlds by making distinctions between the in-groups to which they see themselves belonging (e.g. practitioners or academics) and out-groups (e.g. academics or practitioners). These groups are delineated by particular characteristics that allow individuals to establish themselves within the in-group and distinguish themselves from the out-group(s) (Turner, 1987, 1999). Social identification then leads the individual to acknowledge and adopt the norms of the group(s) with which he or she identifies. This may lead to the idealization of such groups. Once the individual has identified with a particular group, comparisons are made with other groups. However, to maintain self-esteem, the comparison needs to favour the in-group. This can occur through the valorization of the in-group and/or the derogation of out-groups (Tajfel, 1978; Tajfel and Turner, 1979; Watts, 2009). Furthermore, intergroup comparisons may result in individuals showing strong in-group favouritism when their group is perceived to be unfairly placed into a low-status position (Ellemers, Wilke and van Knippenberg, 1993; Ellemers, Spears and Doosje, 2002; Watts, 2011).

This project was intended to address some of these failings through intra-sectoral collaboration. To achieve this collaboration, the academics and practitioners needed to acknowledge each other's contributions and work together. Most were able to do so, but some of the academics were resistant to the collaboration. From a social identity perspective, the researchers came to the project with their in-group identification – as practitioners/policy makers and academics – and most of them formed a new in-group as researchers. Researchers from both sectors initially repeated the stereotypes of their colleagues from the other sector even though most of them had not had any meaningful engagement with them prior to this project. It was enough for them to know that there were significant differences between the representatives of the different sectors. The formation of the new in-group was facilitated by working together and recognizing the value of everyone's contributions. This allowed most of the researchers to identify with the new in-group.

The resistance of some of the academics can be traced to their strong in-group identification and the consequent out-group derogation of the practitioners/policy makers. This was evident in their repeated assertions that their research was ignored, and, for some, this had even become a point of pride. The project, especially in the early stages, was seen as an academic rather than an intra-sectoral study. This was promoted by the academics and accepted by the practitioners. This established a hierarchy between the original in-groups with the academic in-group clearly dominant (the practitioners were typically more enthusiastic about what they could learn from the collaboration than the academics). However, the methodological approach favoured by the collaboration-averse academics was deemed inappropriate by the facilitators, who effectively overruled it. This became the catalyst for a renewed intra-sectoral divide. At this point these academics felt their authority threatened and retreated to the security of their original in-group identification. However, their out-group derogation now focused on both the original in-group of practitioners and the newly forming in-group of collaborative researchers.

They continued to deny the value of the practitioners' contributions as co-researchers and maintained that future research should involve only them as research participants (e.g. through being interviewed). Moreover, a year into the project, and despite repeated discussions about the problems of over-theorized research with limited, if any, practical application, they also maintained that the study's findings should be theorized. The practical consequence of the strong in-group identification built around these arguments was limited interest in the intra-sectoral collaboration at the heart of the RCSS.

The RCSS and social choice

The limitations on the researchers' identification with the newly formed in-group necessarily limited their meaningful contributions to the decisions the group made about the conduct of the research. Some of them disengaged because they were unwilling to accept the conditions for joining the new in-group. Others were disengaged because the legitimacy of their identification with the newly formed in-group was undermined by others. Their agency in these processes offers insight into the significance of group identification and social choices.

The development of the research designs provides a good illustration of this. Using a simple understanding of social choice, the teams' willingness to change their initial designs was – at first sight – fair and just. They were given advice, guidance and information about different approaches, and most team members agreed that what had been proposed by the facilitators was more appropriate than what they had proposed. That is, the process of choosing was informed and had acknowledged the opinions of all team members. Moreover, the choice was acceptable to most of them. However, the role of the facilitators – who had an effective veto – cannot be ignored here, and so the fairness and justness of the teams' decisions need to be questioned.

The facilitators had a clear sense of how the research should proceed and were ready to impose that on the teams if they did not agree with them. The underlying choice was not so much 'Take it or leave it' as 'Take it or leave', and this would seem to contravene the principle of non-dictatorship (Arrow, 1951). Arguments that the facilitators had

Table 6.1 *Participation, contribution and feasibility*

	Contribute	Not contribute
Participate	Feasible	Not feasible
Not participate	Not feasible	Not feasible

responsibilities to the funders (the DFID) and the intended beneficiaries (the primary school teachers and their pupils) may be important but seem redundant in this context of apparent choice. The individual researchers had two options concerning their work on the project: (1) whether or not to participate in the study; and (2) whether or not to contribute to the teams (which included using the 'chosen' research designs). The matrix in Table 6.1 highlights the lack of choice available to them. Three of the four choices available to them were unfeasible, leaving only the one feasible 'choice' together with the allegation of dictatorship.

It must be remembered, though, that the main study had the RCSS built into it, and it was therefore expected that the researchers would learn from their colleagues and the facilitators. The request for proposed research designs was primarily a means of selecting the research teams but it also functioned as a starting point for the intra-sectoral collaboration developed throughout the project. There was a presumption of learning – including learning about different approaches to the conduct of the study – that shifted the balance of choices available to the researchers. Here (Table 6.2), the options were to (1) choose whether or not to apply to the project or (2) choose whether or not to learn from it, including learning from the co-researchers and facilitators.

Three of the four options are now seen to be feasible (the RCSS, which included cascading the learning beyond the teams, accounts for the feasibility of not applying but still learning), and so there was a greater choice of desirable outcomes. The most desirable of these outcomes was (successful) application leading to new learning, including learning about the different approach to the project that most researchers agreed was most appropriate.

This undermines the allegations of dictatorship, but does not necessarily explain them. The issue is that there was no choice – it was, as noted above, a matter of 'Take it or leave' – but there was the illusion

Table 6.2 *Application, learning and feasibility*

	Learn	Not learn
Apply	Feasible	Not feasible
Not apply	Feasible	Feasible

of choice. This illusion arose from a misunderstanding about the purpose of the teams' proposed research designs and the intra-sectoral sharing of skills and knowledge that was a key element of the RCSS. Most of the academics accepted the approach that had been imposed on them but some, feeling their authority undermined, reified their social identities as academics and derogated the newly forming out-group of researchers – the practitioners and other academics working together – to enhance their own sense of status.

This derogation concerned their perception of the status of the practitioners and their belief that they did not need to be engaged in the study as co-researchers. It did not prevent the study taking place, but it did undermine it. It led to some friction within the teams and inhibited the collaboration that should have been taking place. These academics agreed to work in the teams but chose to do so reluctantly and without full participation. Their agency (in the sociological rather than the capability sense) enabled them to make this choice of limited participation. However, their choice influenced the opportunities of other researchers to fully participate.

The junior practitioners – who were closest to the schools where the research took place, and so had much to offer the project – had typically been nominated to join their teams but were pleased to be involved. They anticipated learning from their colleagues, particularly the academics, but were uncertain about their own experience-based contributions. Such contributions were a key element of full participation in the teams. With the encouragement of the facilitators, some did share experiences, which helped shape the first part of the study. However, others were less forthcoming, and their engagement was limited to acting as research assistants to the academics.

As with some of these academics, they chose to limit their participation. Unlike the academics, though, their participation was further limited by the reluctance of some of their colleagues to recognize their potential contributions. In other words, their agency to fully participate was limited because their choices were constrained by the derogation of the groups to which they belonged and with which they were identified. This meant they could not fully join the newly forming in-group with which they wished to identify.

The processes of engaging with the RCSS highlighted two significant issues concerning social choice. The more obvious was the substantive freedoms the researchers had to contribute to the decisions made by the research teams. Underlying this, though, was the more significant issue of how their identification with the in-group making the decisions contributed to the knowledge base informing the decisions made by that in-group.

The RCSS and capability

The long-term focus of the 'Effective Teachers Study' was improvement to recruitment policies and practices in northern Nigeria. Here, though, we focus on what we might call the professional capabilities (Devecchi and Watts, 2018) of the researchers – that is, the substantive freedoms they had to contribute to this long-term aim.

The relevant functionings concerned the use of professional skills as well as the acquisition of new skills. They also concerned the sharing of extant skills with their colleagues. Previous work had failed to enhance the professional well-being of primary teachers and the educational well-being of their pupils. Policy is rarely evidence-based and often capricious (Bridges and Watts, 2008; Watts, 2010). Academic studies – particularly, but not exclusively, in Nigeria – typically do not extend beyond criticism and usually fail to explain how policies and practices can be improved (Watts and Akogun, 2017). Simply using, sharing and acquiring the skills that had generated this slough of educational despond therefore had limited value in terms of the wider context. To be of real value, those skills needed to be deployed in the improvement of primary education.

The aim of the study was to act as a catalyst for such improvement. It created the space for capability enhancement through financing dedicated time and providing appropriate support. However, it was important that this was not just another top-down development project. The researchers from the two subsectors had to work together and learn from each other. They all acknowledged that similar opportunities had been non-existent. Moreover, the out-group derogation exhibited by the two in-groups of practitioners and academics produced and reproduced conditions that made such collaboration under other circumstances difficult at best. By acting as broker, as well as financer and facilitator, EDOREN provided the space necessary for collaboration.

The freedom to use and acquire professional functionings within this space was necessarily subject to the conditions framing it. This freedom was dependent on the researchers' willingness to share knowledge and skills that were relevant to the study and its long-term aim. The conversion of the professional resources was subject to the negotiation of the mutual intra-sectoral mistrust and the initial perception of the study as an academic exercise. This required the interventions of the EDOREN facilitators.

However, the main concern was intra-sectoral learning, and the freedom to acquire these professional functionings was constrained by the researchers' willingness to learn from their colleagues. In the first phase (i.e. the data collection) there was more recognition from the practitioners about what they had learnt from the academics (e.g. fieldwork skills). There was significantly less recognition from the academics that the methodology was shaped by the experiences of the practitioners. This lack of recognition continued into the second phase (i.e. the policy engagement) when most, but not all, of the academics acknowledged the contributions of the practitioners. Learning theories offer many complex reasons why people are reluctant to learn but here they have been summarized by social identity theory: the out-group derogation of some academics, exacerbated by the sense that their authority had been undermined, meant they were simply unwilling to recognize the legitimacy of the practitioners' contributions to the study.

This then leads into the next concern: the freedom to share extant experience, knowledge and skills. Again, it is important to note the need to share what is pertinent to the project and its aim. It was also important that the researchers recognized the value of what they had to share. The facilitators encouraged the practitioners to contribute, and most of them did, even though some of them, particularly the junior practitioners, did so reluctantly.

As indicated above, these contributions were not always taken seriously. The freedom to share, then, was mediated by personal characteristics but, more importantly here, the responses of others. These responses were mediated by the in-groups with which the researchers identified: the original subsector-based in-groups or the newly formed intra-sectoral in-group of researchers.

The strength of in-group identification influenced the researchers' freedom to take part in the collaborative work of the research teams – that is, it influenced their freedom to appear in public (albeit the very limited public of the study) without shame. The researchers typically saw the study as an academic project, and this meant the practitioners, especially the junior practitioners, were constantly playing catch-up to be part of it. The academics started taking them more seriously when they demonstrated their worth in conducting the fieldwork in phase one – in other words, when they demonstrated that they could be more academic.

This inevitably distorted the defining characteristics of the newly emerging collaborative in-group. It also disadvantaged the practitioners in being able to contribute their own extant skills, knowledge and experience to the study. It is not that what they had to contribute had no value – the value of their contributions was clear from the design of the first phase of the study – but that they struggled to have it properly recognized by their colleagues.

The formation of a new in-group of researchers was a necessary condition for effective learning. The new in-group went some way to redressing the imbalances embedded in the mutual mistrust shaped by the derogation of the out-groups – whether of academics or practitioners. Willing participation in the new in-group clearly facilitated the achievement of the professional functionings (i.e. the use, sharing and acquisition of knowledge and skills aimed at improving the primary education sector), and this was clearly important. Most of the researchers achieved these functionings, but two subgroups fell short of it: the collaboration-resistant academics and most of the junior practitioners.

However, there were significant differences in their substantive freedoms to achieve these functionings. The collaboration-resistant academics could have learnt more if they had been willing to acknowledge their need to learn more. The junior practitioners could have contributed more – and been taken more seriously – if they had not been the target of the out-group derogation of the collaboration-resistant academics. These academics therefore had greater capability because they chose not to learn. The practitioners had less capability because their freedom to contribute was dependent on how they were seen by their academic colleagues.

Conclusions

This particular study has a very particular focus: the intra-sectoral collaboration of academics and policy makers/practitioners in northern Nigeria. However, these conclusions have a much wider significance and are relevant to the ways in which social identities and social choice can influence capability. Our concern here has been with the researchers' professional capabilities and their substantive freedoms to progress from simply doing a job to making it personally meaningful and satisfying (Alkire, 2002; Watts and Bridges, 2006) by potentially enhancing the well-being of others (Devecchi and Watts, 2018), and so being able to appear in public without shame (Sen, 1999; Alkire, 2002) by doing the job properly.

Importantly, the detailed approach to the evaluation of the RCSS, with the individual researchers being repeatedly observed and interviewed about their collaborative experiences throughout the first year of the project, allowed us to carefully examine the evolution of the group capabilities. The rhetoric expressed during the workshops and in the interviews indicated the development of harmonious relationships only occasionally interrupted by disagreement. These disagreements should not in themselves be seen as disruptive, as they are perhaps inevitable aspects of collaborative work. They can even be seen as necessary reminders that different group members have different opinions and views.

If the mid-term evaluation of the RCSS (Watts and Akogun, 2017) indicated that most of the key indicators (with the exception of mentoring for the practitioners) were being met, it also highlighted the issue of the intra-sectoral mistrust that influenced the collaboration underlying the strategy. This mistrust also influenced the capabilities of the researchers. It was shaped by social identity processes influencing the agency – and therefore the social choice, and so the capability – of others.

In terms of the freedom to achieve the professional functionings, there was greater capability when the research teams worked together and recognized the contributions of the individual team members. The sense of individual and group identities acted as a conversion factor. The reluctance of team members with greater authority to identify with the newly formed in-group of intra-sectoral researchers limited their achievement of the professional functionings. However, they had the opportunity to identify with that in-group, and so their capability was not limited. Unfortunately, that reluctance impacted on the capability of others, particularly the junior practitioners. Some of them were reluctant to fully participate in the team activities but their freedom to do so was constrained by the social identification of colleagues with greater authority. In other words, their freedom to contribute – more specifically, within the capability approach, their freedom to contribute without shame – was limited. This limitation was not of their choosing.

These social identity processes also played a part in the social choices of the study, particularly the ways in which they enabled or inhibited individuals from properly participating in collective decision-making processes.

Perhaps most obviously here they were evident in the refusal of some academics to accept the majority decision of their colleagues to adopt the research design advocated by the facilitators. However, as noted above, this was not a meaningful choice, despite the veneer of the majority decision; it was a choice made in the best interests of the teams in the wider context of the study, but it was underpinned by the violation of the non-dictatorship principle. The real choice – the real meaningful choice – was in the application to take part in the study. This made clear the need for intra-sectoral collaboration and guidance from the facilitators. The implication was clear: that learning was a condition of participation. Most of the researchers acknowledged and accepted this. However, some did not. Their choices were made on the basis of distorted interpretations of the study as an academic exercise, and its conditions and their decisions disrupted, but did not derail, the study.

Here, then, is the first tentative conclusion. Social choices need to incorporate legitimate options but they need to be properly informed (Sen, 1999). Uninformed choices can undermine the outcome and so call into question the choice process.

Second, and perhaps unsurprisingly, group capabilities are more likely to be enhanced when all members of the pertinent social group work together and recognize the value of the resources that each member brings to the group. One issue in this study was that the academics and practitioners alike initially saw it as an academic exercise. This emphasized the value of the academics' contributions and de-emphasized the value of the practitioners' contributions. It was only during the second phase, when the knowledge and the experience of the practitioners were more fully recognized, that the wider in-group of researchers began to form.

Third, and recognizing the difficulties of that last point, the individualistic nature of the capability approach demands recognition of the complex nature of individuals. Here, that complexity can be seen in the potentially significant destabilization of the RCSS because some individuals felt their authority had been unfairly challenged. Capability assessments, if they are to be true to their fundamental purpose, must be able to recognize such complexities.

Here, the careful approach to the evaluation of the RCSS allowed us to recognize such complexities as the two in-groups of academics and practitioners formed the wider in-group of researchers. This did not require them to abandon their membership of the initial groups but to reflect on key aspects of what defined them. As indicated here, the failings of the primary education sector in northern Nigeria, and the consequent urge to apportion blame elsewhere, can cause those who feel their own identities may be under threat to retreat to the safety of their in-groups. This can influence the social choice and the capabilities of others, especially those considered to have fewer resources or whose resources are not necessarily valued.

Appropriate reflection, though, can lead to the redefinition of individual and group identities. The role of EDOREN as funder and facilitator of the main study was necessary to that reflection in this case because the two initial in-groups had become so deeply entrenched that, in all probability, no intra-sectoral collaboration would have taken place otherwise. However, such interventions may not always be needed. In capability terms, such reflection can lead to the reconsideration of those things we value and have reason to value, including the freedom to take part in the life of the community – here, the community of researchers – without shame.

It is this process of reflecting on and redefining individual and group identities, and the influence of the process on social choice and capability, that makes the findings of this study relevant beyond its focus on the primary education sector in northern Nigeria.

Acknowledgement

This work was supported by EDOREN, which was funded by the United Kingdom's former Department for International Development (contract 5975).

References

Akogun, O., Allsop, T., Watts, M., and Waziri, N. (2017) Evidence-based policy and practice: primary teacher recruitment and deployment in northern Nigeria. Paper presented at the 14th UKFIET International Conference on Education and Development, University of Oxford, 5 September.

Alkire, S. (2002) *Valuing Freedoms: Sen's Capability Approach and Poverty Reduction*. Oxford: Oxford University Press.

Allsop, T., and Watts, M. (2017) *Identifying, Recruiting and Deploying Effective Teachers in Kano and Kaduna States*. Abuja: EDOREN.

(eds.) (2018) *The Use of Evidence in Developing Primary Education Policies in North-Western Nigeria*. Abuja: EDOREN.

Arrow, K. J. (1951) *Social Choice and Individual Values*. New York: Wiley.

Bennell, P., Anyawu, S., and Dodo, M. (2014) *The Supply of and Demand for Primary and Junior Secondary School Teachers in Katsina State, 2014–25*. Abuja: EDOREN.

Bridges, D., and Watts, M. (2008) Educational research and policy. *Journal of Philosophy of Education*, 42 (Supp. 1): 41–62.

Devecchi, C., and Watts, M. (2018) Other people's adaptations: teaching children with special educational needs to adapt and to aspire. In *New Frontiers of the Capability Approach*, Comim, F., Fennell, S., and Anand, P. B. (eds.): 571–96. Cambridge: Cambridge University Press.

Ellemers, N., Spears, R., and Doosje, B. (2002) Self and social identity. *Annual Review of Psychology*, 53: 161–86.

Ellemers, N., Wilke, H., and van Knippenberg, A. (1993) Effects of the legitimacy of low group or individual status on individual and collective status enhancement strategies. *Journal of Personality and Social Psychology*, 64 (5): 766–78.

ESSPIN (2013) *Overall Findings and Technical Report of ESSPIN Composite Survey 1 (2012)*. Abuja: EDOREN. www.esspin.org/resources/reports/composite-survey-1-reports [accessed 28 July 2017].

Kontagora, H. L., Watts, M., and Allsop, T. (2018) The management of Nigerian primary school teachers. *International Journal of Educational Development*, 59: 128–35.

Ogundahunsi, O. T., Vahedi, M., Kamau, E. M., Aslanyan, G., Terry, R. F., Zicker, F., and Launois, P. (2015) Strengthening research capacity: TDR's evolving experience in low- and middle-income countries. *PLoS Neglected Tropical Diseases*, 9 (1): 1–6.

Sen, A. K. (1999) *Development as Freedom*. Oxford: Oxford University Press.

Steenbergen, V. (2016) EDOREN thematic research on 'identifying, recruiting and deploying effective teachers'. Abuja: EDOREN.

https://edorennigeria.files.wordpress.com/2014/07/edoren_thematic_research_identifyin_recruiting_deploying_teachers_jan-24_2017_2-51pm.pdf [accessed 28 July 2017].

Tajfel, H. (ed.) (1978) *Differentiation between Social Groups: Studies in the Social Psychology of Intergroup Relations.* London: Academic Press.

Tajfel, H., and Turner, J. C. (1979) An integrative theory of intergroup conflict. In *The Social Psychology of Intergroup Relations*, Austin, W. G., and Worchel, S. (eds.): 33–7. Chicago: Nelson Hall.

Turner, J. C. (1987) A self-categorization theory. In *Rediscovering the Social Group: A Self-Categorization Theory*, Turner, J. C., Hogg, M. A., Oakes, P. J., Reicher, S. D., and Wetherell, M. S. (eds.): 1–18. Oxford: Blackwell.

(1999) Some current issues in research on social identity and self-categorization theories. In *Social Identity: Context, Commitment, Content*, Ellemers, N., Spears, R., and Doosje, B. (eds.): 6–34. Oxford: Blackwell.

Watts, M. (2008) Narrative research, narrative capital, narrative capability. In *Talking Truth, Confronting Power*, Satterthwaite, J., Watts, M., and Piper, H. (eds.): 99–112. Stoke on Trent: Trentham Books.

(2009) Sen and the art of motorcycle maintenance: adaptive preferences and higher education in England. *Studies in Philosophy and Education*, 28 (5): 425–36.

(2010) Drugs and drug education policy: what counts as evidence. *Power and Education*, 2 (3): 322–34.

(2011) Symbolic capital and the capability gap. In *Closing the Capability Gap: Renegotiating Social Justice for the Young*, Leßmann, O., Otto, H. U., and Ziegler, H. (eds.): 199–214. Farmington Hills, MI: Barbara Budrich Publishing.

(2018) *The Research Capacity Strengthening Strategy for Evidence-Based Education Policy and Practice in Northern Nigeria: Year Two Report.* Abuja: EDOREN.

Watts, M., and Akogun, O. (2017) *The Research Capacity Strengthening Strategy for Evidence-Based Education Policy and Practice in Kaduna and Kano States, Nigeria.* Abuja: EDOREN.

Watts, M., and Bridges, D. (2006) The value of non-participation in higher education. *Journal of Education Policy*, 21 (3): 267–90.

Watts, M., and Ridley, B. (2007) Evaluating musical dis/abilities: operationalising the capability approach. *International Journal of Research & Method in Education*, 30 (2): 149–62.

PART II

Inclusiveness, Social and Individual Agency

7 In defence of inclusiveness
On sustainable human development, capability and indicators of progress[*]

MOZAFFAR QIZILBASH

Introduction

The paradigm of sustainable human development (hereafter SHD) developed by Mahbub ul Haq, and the capability approach (hereafter CA) advanced by Amartya Sen, are examples of inclusive views: views that are constructed so that they do not exclude certain other views and can be the basis of reasoned agreement between people holding diverse views. This chapter examines distinct strategies deployed in ensuring that these views are inclusive. Although Haq's paradigm and Sen's approach both suggest that human beings are the ends of development, they are inclusive in different ways. The critical perspective involved in endorsing Sen's CA may exclude various other perspectives focused on the priority of basic needs or a focus on 'utility' or income. While Haq's formulation of the SHD paradigm was influenced by Sen's CA, I argue that it was constructed so that it can be endorsed by distinct views and perspectives of the sort that capability advocates might reject. For this reason, the paradigm was the basis of a coalition of people advocating diverse views, of which the capability perspective was only one. This is an important difference between Haq's paradigm and Sen's perspective.

This chapter traces the emergence of these views and initial tensions between them, which related to the role of income in Haq's

[*] A very early version of this chapter was the basis of a keynote talk at the Cambridge Capability Conference from 22 to 23 June 2018, and was also presented at the conference on 'Happiness, capabilities and opportunities', University of Napoli, 'Federico II', from 15 to 17 November 2018. I thank all those who commented on the paper at these events. I also thank Flavio Comim, Siddiq Osmani and Amartya Sen for their comments about different aspects of this chapter. Finally, Mahbub ul Haq introduced me to the idea of human development. I acknowledge my debt to him. Any error is mine.

139

paradigm and in the construction of the Human Development Index (HDI). In recent years these tensions have subsided and the ideas of human development and capability have become more closely intertwined. There are both risks and potential benefits from a full 'merger' between these views. One risk – that the paradigm becomes grounded in an approach that is, arguably, rather hard to 'operationalize' – is, I suggest, minimal if, like Sen himself, advocates of the CA take a pragmatic approach to the variety of indicators that can be used in applying the approach, and do not restrict themselves to direct measures of what people are able to be and do. Another risk is that Haq's paradigm becomes inextricably linked with one particular perspective so that it is unable to ground a multi-perspectival consensus among a variety of conflicting views. I argue that the fact that the paradigm is inclusive and can accommodate distinct perspectives has been, and may once again be, important for exercises involving indicators for evaluating progress. These exercises can include the use of multidimensional development indicators as well as indicators used in other exercises for which consensus is important, such as the setting of targets such as the Millennium Development Goals and the Sustainable Development Goals. For this reason, I defend this aspect of the inclusivity of the paradigm, which would be threatened by its complete 'merger' with the CA.

The chapter is organized as follows. The second section explains the idea of an inclusive view of development (and related topics) and various strategies that are deployed to ensure that a view is inclusive; the next two sections explain the emergence of Haq's paradigm and Sen's CA, the different respects in which these views are inclusive and tensions between them; the fifth section explains how, over time, attempts were made to reconcile and fully 'merge' these views; the sixth section argues that there are risks in the potential merger between these views and makes a case for not fully 'merging' them; and there is a concluding section.

Conceptual preliminaries

Any view of development – or, indeed, of related topics such as the quality of life, morality and justice – usually makes significant commitments that distinguish it from other views. Sometimes these commitments can make holding one view incompatible with holding others. To the degree that they do so, I shall say that these commitments are *exclusionary*. For example, to the degree that a view of development is committed to a particular view of what makes a life good, one cannot hold that view while holding alternative views of the good life. *Inclusionary* strategies are aspects of a view that ensure that it does not make certain sorts of exclusionary commitments and that it can be the basis of agreement between people who hold different views. Inclusive views restrict their exclusionary commitments and deploy inclusionary strategies with a view to achieving some degree of reasoned consensus among people who hold diverse views. But any inclusive view must make *some* exclusionary commitments, in order to be a well-articulated view that can be distinguished from others.

Inclusive views differ in their commitments and also deploy different types of inclusionary strategy. I focus on four types of inclusionary strategy. A view can be inclusive (1) by adopting vague terms that can be filled out differently by different people; (2) by being open-ended and taking no stance on some topic; (3) by developing a general framework within which the specific concerns and insights of other views can be encompassed; and (4) by focusing on areas of 'intersection' or 'overlap' between different views. As a candidate example of (1), consider the well-known Brundtland Commission definition of sustainable development (hereafter SD), according to which SD is 'development that meets the needs of the present without compromising the ability of future generations to meet their own needs' (World Commission on Environment and Development, 1987: 43). It is sometimes claimed that the concept of SD has commanded quite wide consensus because it is vaguely articulated. As Sharachachandra Lélé (1991: 607) puts it: 'There are those who believe that one should not try to define SD too rigorously. To some extent, the value of the phrase does lie in its broad vagueness. It allows people with hitherto irreconcilable views in the environment and development debate to search for common ground.' The Brundtland definition of SD is couched in terms that invoke a basic needs view. This may be an inclusionary strategy, to the extent that people who hold different views of the good life may still agree on the importance of satisfying certain basic needs (see Qizilbash, 1997). Nonetheless, some reject the basic needs view, and, to some degree, this might limit the consensus it supports. The use of a term that is vaguer, such as 'interests', in place of 'needs' might make the view open to people who take different views – whether they view SD in terms of needs or some other concept such as 'capability' (see Anand and Sen, 2000b) or 'utility' and in that way more inclusive.

As an example of (2), consider the question of whether use of the market mechanism or state intervention is the best way to pursue SD in some context. A view of development can be 'incomplete' or open-ended in not taking a stance on this topic, so that it can be held by people who hold different views on this question. As an example of (3), consider a general framework that can accommodate both basic and non-basic needs within its frame (see, for example, Doyal and Gough, 1991). Such a framework would potentially avoid exclusionary commitments, since people might endorse it while taking different views on the priority of basic needs. Finally, an example of (4) is a view of development that might focus on certain shared values – such as equity – which might be endorsed by, and filled out in different ways by, views with different philosophical groundings.

The idea of an inclusive view is distinct from, if related to, some terms used in the literature in moral philosophy. In defining the concept of 'welfarism', Amartya Sen (1979: 471) had in mind views that exclude all non-welfare or non-'utility' information in making *moral judgements*. Welfarist views make an exclusionary commitment, since if one holds such a view one must reject all non-welfarist views. But the term 'exclusion' here relates to the information excluded rather than the views that are excluded. One might impose an information constraint of this sort in the context of views of development. By doing so, one would make an exclusionary commitment. Nonetheless, in Sen's terms, welfarists believe that welfare is taken to be the only object of *ultimate value*. The exclusion is not necessarily of specific *indicators* of welfare or development. Sen (2000: 19–20) has compared the exclusive concentration on welfare in welfarism with the 'mono-concentration' on one indicator – real national income – in the context of development. But these forms of exclusion are distinct. In the penultimate section, I take up the question of whether, or to what extent, exclusion of information about the ultimate objects of value implies exclusion of particular indicators.

Before moving on to specific inclusive views of development, I should mention two leading views in moral and political theory and how these would be categorized in the terms I am using. An example of a non-inclusive view of *morality* is utilitarianism in any of its many forms. Take the version of this view that was advanced by Jeremy

Bentham (see Mill, 1962) and that favoured maximizing happiness in society. Bentham took a specific view of the quality of life, of the weight to give to the welfare of different people in judging aggregate happiness, and so on. If *development* is judged – as it might be in this view of morality – in terms of an expansion of the sum of, or average, happiness, this view clearly excludes many other views – views that take a different view of the quality of life, or of how to make social welfare judgements or that do not exclude non-happiness information. But, since utilitarian views are concerned with what is (morally) right, they may not be concerned with achieving consensus. Indeed, it may not be seen as a weakness of these views that they do not allow one to achieve one. By contrast, later statements of John Rawls' theory of justice (see Rawls, 1993, and 2001) are concerned with achieving an 'overlapping consensus' among people who hold diverse moral doctrines and views of the good life. To this degree, these later statements clearly constitute an inclusive view. It is in part because of the search for agreement that Rawls (1993, 1999: xiii) focuses on the needs of citizens (whatever their conceptions of morality or the good life) in adopting 'social primary goods' (or all-purpose means) in these later statements of his view. In the context of development, this approach may be classified as a variant of the needs approach. Indeed, in these later statements, Rawls notes that prior to his first principle of justice, which states that '[e]ach person has an equal claim to a fully adequate scheme of equal basic rights and liberties' (1993: 5), there may also be 'a lexically prior principle requiring that citizens' basic needs be met, at least insofar as their being met is necessary for citizens to understand and to be able fruitfully to exercise those rights and liberties' (1993: 7). Nonetheless, Rawls' theory is not advanced as a view of development as such but as a theory of justice. In its later statements, it also presupposes the background of a democratic society (see Rawls, 1993). This presupposition distinguishes his views from the views of development on which I focus in what follows.

Two conceptions of human development

The idea of 'human development' – and subsequently of 'SHD' – emerged from a fundamental reconsideration of central issues in development circles in the 1970s and 1980s. In academic debates, the most clear expression of the idea initially emerged in the work of the basic needs school – led by Paul Streeten, Frances Stewart and others, including Mahbub ul Haq (see Streeten et al., 1981) – as well as the work of Amartya Sen, notably in his early articulations of the CA (see Sen, 1983, 1984, 1988 and 1990, *inter alia*). The central insight shared by these various thinkers was that, in the pursuit of income growth, people and their quality of life had been forgotten. Income growth often failed to translate into poverty reduction. And the benefits of income growth had not necessarily been equitably distributed. The basic needs school responded by arguing for the priority of meeting basic human needs in the process of development. However, it did not fundamentally challenge the way in which development was defined. In Sen's work, by contrast, these concerns about a failure to translate the benefits of economic growth into better human lives led him to *(re)define* development as an expansion in what people can *do* or *be*, and, in this sense, an expansion in their 'capability' (see, in particular, Sen, 1984, 1988 and 1990).

Mahbub ul Haq's work for the United Nations Development Programme (UNDP), starting around 1989, led to the publication of a series of *Human Development Reports* (UNDP, 1990, 1991, 1992, 1993, 1994, 1995, 1996, 1997), and brought these ideas to a larger audience. One of Haq's crucial achievements was to bring together a diverse group that rejected the prevailing economic orthodoxy. His formulation of the idea of human development involved putting people back at the centre of development planning. The fear that human beings had got lost in the presentation of national income accounts and growth targets inspired his demand for a 'human balance sheet', and also alternative indicators to chart how people were faring. Haq (1995: 3) argued that people were both the means and ends of economic development. I refer to this central insight as the *core conception* of human development.

The core conception was endorsed by members of the basic needs group, Amartya Sen and others, including Meghnad Desai. Looking back, Sen (2006: 257) observed:

[T]here were several movements of discontent which were seeking an approach broader than what standard economic measurement provided. There were development theorists arguing for the recognition of 'basic needs'. There were advocates of various indicators of 'physical quality of life'. There were writers focusing on disparities in 'living conditions'. There were international organisations ... which emphasised the importance of ascertaining 'the state of the world's children'. There were relief organisations ... concerned with hunger, morbidity and mortality, rather than only income poverty. There were humanists voicing the need for social justice in the opportunities that people have. And there were also some obdurate theory-spinners wondering whether the foundations of economics and social evaluation could be radically shifted from commodities to capabilities, thereby shifting the focus from what people own (or have) to what they can actually do (or be). The human development approach, under Mahbub ul Haq's stewardship, tried to make room for all these concerns.

A variety of concerns thus motivated Haq's 'coalition of discontents'. The success of the core conception rested in part on the fact that it did not have any significant exclusionary commitments or 'theoretical baggage'. To be sure, the core conception would exclude views seeing human beings as only the means of development. It is hard to find anyone who would explicitly take this view, but human capital views in economics might, as Sen (1999: 292–7) suggests, implicitly treat human beings as inputs, and so as merely the means to the end of production. The core conception warns us against that view.

Although several views endorsed the core conception and came to 'own' it, it was also endorsed by others who subsequently became discontented with the pursuit of economic growth in more developed nations when this did not deliver happiness. A utilitarian perspective – of the sort originally advanced by Jeremy Bentham, concerned with the maximization of happiness – may also raise concerns with income-growth-focused views of progress. The modern utilitarian view, endorsed by Richard Layard (2005), does precisely this. Indeed, even Sen – who is a leading critic of utilitarianism – has noted that utilitarianism has the merit that it focuses on people and their well-being. As he puts it, the 'utilitarian approach ... does pay attention to the *well-being* of the people involved when judging social arrangements and their results' (Sen, 1999: 60, emphasis in original; see also Sen, 2009: 269–84). And earlier work had also argued that some views of welfare (see Griffin, 1986) that emerged from the utilitarian tradition are compatible with the core conception (Qizilbash, 1996a, 1996b, 2002). Nonetheless, on this reading, the core conception is not a full-blooded view of development. Rather, it is a basic *tenet* that can be endorsed by a wide variety of views, all of which are, to this extent, views of human development.

In further elaborating the idea of human development, Haq went beyond the core conception in various ways. First, he did so by suggesting that development involved expanding people's 'choices', not just their incomes. The fact that income was nonetheless treated as a 'choice' still appears puzzling. In ordinary language, income is the sort of thing that can open up the range of choices available, rather than itself being a 'choice'. The way in which Haq was using the term 'choice' more closely matches the delineation of a *domain of value* or *an aspect of the quality of life* or *a valued dimension of life*. And it is unsurprising that, in an early academic discussion of the Human Development Index, which Haq pioneered in collaborating with others – including Meghnad Desai and Sen – Desai (1991: 354–5) uses the term 'choice' interchangeably with the word 'dimension' of well-being. Desai's framework is consistent with my reading of Haq's text. On this reading, income is in the economic domain; but there are other valued dimensions of life, in the social and cultural domains, that might be unconnected with income. As he puts it, 'The defining difference between the economic growth and human development schools is that the first focuses exclusively on the expansion of only one choice – income – while the second embraces the enlargement of all human choices – whether economic, social, cultural or political' (Haq, 1995: 14). If one reads Haq's concern with 'choices' in this way, the chief inclusionary strategy deployed is to advance a more general framework – one that is concerned with all valued dimensions of life rather than just the economic dimension. On this reading, it is clearer why Haq advanced the HDI as an index of people's 'choices': he thinks of it as a 'more comprehensive measure of development that could capture all, or many more, of the choices people make – a measure that would serve as a better yardstick of the socio-economic progress of nations' (Haq, 1995: 47). With regard to income, he acknowledges, nevertheless, that this component of the index is 'more troublesome' (49) because some critics did not regard income as an end but only as a means. And, in the early *Human Development Reports* (see, for example, UNDP, 1990 to 1997), the HDI was presented alongside a large amount of information about various aspects of human life.

Although Haq stressed the expansion of various 'choices' involved in development, he also made certain values or 'pillars' central to it. These related to: equity; sustainability; participation and empowerment; and productivity. And Haq notes that, to pursue some of these 'choices', society need not be particularly affluent. It need not be particularly wealthy to pursue gender equality or democracy, for example. And he adds that '[v]aluable social and cultural conditions can be – and are maintained at all levels of income' (Haq, 1995: 15). Haq clearly only thought of one of these pillars – productivity – as primarily economic in nature. He writes that '[a]n essential part of the human development paradigm is productivity', which requires 'investing in people and an enabling macroeconomic environment for them to achieve their maximum potential' (19). With regard to 'sustainability', he suggests that '[t]he next generation deserves the opportunity to enjoy the same well-being that we now enjoy' (19), which – while it is not expressed in terms of basic needs – is a close relative of the notion of SD advanced by the Brundtland Commission. In this initial articulation, he thinks that '[i]t matters little whether the paradigm is labelled "sustainable human development" or "sustainable development" or "human development"' (19). The labelling of the paradigm did nonetheless matter, because the use of 'sustainable human development' reminds us of the central position of sustainability as one of the pillars of the paradigm.

Like the core conception, the paradigm of SHD is a conception that most people who wish to prioritize basic needs and those who argue in favour of development as an expansion of capability, as well as many others including those who are concerned with SD or participatory development (e.g. Goulet, 1989), will have every reason to endorse, especially when they compare this paradigm with a narrow concern with income growth. The values involved are articulated at such a general level that many would find little reason to treat them as exclusionary commitments. Nonetheless, the paradigm does make exclusionary commitments. It is clearly incompatible with any view that rejects any of its four pillars.

Did Haq endorse the CA in articulating the paradigm? Although Haq does use the language of 'capabilities', he does so in a way that does not map well onto Sen's account. And, to the degree that he introduces this language, Haq does so primarily in connection with the 'productivity' pillar of the paradigm. He tells us that the '[h]uman development paradigm is concerned with building up human capabilities (through investing in people) and with using those capabilities (through an enabling framework for growth and employment)' (Haq, 1995: 21). The use of the word 'capabilities' here maps onto ordinary language, and could easily be replaced by 'skills'. To this extent, his use is closer to the language of 'human resource development' (and the concern with human capital in some parts of economics) than it is to Sen's focus on what people can do or be. And, while Sen might endorse the human development paradigm, because he shares the values advanced, it would be a mistake, I suggest, to think that Haq was adopting a version of the CA simply because of his use of words such as 'capabilities' and 'choices'. Rather, his use of language and concepts is, I suggest, better understood as part of an inclusionary strategy to build a consensus or coalition, which might include capability advocates, like Sen, rather than to endorse one or other of the competing views of development on offer. Indeed, success in coalition or consensus building would require that no relevant view was endorsed at the expense of another.

This way of building a consensus is, arguably, connected to one strand of the deliberative democracy literature: Cass Sunstein's idea of 'incompletely theorized agreements' (Sunstein, 1995). Sen (2000: 22) makes this point in recalling Haq's achievements: 'He wanted to build on agreement (what Cass Sunstein, the Chicago legal theorist calls "an incompletely theorised agreement")'. Sunstein makes the case in the legal context. He writes: 'Democracies ... must deal with people who tend to distrust abstractions altogether. Participants in law are no exception. Judges are certainly not ordinary citizens. But neither are they philosophers. Indeed, participants in law may be unwilling to commit themselves to large-scale theories of any kind, and they will disagree with one another if they seek to agree on such theories' (Sunstein, 1995: 1735). He goes on to add (1735–6, emphasis in original):

My suggestion ... is that well-functioning legal systems often tend to adopt a special strategy for producing agreement amidst pluralism. *Participants in legal controversies try to produce incompletely theorized agreements on particular outcomes.* They agree on the result and on relatively narrow or low-level explanations for it. They need not agree on fundamental principle. They do not offer larger or more abstract explanations than are needed to decide the case. When they disagree on an abstraction, they move to a level of greater particularity. The distinctive feature of this account is that it emphasizes agreement on (relative) particulars rather than on (relative) abstractions.

Sen's account of Haq's success in consensus building echoes Sunstein's view. He writes (Sen, 2000: 22) of 'Haq's impatience with theory, which (I have to confess) I sometimes found quite frustrating, was a great help in this'. And, in explaining Haq's contribution in terms of an incompletely theorized agreement, Sen tells us (22, emphasis in original):

Such agreements may emerge pragmatically, on quite diverse grounds, after a general recognition that many things are important. Mahbub transformed the inquiry into an intensely practical one. He told the world: 'Here is a broad framework; if you want something to be included in it, which may deserve a table in the *Human Development Report* (and with incredible luck may even be considered for inclusion in one of the indices like the Human Development Index, or the Human Poverty Index), tell us *what* and explain *why* it must figure in the accounting. We *will listen.*

Haq's paradigm deploys various inclusionary strategies with a view to building a coalition. It invokes values that are endorsed in different views, and so focuses on areas of overlap; it is also, on my reading, inclusive to the degree that it avoids taking a stand on controversial questions about the nature or constituents of the good life, or on the respective roles of the market and the state. Furthermore, Haq's somewhat unusual and vague use of the term 'choices' relates to dimensions of value and was inclusive to the extent that people holding different views of value could fill it out in different ways.

Development as capability expansion

The CA, unlike the conceptions of human development I have just discussed, initially emerged in the context of egalitarian justice. It emerged in Sen's answer to the question of what, if we are egalitarians, we should aim to equalize (Sen, 1980). In the early 1970s and 1980s the discipline of development economics also came under intense scrutiny from a variety of critics. Sen began to respond to these criticisms, first in an important paper entitled 'Development: which way now?' (Sen, 1983), by endorsing the core conception of human development. In particular, he writes (Sen, 1983: 754):

Perhaps the most important thematic deficiency of traditional development economics is its concentration on national product, aggregate income and total supply of particular goods rather than on the 'entitlements' of the people or the 'capabilities' they generate. Ultimately, the process of economic development has to be concerned with what people can and cannot do, e.g. whether they can live long, escape avoidable morbidity, be well nourished, be able to read and write and communicate, take part in literary and scientific pursuits, and so forth.

Sen (1988, 1990) went on to articulate his notion of 'development as a capability expansion'. Although he endorses the core conception of human development – through a shift in focus from national product or income to people – his use of terms is very different from Haq's. In these and later statements (see, for example, Sen, 1993, 1999, 2009 and 2017) of the CA, Sen's core concepts are functioning and capability. *Functionings* are 'beings' and 'doings' that are states of the person, such as being well nourished, sheltered, or reading or writing. *Capability*, by contrast, refers to the combinations (or *n-tuples*) of valued functionings from which one can choose one collection. In as much as lives are constituted by combinations of functionings, a person's capability reflects the range of lives from which he or she can choose one. In this sense, capability is an opportunity concept: it refers to the opportunities or freedom a person has. Although this is the formal definition of capability that Sen typically uses, he also often uses 'capability' less formally to refer to the ability to do or be something specific, such as to avoid hunger or to appear in public without shame. Sen (2009: 233) has acknowledged these 'multiple' uses of the term 'capability', and I distinguish them only when the difference between them is relevant. Nonetheless, it should be clear that Sen's use of 'capability' is different from Haq's.

It is also important to note that Sen includes in his notion of capability not just the freedom to pursue well-being but also other goals that an agent may have reason to pursue. He covers the range of such goals under the notion of 'agency', which includes as a subset 'well-being goals'. A person's capability – as it is formally defined – covers both freedom to pursue well-being – 'well-being freedom' – and freedom to pursue goals more generally – 'agency freedom'. In this respect, the CA differs from some other approaches – notably basic needs and 'utility'-based views – in as much as those are concerned primarily or exclusively with welfare. The CA is concerned with welfare understood in terms of an evaluation of achieved functionings. But, unlike some of these other views, it gives freedom a value independent of well-being.

Sen distinguishes functionings and capability from other 'spaces' of evaluation, such as income and resources, as well as Rawls' social primary goods and 'utility' understood in various ways, such as desire satisfaction, happiness and pleasure. He makes a strong case for including functioning and capability as focal spaces in social evaluation. However, it is not always clear that Sen intends to replace these alternative spaces with an *exclusive* focus on capability or functioning. There are, arguably, two conflicting tendencies in Sen's writings. One of these may involve more exclusionary commitments than the other. In most statements of the approach, Sen claims that there are deficiencies in some alternative views. Consider views focused on income or resources: different people need distinct amounts of income and resources to be able to do and be various things. To the degree that we are concerned with what they are able to do and be, income and resources are misleading spaces for the evaluation of advantage. Or consider a singular focus on 'utility', understood as desire satisfaction or pleasure or happiness. This focus might be misleading, because people can adapt their desires and expectations so that they are easily satisfied or contented and 'happy'. In addition, Sen (1984: 513–15) distinguishes the CA from the basic needs approach, for a variety of reasons, not least because the basic needs approach sometimes focuses on commodity requirements, and this focus is potentially problematic for the same reasons a singular focus on income or resources might be.

By raising these objections, the CA gives us reason to reject utilitarian views as well as those that focus purely on the growth of income or purely on prioritizing basic needs. For example, when, in an early statement, Sen (1984: 511) writes that '[d]evelopment is not a matter, ultimately, of expanding supplies of commodities, but of enhancing the capabilities of people. The former has an importance only in an instrumental and strongly contingent way, traceable to the real importance of the latter', he is rejecting commodity- or income-focused approaches outright, to the extent that they focus on means rather than ends. Similarly, when he writes that the 'utility-based narrow vision of traditional welfare economics … is fundamentally inadequate as a basis for evaluating action and policy, in general, and development and structural change, in particular', Sen (1984: 513) is rejecting the view of development as an expansion of 'utility'. To this extent, the notion of development as capability expansion involves significant exclusionary commitments. Indeed, Sen is quite explicit about the fact that, by focusing on a particular space, the CA excludes other spaces. He writes that '[t]he CA is concerned primarily with the identification of value-objects, and sees the evaluative space in terms of functionings and capabilities to function' (Sen, 1993: 32). He adds: 'The selection of the evaluative space has a good deal of cutting power on its own, both because of what it *includes* as potentially valuable and because of what it *excludes*' (33, emphasis in original). Sen goes on to make this the basis for distinguishing the capability approach from various alternatives. I refer to this as the 'more exclusive' interpretation of the capability approach.

Nonetheless, because it is an inclusive view, Sen's view adopts various inclusionary strategies. The first of these is to make space for the views it criticizes. For example, Sen argues that poverty might be conceived of in terms of 'basic capability failure': in terms of being unable to do and be certain basic things (an inability to exercise certain crucially important functionings up to certain minimally adequate levels). To this degree, Sen attempts to make room for the concerns of the basic needs school within a more general framework. Similarly, because Sen (1984: 513) recognizes 'being happy' as a valued functioning, he makes space for those who are concerned with 'utility'. Second, the CA does not specify what the good life consists in. That is, it takes no specific view about the content of that life, beyond the fact that certain functionings are crucially important in the context of poverty evaluation. It also takes no view of the relative weight to give to distinct functionings. Here, Sen's approach is intentionally 'incomplete', allowing advocates who agree about the importance of the spaces of capability and functioning to disagree on their views of the good life, its components and the weights and priorities to be given to those components. Third, Sen is concerned with areas of overlap and reasoned consensus. He (Sen, 1992: 46–7) intentionally stresses the possibility of interpersonal comparisons of the quality of life when there is an 'intersection' between people's weights, or, indeed, when all the functionings point in the same direction (the so-called 'dominance partial ordering'), which can yield shared judgements.

Indeed, given Sen's desire to be inclusive, there are passages in his writings that appear to run counter to the 'more exclusive' reading of the approach discussed earlier. In his Nobel lecture, Sen (2002: 85) discusses his CA as well as the contribution of the *Human Development Reports* in the context of an expansion of information for interpersonal comparisons of the quality of life that go beyond information on 'utility'. If this is the right way to think about the CA, it is not exclusionary with regard to information about what is of fundamental value, in the way in which welfarism is. And, after introducing the capability approach in the Nobel lecture, he continues by remarking that, 'given the nature of the subject and the practical difficulties of informational availability and evaluation, it would be overambitious to be severely exclusive in sticking only to one informational approach' (Sen, 2002: 84). Because of the context in which Sen makes this remark (in which information relates to both values and measures), it is not clear that Sen intends here to refer to exclusiveness at the level of the objects of ultimate importance. Nonetheless, this anti-exclusionary tendency arguably goes back to Sen's first paper on capability (Sen, 1980). In the context of egalitarian justice, Sen argues that there is a case for considering information on functioning and capability, as opposed to an *exclusive* focus on income or resources or 'utility' of the sort we find in some other approaches. And Sen (1982: 369) argues that his is not a *singular* concern with (basic) capability equality. For example, he writes that, 'while it is my contention that basic capability equality has certain clear advantages over other types of equality, I did not argue that the others were morally irrelevant' (369). His purpose is to provide information that is not available in some of the other approaches. And in a recent statement he writes, along similar lines, 'In this view, individual claims are to be assessed not just by the incomes, resources or primary goods people respectively have, not only with reference to the pleasures or utilities people enjoy, but in terms of the freedom they have to choose between different ways of living they have reason to value' (Sen, 2017: 357). If one reads Sen's views in this 'more inclusive' way, his contribution to the development literature may not necessarily be to redefine development altogether but to provide an additional perspective that can enhance, and correct errors in, those preceding it. It is hard to reconcile this view with the reading of Sen with the 'more exclusive' interpretation. This is in part because, on this reading of Sen's views, an 'exclusive' focus on capability would also be mistaken, not least because there are other aspects of freedom – such as 'process freedom', including autonomy of choice (see Sen, 2002: 585–7) – that matter. For this reason, he argues, in the context of justice, that capability is not the only thing that ultimately matters, and he argues against what he terms 'an exclusively "capability approach"' (Sen, 2017: 358). He writes that 'it would be misleading to see the capability approach as standing on its own as a guide to justice, since it focuses only on specific aspects of well-being and freedom' (358). And, elsewhere, he rejects any 'unifocal' view of the demands of equality, and adds: 'The central issue here concerns the multiple dimensions in which equality matters, which is not reducible to one space only, be that economic advantage, resources, utilities, achieved quality of life or capabilities. My scepticism about a unifocal understanding ... (in this case applied to the capability perspective) is part of a larger critique of a unifocal view of equality' (Sen, 2009: 297).

Clearly, with regard to the informational constraints on what is of *ultimate* value, a version of the CA that avoids some such constraints makes fewer exclusionary commitments. Advocates of the CA may have to choose between these different interpretations of the approach. Alternatively, they may attempt to reconcile the more or less exclusive readings arguing that, whereas capability and functioning are the right spaces for the evaluation of *advantage*, there are other dimensions (such as 'process freedom') that are also relevant to moral and political evaluation and the comparison of social states.[1] Equally, they may suggest that Sen's comments about the limitations of any single focal informational space are made in the contexts of equality and social choice rather than development. Nonetheless, my reading of the CA is that, to the degree that it gives us reasons to reject various other perspectives (involving basic needs or income or 'utility'), it contains exclusionary commitments that are absent in Haq's paradigm.

Tensions and 'reconciliation': the justification of the HDI

It is hardly surprising, given the quite distinct uses of language in articulations of Haq's and Sen's views, including the rather different use of words such as 'capabilities' and 'choices', that – in spite of the fact that they both clearly advanced the core conception of human development at different times in the 1980s – some of those who were working on the CA found it hard to endorse the HDI.[2] After all, the CA sees development as a capability expansion *rather than* as a growth

---

[1] I thank Siddiq Osmani for raising, and for discussions of, this point.

[2] I have in mind here views expressed at the time of the first international conference on the CA ('Justice and poverty: Amartya Sen's capability approach'), held in Cambridge in June 2001. The flavour of those discussions can, to a limited degree, be inferred from the published papers that emerged from that (and similar) event(s). See, *inter alia*, the chapters in Comim, Qizilbash and Alkire (2008), as well as Alkire (2005) and Brandolini and D'Alessio (2009). Often the failure to endorse the HDI among capability researchers is manifested in these articles by a lack of much, if any – rather than overtly critical – engagement with it.

in per capita income. It was immediately problematic for some capability advocates that the HDI included income among its constituent measures. On the CA, as we have seen, income is only a means and does not necessarily accurately reflect what people are able to do and be. Furthermore, to the degree that the other measures included in the HDI were non-income measures, they were not measures of capability either, if capability refers to a combination (or *n-tuple*) of functionings from which one might choose. If anything, the remaining component indices appeared to be (aggregate or average) indicators of achievement in specific *functionings*. To some advocates of the CA, the HDI represented a measure of *well-being* (rather than freedom), combining aggregate measures of functioning and income, where income was a proxy measure of welfare. Indeed, this is consistent with Desai's early account of the index, which – as we saw – interpreted the HDI in terms of a 'well-being function'. To this extent, the HDI was *not* a measure of progress in capability expansion. For these advocates, Sen's involvement in the construction of the HDI appeared to be an uncomfortable compromise. And Sen (1993: 73) himself wrote that the *Human Development Reports* provided a picture of 'actual lives lived by people' (and thus of achieved functionings) rather than their capability or freedom to choose between different lives.

At the same time, within Sen's own writings, there was already a question about how one might measure people's capability, given that data for the most part related to observations that reflected choices people had made, rather than to the combinations (or *n-tuples*) of functionings from which choice was made. For this reason, some argued that *capability* indicators were simply impractical. Nonetheless, Sen (1992: 50–2) had already addressed these issues in some of his writings. In particular, he had noted that a person's achieved functionings might be seen as a measure of his or her capability under certain assumptions. The relevant assumptions were (1) that we can evaluate the set of valuable beings and doings simply through the value of just one element in that set – so-called 'elementary evaluation'; and (2) the relevant element reflects welfare-maximizing choice (so that it is a 'best element' – one that is at least as good as any other available). Sen noted that such elementary evaluation is actually used in most standard consumer theory, since, in this theory, the value of the budget set (of alternative commodity bundles that are available to the consumer) is measured through the observed choice made. This approach obviously takes out the value of freedom to the degree that it would treat the value of the set as the same even if the same functioning(s) were observed and no exercise of choice was involved. But Sen (1992: 52–3, emphasis in original) conceded that

[t]here is, in principle, some real advantage in being able to relate the analysis of *achieved* well-being on the wider informational base of the person's *capability set*, rather than just on the selected element of it. This is, however, not to deny that quite often this advantage would have to be foregone given the difficulty of getting information regarding the capability set as opposed to the observed functionings. In fact, the capability set is not directly observable, and has to be reconstructed on the basis of presumptions ... Thus, in practice, one might have to settle often enough for relating well-being to achieved functionings, rather than bringing in the entire capability set ... But we must distinguish between what becomes acceptable on grounds of practical difficulties of data availability, and what would be the right procedure had one not been so limited in terms of information. In arguing for the importance of the capability set in analysis of achieved well-being, we are not closing our eyes to the problems of informational availability, nor to the value of the second-best analysis that we can do even with limited data ... Practical compromises have to be made with an eye both to (1) the range of our ultimate interests, and (2) the contingent circumstances of informational availability.

On this rationale there was a case for treating some functioning measures as 'second-best' capability measures. Thus, the measures of knowledge (e.g. adult literacy and enrolment ratios or mean years of schooling) and health (e.g. life expectancy) used in some of the components of the HDI and related measures – such as the 'human poverty index' (UNDP, 1997) – could be treated as 'second-best' measures that could be *justified* using the CA. However, in making this transition, the term 'capability' was not used in the formal sense advanced in Sen's work (where it relates to the combinations of functionings from which one can choose one collection) but, rather, less formally to refer to the ability to do or be specific things – such as the ability to read or write, the ability to learn in school or the ability to lead a long life. But, going beyond this (and aside from the problems associated with data collection), the obvious problem lay in the 'presumptions' that were involved, notably the underlying assumption of prudential rationality (i.e. that people were maximizing welfare). Quite aside from the assumption of (optimizing) rationality (i.e. that people would choose options that are at least as good as others that are available), there was the question of the goals an agent pursues. If we find a person starving in a famine situation, we would not usually be able to say, simply on the basis of the observation, that he or she is starving, whether he or she has chosen to do so by, say, giving the food available to another member of the family or whether he or she had no choice in the matter. If a person chose to starve because he or she decided to give the food available to his or her son, then he or she had the freedom or capability to avoid starvation. This person had well-being freedom but chose not to pursue it. If observed choice involves rationality – which might be other-regarding or moral – but not prudential rationality, it would be mistaken to assume that the observed functioning accurately reflects capability (or well-being freedom).

Although the components of the HDI that related to education and health could be justified within the CA, it was harder to make the case for the income component. Nonetheless, Anand and Sen (2000a) provided a fuller defence of it. They write (86):

The first report, *Human Development Report 1990*, identified three key aspects of the quality of life of people, to be enhanced by the process of development: longevity, education and 'command over resources to enjoy a decent standard of living' ... There is a clear asymmetry here. Both longevity and education are clearly valuable as aspects of a good life, and also valued as constituents of the capability to do other things. In contrast 'command over resources' is only an instrument for other ends – indeed income is just one way of seeing this command. The purpose of including the income component in the HDI was to note the fact that there are many important capabilities which are critically dependent on one's economic circumstances. The income level enjoyed, especially close to poverty lines, can be very crucial information on the causal antecedents of basic human capabilities.

Anand and Sen (2000a: 87) thus treat the income component as an indirect measure of 'some capabilities not well reflected, directly or indirectly, in the measures of longevity and education'. And the fact that income is of purely instrumental value leads them (100) to argue that that is one reason why the income component is given diminishing returns in the construction of the HDI:

As a crucial means to a number of important ends, income has, thus, much significance even in the accounting of human development. While something is lost in terms of 'purity', in not sticking only to variables such as life expectancy and being educated which are valuable in themselves, a major practical gain is made in indirectly extending the coverage to take note of various capabilities that people do value intensely and which cannot be adequately reflected in figures for life expectancy and literacy. The need to take a transformation – to be exact a strictly concave transformation – of the income variable relates to the fact that the valued object is not income itself, but the things that we are able to do with income, and it gives some recognition to the further fact that there are likely to be some diminishing returns in the conversion.

Here Anand and Sen explicitly use the language of *capability* rather than functioning in the justification of the income component of the HDI, even if the more obvious term to use – for advocates of the CA – in this context would have been 'functioning'. In his subsequent work Sen also argues, in defence of the HDI, that 'education enhances the ability of people to do what they value doing' (Sen, 2006: 258). Similarly, in the case of longevity, Sen argues that '[t]he value of living must reflect the importance of our valued capabilities – our ability to do what we would like to do – since living is typically a necessary condition of having those capabilities' (258). What emerges is a defence of the HDI in terms of *capability* rather than *functioning*. And explicit in this defence is the need to give up some 'purity' in the construction of indices given the prospect and importance of 'practical gain'. This logic is consistent with Sen's earlier discussion of the need for practical compromise in the application of the CA.

Although Haq had originally advanced the human development paradigm in such a way that it might be endorsed by people with diverse views and agendas, defences of the HDI and related measures led to the increasing use of the CA in discussions of the human development paradigm. This use emerged most prominently in the most significant reconsideration of the indices annually reported in the *Human Development Reports*. Changes made in the light of this exercise were presented in the 2010 *Human Development Report* under the leadership of Jeni Klugman (see UNDP, 2010, and Klugman, Rodríguez and Choi, 2011). And the detailed differences between the CA and the human development paradigm are here, again, considerably obscured. So, for example, Klugman, Rodríguez and Choi (2011: 254–5) write:

The human development approach is closely related to the idea of human capabilities proposed by Sen and developed by, among others, Nussbaum … and Robeyns. In fact, the intellectual origins of both approaches are tightly intertwined. In 1989, as he was joining the team of collaborators that wrote the first HDR, Amartya Sen published the paper 'Development as Capability Expansion' ... The idea of the HDI as an index of capabilities was clearly stated at the outset and in other writings by the report's authors. The 1990 HDR, for example, describes the HDI as 'an index which captures three essential components of the quality of life ... longevity and knowledge refer to the formation of human capabilities, and income is a proxy measure for the choices people have in putting their capabilities to use'.

It is certainly true that, in some passages, Sen's influence comes out very forcefully in the 1990 *Human Development Report*. Nonetheless, it is also clear that the characterization of human development in that report aims to bring together the insights of multiple perspectives – including the basic needs approach, and participatory views of development. To cite another passage from the 1990 report: 'Human development is, moreover, concerned not only with basic needs satisfaction but also with human development as a participatory and dynamic process. It applies as much to less developed countries and to highly developed countries. Human development as defined in this Report thus embraces many of the earlier approaches to development' (UNDP, 1990: 11). This point gets rather lost, as the human development paradigm and the CA tend to get further 'merged', especially in the later reports. Indeed, even in academic texts dating from this period, the two ideas are increasingly merged into one view. For example, Sabina Alkire and Séverine Deneulin talk of the 'human development and capability approach' as 'an approach to development in which the objective is to expand what people are able to do and be – what might be called their real freedoms' (Alkire and Deneulin, 2009: 23; see also Fukuda-Parr, 2008).[3] These attempts at further 'merging' Haq's paradigm and the capability perspective into one approach would have the effect of grounding the human development paradigm on one specific perspective. They thereby risk excluding and alienating

---

[3] This attempt at a full merger *might* mistakenly be associated with the emergence of the Human Development and Capability Association in 2004. Although the title of the association 'acknowledged the deep connections between work on human development and capability' (Qizilbash, 2005: 145), there was no suggestion that the two views could be fully merged, not least since there were fellows of this association (such as Frances Stewart) who endorsed the human development paradigm while being critics of the CA or who took alternative views of well-being (see Qizilbash, 1996b). Robeyns (2017:198–9) has made similar points in her discussion of this issue.

other perspectives that were part of the coalition that endorsed the paradigm. It would also exclude those – needs advocates, utilitarians and others – who were critics of the CA but might or did endorse the paradigm. To this degree, it makes the paradigm less inclusive than it was when it was initially articulated, by binding it to any exclusionary commitments that are present in the CA. These attempts to completely 'merge' the human development paradigm and the CA have, unsurprisingly, not passed without some dissent. The most obvious reason for this, noted by Ingrid Robeyns (2017: 197–204), is not primarily about the detailed differences between Haq's paradigm and Sen's approach. Rather, it is that the CA is concerned with many subjects, of which development is only one. My chief concern, by contrast, is about the way in which any attempt to fully 'merge' these distinct views impoverishes the human development paradigm, identifying it with one particular perspective.

Inclusivity, indicators and Haq's paradigm

The paradigm of SHD that was the basis of a multi-perspectival consensus led by Mahbub ul Haq has, I have argued, increasingly become very closely associated with a single perspective. In historical terms, this is in some respects unsurprising, since there has been a large growth in work on the CA in recent decades, and that work has influenced the direction of work on human development. But, because of various challenges faced by work on capability, there is a natural tendency to focus on issues within that approach and its 'operationalization' rather than on the question of how a variety of approaches might help to operationalize the paradigm. This is one reason why completely intertwining the human development paradigm and the CA risks weakening some of the motivating force of the paradigm. The second reason why the complete intertwining of the two approaches poses a risk is that the paradigm was used to create consensus between different perspectives. Grounding the paradigm in one of these perspectives must undermine its ability to build cross-perspectival coalitions. In the remainder of this chapter I consider these two risks.

With regard to the risk that intertwining the CA and human development paradigm will undermine the motivational force of the paradigm by focusing on issues internal to the CA, there is at least one person for whom human development and the capability perspective remain very close and powerful *at a motivational level*: Amartya Sen himself. And his co-authored work with Jean Drèze (Drèze and Sen, 2013), *An Uncertain Glory: India and Its Contradictions*, shows the continued relevance and force of the core conception of human development as well as the continued relevance of some of the pillars (relating to sustainability, equity and empowerment) of Haq's SHD paradigm. Informed by the capability perspective and the core conception, Drèze and Sen (1995) show that India has achieved considerable success in terms of growth per capita, but that growth has not been equitably distributed, nor has it translated into the sorts of achievements in the areas of health, basic education and poverty reduction that one would expect. And India is not the only country where these sorts of points remain relevant. Indeed, the *Human Development Reports*, published nationally, regionally and internationally, continue to highlight these sorts of concerns.

Nonetheless, it might be argued that, with the exception of Sen's contributions and other successful public interventions, there are risks that human development work faces through its ever closer association with one intellectual perspective. The capability perspective can, as I have argued, be interpreted in more or less inclusive ways. The risks in terms of a narrowing of work on human development might *appear* to be at their greatest when the human development paradigm becomes associated with just one perspective, excluding others, and with only one space of evaluation, thereby potentially implying that only one sort of indicator – one that is interpreted in terms of *capability* – should be the focus of work on human development. The more exclusive interpretation of the CA – focused on 'capability only' – may even lead its advocates to eschew interest in indicators of functionings. This would make the CA difficult to operationalize, especially if it is admitted that the capability set is unobservable – notwithstanding the important work that has been done on using a variety of methods to get at information on capability and other aspects of freedom such as agency (see, *inter alia*, Krishnakumar, 2021; Anand et al., 2009; and Comim, Qizilbash and Alkire, 2008).

It is unsurprising that this concern, even if it is fair in describing certain risks, is not supported by Sen's own writings on the CA – and for rather specific reasons. First, Sen's CA is not concerned exclusively with capability; it also recommends the space of functioning (and capability is itself an *n-tuple* of functionings). Second, Sen has himself discussed at some length the pragmatic considerations that are relevant given data and informational limitations when capability is not observable. He has been extraordinarily explicit on this point, arguing that the best practical applications of the approach may involve using indicators that are *not* capability measures. For example, he writes (Sen, 1999: 81, emphasis in original):

> The capability perspective can be used in rather distinct ways. The question as to which practical *strategy* to use for evaluating public policy has to be distinguished from the *foundational* issue of how individual advantages are best judged and interpersonal comparisons most sensibly made ... At the foundational level, the capability perspective has some obvious merits ... This does not, however, entail that the most fruitful focus of practical attention would be measures of capabilities.

Sen goes on to distinguish three 'practical approaches' (83) to application: (1) the direct approach, which focuses purely on direct observation of functioning or capability; (2) the supplementary approach, which focuses on income, but supplements this focus with capability considerations, 'often in rather informal ways'; and (3) the indirect approach, which continues to focus on income but adjusts this to take into account influences on capability (notably factors that influence the transformation of income into capability and functionings). One implication is that, *even if* a version of the CA is exclusive at the level of information about what is ultimately valuable, this exclusiveness need not extend to the level of indicators. Indeed, on Sen's view (however this is interpreted), a very wide variety of measures can be justified by pragmatic application of the CA.

This conclusion is unsurprising, because much the same point can be made about the most exclusive of all the approaches discussed here: utilitarianism. As we have seen, utilitarianism is a form of welfarism, and restricts information about what is ultimately valuable to welfare or 'utility'. Does this imply that utilitarians should focus only on indicators of happiness or pleasure satisfaction or some other concept of 'utility'? This question is not unrelated to questions that arose at the outset in the development of neoclassical economics. When William Stanley Jevons (1871) advanced neoclassical economics and used the idea of a 'utility'-maximizing agent as the basis of consumer theory, he was aware that 'utility' may be both unobservable and unmeasurable. That concern did not hamper the development of a formal 'utility'-based calculus. Rather, it led to the use of numerous proxies for 'utility' – each of which was plausible only under certain assumptions. Hence, income and consumption emerged as proxy measures of welfare. Furthermore, utilitarian views were also concerned with the measurement of other values, such as equality. Given the assumption of diminishing marginal 'utility' of income, Hugh Dalton (1920) proposed a normative measure of *income* inequality that would rise as aggregate 'utility' fell. The foundational space that motivated Dalton's indicator was 'utility', but the actual space used for the indicator was income. And a utilitarian view need not be restricted to measures of 'utility' or income. If one considers a wide range of utilitarian views, even if they focus on 'utility' as the object of ultimate value, they may also advance a set of causes of happiness (see, for example, Layard, 2005); and they may also endorse the importance of freedom to the extent that this promotes aggregate 'utility'. The fact that, for welfarists, 'utility' is the only value of ultimate importance does not exclude the use of indicators of the causes of happiness or of freedom. Here also exclusivity at the level of the space of ultimate value is compatible with pragmatic use of a wide range of socio-economic indicators. These examples suggest that the potential risks with regard to the merging of the CA and the SHD paradigm may not undermine the fruitful application of the paradigm. And, given the considerable growth in the literature on the CA in recent decades, the attempt to 'merge' the two approaches may have given a lease of life to, and provided a formal foundation for, that paradigm. So, the first risk may not be significant, and the reward of a fuller 'merger' may outweigh that risk.

Now consider the second risk: that the rooting of the paradigm in one single intellectual perspective will undermine its ability to ground cross-perspectival coalitions. One of Haq's most important contributions was to develop a paradigm that could be the basis of 'incompletely theorized agreements' between people advocating different perspectives. The paradigm simply cannot play that role if it is 'merged' with just one perspective. When Sen points briefly to Haq's success in achieving 'incompletely theorized agreements', his discussion refers to proposals about indicators. And it is easy to see how very different philosophical perspectives can achieve agreement about indicators. Consider happiness. In some utilitarian views – such as Bentham's – this is of ultimate importance, and it would be an obvious measure to focus on if it is available. But the inclusion of a happiness index might also be justified through the capability perspective, because that perspective can treat 'being happy' as a valued functioning (Sen, 2009: 276–7). Similarly, a measure of life satisfaction might be of obvious interest to those who endorse a desire satisfaction version of utilitarianism, while the CA might justify that index on the grounds that life satisfaction provides evidence of how a person's life is going even if it is a misleading index of welfare (Sen, 1985: 189). Even one of the leading advocates of the basic needs approach who is also one of the most ardent critics of modern happiness research, Frances Stewart (2014: 304), acknowledges that life satisfaction might, for informational reasons, be used in a 'dashboard of multiple indicators'. Turning to a different sort of index, although the CA might endorse an index of political freedom on the grounds that freedom is of ultimate importance, a utilitarian view can endorse the same index on the grounds that freedom is either of instrumental importance or actually promotes happiness. Because the SHD paradigm does not exclude any of these views, it can ground a cross-perspectival consensus on indicators between utilitarian, needs and capability advocates in the absence of agreement about what ultimately matters.

The SHD paradigm might thus continue to play a role in building consensus across different philosophical perspectives. Might such a consensus extend beyond indicators to the pillars of the paradigm? Consider the utilitarian happiness perspective recently advanced by Richard Layard. While Sen advances reasons to reject utilitarianism, Layard (2005: 60) provides reasons to reject the CA. The two views are mutually exclusive, and, unsurprisingly, may sometimes diverge dramatically at the level of policy (see Qizilbash, 2008). But it turns out that happiness research might also endorse not merely the core conception but something very close to Haq's paradigm. The evidence supporting this claim comes from the 2012 *World Happiness Report*, of which Layard was one of three co-editors. The report notes that modern happiness research starts with challenges facing more wealthy nations, and with the observation that as nations become richer, people do not necessarily become happier (Sachs, 2012: 4). If one is concerned with human happiness, this gives one pause for thought, and reason to go beyond any exclusive focus on per capita income as a measure of progress. But might happiness research also endorse elements of the SHD paradigm as it was presented by Haq? Recall the four pillars of Haq's paradigm: productivity; sustainability; empowerment; and equity. The 2012 *World Happiness Report* considers the prospect of the Sustainable Development Goals which have now replaced the Millennium Development Goals. In his introduction to the report, Jeffrey Sachs (2012: 7) argues that these goals should have 'four pillars': ending extreme poverty (which he argues will significantly improve happiness); environmental sustainability (with a view to humanity avoiding the breach of specific thresholds for environmental damage, which will lead to irreparable damage to the Earth and future generations); social inclusion (which means that the benefits of development technology etc. should be enjoyed by all members of society, not just the few); and good governance (which involves societies acting collectively through participatory institutions, and the ability of people to shape their own lives and reap the happiness that comes from political participation and involvement). Now, although the goal of poverty reduction is central to the SHD paradigm (so much so that it is not explicitly mentioned as a pillar), it is striking how closely three of the pillars of that paradigm – equity, sustainability and empowerment – track the remaining three pillars recommended by the 2012 *World Happiness Report*. This convergence between the pillars that Sachs recommends for the Sustainable Development Goals and the pillars of Haq's paradigm suggests that that paradigm, or some adapted modern version of it, can be the basis of agreement about indicators and goals between people who hold quite different views – and, indeed, between people who would never agree on the objects of ultimate importance – in a way that the CA may not. The capacity of Haq's paradigm to ground 'incompletely theorized agreements' is an important part of his legacy, which might continue to bear fruit. And a full merger between the CA and the paradigm of SHD would undermine that legacy.

Conclusions

The view of development as capability expansion and the human development paradigm are inclusive views that can be the basis of consensus between people with different views. Nonetheless, they are distinct ideas and deploy different inclusionary strategies, and the capability perspective is only one of a range of perspectives that is consistent with the paradigm, as Mahbub ul Haq conceived it. There are at least two different ways of interpreting Amartya Sen's writings on capability, one of which makes his view more exclusive than the other. But, whichever reading one adopts, Sen's writings advance reasons for capability advocates to reject some views – such as the basic needs view and utilitarianism – that are consistent with the core conception of human development and may also endorse the four pillars of the SHD paradigm. This is an important difference between the SHD paradigm and the CA.

Although Sen was one of the first to endorse the core conception in his work in development economics, because of differences between Haq's articulation of the SHD paradigm and the CA – notably because income was listed as a 'choice' and a component in the HDI – there were tensions between these views. These tensions were resolved in part through Sen's defence of the HDI. In the light of this 'reconciliation' there have been attempts to 'merge' the CA fully with Haq's paradigm in the subsequent literature. There are various risks involved in any such complete 'merger'. One of these is that, if the paradigm is grounded in one particular perspective, it will not be able to ground a cross-perspectival coalition of the sort that Haq was able to build. Building such a coalition was one of Haq's chief achievements, and part of the reason for the success of the paradigm. Indeed, in the current context, an updated version of the paradigm may once again ground such a consensus based on the core conception and something akin to its four pillars, which might include modern happiness researchers as well as capability and needs advocates. That consensus may prove to be important at the level of indicators of progress, because very diverse indicators can be justified by distinct theoretical and philosophical perspectives. For these reasons, I defend the inclusiveness of the paradigm, which is an important part of Haq's legacy.

References

Alkire, S. (2005) Why the capability approach? *Journal of Human Development*, 6 (1): 115–35.

Alkire, S., and Deneulin, S. (2009) The human development and capability approach. In *An Introduction to the Human Development and Capability Approach: Freedom and Agency*, Deneulin, S., and Shahani, L. (eds.): 22–48. London: Earthscan.

Anand, P., Hunter, G., Carter, I., Dowding, K., Guala, F., and van Hees, M. (2009) The development of capability indicators. *Journal of Human Development and Capabilities*, 10 (1): 125–52.

Anand, S., and Sen, A. K. (2000a) The income component of the Human Development Index. *Journal of Human Development*, 1 (1): 83–106.

(2000b) Human development and economic sustainability. *World Development*, 28 (12): 2009–49.

Brandolini, A., and D'Alessio, G. (2009) Measuring well-being in the functioning space. In *Debating Global Society: Reach and Limits of the Capability Approach*, Chiappero-Martinetti, E. (ed.): 91–156. Milan: Fondazione Giangiacomo Feltrinelli.

Comim, F., Qizilbash, M., and Alkire, S. (eds.) (2008) *The Capability Approach: Concepts, Measures and Applications*. Cambridge: Cambridge University Press.

Dalton, H. (1920) The measurement of the inequality of incomes. *Economic Journal*, 30: 348–61.

Desai, M. (1991) Human development: concept and measurement. *European Economic Review*, 35 (2/3): 350–7.

Doyal, L., and Gough, I. (1991) *A Theory of Human Need*. Basingstoke: Macmillan.

Drèze, J., and Sen, A. K. (1995) *India: Economic Development and Social Opportunity*. Oxford: Oxford University Press.

(2013) *An Uncertain Glory: India and Its Contradictions*. London: Allen Lane.

Fukuda-Parr, S. (2008) Human rights and human development. In *Arguments for a Better World: Essays in Honor of Amartya Sen*. vol. 2, *Society, Institutions, and Development*, Basu, K., and Kanbur, R. (eds.): 76–99. Oxford: Oxford University Press.

Goulet, D. (1989) Participation in development: new avenues. *World Development*, 17 (2): 165–78.

Griffin, J. (1986) *Well-Being: Its Meaning, Measurement and Moral Importance*. Oxford: Oxford University Press.

Haq, Mahbub ul (1995) *Reflections on Human Development*. Oxford: Oxford University Press.

Jevons, W. S. (1871) *The Theory of Political Economy*. London: Penguin.

Klugman, J., Rodríguez, F., and Choi, H.-J. (2011) The HDI 2010: new controversies, old critiques. *Journal of Economic Inequality*, 9: 249–88.

Krishnakumar, J. (2021) Econometric and statistical models for estimating the capability approach. In *The Cambridge Handbook of the Capability Approach*, Chiappero-Martinetti, E., Osmani, S., and Qizilbash, M. (eds.): 453–76. Cambridge: Cambridge University Press.

Layard, R. (2005) *Happiness: Lessons from a New Science*. London: Penguin.

Lélé, S. (1991) Sustainable development: a critical review. *World Development*, 19 (6): 607–21.

Mill, J. S. (1962) *Utilitarianism: Including Mill's On Liberty and Essay on Bentham and Selections from the Writings of Jeremy Bentham and John Austin*, Warnock, M. (ed.). Glasgow: William Collins & Sons.

Qizilbash, M. (1996a) Ethical development. *World Development*, 24 (7): 1209–22.

(1996b) Capabilities, well-being and human development: a survey. *Journal of Development Studies*, 33 (2): 143–62.

(1997) Needs, incommensurability and well-being. *Review of Political Economy*, 9 (3): 261–76.

(2002) Development, common foes and shared values. *Review of Political Economy*, 14 (4): 463–80.

(2005) Special editor's introduction. *Journal of Human Development*, 6 (2): 145–50.

(2008) The adaptation problem, evolution and normative economics. In *Arguments for a Better World: Essays in Honor of Amartya Sen*, vol. 1, *Ethics, Welfare, and Measurement*, Basu, K., and Kanbur, R. (eds.): 50–67. Oxford: Oxford University Press.

Rawls, J. (1993) *Political Liberalism*. New York: Columbia University Press.

(1999) *A Theory of Justice*, rev. edn. Oxford: Oxford University Press.

(2001) *Justice as Fairness: A Re-Statement*. Cambridge, MA: Belknap Press.

Robeyns, I. (2017) *Wellbeing, Freedom and Social Justice: The Capability Approach Re-Examined*. Cambridge: Open Book Publishers.

Sachs, J. (2012) Introduction. In *World Happiness Report*, Helliwell, J., Layard, R., and Sachs, J. (eds.): 2–9. New York: Earth Institute, Columbia University.

Sen, A. K. (1979) Utilitarianism and welfarism. *Journal of Philosophy*, 76 (9): 463–89.

(1980) Equality of what? In *The Tanner Lectures in Human Values*, vol. 1, McMurrin, S. M. (ed.): 197–220. Cambridge: Cambridge University Press.

(1982) *Choice, Welfare and Measurement*. Oxford: Blackwell.

(1983) Development: which way now? *Economic Journal*, 93: 745–62.

(1984) *Resources, Values and Development*. Oxford: Blackwell.

(1985) Well-being, agency and freedom: the Dewey lectures 1984. *Journal of Philosophy*, 82 (4): 169–221.

(1988) The concept of development. In *Handbook of Development Economics*, Chenery, H., and Srinivasan, T. N. (eds.): 9–26. Amsterdam: North-Holland.

(1990) Development as capability expansion. In *Human Development and the International Development Strategy for the 1990s*, Griffin, K., and Knight, J. (eds.): 41–58. Basingstoke: Palgrave Macmillan.

(1992) *Inequality Reexamined*. Oxford: Oxford University Press.

(1993) Capability and well-being. In *The Quality of Life*, Nussbaum, M. C., and Sen, A. K. (eds.): 30–53. Oxford: Clarendon Press.

(1999) *Development as Freedom*. Oxford: Oxford University Press.

(2000) A decade of human development. *Journal of Human Development*, 1 (1): 17–23.

(2002) *Rationality and Freedom*. Cambridge, MA: Harvard University Press.

(2006) Human Development Index. In *The Elgar Companion to Development Studies*, Clark, D. A. (ed.): 256–9. Cheltenham: Edward Elgar.

(2009) *The Idea of Justice*. London: Penguin.

(2017) *Collective Choice and Social Welfare*, expanded edn. London: Penguin.

Stewart, F. (2014) Against happiness: a critical appraisal of the use of measures of happiness for evaluating progress in development. *Journal of Human Development and Capabilities*, 15 (4): 293–307.

Streeten, P., Burki, S., Haq, M, Hicks, N., and Stewart, F. (1981) *First Things First: Meeting Basic Needs in Developing Countries*. Oxford: Oxford University Press.

Sunstein, C. (1995) Incompletely theorized agreements. *Harvard Law Review*, 108 (7): 1733–72.

UNDP (1990) *Human Development Report 1990*. New York: Oxford University Press.

(1991) *Human Development Report 1991*. New York: Oxford University Press.

(1992) *Human Development Report 1992*. New York: Oxford University Press.

(1993) *Human Development Report 1993*. New York: Oxford University Press.

(1994) *Human Development Report 1994*. New York: Oxford University Press.

(1995) *Human Development Report 1995*. New York: Oxford University Press.

(1996) *Human Development Report 1996*. New York: Oxford University Press.

(1997) *Human Development Report 1997*. New York: Oxford University Press.

(2010) *Human Development Report 2010: The Real Wealth of Nations: Pathways to Human Development*. New York: Oxford University Press.

World Commission on Environment and Development (1987) *Our Common Future*. Oxford: Oxford University Press.

8 | *Exploring Sen on self-interest and commitment**

GAY MEEKS

Amartya Sen's work on capabilities is characteristically rich in deeply systematic analysis that leads to the offer of new categorizations to clarify and illuminate the conceptual space. Yet this very richness sets a challenge to his readers in digesting fresh terminology and keeping hold of the relationships between multiple fine distinctions, sometimes set against the background of specific moves by other authors within the fields of political theory, philosophy, law or (especially) economics. With that challenge in mind, this chapter explores aspects of Sen's analysis of self-interest and commitment and seeks to highlight their interplay by probing some imagined situations.

The first section ('Concepts') presents the alternative forms of commitment Sen's analysis distinguishes as important departures from facets of self-interest. He identifies 'three different ways in which the self may be central to one's self-interested preferences and choices' – all of which are 'imposed in the traditional models of economic theory', with two retained in the broader approach of modern rational choice theory. But a fourth feature of the self, contrasting with the others, is the foundation for the committed behaviours he argues self-interest approaches fail to recognize. It involves a dimension of reasoned self-scrutiny that is central to his conception of agency (Sen, 2002: 33–6, 214).[1]

Sen tells us that the three components of the self he has separated out in standard approaches to rationality are in fact 'independent of each

* A preliminary version of this chapter was presented with support from David Clark at the annual Cambridge Capabilities Conference in June 2017 (whose general theme was social choice and capabilities). David has been instrumental in encouraging me to pursue the topic and keeping me abreast of developments in the literature. I am most grateful to CCC participants in both 2017 and 2018 for their very valuable comments and suggestions. I have also benefited greatly from discussions with students in my MPhil classes and with Polly and Kitty Meeks.
[1] Unnamed quotation references in the text are to works by Sen.

other, and can be used – or not used – in any combination' (2002: 34, 214). His threefold typology of these distinct aspects of self-interest thus prompts consideration of attributes of the implied eightfold pattern of combinations of their respective presence or absence, and their linkage to the two forms of commitment Sen defines: I set out this pattern in the second section ('Relationships') and examine its nuances through posing an imaginary internet dating conundrum.

The third section ('Implications and applications') revisits Sen's stress on the self as agent in outlining the role Sen accords to commitment and examples he gives of its empirical importance.

The next section ('Arguments, knock-down arguments and Humpty Dumpty') addresses some complexities in and disputes over establishing cases of commitment. After a comment on debate over one of the twin forms of commitment Sen defines that has been particularly contentious, I sketch some hypothetical voting dilemmas that could have arisen in the United Kingdom during parliamentary procedures in 2017 relating to Brexit and speculate over how ideas of committed behaviour might enter into them. Giving reasons for pinning my colours to the commitment mast, I conclude the chapter by inviting readers to count the cost of over-exploiting the malleability – the 'Humpty-Dumptyness' – of language.

Concepts

Highlighting the limitations of modelling behaviour as purely related to a simplistic concept of the rational self has been a persistent theme of Sen's, from his early paper 'Rational fools: a critique of the behavioural foundations of economic theory' (Sen, 1977) to the recently expanded edition of his seminal book, *Collective Choice and Social Welfare* (2017, esp. pp. 300–304), with many significant contributions in between (notably Sen 1982, 1985a, 1985b, 1987, 1993, 1997, 1999, 2002, 2005, 2007 and 2009). Concluding the initial 1977 paper, he writes: 'the main issue is the acceptability of the assumption of the invariable pursuit of self-interest in each act', his central challenge to this being 'the need to accommodate commitment as a part of behaviour' (1977: 343–4). This was against the backdrop of his disquiet that, out of step with the broader approach of early economic writers (including Adam Smith), 'a very large part of modern economics has increasingly fallen for the simplicity of ignoring all motivations other than the pursuit of self-interest, and brand-named "rational choice theory" has even elevated this falsely alleged uniformity in human behaviour into the basic principle of rationality' (2009: 187). The features of the self that Sen goes on to distinguish stem from this specific critical context.[2]

It might at first seem that a critique of the dominant trend Sen finds in modern economics need only confront the narrowness of assuming universal self-regarding greed, according to which our personal well-being relates only to what we possess ourselves or directly experience and not to any other considerations, such as the well-being of others.[3] He designates this traditional characterization of self-interest as 'self-centred welfare', under which 'a person's welfare depends only on her own consumption and other features of the richness of her [own] life …' (2002: 33).[4]

However, Sen is well aware that this particularly 'restricted version' of rational choosing – taking 'rational persons … not only [to] be self-seeking, but … also [to] be … completely unaffected by the well-being or achievements of others' – is 'increasingly out of fashion now' (2009: 188). Classifying it as one, albeit extreme, feature of the self that theorists in this vein have standardly invoked, he moves on to identify another that, following the economist Gary Becker (1976, 1981, 1996), they tend to appeal to nowadays. This allows for other-regarding behaviour – 'taking an interest in others' – *in so far as* this still 'promot[es] their own welfare', thus, for instance, 'taking note of their own enjoyment – or suffering – from the welfare of others': in this important broadening of the concept to include non-self-centred behaviour, self-interest includes gains or losses in one's own welfare that result from experiencing sympathetic fellow feeling with others' joy or pain – and, less appealingly, any that might result instead from antipathetic feeling (Sen, 2009: 188).

---

[2] They may for that reason not immediately match up with features and concepts familiar in other disciplines. John Davis (2007: 332) comments that his discussion of Sen on identity and commitment relates specifically to 'a particular history of thinking about individuals in economics', noting its separation from the approach to personal identity 'in philosophy and elsewhere', where 'different sorts of issues' have been the main focus of concern. Des Gasper makes the case for fruitful insights being gained by paying more regard to work in social psychology (see, for example, Gasper 2000).

[3] On attributing 'greed' here, see note 20.

[4] The definitions as given in Sen (2002) differ slightly in wording from those originally set out in Sen (1985a), and from various other statements of them: see notes below detailing and sometimes explaining these minor variations.

Sen also pays regard to the explanatory value of the work of Christine Jolls, Cass Sunstein and Richard Thaler (1998) in law and economics, who take account of process factors in 'extend[ing] Becker's extension' of self-interest (Sen, 2002: 31), recognizing, for instance, that emotional or reciprocal benefit to oneself can come from treating others fairly. And he makes due allowance too for the 'large literature on skilfully "elongating" the self-interest model' by means of 'ingenious' attempts to explain in 'instrumental' terms, as indirect means to a self-interest-maximizing end, observed behaviours such as cooperation, kindness and public-spiritedness (24–5). Wherever seemingly non-selfish action is undertaken *because* of its contribution to one's own welfare (whether through sympathy or antipathy, through the effects of process concerns or through other self-benefiting effects, such as enhanced reputation or easing the conscience by guilt avoidance), it can enter into rational choice theory's modern wider understanding of self-interest and factor into the second component of the self that Sen presents: this he names 'self-welfare goal', under which 'a person's only goal is to maximize her own welfare', whether very narrowly or more broadly understood (2002: 34).

However, Sen forcefully points out that this second feature of the self cannot be assumed to exhaust the domain of acting with regard to others: it does not prove 'the adequacy of simple and selfish values' to represent the full 'breadth of our values and priorities' (2002: 25). Once released from the still restricted confines of rational choice theory, 'the power of reason ... allows us to consider our obligations and ideals as well as our interests and advantages' (1999: 272). Introducing his original concept of commitment in 1977, he contrasts it with sympathy, sharply at first: 'If the knowledge of torture of others makes you sick, it is a case of sympathy: if it does not make you feel personally worse off, but you think it is wrong and you are ready to do something to stop it, it is a case of commitment' – or, in the more nuanced comparison that immediately follows, even if you do feel personal pain (as you very naturally might), you show commitment so long as making yourself feel better is not the *reason* for your being ready to take action (1977: 326–7; 2002: 35; see also 2009: 179).[5]

---

[5] Or again, in later presentations (e.g. 2002: 34–5), at least it is not the *prime* reason.

Since behaviour based on sympathy opens up space for other-regarding behaviour that nonetheless benefits the self, application to it of terms such as 'selfish' (or even 'self-interested'[6]), on the one hand, or 'altruistic', on the other, is not straightforward without adding qualification. Sen writes with Becker in mind when he allows that conforming to 'self-welfare goal' causes 'no problem in accommodating altruism' (2002: 36);[7] but he also describes 'altruism through sympathy' as being 'ultimately self-interested benevolence' (1997: 760, n.33). He sees altruism in this sense as accompanying egoism in one interpretation of that term, stating that behaviour based on sympathy, as incorporated in rational choice theory and amounting to 'the pursuit of one's own utility ... is in an important sense egoistic' – whereas 'action based on commitment [whether or not accompanied by sympathy] ... would be non-egoistic in this sense' (1977: 326). I take it that 'mean' also has a suitably qualified sense in Sen's central argument here: 'A person can indeed choose to be mean without being irrational ... [but] rationality does not actually *require* such meanness', as the prevalent rational choice view supposes: rather, rationality 'can allow the acknowledgement of goals that are not exclusively reduced to one's own welfare' (2002: 36–7, emphasis in original).

Pursuing goals beyond own welfare allows for the possibility of such pure self-sacrifice as might be associated with saintly actions by secular heroes. But many kinds of goal might come into the category of not being driven by personal gain, as Sen points out: commitment 'may relate to the working of some universalized morality, [but] it need not necessarily be so broad-based ... [A] sense of commitment to one's community, race, class, fellow-workers, fellow-oligopolists, etc., could be important in the choice of actions' ... [T]he 'morality or culture underlying [commitment] may well be of a limited kind – far removed from the grandeur of approaches such as utilitarianism'

---

[6] Davis (2007) suggests instead using the term 'self-regard' in this connection.
[7] Consider how Becker uses the term in his renowned treatise on the family, which 'assume[s] that parents are altruistic: their utility is raised when their children are better off. Altruistic parents are willing to contribute to the cost of investing in their children's human capital, but their contribution is limited by the recognition that greater spending on children means less spending on themselves. Therefore, even altruistic parents may underinvest in children' (Becker, 1981: 5).

(1982: 8; 1977: 335). And committed behaviour does not have to be newsworthy; it can instead be a familiar feature of day-to-day life: 'We do not have to be a Gandhi, or a Martin Luther King Jr, or a Nelson Mandela, or a Desmond Tutu,[8] to recognize that we can have aims or priorities that differ from the single-minded pursuit of our own well-being only' (2009: 18).[9]

Sen goes on to draw attention to yet a further component of self-interest: this comes in sticking doggedly to one's goals, whether own-welfare-focused or not, and seeking 'maximum fulfilment of [them] (irrespective of the goals of others)' (2002: 36–7). He terms this third, determinedly own-goal-seeking, feature of the self 'self-goal choice', under which 'a person's choices must be based exclusively on the pursuit of her own goals' (34).

What Sen holds self-goal choice to leave out of account is showing due consideration for other people's plans: it fails to 'respect the agency aspect of others' (1987: 55). Of course, just as feeling for the fate of others can affect own welfare, so appreciating others' goals can sometimes affect the goals one adopts oneself, transforming some own-goal-driven behaviour in such a way as to stop it cutting across goals influencing the aims of other people. But this need not happen in general, and the possibility remains of own goal pursuit impacting on the goals of others in one's sphere of action. Here, Sen insists once again that rationality is not tied to one's own interests: it does not exclude generosity and – giving rise to a further form of commitment – it 'can allow … the recognition of values of appropriate social behaviour' (2002: 36), with acceptance of

certain self-imposed constraints of 'decent behaviour' (varying from following safety rules of orderly exit without jostling one's way to the exit door as the fire alarm sounds, to more mundane practices like not racing to take the most comfortable chair in a social gathering, leaving others far behind) … There is nothing very peculiar, or silly, or irrational about [a] decision to 'let others be' … Being considerate of the desires and pursuits of others need not be seen as a violation of rationality. (2009: 182, 193)

---

[8] Nowadays it is tempting to add 'or a Malala Yousafzai or a Greta Thunberg'.
[9] Davis (2007) persuasively suggests the influence of Williams' (1973, 1981) account of committed behaviour. Schmid (2005) refers to Williams (1979), and points also to Searle's (2001) analysis of commitment.

Sen contends, then, that the nature of rational choice extends well beyond the limits set by 'so-called rational choice theory',[10] whose 'insistence on defining rationality simply as intelligent promotion of personal self-interest sells human reasoning extremely short' (2009: 194). He contrasts the three features of the self he has identified as constituting aspects of self-interest with a fourth feature that he regards as crucial if justice is to be done to rationality. This is the capacity for 'self-scrutiny and reasoning' (2002: 33). Proposing that rationality be viewed as 'conformity with reasons that one can sustain, even after scrutiny, and not just at first sight' (2009: 180, n.), he stresses that, 'to use a medieval distinction, we are not only "patients" whose needs deserve consideration, but also "agents" whose freedom to decide what to value and how to pursue what we value can extend far beyond our own interests and needs' (2009: 252; and, similarly, 2005: 10).[11] We are free to recognize that 'there are goals other than well-being, and values other than goals' (1985b: 186). As agents, it is open to us to act from either or both forms of commitment, for 'our choices need not relentlessly follow our experiences of consumption or welfare, or simply translate perceived goals into action … The reach of one's self is not limited to self-interest maximization … [and] even as … the self-interest approach to rationality … privileges self-interest, it also undermines self-reasoning … [It] subverts the "self" as a free, reasoning being, by overlooking the freedom to reason about what one should pursue' (2002: 36, 37, 46).

Relationships

It will be convenient now to bring together the definitions of self-centred welfare, self-welfare goal and self-goal choice explained above, in the form in which Sen spelt them out in 2005, and to refer to them as S1, S2 and S3, respectively (2005: 6, emphasis in original):

[10] 'So-called', 'misleading[ly]' in its 'puny view of reason', 'ambitious[ly] … brand-named' (2005: 5; 2009: 179, 187; 2007: 342–4).

[11] Davis (2007), building on his earlier work, revealingly explores Sen's association of commitment with the fourth aspect of the self and the agent's sense of identity, defining 'personal identity for Sen as a special capability whereby individuals exercise a reflexive capacity to make commitments in a social setting in a sustained way' (330). See also Kirman and Teschl (2006).

S1 (self-centred welfare): 'A person's welfare depends only on his or her own consumption, which rules out sympathy or antipathy toward others, as well as the effects of processes or relational concerns on one's own welfare.'[12]

S2 (self-welfare goal): 'A person's only goal is to maximise his or her own welfare, which rules out incorporating within one's own objectives other considerations (such as the welfare of others), *except to the extent that it influences the person's own welfare*.'[13]

S3 (self-goal choice): 'A person's choices must be based on the exclusive pursuit of his or her own goals, which rules out being restrained by the recognition of other people's goals, *except to the extent that these goals shape the person's own goals*.'[14]

It will similarly be convenient in what follows to summarize the two forms of commitment that Sen identifies as analytically distinct (for example, in 2007: 350 and 354–5)[15] and to refer to them as Ci and Cii, respectively:

Ci: a person has goals other than maximizing his or her own well-being [whether that well-being depends just on own consumption or not]. This violates S2.

Cii: a person's choices need not be based on the exclusive pursuit of his or her own goals [one can restrain the single-minded pursuit of one's own goals]. This departs from S3.

[12] Only Sen's (2002: 33) version includes the apparently less materialistic phrase 'and other features of the richness of her life'. Mention of exclusion from S1 of process and relational concerns enters into the self-centred welfare definitions from 2002 onwards, in response to Jolls, Sunstein and Thaler (1998).

[13] This '*except to the extent ...*' wording of the Becker-et-al.-sensitive qualification was introduced in 2005. The original 1985 statement of S2 phrased this as self-welfare goal not involving '*directly* attaching importance to the welfare of others' (1985a: 347, emphasis added). Both the 1985 and 1987 definitions incorporated allowance for uncertainty, making the maximand the expected value, or in 1987 the probability-weighted expected value, of own welfare (1987: 80).

[14] 1985's wording for S3 was: 'Each act of choice of a person is guided immediately by the pursuit of one's own goal ...' (1985a: 347). In contrast with the simpler 2002 definition (2002: 33), both the 1985 and 1987 statements, like the 2005 statement (2005: 6), explicitly mention other people's goals, specifying not being 'restrained by the recognition of other people's pursuit of their goals' (1985a: 347) or not being 'restrained or adapted by recognition of mutual interdependence of respective successes, given other people's pursuit of their goals' (1987: 80).

[15] Similarly: Sen (2002: 36-7; 2005: 7; 2009: 190, 193).

In Sen's analysis, S1, S2 and S3 are all 'imposed in the traditional models of rational behaviour (for example, in the "general equilibrium theory" of Arrow and Debreu)' (2005 : 6)[16] and are 'invoked, in one form or another, in the standard characterization of self-interest' (2002: 33); and, although 'the later sophisticated version of RCT [rational choice theory] ... avoids the limiting assumption of [S1] ... there is still complete adherence to [S2 and S3]' (2007: 354). Yet, as agents exercising reasoned scrutiny of our values and objectives, we need not conform to S1, or to S2 or to S3 – although we may; and Sen stresses that, since S1, S2 and S3 are independent of each other, behaviour violating any one of them leaves open the question of whether behaviour accords with either of the other two. S1, S2 and S3 'can be used – or not used – in any combination' (2002: 34).

In further description, Sen points clearly to the eightfold pattern here implied of possible combinations of presence or absence of the three self-interest features.[17] However, he does not dwell long on this pattern, and, since it is revealing in showing the variety of routes in principle to committed behaviour forms, I display it more explicitly here, exploring its various branches by means of a hypothetical foray into the modern dating scene.

Imagine a young person (let us call her Irene), an ardent student of Sen's work, who is about to embark on internet dating. Familiar with his categories of self-centred welfare, self-welfare goal and self-goal choice and with the two forms of commitment he describes, she decides to weigh up which combinations of S1, S2 or S3 or their denials, with links to Ci or Cii, might be most attractive or alarming if declared as character traits. To this end, she draws up a chart showing eight potential dates, each of whom exhibits a rationally supportable combination. The implied character combinations are shown in Figure 8.1.

At first blush, one might suppose that Irene, who we will assume is a generous soul herself, would lean towards proffered attributes showing commitment and be more wary of avowed self-interest. As an aide-memoire, she has loosely tagged S1 in her mind as drawing well-being

---

[16] However, see Sen (1999: 118–19) for a summary of the departure his 1993 paper ('Markets and freedoms') develops from the classic Arrow–Debreu framework, allowing its central efficiency conclusion to be translated to relate to substantive freedoms rather than self-interest maximization.

[17] See note 25 below.

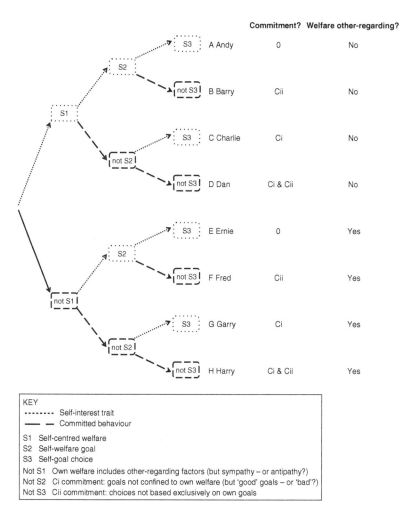

Figure 8.1 Behavioural traits: mixing – and matching

just from what you yourself get; S2 as really just in things for your own sake, even if caring too; and S3 as sticking to your own path regardless of knocking others out of the way. Put in this way, none of these characteristics seems very desirable in a partner. Won't a person characterized by commitment Ci – not motivated just by own gain – or Cii – not elbowing people aside – be bound to seem more appealing?

But, on looking closely at Figure 8.1 and carefully considering Sen's definitions, Irene feels the answer is 'No, not necessarily'. Admittedly, combination A – Andy's profile – has very marked limitations: offering S1, S2 and S3, with no hint of commitment, he pursues his goal of enhancing his own self-centred welfare, with no other-regarding feelings and no allowance for priorities that others might have. In terms of her tags, he cares only for what he gets, he's in it just for himself and he's wedded to that even if it means trampling on other people's plans. How could combination H at the other extreme – Harry's profile – fail to shine in comparison? Here are Ci and Cii, without S1, S2 or S3, which is an offer of other-regarding feelings together with goals beyond self-gain, combined with a considerate attitude to other people's aims. This might indeed be the definitive dream date – were it not for three possible snags.

The first drawback worrying Irene is that, on the information given, she cannot in principle rule out the risk that Harry's non-self-centred welfare, far from being driven by sympathy for others, is fuelled instead by antipathy towards them. Sen has been clear that both possibilities are compatible with experiencing pleasure or pain at the fate of others. Second, she must take into account the risk that Harry's goals, while extending beyond his own welfare and on occasion set aside to accommodate others' goals, might nevertheless be for her a turn-off: he might be committed to what she – and perhaps others – would regard as unpalatable projects. Sen has explained that commitment can be to a limited group, and Irene might not relish their aims.[18] Third, it could be that, in accommodating the goals of others rather than sticking to his guns, Harry's acquiescence goes too far for her: she might be content with his goals but yet be appalled at the goals of others to which he is prepared to give way – or she might so admire his goals as to spurn his restraint – in either case giving her reason again to contemplate dismissal with a swipe left.[19] Lest the dream date should deteriorate into a nightmare, she could do with some assurance that Harry's combination of characteristics comes in a benign version (with sympathy for

---

[18] At the extreme, there are possibilities such as commitment to the aims of a terrorist group.

[19] For example, the desirability of 'letting others be' would surely falter if it came to collaborating with Nazi goals, as it might do also for contrasting reasons if disrupting others' daily goals was integral to a civil disobedience strategy with a valued aim (for example, continued blocking of access to public roads by Extinction Rebellion in London in April 2019, though not uncontroversial, had considerable public support). See also note 21.

others, welcome goals and, alongside general considerateness to others, refusal to yield to goals of a malevolent kind) before plumping for him in preference to Andy – who, in his deep all-round self-interest, at least avoids enjoying doing people down and adopts and yields to no goals *more* regrettable than complete self-absorption.[20]

Are there grounds on which Irene could narrow the field? Reflecting on commitment in form Cii, she might note that the declared willingness of four of the potential dates to reject S3 – restraining their own goals in order to 'let others be' – is framed in their profiles in terms chiming with Sen's description of this as '*decent* behaviour' (2009: 182, emphasis added). That being so, she may decide that their sense of decency can be presumed to extend beyond just the making of concessions, to encompass also sensitivity to the nature of what is being conceded, so that it is safe for her to trust in their limiting appropriately their consideration for others' plans, remaining unyielding to behaviour that is malign.[21] This would give the edge to proffered profiles B, D, F and H, for on this ground Barry outpaces Andy, Dan trumps Charlie, Fred trounces Ernie and Harry beats Garry.

However, the argument persists that antipathy rather than sympathy could be significant in the non-self-centred welfare of declarations against S1, made by Fred and Harry (as well as Ernie and Garry). This leaves Irene concerned over the risk in elevating their profiles over the profiles A, B, C and D declared by Andy, Barry, Charlie and Dan from the self-centred set. And, in the same way, the argument on goals beyond own welfare perhaps being unwelcome ones – relevant to the S2-denying, Ci-commitment-promising, profiles of Dan and Harry (as well as Charlie and Garry) – makes her feel it is problematic to pick one of them rather than profiles A, B, E and F offered by Andy, Barry, Ernie and Fred. When all these considerations are taken together, it is profile B that comes out well; so, if Irene has no further information and proceeds on a 'safety first' basis, she may feel impelled to award her right-swipe acceptance to Barry. Stealing a march on Andy in his

---

[20] Is Andy necessarily *greedy*? Is his welfare greater the more he is able to get, or might he be satisfied with a mere sufficiency? The definition of S1 seems to leave both possibilities open, but it would be in keeping with the traditional approach S1 is designed to capture if Andy is taken to prefer more to less.

[21] This accords with an example in which Sen qualifies not imposing 'barriers to the pursuit of other people's goals' with the addition, 'when these goals are not in any sense evil' (2009: 192).

considerateness in not unreasonably pushing his own goals forward, he could triumph in spite of his 'S1, S2' pairing of self-interest traits – indeed, as things stand, triumphing *because* of them, since they calm Irene's fears by ruling out antipathetic characteristics and potentially vicious or dangerous goals: in choosing self-seeking Barry, she would at least be able to anticipate what she is in for.

But, understandably, she is not thrilled at the prospect of dating Barry. At this point she might begin to ask herself how likely it is that, on starting internet dating for real, she will encounter the full range of profile characteristics represented by the hypothetical partners represented in Figure 8.1. Although each combination is conceived as rationally supportable, their probabilities of being adopted and sustained might vary in practice. Sen suggests himself that, even though there is no contradiction in entirely self-centred welfare coming in tandem with eschewing exclusive own welfare pursuit [the 'S1, not S2' combination offered by Charlie and Dan], it is perhaps 'more realistic' to expect this [Ci] form of commitment to accompany welfare sensitivity to others [as it does for Garry and Harry with their 'not S1, not S2' combination] (2002: 34) – so the likes of Charlie and Dan may prove thin on the ground. One might also surmise that commitment in the [Cii] form of 'decent behaviour' considerateness could seem somewhat out of step, though not strictly inconsistent, with exclusive pursuit of a purely self-centred welfare goal – precisely the 'S1, S2, not S3' combination being offered by Barry, who might therefore prove to be a rare character type. Irene may then wish all the more that she could quiz those not wedded, as is Barry, to S1, about the kind of response they feel to the fate of others (for it could be hearteningly sympathetic) – or those who are not tied, like him, to S2, about which goals beyond own welfare they are committed to (for these could be captivating ones). She does feel it would be taking a poor view of human nature and society to suppose antipathy as common as sympathy, and off-putting goals as prevalent as laudable ones, and on these factors flirts with the idea of therefore trusting to luck – but only fleetingly, for in the matter of dating she is risk-averse.

In her hypothetical dating dilemma, having endorsed Cii considerateness (shown by Barry, Dan, Fred and Harry) and noted worrying ambiguities over the nature of sensitivity to others and of other-regarding goals (affecting Dan, Fred and Harry but not Barry), Irene needs more depth of information than is shown in the Figure 8.1 skeleton profiles on self-interest and commitment if she is to progress beyond settling for Barry. Suppose she has it. If it then turns out that Fred does feel antipathy to other people, that Dan has damaging goals and that Harry is risky on both counts, perhaps still Barry it had better be (if she can find him when she takes the plunge).[22] But, if instead Dan's goals should prove to extend beyond his own welfare in encouraging ways, he would outpace Barry, for, while the pure self-centredness in which his welfare consists is, like Barry's, not very appealing, his wider – firmly non-egoistic – goals can be. Equally, if the evidence indicates that Fred's character is sympathetic, he will also trump Barry, for, although his motivation. Like Barry's, is his own welfare gain, he may accomplish much for those with whom he sympathizes[23] – and warmth of feeling is not unattractive in itself.

As for Harry, who initially appeared the star of the bunch, if the extra data put him too in the clear on sympathy and goals, he will indeed become the first pick: with the lurking risks quashed, he heads the whole field after all. But to secure this it has not been enough that his welfare is not self-centred and that he shows commitment in both forms. It is only when Irene is assured of the sympathetic quality of his nature and the benign character of his goals that Harry decisively prevails for her over his rivals – each a more self-interested contender in one way or another – and truly comes into his own.[24]

---

[22] Only 'perhaps' because she may take into account the fact that the order in which factors are considered can bias the conclusion reached (one aspect of Herbert Simon's concept of procedural rationality: see Simon, 1976). In these 'Barry wins' circumstances, she may wish to reconsider her first move in prioritizing the 'let others be' candidates. If there is evidence to show that Charlie's goals are ones she finds good, or that Ernie sympathizes with others or that Garry ticks both these boxes, she might feel these factors can come ahead of Barry's otherwise self-seeking Cii considerateness after all.

[23] As noted in the first section, Sen does not regard S2 as incompatible with (an egoistic version of) altruism (2002: 36).

[24] It may be helpful to list now, and summarize in terms of my notation, how the references Sen makes to combination groupings in a number of different sources relate to profiles A to H in Figure 8.1.

    (a) All the possibilities are covered in the brisk descriptions given in his 1985a and 2005 papers: see Sen (1985a: 347, and 2005: 6), also detailed below.

    (b) The traditional models' combination of S1, S2 and S3 [profile A] is noted in Sen (1985a: 347, 2002: 34, and 2005: 6).

    (c) Retaining S2 and S3 but not demanding S1 [in line with profile E] is referred to in the same sources, as well as in Sen (1987: 80, and 2007: 354).

Implications and applications

This dating conundrum serves to illustrate the nuances in Sen's account of the concepts of self-interest and commitment.[25] It is apparent that a person can rationally show commitment in one form yet not in another, and self-interest in one, two or three different ways; that each self-interest feature can combine with at least one form of commitment; that there is a sense in which self-interest can include other-regarding, sometimes tender-hearted, elements; and that, although the essence of commitment is its non-self-regarding nature, the particular objects of people's commitments will affect how far and by whom their commitment is likely to be regarded as a virtue.

Sen's central critique is of theorists, especially theorists influential within the discipline of economics, *restricting* the domain of rational choice to the furthering of self-interest and, when assuming further that choices are in fact rationally made, interpreting actual behaviour through that limiting unifocal lens. In arguing for recognition of the greater breadth of rationality, he does not deny self-interest its due place in rational assessments, and he is sensitive to the heterogeneity of possible reasoned commitments. The concept of commitment is crucial to the critique – for 'as soon as commitment is admitted as an ingredient of choice ... the basic link between choice behaviour and welfare achievement in the traditional models is severed' (1977: 329) – but challenging

(d) As mentioned above, the lack of contradiction in the (not necessarily realistic) 'S1, not S2' combination [see C and D] is pointed out in Sen (2002: 34), as well as in (1987: 81).

(e) That the 'not S1' set [as in profiles E, F, G and H] includes both members satisfying and members not satisfying S2, and, similarly, satisfying or not satisfying S3, is stated in Sen (1985a: 347, 2002: 34, and 2005: 6).

(f) Similarly, the observation that, if social justice is pursued as a non-S2 choice, this leaves it open whether or not other self-interest features, S1 or S3, will apply [as illustrated by C, D, G and H] is made in Sen (1985a: 347, and 2005: 6).

(g) And that departing from S3 may, but need not, involve violating self-interest features S1 or S2 [profiles B, D, F and H] is noted in the same sources as in (f).

(h) Sen comments in (2007: 355) that [in terms of my Ci, Cii notation] the Ci form of commitment can occur in the absence of Cii [see the C and G profiles], that form Cii can occur without Ci [see B and F] but that both 'may, of course, act together' [as in D and H].

[25] Of course, Irene's experimental dating chart is a purely heuristic device: it would be unfortunate if it gave the impression that Sen's forensic analysis of rational choice is designed for the purpose of relationship counselling.

'the allegedly peerless status of self-interest as the exclusive navigator of rational behaviour' does not mean that 'exclusive pursuit of self-interest is ... banished ... from the domain of rationality ... [rather] its role in rationality is *contingent on self-scrutiny*' (2002: 46–7, emphasis added).

It is Sen's 'fourth aspect of the self' that is at the heart of his own account of rational choice.[26] This fourth aspect – the self as reasoning, self-scrutinizing agent, rather than mere responder to the stimulus of self-interest – is on a different plane from the three self-interest aspects he has identified.[27] For Sen, choosing rationally involves 'basing ... our choices on reasoning that we can reflectively *sustain*, and it demands that our choices, as well as our actions and objectives, values and priorities, can survive our own seriously undertaken critical scrutiny' (2009: 194, emphasis in original). The scrutiny is to be 'exacting', going well beyond 'uncritical rumination' (2002: 49).[28] And it would not be 'particularly unusual' for this scrutiny process to yield reasons for action that 'are not

---

[26] His original 'rational fools' argument was primarily concerned with showing the 'far-reaching consequences on the nature of many economic models ... [of] admitting behaviour based on commitment', and, aware of the 'many alternative characterizations ... [of] the concept of rationality', he included in a concluding section the disclaimer that 'there is not much point in debating the "proper" definition', pointing out that his behavioural critique did not hang on whether departures from self-interest were termed rational. However, he also noted that 'admitting commitment as a part of behaviour implies no denial of reasoned assessment as a basis for action'; and that, although 'commitment as a part of behaviour ... does not presuppose reasoning, ... it does not exclude it; in fact, in so far as consequences on others have to be more clearly understood in terms of one's values and instincts, the scope for reasoning may well expand' – as his later writings indicate. And the title of this early paper suggests already the presence of concern over the breadth of characterization of rationality, for, although the orthodox consistent chooser of the paper's title may be called 'rational' in one sense, Sen does also characterize him or her as a 'fool' – because he or she 'has no use for ... distinctions between quite different concepts' (1977: 336, 343–4).

[27] It is tempting, but might be misleading, to label this aspect S4. Davis notes, similarly, that 'this fourth aspect of the self [is] different in kind from the three self-interest-based aspects of the self employed in neoclassical behavioural models' (2007: 313).

[28] This does not make the requirement unrealistic, says Sen (2002: 50–1), for we need not 'undertake [it] before each and every act of choice', often relying instead on rules built up from past experience but always subject to potential reassessment (there are clear parallels here with the rationale of rule rather than act utilitarianism). In addition, allowing instinctive responses to factor in so long as 'choices instinctively made would survive closer scrutiny if one were to undertake it' would chime in with Kahneman's (2011) account of 'system 1' thinking.

entirely self-serving ... [A]s Adam Smith noted ... some of these motivations, like "humanity, justice, generosity and public spirit", may ... be very productive for society [Smith 1759]' (Sen, 2009: 189, 191).

But disciplined self-scrutiny combines with agent freedom, so, although the scrutiny process is exacting, it is also 'permissive ... [C]ritical self-scrutiny ... can still allow a variety of competing reasons to receive contending attention ... [W]e can have sustainable reasons for action that reflect our inclinations and our own individual lines of self-scrutiny ... [and consequently] rationality as a characteristic of choice behaviour rules out neither the dedicated altruist, nor the reasoned seeker of personal gain' (2009: 182–3, 194–5). Although

the socially responsive conduct that John Rawls [1971, 1999, 2001] calls 'reasonable' behaviour (... a species of sensitive rationality) ... may well emerge victorious in the critical scrutiny ... there is no necessity for this to happen ... based simply on the demands of reasoned scrutiny ... It is possible that morality and fairness may demand just that ... but ... moral reasoning is only one kind of reasoning ... [T]he need to give weight to this type of consideration may or may not be accepted by the person on the basis of her own deliberations. (2002: 40, 46–7)

Thus Sen stresses that, although we might ourselves think it more 'reasonable' if such scrutiny sometimes results in pursuit of the social good rather than in always being a 'no-nonsense maximizer of self-interest', the scrutinizing remains up to the agent: agency freedom keeps its central place (2009: 195).[29]

The admission of committed behaviour is seen then as 'enrich[ing] our conceptual understanding' by advancing beyond the traditional 'remarkably miniaturized view of human rationality' (2005: 10; 2009: 180), but – even if we could suppose people always to behave rationally – 'in making predictions of behaviour ... it is important to avoid the error of assuming that people are peculiarly virtuous and desperately keen to be just'. Although Sen holds the role of broader values

---

[29] Sen candidly recognizes that this means the approach 'does not yield a way of bearing down on [a] recalcitrant scrutinizer' – a person who 'has not really undertaken that scrutiny with an adequate open-mindedness' but yet judges his or her choices as resulting from duly exacting scrutiny 'even though others are far from convinced'. But he questions whether this latitude is a defect at all, adding: '[I]f the freedom which this approach to rationality gives to the person *is* a defect, it is also at the same time one of its principal assets' (2002: 49–51, emphasis added).

to be 'crucial' in some contexts, he also stresses that 'we must not fail to note the extensive role of intelligent self-seeking' too: 'It is a question of having a balance in our behavioural assumptions' (1999: 280). This leaves open the issue of how widespread committed behaviour is likely to be in practice; but, once commitment-based action is recognized as a possible outcome of duly scrutinized choice, there are implications for explaining those observed patterns of behaviour that do not sit easily with purely gain-maximizing accounts. Sen refers to the 'many empirical studies that indicate that commitment behaviour has its actual domain' (2005: 9–10).

It is to be expected, as Sen argued in his original paper, that 'the empirical importance of commitment ... would vary ... from field to field' (1977: 342). He grants that 'normal economic transactions would break down if self-interest played no substantial part at all in our choices' (1987: 19)[30] and acknowledges that 'for many types of [economic] behaviour ... [such as] the private purchase of many consumer goods ... commitment is unlikely to be an important ingredient'; for example, in the supermarket, where self-interested choices typically hold sway, it might 'show up rather rarely' (1977: 330). The shopping basket could occasionally reflect committed behaviour – an example he had cited in the 1970s was the boycotting of South African avocados – and, some decades on, in an era of environmental fears and in a transformed media world, it is arguable that there is considerably more widespread consumer commitment to holding producers and retailers to account over ethical issues (as in the blacklisting of consumer outlets or particular products or brands if, for instance, there is felt to be a dragging of heels in reducing plastic pollution, ensuring safe working conditions in supply industries or limiting food miles to cut carbon emissions). But, even so, at the current time his broad expectation for the generality of consumption would seem to stand.

However, Sen describes a number of other economic contexts in which the assumption that behaviour depends only on individual economic incentives runs into systematic trouble, and commitment 'helps us understand actual behavior better' (2005: 9). He details, for instance, the provision of public goods, issues of business ethics, the

---

[30] He allows also that 'it would be extraordinary if self-interest were not to play quite a major part in a great many decisions' (1987: 19), for 'self-interest is ... an extremely important motive' (1999: 261).

functioning of cooperatives, collective bargaining practices and the varying work motivation norms across countries. And he sees purely gain-maximizing explanations of behaviour as similarly falling short in a wide range of fields beyond economics – referring to examples such as individual voting in large elections, political solidarity, non-littering behaviour and navigating prisoners' dilemma situations (1977: 329–34; 2002: 26; 2005: 8–9). To these can be added a host of 'goal-restraining' commitment cases, as illustrated in the first section (not jostling ahead of others to the fire exit, and so on). So, on the empirical front, Sen takes commitment to have general importance 'for explaining behavioral variations between different societies and over time … [and] in different social circumstances' and holds there to be 'many cases that would be hard to fit within the narrow limits of self-welfare goal and self-goal choice' (2005: 9, 10).

Although commitments may be made to limited groups or projects and will often involve culture-dependent habits and social norms, the idea of commitment – in its denial of the unvarying pursuit of self-interest – also makes room for the wider ethical motivations that can come from agents' scrutiny of their values. As Sen puts it, 'Ethics is somehow mixed up with the idea of commitment.' He goes on to argue that 'the role of commitment in the ethics of behavior can be investigated in nearly every field of practical reason' (2005: 10, 12). His prime illustration of this is 'environmental reasoning and conduct', in which he brings out the ethical dimension of the concept of commitment through a striking discussion of the characterization of sustainable development and of our responsibility towards future generations and to other species, urging that 'not all [the] … reasons for our conservational efforts … are parasitic on our own living standards (or need fulfilment) and some of which turn precisely on our sense of values and on our acknowledgement of our fiduciary responsibility' (2005: 11–12; 2009: 249–52).

The reference in this argument to fiduciary responsibility points up a distinct element in the idea of commitment. In his 1997 paper 'Maximization and the act of choice', acknowledging Ragnar Frisch's discussion of 'the far-reaching impact of responsibility when one is trusted with acting for others', he drew on the domestic illustration given. This was of the responsibility Frisch felt he bore in making a modest decision as to which of two 'very different, but both very fine' cakes to select, knowing his wife would be left with the other.

Sen notes that 'this is a case which involves "commitment", not just "sympathy"', relating that Frisch regarded his 'own total utility function ... [as] completely irrelevant' and held that the 'relevant [choice] problem' facing him was simply 'which one of the two cakes does my wife prefer?' (1997: 759–61).[31] This meant seeing the choice not as a matter of wanting to share in his wife's pleasure but, rather, as fulfilling a *duty* he owed to her.[32] In later associating this idea of fiduciary obligation – being charged to act on behalf of others – with 'our sense of responsibility towards the future of other species that are threatened with destruction', Sen appeals to an argument of Gautama Buddha to show how it can come about that we are charged with such a duty, implying a particularly binding moral commitment.[33] The argument bases our responsibility on the fact of 'asymmetry of power': we have much greater power than other species, and therefore bear some responsibility for their fate (2005: 12; 2009: 251). This responsibility-conferring power asymmetry line of thought has, potentially, very extensive reach. It might therefore engender, but may be ready to meet, objections paralleling the 'too demanding of us' attack sometimes mounted against utilitarian ethics (see the utilitarian case put forward by Peter Singer, 2009, in *The Life You Can Save: Acting Now to End World Poverty* and the discussion of demandingness in Judith Lichtenberg, 2014, and Clark and Meeks, 2018).

The overall significance of admitting 'committed' behaviour, then, is threefold for Sen: 'The importance of understanding the role of commitment in rationality applies to ... behavioral ethics in general, as it does also to the conceptual clarification of the very idea of rationality and the investigation of its implications for predicting behavior and actions' (2005: 12).

---

[31] Frisch's account could perhaps raise a doubt as to whether this was misplaced chivalry on his part (we do not know his wife's wishes, but are told she handed him the tray asking him to help himself; it could be that her only interest was in him taking the cake *he* liked better).

[32] Sen draws a distinction (with respect to menu dependence) between fiduciary obligation, as in Frisch's cake selection case, and commitment to following a social norm, as in the conventional etiquette of cake choosing when in company (1997: 760–1). On selecting the size of a slice of cake, see Baigent and Gaertner's paper 'Never choose the uniquely largest: a characterization' (1996).

[33] Cramp writes that, in Judaeo-Christian thought, environmental responsibility follows from the principle of stewardship (Cramp, 1991: 65, 67).

Arguments, knock-down arguments and Humpty Dumpty

Since Sen's analysis of commitment challenges so much conventional theory, it is not surprising that it has been subject to attack from several quarters. Perhaps the most controversial element has been commitment in the second [Cii] form. A preliminary but little-discussed question here might concern some complexity in separating the two forms of commitment, since there can be cases when instances of Cii seem intertwined in various ways with Ci behaviour. Sen himself is careful to note that 'the two types of departure may, of course, act together and sometimes they may be hard to disentangle precisely'; but he does find clear analytical distinction between, on the one hand [Ci], pursuing goals that are not 'simply a reflection of one's own well-being' and, on the other [Cii], 'restrain[ing] the pursuit of one's goals to make room for others to pursue their goals' (2007: 355). He formally introduced the latter type of commitment in his 1985 paper 'Goals, commitment, and identity'[34]: this followed a conference presentation of the paper in the preceding year, and Sen was already aware that disputing self-goal choice met with particular resistance (1985a: 349). In spite of powerful responses from him over the intervening years, this is still a topic of debate (a recent suggestion on possible resolution, for instance, being offered by Ann Cudd, 2014).

The main bone of contention is whether commitment in Cii form is possible at all. Most prominent among the critics is the philosopher Philip Pettit, who accuses Sen of offending against 'our common sense psychology, that rational agents aim at satisfying their desires,

---

[34] This may not be so sharp a departure from his 1977 paper as might at first appear. It could be held that the idea was implicit in the earlier paper, presaged in some of its examples – including the well-known illustration of a boy offering his companion the first choice from a large and a small apple when his own wish was for the big one, but being miffed when his pal, taking the larger fruit, does not afford the same courtesy to him (1977: 328). The apple example (also cited by Sen, 2002: 50) shows, as intended, the significance of reasons lying behind choice and can chime in with Cii acceptance of 'decent behaviour'. But it is capable of alternative interpretations too, one of which relates to Sen's 1997 analysis of 'strategic nobility' (1997: 760–2): might the first boy, by setting a polite example, conforming to the restraint of a social norm, actually have been pursuing a sneaky strategy to get the bigger apple for himself in the end? (This might seem the more likely, since, had he simply been thinking it impolite to deny the larger fruit to boy 2, he could have taken the small apple himself in the beginning.)

according to their beliefs ... [In departing from self-goal choice,] he is setting himself against our basic common sense about action' (Pettit, 2005: 21). Pettit then proceeds to spin a 'charitable account ... of why Sen should say what he does ... [an account] that does not find anything deeply amiss in his ideas' after all – proposing that, on this basis, the 'charge against him ... might even reduce' to one of 'idiosyncrasy' and 'terminological infelicity' rather than 'intellectual oversight' (31–2). To both the central charge and the unsolicited plea in mitigation, Sen – expressing himself 'touched' by Pettit's efforts – gives a robust and suitably wry reply (see 2007: 347–52).

One element in the critical attack is an idea that a person restraining his or her goals so as to allow for the goals of another will nevertheless be acting on his or her own goals through having adopted the other's goals as his or her own. But Sen presents for consideration a situation in which a woman complies with a request to lower a plane window blind (or 'shade') – shutting out the sunshine she had been aiming to enjoy from her window seat – so that her neighbour can see his computer screen better as he continues to play what the shade lowerer holds to be a foolishly mind-numbing game. It would seem odd to say that the neighbour's goal of playing his game has now been adopted by the shade lowerer as her own novel goal and that she acts to satisfy her desire, when this is far from being a goal she endorses (she thinks his well-being would be boosted if he switched to doing something else, such as reading the newspaper she could lend him). 'Rather,' says Sen, she is 'just following a norm of good behaviour [she] happen[s] to approve of (let others do what they really want), which is a self-imposed behavioural restraint [she] accept[s]'; 'there is, after all, a difference between *restraint* and *conversion*' (2009: 192–3; 2007: 348–9, 355, emphasis in original).

A good deal of ink has been spilt – or, more accurately, keyboard time has been spent – on this dispute over whether Sen's second form of commitment as he defines it is too much at odds with the prevailing understanding of intentional action, with some intensive discussion of the plane window shade case. A common response to debate over the blind is to agree with Sen on the neighbour's goal not being adopted but to insist that the shade lowerer must be pursuing a different goal she has, which is now prioritized over her desire to enjoy the sun. This might perhaps be a goal of forestalling a hostile atmosphere (although no hostility avoidance would be involved if the shade lowerer had been assuming, as she might, that a refusal to lower would have been taken well). Yet, if exercising what Sen views as goal constraint – which might naturally be accompanied with an internal sigh of resignation – is to be regarded instead as desire fulfilment, the satisfying of a preferred goal, there seems a risk of draining away the usual meaning: the internal sigh may be out of place if, whenever you hold back from what it is your goal to do, you are still pursuing your goal.[35]

The suggested resolution advanced by Cudd in her 2014 contribution is constructive but does not cover all the departures from self-goal choice identified by Sen. Seeking to resolve the tension between his 'potentially illuminating' position on goal-constraining commitment, which she wishes to retain, and its 'problematic' divergence from the conventional philosophical account of agency as goal-directed (Cudd, 2014: 36), she proposes that the conventional account should be broadened so as to allow for 'a type of goal-displacing commitment'[36] that she calls 'tacit commitment' – whereby 'tacit commitments regulate behaviour without being made conscious and explicit' (35–6). This suggestion is useful in so far as commitment behaviours are governed by implicit norms, but the scope of Cii commitment extends further: if its other elements are to be accommodated within the theory of agency, the proposed broadening would need to be broadened. Sen speaks of the role of 'rational deliberation' (alongside evolutionary selection) in the emergence of behavioural norms (1999: 273) and describes violation of self-goal choice 'arising ... from the normative restraint we voluntarily impose on ourselves on grounds of recognising other people's pursuits and goals' (2007: 353–4). A conscious decision on restraint appears part of the plane shade story; the shade lowerer seems well aware of what she is doing.

Although commitment in form Cii rouses most opposition, Sen's wider account of commitment has not been immune from criticism. More general questioning is sometimes based on the idea that it adds unnecessary clutter that could be avoided without loss in a more familiar approach (see Hahn, 1991, and Hausman, 2005, 2011). This streamlining move can apply to Cii commitment, since, as Sen writes, 'We do of course know that mathematically any constraint can be seen as a *surrogate* goal' (2007: 354, emphasis added); but it relates also to

---

[35] This echoes Meeks (2017: 1058, and 2018: 36–7).
[36] 'Goal-displacing' is Pettit's term, not Sen's.

choices made from Ci commitment, which, though not in accord with self-welfare goal, can still be formally represented as made in accordance with a person's own 'all things considered' preference ranking. Sen does not quarrel with the formal modelling possibilities, which indeed he has often drawn attention to himself; but he stresses the need for care and clarity in employing them, cautioning that perfectly sound technical devices can have the effect of submerging distinctions it is important to retain, with risk of confusion when the technical usage of a term differs from that in prevailing language (see, for instance, 1991: 13–14; 1993; 1997: 768–71; 1999: 118–19, 348–9 n.36; 2002: 37–42; and 2007: 344–5, 353–4).[37]

In the background of challenges to Sen's commitment approach there may sometimes lurk also the idea that what might appear to be committed behaviour does genuinely result in some way from underlying gains in personal welfare. However, claiming there will be universal success in 'the detection of hidden instrumentality', as Sen calls it (2002: 28), seems to rely more on theoretical possibilities than likelihood in reality. I recall my class discussing possible examples of commitment one year when a student declared she had recently become a vegan because of concern about climate change: upon the rest of the class[38] maintaining she must be feeling so good about that virtuously 'green' decision as to outweigh the discomfort of missing other foods, we felt her sincerity as she protested vehemently: 'No! I really loved eating meat and I feel absolutely *dreadful*'.

Suspicion of disguised self-interest in the actions of one group purportedly committed to act in the public interest – Members of Parliament – may well have been on the increase recently in the United Kingdom. Years of government inability to implement the decision taken to leave the European Union following the outcome of a 2016 referendum made many 'Leave' supporters, in a general public becoming cynical about the motivations of politicians, sceptical about the degree of commitment to 'Brexit' of a majority of their elected representatives, who had repeatedly voted against ratifying a withdrawal agreement negotiated with the European Union. There was speculation about the

---

[37] An arresting illustration he gives of the contrast between formal explanation in terms of 'as if' preferences and psychological explanation drawing on social perceptions of duty relates to the Japanese phenomenon of *karoshi* (death through overwork).

[38] Save for another new vegan, who entirely agreed with the first.

pursuit of personal agendas and neglect of fiduciary responsibility, and yet it is arguable that a high degree of commitment was shown in the behaviour of some, perhaps many, Members of Parliament, who, with more than one fiduciary duty at issue, faced complex decisions. I offer a constructed example related to the parliamentary aspect of the Brexit saga as an illustration of how attempts to argue the universal dominance of self-interest might be made, might struggle but could resist decisive elimination.

Imagine reviewing decisions taken by two – hypothetical – MPs each of whom might have been held to be acting from commitment in a crucial early vote. In the 2016 referendum, on the question 'Should the United Kingdom remain a member of the European Union or leave the European Union?', 48.1% of those voting chose 'Remain' while 51.9% voted 'Leave'. The prime minister pledged to deliver Brexit in accordance with the referendum result but would be able to give the European Union notice of the United Kingdom's intention to withdraw from the European Union (as required under treaty) only if a majority of MPs in the House of Commons voted to confer that power on her. Call the voting options *Confer* and *Not Confer*. Suppose, then, that the situations and actions of the two MPs when the bill to confer power was put to a parliamentary vote in 2017 were these.

MP X

- Campaigned in the referendum for 'Remain', believing it to be in the interests of the United Kingdom as a whole and of her constituents to remain in the European Union
- Feels it her prime duty to protect the interests of the country and her constituents
- Is conscious of representing a constituency in which the vote was 75 per cent in favour of 'Leave', more than matching the referendum result
- Will be dependent on her constituents' votes for re-election as their MP
- Is a member of the governing party and has been spoken of as likely soon to be offered a ministerial post
- Is subject to an understanding that she will toe the party line in parliamentary votes
- The party line, based on respecting the 'Leave' result of the referendum, is to vote *Confer*
- She votes *Not Confer*

MP Y

- Campaigned in the referendum for 'Remain', believing it to be in the interests of the United Kingdom as a whole and of her constituents to remain in the European Union
- Feels it her prime duty to respect the 'Leave' result of the referendum
- Is conscious of representing a constituency in which the vote was 75 per cent in favour of 'Remain', the position she herself believes to be in the best interests of the country
- Will be dependent on her constituents' votes for re-election as their MP
- Has been spoken of as a potential future leader of her 'Remain'-supporting party
- Is subject to an understanding that she will toe the party line in parliamentary votes
- The party line, based on what it believes to be in the best interests of the country, is to vote *Not Confer*
- She votes *Confer*

For both X and Y, there is a clash of fiduciary duties, which impose stronger responsibilities than the obligation that might be felt to stay loyal to a political party. Circumstances had pitted the duty of an MP – in the United Kingdom's system of representative democracy – to support the interests of her constituents in accordance with her own judgement on the merits of the case (rather than acting as a delegate simply on the basis of constituents' majority opinion) against an apparent democratic duty to abide by the result of a referendum – albeit an 'advisory' one – in which Parliament itself had delegated decision to the electorate. In the hypothesized cases, MPs X and Y have each addressed this dilemma by relegating one fiduciary duty to a secondary place, and, although they have opposing views over which duty should have precedence, both act in accordance with the strict obligation they have prioritized.

On the face of it, then, it seems natural to describe both imagined MPs as having acted from commitment in their voting behaviour, departing from self-welfare goals in deciding to go with prioritized duty and vote against their own strong interests – departing from S2 with Ci commitment.[39] In order to do what they see as their prime

---

[39] Might Cii commitment be involved? With this form of commitment depending on 'self-imposed behavioural restraint' of 'what can be rightly described as your actual goals that you want to pursue' (2007: 349, 354) – *but* after allowance for the extent to which the goals of others 'shape [your] own goals'

duty, each has put at risk her re-election as an MP and has sacrificed the likelihood of advancement within her parliamentary party. This would seem to make it hard to categorize these votes convincingly as resulting from self-interest.[40]

Nevertheless, as usual, a story of apparent compliance with self-interest can be composed. One contention could be that self-interest has so far been reckoned narrowly just in terms of career prospects and it is one-sided to leave feelings out of account. For example, our MPs may have gained satisfaction from having done what they believe to be right overall. However, here, resolving the conflict in duties may have been a close-run affair, leaving any such gain in own welfare at least somewhat tempered by regret over compromising a secondary duty. Then there is the question of sympathy with others, which can enter into the self-welfare goal. But – assuming that sympathy rather than antipathy is at issue here – it would seem that the voting decisions taken might well on balance reduce own welfare on this count, since, although they gain succour from the pleasure they are affording to some, our hypothetical MPs will be forgoing reflected benefit from the satisfaction that, had they acted differently, they would have created in others by respecting the position of most of those they represent and showing loyalty to party colleagues in Parliament too. It is questionable how plausible it would be to suppose there to be sources of satisfaction sufficient to outweigh the denting of own welfare stemming from upset to constituents and colleagues combined with career jeopardy. If the story becomes too tortuous, the assertion of self-interested behaviour will appear contrived. Nor would putative welfare gain be enough to undermine commitment, if the MPs' reason for voting as they did was indeed to do their duty.

Consider for comparison how the behaviours might be described if, facing the same situation and holding the same beliefs as beforehand, MP X had voted in the opposite way – to *Confer* – and, similarly, MP Y had voted *Not Confer*. Now each is going *against* what she feels to be her prime duty – against what she judges it would be right to do, all

---

(2005: 6) – the question is perhaps whether it is the nature of fiduciary duty to shape a person's own goals, rather than constraining them.

[40] Cases may come to mind in which self-interest categorization would be even harder to justify (such as doctors and nurses volunteering in 2019 to treat Ebola patients in the Democratic Republic of the Congo in areas of community hostility towards treatment centre staff).

things considered – but in so doing she bolsters her career prospects, shares in the pleasure her decision gives to her colleagues and the majority of her constituents and can ease her conscience with the comfort of having fulfilled a lesser duty (as she sees it). Might it not be desirable to retain the ability to distinguish as self-interested these reverse choices from the original ones in which the MPs stood by – were committed to – their principles?

However, there is a line of thinking on which you will count as self-interested however you choose to act. Sen refers to a frequent argument drawn from supposed demands of rationality – 'an allegedly knockout argument'– which takes the form of asking 'If it is not in your interest, why would you have chosen to do what you did?' (2006: 21).

Sen's reference to a 'knockout argument' may awaken in devotees of Lewis Carroll's 'Alice' books recollection of Humpty Dumpty's claims (in chapter 6 of *Through the Looking-Glass*) about the meaning of words. When he tells Alice that, by 'glory', he meant 'a nice knock-down argument', and Alice objects that this is not what 'glory' means, he famously retorts: 'When *I* use a word, it means just what I choose it to mean – neither more nor less.' And, to Alice's protest 'The question is whether you *can* make words mean so many different things', he replies: 'The question is which is to be master – that's all.' Then – revealingly – after attributing a long and unnatural meaning to 'impenetrability', he adds: 'When I make a word do a lot of work ... I always pay it extra'. No doubt he has to pay it extra – because it is being pushed to work beyond its job description.

Can the term 'self-interest' be employed to cover (as Alice might say) 'so many different things', as it must if it is to underlie all decisions on action? In parallel with the discussion above of 'surrogate' goals and 'all things considered' preferences, elasticity of usage and freedom in definition – as it were, the Humpty-Dumptyness of language – would indicate the answer is 'Yes'. But at what cost?

Discussing egoism in his 1977 paper, Sen recognizes – and exposes the limitations of – 'revealed preference' theory, which, by linking a chosen alternative with achieving higher personal utility, reduces 'man to a self-seeking animal ... [simply through] careful definition ... [I]f you are consistent, then no matter whether you are a single-minded egoist or a raving altruist or a class-conscious militant, you will appear to be maximizing your own utility in this enchanted world of definitions'

(1977: 322–3). He argues that the price of this 'definitional egoism' (as he dubs it) was a failure to reflect 'personal welfare ... as ... usually understood' (323). Similarly, but more generally, he acknowledges that, in spite of the downsides, it is '*possible* to define "interest" in such an expansive – and capacious – way that it encompasses all the concerns that a person chooses to pursue, irrespective of motivation' (2009: 379, emphasis added). But, in their book *Free to Choose*, Milton and Rose Friedman make the bold claim that so capacious a definition *must* be used. Asserting that a 'broad meaning must be attached to the concept of "self-interest"', they do not mean just to point out the narrowness of interpreting 'self-interest as myopic selfishness, as exclusive concern with immediate material rewards', for they contend further that 'self-interest is ... whatever it is that interests the participants, whatever they value, whatever goals they pursue. The scientist seeking to advance the frontiers of his discipline, the missionary seeking to convert infidels to the true faith, the philanthropist seeking to bring comfort to the needy – all are pursuing their interests, as they see them, as they judge them by their own values' (Friedman and Friedman, 1980: 47).

Yet judging which goals to pursue in the light of one's values could accord with commitment, so to describe one's choice of goals as automatically self-interested is either to deny the possibility of committed behaviour (taking self-interest as ordinarily understood) or else to stretch the sense of self-interest almost to vanishing point – with potentially damaging ambiguity as to which (there is a risk of theoretical argument relying on the latter, watered-down meaning but policy makers believing that the case has been made for the former, undiluted one). Although self-interest in the Becker sense is not tied to the 'myopic selfishness ... [of] exclusive concern with immediate material rewards', any more than committed behaviour is intrinsically noble, it is divorced from the range of goals that go beyond own welfare pursuit, and, even if they can be incorporated in an artificially extended sense of self-interest, only the concept of commitment is transparent in recognizing them.

Commitment is 'up front' in admitting the possibility of pure selflessness. If Humpty Dumpty, hell-bent on being master of words, wants the descriptor 'self-interested' to take on covering that celebrated category of human behaviour, he will surely have to 'pay it extra' and, further, force commitment – currently doing the job – into redundancy. But that seems a peculiarly costly and confusing way of going about things – best fitted to a 'through the looking-glass' world.

References

Baigent, N., and Gaertner, W. (1996) Never choose the uniquely largest: a characterization. *Economic Theory*, 8 (2): 239–49.

Becker, G. (1976) *The Economic Approach to Human Behavior*. Chicago: University of Chicago Press.

(1981) *A Treatise on the Family*. Cambridge, MA: Harvard University Press.

(1996) *Accounting for Tastes*. Cambridge, MA: Harvard University Press.

Carroll, L. (1871) *Through the Looking-Glass, and What Alice Found There*. London: Macmillan.

Clark, D. A., and Meeks, J. G. (2018) The canniness of ought. *Journal of Human Development and Capabilities*, 19 (1): 103–11.

Cramp, A. (1991) Pleasures, prices and principles. In *Thoughtful Economic Man: Essays on Rationality, Moral Rules and Benevolence*, Meeks, J. G. (ed.): 50–73. Cambridge: Cambridge University Press.

Cudd, A. E. (2014) Commitment as motivation: Sen's theory of agency and the explanation of behavior. *Economics and Philosophy*, 30 (1): 35–56.

Davis, J. B. (2007) Identity and commitment: Sen's fourth aspect of the self. In *Rationality and Commitment*, Peter, F., and Schmid, H. B. (eds.): 313–35. Oxford: Oxford University Press.

Friedman, M., and Friedman, R. D. (1980) *Free to Choose: A Personal Statement*. London: Penguin.

Gasper, D. (2000) Development as freedom: taking economics beyond commodities – the cautious boldness of Amartya Sen. *Journal of International Development*, 12 (7): 989–1001.

Hahn, F. H. (1991) Benevolence. In *Thoughtful Economic Man: Essays on Rationality, Moral Rules and Benevolence*, Meeks, J. G. (ed.): 7–11. Cambridge: Cambridge University Press.

Hausman, D. M. (2005) Sympathy, commitment, and preference. *Economics and Philosophy*, 21 (1): 33–50.

(2011) *Preference, Value, Choice and Welfare*. Cambridge: Cambridge University Press.

Jolls, C., Sunstein, C., and Thaler, R. (1998) A behavioral approach to law and economics. *Stanford Law Review*, 50 (5): 1471–550.

Kahneman, D. (2011) *Thinking, Fast and Slow*. London: Allen Lane.

Kirman, A., and Teschl, M. (2006) Searching for identity in the capability space. *Journal of Economic Methodology*, 13 (3): 299–325.

Lichtenberg, J. (2014) *Distant Strangers: Ethics, Psychology, and Global Poverty*. Cambridge: Cambridge University Press.

Meeks, J. G. (2017) Amartya Sen (1933–). In *The Palgrave Companion to Cambridge Economics*, Cord, R. A. (ed.): 1045–77. London: Palgrave Macmillan.

(2018) On Sen on the capability of capabilities: the story of a not-for-profit enterprise. In *New Frontiers of the Capability Approach*, Comim, F., Fennell, S., and Anand, P. B. (eds.): 12–50. Cambridge: Cambridge University Press.

Pettit, P. (2005) Construing Sen on commitment. *Economics and Philosophy*, 21 (1): 15–32.

Rawls, J. (1971). *A Theory of Justice*. Cambridge, Mass.: Harvard University Press.

(1999) *Collected Papers*, ed. Freeman, S. Cambridge, MA: Harvard University Press.

(2001) *Justice as Fairness: A Restatement*, ed. Kelly, E. Cambridge, MA: Harvard University Press.

Schmid, H. B. (2005) Beyond self-goal choice: Amartya Sen's analysis of the structure of commitment and the role of shared desires. *Economics and Philosophy*, 21 (1): 51–63.

Searle, J. R. (2001) *Rationality in Action*. Cambridge, MA: MIT Press.

Sen, A. K. (1977) Rational fools: a critique of the behavioural foundations of economic theory. *Philosophy & Public Affairs*, 6 (4): 317–44.

(1982) *Choice, Welfare and Measurement*. Oxford: Blackwell.

(1985a) Goals, commitment, and identity. *Journal of Law, Economics, and Organization*, 1 (2): 341–55.

(1985b) Well-being, agency and freedom: the Dewey lectures 1984. *Journal of Philosophy*, 82 (4): 169–221.

(1987) *On Ethics and Economics*. Oxford: Basil Blackwell.

(1993) Markets and freedoms: achievements of the market mechanism in promoting individual freedoms. *Oxford Economic Papers*, 45 (4): 519–41.

(1997) Maximization and the act of choice. *Econometrica*, 65 (4): 745–80.

(1999) *Development as Freedom*. Oxford: Oxford University Press.

(2002) *Rationality and Freedom*. Cambridge, MA: Harvard University Press.

(2005) Why exactly is commitment important for rationality? *Economics and Philosophy*, 21 (1): 5–14.

(2006) *Identity and Violence: The Illusion of Destiny*. New York: W. W. Norton.

(2007) Rational choice: discipline, brand name, and substance. In *Rationality and Commitment*, Peter, F., and Schmid, H. B. (eds.): 339–61. Oxford: Oxford University Press.

(2009) *The Idea of Justice*. London: Penguin.

(2017) *Collective Choice and Social Welfare*, expanded edn. London: Penguin.

Simon, H. A. (1976) From substantive to procedural rationality. In *Method and Appraisal in Economics*, Latsis, S. J. (ed.): 129–48. Cambridge: Cambridge University Press.

Singer, P. (2009) *The Life You Can Save: Acting Now to End World Poverty*. New York: Random House.

Smith, A. (1790 [1759]). *The Theory of Moral Sentiments*, 6th edn. London: A. Millar [repub., with Introduction by Sen, A. K. (2009), London: Penguin].

Williams, B. (1973) A critique of utilitarianism. In *Utilitarianism: For and Against*, Smart, J. J. C., and Williams, B. (eds.): 77–150. Cambridge: Cambridge University Press

(1979) Internal and external reasons. In *Rational Action: Studies in Philosophy and Social Science*, Harrison, R. (ed.): 17–28. Cambridge: Cambridge University Press.

(1981) *Moral Luck: Philosophical Papers 1973–1980*. Cambridge: Cambridge University Press.

9 Incorporating an emotional dimension in the capability approach

JOHN CAMERON

As you pass from the tender years of youth into harsh embittered manhood, make sure you take with you on your journey all the human emotions. Don't leave them on the road.

Nikolai Gogol, *Dead Souls*

An explanatory and apologetic introduction

Both Martha Nussbaum (1995) and Amartya Sen (2009) have written on the necessity of an emotional dimension in the capability approach (hereafter CA). Nussbaum, from an Aristotelian eudaimonia holistic position on human well-being, critiques the view that emotions are a weakness and claims emotional expression in the form of compassion to be invaluable for collective capability development (Nussbaum, 1990). Sen brings in emotions as a critique of the 'rational fools' model that underpins mainstream/neoclassical economics. The authors in Comim, Qizilbash and Alkire (2008) develop a rich account of the CA with an important role for collective agency, with hints that positive emotional bonding may be necessary for that agency to be effective.

This chapter accepts that Nussbaum and Sen and other writers on the CA have acknowledged an emotional dimension as being desirable in the CA to realize fully its positive influence on developing more equitable public policy. But the argument developed here is richer, more nuanced and ambiguous on the roles of emotions, seeing possibilities for both positive and negative influences on individual and collective capability and resulting choices of functionings and levels of well-being.

To enrich the concept of 'emotions', it is useful to explore a continuum from what most people would recognize as purer expressions of emotion found in dreams (Robb, 2019), through a position where emotions engage with rational thought in the form of metaphors, memes and tropes to a position that aspires to representation in mathematical logic and statistical calculation as an impartial rational ideal.

Emphasis on emotions   Emphasis on impartial calculation

←——————————————————————————————————→

Samaritan 'listener' stance   This chapter's stance   Adapted preferences stance

Figure 9.1 A schematic continuum mixing emotions and impartial, 'objective' calculation available to CA researchers

Part of the inspiration for this chapter is my research experience in using ethnographic methods and the recognition that my data processing and analysis tends to neglect, to the point of omission, the more emotional moments in the semi-structured interviews. The Annex offers a synthetic example of a transcript in which moments of strong emotion are explicitly present but are vulnerable to being analytically erased. It was my analytical task to distil a pure 'rational' narrative from a complex soup that could be presented as the 'real' story acceptable to readers with more positivist epistemological inclinations (see, for example, Gasper and Cameron, 2000). My growing discomfort with this tendency increased as I approached formal retirement and reflected on my research 'history' (Cameron, 2005).

Perhaps it was an unconscious, literally conscientious, response to my discomfort with my own past research practice that I decided to train as a UK Samaritan volunteer. The UK Samaritan organization is a charity that engages with people who feel stress to the point that they are willing to talk/write to a complete stranger and express suicidal thoughts The Samaritan volunteer is trained to listen without judgement and without prescription. The listeners are focused on helping the callers explore their feelings ('How do you feel about ... ?'). Gradually the interaction may move towards the callers identifying possible courses of action and prioritizing between those actions. In the language of the CA, the callers are coming from a position in which they see themselves as emotionally incapable of converting their capability set into functionings (other than possibly ending their lives). The listeners aim to help the callers explore their feelings and self-connect existing capability to possible actions/functionings that are consistent with those feelings.

The Samaritan approach can be seen as approaching one end of the above continuum (see Figure 9.1), in which the emotional dimension is the primary focus as the human subjects of the Samaritan gaze are in a state of great emotional stress. As in any continuum, there is a sub-stantial middle ground where most 'normal' subjects have their mixes of calculative and emotional aspects to their identities. The claim of this chapter is that the CA could and should be more willing to explore these mixes to enrich claims to 'know' the researched subjects.

The concept of adaptive/adapted preferences has some capacity to include an emotional dimension. The claim that a person's pref-erences have been adapted suggests a deviation from some superior set of preferences as perceived by an impartial, 'objective' outsider. Adapted preferences are in the eye of the beholding researcher, but the researched subject owns those adapted preferences and chooses functionings consistent with those preferences. The 'failure' to rec-ognize the possibility of alternative functionings and the capability to achieve those functionings may have emotional foundations; for example, saying 'Higher education is not for people like us' suggests a cultural attitude with deeply felt values. Adapted preferences as a basis for public policy may seek to 'cure' the adaptation in terms of rational persuasion, rather than explore, understand – and possibly accept – those emotional foundations.

I am very conscious that the sources used in this chapter are over-whelmingly 'white' men from Europe and North America, albeit from a range of historical periods and with diverse mother tongues. In slight mitigation, I can suggest we are all products of our cultural past histo-ries, and the journeys we make through life are marked by the biases of those pasts, including the texts with which we feel most emotional affinity. I hope that readers, with their own cultural histories, can identify authors with whom they feel such affinity that may reflect the range of positions found in this chapter and perhaps identify other perspectives. The limited claim of this chapter is that the range found here will stimulate deliberation.

So, which texts have I selected to help bridge between people capa-ble of logical calculations and people capable of emotional desires? For the purpose of this chapter, the choice of texts to answer to this question can be framed in terms of five positions, each with two exem-plary texts (one more philosophical, the other a work of fiction imag-inatively developing the philosophical theme).

- Emotions as another reality (Sartre and Mann)
- Emotions as the key to progress (Nietzsche and Stoker)

- Emotions as an obstacle to progress (Erasmus and Fitzgerald)
- Emotions as essential to being a communicating human (Eco and Melville)
- Emotions as key to understanding power (Foucault and Kafka)

These five positions are not intended to be mutually exclusive or hierarchical in terms of analytical or empirical superiority. All may be applicable in various combinations in differing contexts.

A vital methodological point needs to be made before ending these introductory thoughts. Making emotions an explicit part of CA research raises ethical issues. Asking people about their feelings requires great sensitivity (see Abbott, 2007, and Ayers, Vydelingum and Arber, 2017). There are frontiers where the strength of the research subjects' feelings becomes troubling to the researcher in terms of psychic unmanageability. These frontiers will be felt as a desire to adopt therapeutic and/or prescriptive roles. At such moments researchers need to recognize their professional limitations and step back gently to create space for reflection on how to proceed. This suggests an area of training such as that offered by organizations, such as the UK Samaritans, in not only listening to strong feelings but also learning how to 'exit' without damage to either researcher or researched, as two human beings in processes of – hopefully – becoming more capable to achieve valued functionings.

Emotions as another reality

Jean-Paul Sartre (2015 [1939]) situates strong human emotions in an area of consciousness separate from the capacity for rational thought. This area is where we experience joy, sadness, love, hate, compassion and disgust. He notes that some expressions of emotions can be simulated and remain under the control of rational consciousness, and so he focuses on what may be termed 'real' emotions.

We shall call emotion an abrupt drop of consciousness into the magical. Or if one prefers, there is emotion when the world of instruments abruptly vanishes and the magical world appears in its place. Therefore, it is not necessary to see emotion as a passive disorder of the organism and the mind which comes from outside to disturb the psychic life. On the contrary, it is the return of consciousness to the magical attitude, one of the great attitudes which are essential to it. (Sartre, 2015 [1939])

Emotions are 'essential' to human consciousness (see also Hegel, 1967 [1807]). There is a tension in emotion being both real and magical. The key to resolving this tension appears to be that real emotion temporarily takes over consciousness and becomes the totalized real world for the human subject experiencing the emotion. The magic comes from a flight into a world where previously unexplored behaviour becomes a real possibility. Feeling an intense emotion can be seen as demanding a radical change in behaviour, such as fight or flight in a situation of perceived threat, or a radical reorganization of relationships with other people. The emotion-driven desires for radical changes in functionings may utilize pre-existing capabilities in a different patterning or stimulate a need for new capabilities to achieve the desired functionings.

Sartre, as an existentialist, sees no reason to evaluate or rank emotions. Anger in one context may have a positive outcome in terms of a move away from a capability-damaging situation, or it can result in behaviour that itself damages capability. Thomas Mann (2016) vividly captures the latter possibility in his novella *Death in Venice*. The main protagonist, Gustave von Aschenbach, is a man who appears to represent the epitome of a rational, ordered life, exercising a capability for intellectual activity rigorously excluding deep emotions. But, in the chaos represented by Venice as the city drifts into an outbreak of plague, Aschenbach experiences erotic love for a young man as an overwhelming emotion. The book traces intimately the effects of this infatuation on Aschenbach's consciousness and behaviour up to the moment of his death. The narrative moves between Aschenbach's internal dialogue and his actions in the world to convey his life as a totalizing reality. It is not surprising that the richness of the narrative has inspired a film (Dirk Bogarde in one of his greatest roles) and an opera by Benjamin Britten.

The implication for the capability approach of Sartre's and Mann's position is that any view of personhood that omits the emotional dimension will miss vital critical moments in being fully human and making decisions about future well-being. From this position, strong emotions have the potential to open an experiential door to different perceptions of realities and desires to change functionings in radical directions that may lead to using the pre-existing capability set differently or stimulate the acquisition of different capabilities.

Emotions as a key to progress

As a writer and philosopher, Friedrich Nietzsche (2003 [1886]) in *Beyond Good and Evil* has a style that bristles with emotion. Despite his many excursions into totally unacceptable anti-Semitism and sexism, he is useful for this chapter in that he offers a critique of emotional passivity, although he includes Christian religious ecstatic emotional expressions as a socially pacifying force. For Nietzsche, progress depends on the expression of will, and will is not reducible to rational calculation. Progress requires people to break out from the norms that constrain both their actual and perceived range of capabilities and their choices of functionings. Modernity requires subservience to conventions that diminish expressions of values that challenge the rationale of the structure – a rationale that inhibits spontaneity. This is an aspect of Nietzsche's thought that can be seen as influencing Foucault's thinking on critical theory.

But Nietzsche is unclear about the origins of the people who will challenge the structure by living their emotions authentically. The implicit explanation is that these people will have individual emotional wills (or 'Wille', in Nietzsche's formulation) to transcend the barriers to radical change. To turn the expression of authentic emotions into a force for societal change, Nietzsche seems to envisage a conglomeration of 'noble' people ('supermen' in other writing), who possess this quality of authentic intellectual/emotional completeness. Nietzsche's primitive 'sociology' is obsessively focused on ethnic/national group characteristics. He finds some collective strengths and weaknesses in all groups; for example, the 'English' are regarded as bringing about a 'mechanical stultification of the world'.

A more institutional approach to social change may be able to rescue some of Nietzsche's ideas on the significance of authentic emotional expression as a social phenomenon. Bram Stoker's *Dracula* (1998 [1897]) explores the struggle between good and evil. A small group of people explore ways of combating a personification of evil (although the term 'evil' needs qualification, as Count Dracula can be seen as being driven by the necessity of his own survival). While one character applies rational 'scientific' knowledge in the combat, the narrative builds to a crescendo in which the emotionally charged 'hero' overcomes fear and horror with rage and courage to destroy Dracula, who has threatened the woman he loves. The story concludes:

We want no proofs. We ask none to believe us! This boy will some day know what a brave and gallant woman his mother is. Already he knows her sweetness and loving care. Later on he will understand how some men so loved her, that they did dare much for her sake. (Stoker, 1998 [1897])

The sense of emotional authenticity is very strong in this quote. But Nietzsche's sexism has been banished along with the need for rational/empirical 'proofs'. The social outcome can be seen as driven by emotions and achieving a 'progressive' outcome.

The implication for the capability approach of this position on the role of emotions is a need to recognize the power of emotions as key to achieving 'progressive' social goals. A challenge for this position is to conceptualize emotions as social phenomena. Can we speak meaningfully about emotions as collective, as well as individual, phenomena? Nietzsche devotes a significant part of *Beyond Good and Evil* to discussing music and other art forms as clues to how emotions appear as shared cultures. If this is accepted, then this suggests that reflections on broadly defined socially critical artistic products may be desirable as part of a humanities-influenced capability approach (such as films directed by Ken Loach and the 'orientalist' literary criticism of Edward Said).

Emotions as an obstacle to progress

Erasmus's *In Praise of Folly* (2004 [1511]) is a delightfully engaging ironic text. Erasmus uses the text to demonstrate the virtual inevitability of emotional 'folly' in human affairs. He aspires to cool, areligious rationality as the quality that should guide human decision making and the creation of a progressive social order. But Erasmus is sympathetic to the 'reality' of vulnerability and uncertainty and the temptation to live life through strong emotional reactions to unforeseen events. His project is to persuade us to recognize our universal capacity to make rational decisions beyond the claims of folly:

I am so necessary to the making of all society and manner of life both delightful and lasting, that neither would the people long endure their governors, nor the servant his master, ... nor the wife her husband ... unless all of them had their interchangeable failings, one while flattering, other while prudently conniving, and generally sweetening one another with some small relish of folly. (Erasmus, 2004 [1511])

Greater emphasis on our shared rationality could lengthen the time horizon and increase the spatial coverage of our decision making. Erasmus lived in a period when it was possible to think about a pan-European intellectual culture with Latin as its shared language. But as religious division became harnessed to emergent nationalism, as in England, where the execution of Erasmus's close friend, Thomas More, had great symbolic significance, Erasmus's vision faded for nearly 500 years until the creation of a new pan-European project. It may be ironic in the sense of Erasmusian folly that England is also emotionally seceding from this project.

F. Scott Fitzgerald (2002) exposes human folly in all his writings, notably in *The Beautiful and Damned*, but also in *The Great Gatsby*, where strong emotions govern and surround the eponymous character leading inevitably to an inglorious death. Fitzgerald in *The Beautiful and Damned* frees his two major characters initially from any necessity for economic activity and leaves them free to choose how to exercise their capabilities without constraints until late in the book. Their lives are full of folly, their choices are all based on mutually reinforcing petty snobberies and their lives are pickled in an alcoholic lack of rationality. In the conclusion to the book, Fitzgerald allows them to live, but in a state of chronically reduced consciousness and lacking any decision-making capability.

Scott Fitzgerald was in a position to reflect on what happens when human beings are permitted by material circumstances to exercise financially unconstrained choices. Thorstein Veblen looked at such people through an economic lens and proposed a theory that became known as the 'snob/Veblen effect', in which people behaved irrationally by conventional economic rules in choosing to purchase more of goods and services when their prices rose. Fitzgerald's and Veblen's observations of the behaviour of the super-rich do suggest Erasmusian folly, in which the emotional dominates the rational in choices with negative consequences for social progress, and possibly individual well-being.

The surface lesson of this position for the capability approach is close to the implicit position, often adopted by proponents of the CA, that the approach should be stripped of emotional content and reduced to logical calculation. But such 'stripping' may be counter-productive if it reduces our understanding of social choices being made by powerful people when they are driven by emotions in the allocation of substantial resources (see Cameron, 2000). While the CA may strip out emotions for analytical convenience, it has to recognize a deeper lesson, in that such emotional stripping is undesirable in practice, as emotional 'folly' can be essential for human beings for life to be bearable when facing up to mortality and bereavement.

Emotions as essential to being a communicating human

Umberto Eco's *Kant and the Platypus* (2000 [1997]) continues his lifelong engagement with signification and the complexity of human communication. The tale of the platypus relates how the 'scientific community' was thrown into confusion by the discovery of this Australian creature, which appeared to defy the biological classifications of the time. These classifications were believed to be complete and mutually exclusive. The platypus could not 'be' in the scientists' world of tidy, unambiguous language. Eco mobilizes Kant's agonizing over whether human beings can ever 'know things in themselves'. For Kant, language can never become the thing in itself, even if it claims to have signified the thing. In a similar vein, Eco hears human communication as both essential to being human and heavily laden with signs that frustrate all attempts at precision. The following quote captures Eco's position on the ambiguity of any act of defining, which, inevitably, involves the word 'is' (in the sense that 'word we are trying to define' *is* the same as 'word doing the defining'). This is not to say 'that we cannot speak of being: we speak about it all the time, too often perhaps; the problem is that this magic word helps us define almost everything but is defined by nothing' (Eco, 2002 [1997]).

A logical positivist epistemologist may protest that mathematical logic removes ambiguity and provides a basis for universal human communication unfettered by the vagaries within every human language and the impossibility of exact translation between languages (including the translation of Eco's book from Italian to English). But how much human communication is conducted in the language of mathematics and artificially intelligent algorithms?

To extend Eco's argument in *Kant and the Platypus* into the realm of the emotions, it is useful to consider one of his novels. *The Name of the Rose* is, essentially, a detective story. It depends upon careful direct observations and some deductive work to logically connect those observations. The monk detective is coolly rational, but strong emotions prove to be vital to understanding the single motivation that lay behind the multiple murders. The motivation was a desire to suppress the emotions that give rise to human laughter. Interpreting this motivation in the light of Eco's *Kant and the Platypus* suggests that refusing emotions can have dire consequences. Eco also wrote another novel, *Foucault's Pendulum* (on reflection, there may be some irony in the title, given that the book is focused on an ultimate source of power – though it is different from Foucault!). In this book, Eco describes how an irrational, obsessional emotional belief takes the characters on a wild chase through strong emotions in a variety of cultural contexts.

Eco's concern with strong emotions as an essential aspect of human communication and the ambiguity of language can be seen through the lens of Herman Melville's novel, *Moby-Dick* (1988 [1851]). Much of the book is a positivist description of whaling in technical and bio-logical terms. But, for the purpose of this chapter, the focus is on a central human relationship. Early in the book, Queequeg and Ishmael are brought together by circumstance. Their relationship begins with great cultural misunderstandings on the part of Ishmael, in which the emotions of fear and disgust are mixed. Queequeg comes from a Pacific Island culture utterly unfamiliar with Ishmael's upbringing in rural North America. It is easy to assume that Ishmael is 'white' by ethnicity and Protestant Christian by religion, though this is not made explicit.

The two people share very little language and yet they form a close, warm friendship. The story is written from Ishmael's standpoint and describes his learning about Queequeg's culture, including a very dif-ferent attitude to death. Communication is largely delanguaged, and yet emotionally intimate, combining affection and trust in a very demanding physical environment. Of course, there are many fictional accounts of close emotional bonding, but rarely is there so little ver-bal communication without any explicit erotic element, which can be found in much fictional writing. Ishmael's understanding and admira-tion increase as the voyage heads towards its fatal conclusion.

Queequeg in his own proper person was a riddle to unfold, a wondrous work in one volume, but whose mysteries not even himself could read ... And this thought it must have been which suggested to Ahab that wild exclamation of his, when one morning turning away from surveying poor Queequeg – 'Oh, devilish tantalization of the gods!' (Melville, 1988 [1851]: ch. 110)

Captain Ahab can be seen as representing a very different pattern of the interaction between emotions and human communication. Emotions of bitterness and hate restrict his acts of communication to commands. He is successful in communicating his desires to the point of leading the crew (and himself) to their deaths. Unless we understand Ahab's strong emotions, Melville's narrative makes no sense. Emotions are essential to the warm relationships between Queequeg and Ishmael, and to the cold relationship between Ahab and the ship's crew. Elaborated language and rational decision making play very little role in either relationship.

Both Eco and Melville lead their readers to rebalance the rational and the emotional mix in human communication and associated actions. Insofar as the rational requires confidence in the precision of spoken and written language, then Eco throws doubt on this requirement. In the same spirit, Melville gives examples of how human relationships can be driven by emotions.

There are implications for the CA from this standpoint. Communicative agency is perceived as essential to being human; arguably, we know we exist only in interactions with other people. Just a brief perusal of the burgeoning global social media is needed to read and hear how little human communication is conducted in emotionless, logical language in which objective evidence is given priority. Can any conceptual framework that claims to understand the human condition sideline emotional human communicative activity? The CA needs to face up to the accusation that its conceptual model of human personhood is de facto that of artificially intelligent robots. Discourse analysis can help in identifying how emotions are smuggled into public policy by deconstructing metaphors, tropes and memes. Including an emotional language, stripped of claims to scientist logic, is needed for understanding much human communication and actions.

Emotions as key to understanding power

Michel Foucault (2012 [1975]) writes in a style that appears largely to lack emotions. But, arguably, his selection of embodied subjects – punishment, medicalization, sexuality – suggests a starting point in the emotions: possibly indignation, bordering on anger.

Foucault has a central concern with power and the way language works to operationalize and conceal its operation. The unusual step offered in this chapter is a deconstruction of Foucault's thought to 'uncover' an emotional dimension. The bodies 'gazed on' by modernity are rendered as passive victims, accepting the operations of power. But Foucault himself is hardly a passive victim, so how is he able to transcend the embrace of structural disempowerment?

Foucault's stance suggests that the recipients of disempowering experiences have no ways intellectually to react to the enactment of power that threatens their mental and physical integrity. Franz Kafka (1992 [1925]), in *The Trial*, explores a 'bottom-up' response to the arbitrary exercise of power. The victim is accused of an unspecified offence. He believes in the ultimate rationality and legal accountability of the system and pursues every avenue to uncover the specific charge of which he is accused. The narrative describes his journey in terms of his emotions as he faces the operations of a power that refuses to reveal its operational rules. Foucault would recognize the ultimate rationality of an execution of a body that has lost its reason for continuing existence and for whom death is a release.

The emotional journey from anger at perceived injustice to despair and final passive acceptance of a death sentence is vividly described as the victim is frustrated in uncovering what the crime actually is with which he is charged. The characters met argue rationally while the spaces traversed on this emotional journey are dream-like and absurdly surreal. As in much else in Kafka's writing, human beings face a world in which rational calculation is eclipsed by powerful inexplicable forces and responses are 'reduced' to raw emotions. But, for Kafka, these emotional responses render the person dysfunctional in capability terms and unable to contest the powerful forces that render all possible functionings meaningless.

The implication of Foucault's and Kafka's positions for the capability approach is to question any benign donative model of persuadable political power that is often implicit in the approach. Both authors demand that power relationships be recognized as fundamentally disempowering for many people. Responses to such hegemonic disempowerment are likely to be in the realm of negative emotions rather than rationally justifiable actions of resistance. Assumptions of public policies as benign are questionable, no matter how well intentioned, as the 'targets' of those policies have their rational agency denied and are reduced to tears and rage (as vividly portrayed in director Ken Loach's 2016 film *I, Daniel Blake*).

A framework to integrate an emotional dimension into the CA

Integrating a more explicit emotional dimension into the CA can draw on the five positions outlined above. These positions give rise to five questions that anyone conducting CA research may wish to consider.

(1) In the context of CA research, is there a possible alternative emotional reality operating separately from the appearance of rational calculation in converting capability into functioning?

What is sought here is the presence of strong emotions felt by subjects of the research that challenge the 'normal' framing of their decision making: asking what in the context of the research makes the researched subjects feel angry or afraid, which can reveal forces that may tip decisions out of the realm of rational calculation. Similarly, enquiring into the happiness and joys that are hoped for in the future may suggest emotional factors that could influence current decisions. Values, motivations and aspirations may be creatures of the emotions operating independently as both an aspect of capability and a cause of decisions on functionings.

(2) In the context of CA research, are emotions playing a positive role in converting pre-existing capability into more valued functionings and/or developing capability to achieve more valued functionings?

From this perspective, emotions induce positive tendencies in converting pre-existing capability into functionings that generate higher well-being and/or further develop capability to achieve more valued functionings. In its more radical version, emotions, such as anger, can be combined with critical thought to produce an epistemological break with hegemonic social structuring that constrains individual and collective decisions, which can improve the well-being of people outside an elite.

(3) In the context of CA research, are emotions playing a negative role (rather than the positive role in perspective (2) above) in restricting the use of existing capability and obstructing the development of further capability to achieve socially more valued functionings?

This perspective may be associated with the Samaritan position outlined in the introduction to this chapter. The Samaritan position does not resist negative emotions but works with them to understand how they may be transcended. The CA researcher may be able to locate a tension between what appears to be the researched subject's rational decision to achieve more valued functionings and a lack of willingness to make that decision or implement it wholeheartedly. This perspective is closest to the view that emotions need to be stripped out to uncover progressive rational choices.

(4) In the context of CA research, how are the researched subjects communicating at the level of emotions?

This perspective asks the CA researcher to explore the emotional content in the key relationships that are influencing the research context. These emotional interactions may be enhancing or inhibiting collective decision making. Much capability development and access to functionings is dependent on effective communicating, which may have an emotional dimension. This emotional communication may decrease the need for elaborated explanatory extended logical argument. For instance, the emotional states of empathy and trust are prerequisites for effective group decision making and action.

(5) In the context of CA research, what are the relationships between the exercise of power and the emotional responses to that exercise among both the more and less powerful to reproduce and challenge power relationships?

This perspective pushes the CA researcher away from the assumption that the powerful exercise their privileges rationally and benignly, or at least are biddable by evidence-based arguments, to act in the interests of the less privileged. Emotions may be key to the emotional legitimization of power relationships (such as loyalty and patriotism), or the representation of resistance as emotionally irrational (envy, jealousy). Arguably, all power relationships have emotional aspects that govern both strengthening and undermining tendencies that reproduce or challenge those relationships.

Table 9.1 summarizes the five positions in a single framework. It is important not to see the positions as independent. They could all be operating in any single research context. The Annex attempts to apply the framework to a simple synthetic case study.

Table 9.1 *A framework for linking emotional positionalities to research questions*

Position	Key semi-structured research question
(1) Emotions as another reality	How do you feel about the choices you face in your current situation?
(2) Emotions as a positive force	How do your feelings reinforce your choices and current decisions on how to live your life?
(3) Emotions as a negative force	How do your feelings conflict with your choices and current decisions on how to live your life?
(4) Emotions as a communicative essential	How do you feel about your relationships with other people and organizations that influence how you can live your life?
(5) Emotions as a power relationship	When you think about people who have power to influence your life, how do you feel about them?

Conclusion

This chapter has endeavoured to make the case for a greater inclusion of emotional factors in the CA. The argument is that including an emotional dimension does not exclude rational calculation but can be incorporated into a mixed approach (see Figure 9.1). The mixture will be influenced by the context of the research; some contexts will appear to be less 'emotional' than others, but emotional aspects cannot be excluded from any CA research context.

The argument is developed to identify five ways in which emotions may enter into CA research. The five ways range from being an independent influence through positive and negative influences on capability development and expression as functionings. Moving towards social expressions in the CA, the chapter then explores how all human communication has an emotional element and power relationships have an essential emotional dimension.

A unifying framework was developed to offer potential mixes of the five positions (see Table 9.1). The following Annex aims to apply the framework to a synthetic case study. The Annex sets up a scenario for a semi-structured interview and then presents a synthetic transcript that illustrates the various positions identified in the framework.

But, as a final conclusion to the main text of this chapter, it is worth reflecting on reasons for including an emotional dimension more explicitly in the CA.

(1) An ethical reason can be advanced in terms of principles that should guide researching people's lives. A person being 'researched' arguably has a right to be treated as a whole subject and not an object rendered manageable for the purposes of researchers steeped in positivist epistemology. An emotional dimension may be uncomfortable to include for researchers untrained in the reflexivity and sensitivity required to explore people's feelings. But such discomfort is a poor reason for objectifying another human being.

(2) Emotions can be vital to understanding how people:
- perceive their capability set;
- obstruct or enhance the conversion of a capability set into functioning; and
- prevent or facilitate creating economic, social and power relationships that change capability sets and hence choices of functionings.

(3) Including emotions in CA research opens up the CA to learning from the broadly defined humanities (hence the references to works of 'fiction' in this chapter). Including insights from 'fictional' texts (as in Nussbaum, 1995) enriches CA research and renders the CA more fully 'human'.

Annex: applying the framework using a synthetic semi-structured interview

This Annex attempts to apply the framework summarized in Table 9.1 in the main text of this chapter. The interview transcript is annotated with numbered end-notes (in the form of numbers in parentheses at the end of relevant moments in the transcript).

Background

Robust statistical data for a South Pacific island country gathered over the past 30 years indicate that substantial 'lone' migration by married men has been a continuing demographic phenomenon and may be increasing.

Other less robust country statistics suggest this migration has generally had a positive impact on family incomes. But international academic research literature in a number of countries suggests there may be complex effects on the capabilities and functionings of those 'left behind'.

CA *research question*

Are there circumstances in which a husband's migration may damage the family 'left behind' in terms of capability and functionings?

Interview context

This respondent was identified after a conversation with a key informant – the pastor of a well-supported church – identifying women whose experiences of a husband's migration were possibly negative.

The respondent stated she was willing to be interviewed in English as that had been the language of instruction in her primary and secondary schools. She generally seemed at ease to talk about her experiences.

When asked to describe herself for the purpose of the interview, the respondent highlighted (in order stated):

(1) she was a mother of three children under ten years of age;
(2) she was a person of indigenous ethnicity who attends a Seventh Day Adventist church every Saturday;
(3) she could produce sufficient food for subsistence from her own 'garden' – land held under secure communal land allocation arrangements; and
(4) her husband migrated to New Zealand six years ago on an indefinite-duration overseas worker contract, with annual home leave possibilities.

Interview transcription extract

INTERVIEWER: So far, your responses suggest that your husband's migration affected your marriage relationship. Is that correct? (1)

RESPONDENT: Well [*slight hesitation*], yes; but I was surprised by the changes. They seemed to go against the values we shared when we married.

INTERVIEWER: Can you say more about being surprised? (2)

RESPONDENT: We saw his move as improving our economic situation; I did not expect the emotional stresses. (3)

INTERVIEWER: Did your economic situation improve?

RESPONDENT: Not consistently; he does bring money on his visits home, but those visits have become less frequent. He has not come home in the last year and a half.

INTERVIEWER: How did the emotional stress appear? (4)

RESPONDENT: On his visits home, he became angry when I asked him about his life in New Zealand [*appears to be close to tears*]. (5)

INTERVIEWER: I do understand how distressing this must be for you. Do you want me to switch off the recording machine and take a break? (6)

RESPONDENT: No, I am OK, really

INTERVIEWER: When your husband went back to New Zealand last time, did you change anything about your life after he left? (7)

RESPONDENT: I talked to my friends in the church. We agreed that our beliefs would not allow legal divorce, but there was no reason that I should not seek to find extra money for school costs without consulting my husband. (8)

INTERVIEWER: So what did you do then?

RESPONDENT: I joined a group saving and loan scheme organized by the church.

INTERVIEWER: Did that work out?

RESPONDENT: Not really [*hesitates*]. The scheme was aimed at quick profit activities, like chicken rearing or small grocery stores. I wanted to pay school costs. (9)

INTERVIEWER: What did you do?

RESPONDENT: I took the first loan and then borrowed from a relative to repay it. I will stay with the group – they are my friends – making the minimum savings but taking no more loans. (10)

INTERVIEWER: This interview has been very, very interesting, thank you, and has given me much to think about. May I come back and talk to you again if I have some further questions?

RESPONDENT: I hope this helps your research and will help other women like me. (11)

INTERVIEWER: Is there anything you would like to add now?

RESPONDENT: Just that I do love my husband and, please God, I hope we will be happy together in the future. (12)

(1) Creating space to allow emotions to be expressed as an independent dimension of experience (position 1).

(2) Allowing room for the emotion of 'surprise' to induce positive or negative effects on capability (positions 2 and 3).

(3) Suggests the emotional aspect is negative, and possibly undermining capability and choice of functionings in this case (position 3).

(4) Moving back towards the emotional from the material (having established a link to the global literature).

(5) Anger as an emotion that can restrict communication (point 4).

(6) A moment testing the frontier of research and requiring an ethical response.

(7) A challenge of converting capability into new functionings in a new context with emotions possibly hindering the conversion (position 3).

(8) Positive emotional support from others, enhancing capability conversion to new functionings (position 4).

(9) Emotional determination to persist with capability conversion against rules from above (position 5).

(10) Emotional commitment to social relationships at some material cost (point 4).

(11) Another moment of ethical challenge in terms of emotional appeal to prescriptive power.

(12) An emotional block to developing new capability for new functionings (position 3).

References

Abbott, D. (2007) Doing 'incorrect' research: the importance of the subjective and the personal in researching poverty. In *Research Skills for Policy and Development: How to Find Out Fast*, Thomas, A., and Mohan, G. (eds.): 208–22. London: Sage.

Ayers, N. E., Vydelingum, V., and Arber, A. (2017) An ethnography of managing emotions when talking about life-threatening illness. *International Nursing Review*, 64 (4): 486–93.

Cameron, J. (2000) Amartya Sen on economic inequality: the need for an explicit critique of opulence. *Journal of International Development*, 12 (7): 1031–45.

(2005) Journeying in radical development studies: a reflection on thirty years of researching pro-poor development. In *A Radical History of Development Studies: Individuals, Institutions and Ideologies*, Kothari, U. (ed.): 138–56. London: Zed Books.

Comim, F., Qizilbash, M., and Alkire, S. (eds.) (2008) *The Capability Approach: Concepts, Measures and Applications*. Cambridge: Cambridge University Press.

Eco, U. (2000 [1997]) *Kant and the Platypus: Essays on Language and Cognition*, McEwen, A. (trans.). Boston: Houghton Mifflin Harcourt.

Erasmus, D. (2004 [1511]) *In Praise of Folly*. London: Penguin.

Fitzgerald, F. S. (2002 [1922]) *The Beautiful and Damned*. New York: Random House.

Foucault, M. (2012 [1975]) *Discipline and Punish: The Birth of the Prison*, Sheridan, A. (trans.). New York: Vintage.

Gasper, D., and Cameron, J. (2000) Assessing and extending the work of Amartya Sen. *Journal of International Development*, 12 (7): 985–8.

Hegel, G. W. F. (1967 [1807]) *The Phenomenology of Mind*, Baillie, J. B. (trans.). New York: Harper & Row.

Kafka, F. (1992 [1925]) *The Trial*, Muir, E., and Muir, W. (trans.). London: Everyman's Library.

Mann, T. (2016 [1912]) *Death in Venice*. London: Re-Image Publishing.

Melville, H. (1988 [1851]) *Moby-Dick; or, The Whale*, Hayford, H., Parker, H., and Tanselle, G. T. (eds.). Evanston, IL: Northwestern University Press.

Nietzsche, F. (2003 [1886]) *Beyond Good and Evil*. London: Penguin.

Nussbaum, M. C. (1990) *Love's Knowledge: Essays on Philosophy and Literature*. Oxford: Oxford University Press.

(1995) Emotions and women's capabilities. In *Women, Culture, and Development: A Study of Human Capabilities*, Nussbaum, M. C., and Glover, J. (eds.): 360–95. Oxford: Oxford University Press.

Robb, A. (2019) *Why We Dream: The Science, Creativity and Transformative Power of Dreams*. London: Pan Macmillan.

Sartre, J.-P. (2015 [1939]) *Sketch for a Theory of the Emotions*. Abingdon: Routledge.

Sen, A. K. (2009) *The Idea of Justice*. London: Penguin.

Stoker, B. (1998 [1897]) *Bram Stoker's Dracula Unearthed*, Leatherdale, C. (annotated and ed.). London: Desert Island Books.

10 | *Sufficiency re-examined*

JAY DRYDYK

If human rights enjoy the support of public reason, then so must the obligation of every society to ensure that each of its members has an adequate standard of living. This obligation is a hallmark of human rights as they have been understood for the past seventy years, expressed in article 25 of the United Nations' Universal Declaration: 'Everyone has the right to a standard of living adequate for the health and well-being of himself and of his family, including food, clothing, housing and medical care and necessary social services, and the right to security in the event of unemployment, sickness, disability, widowhood, old age or other lack of livelihood in circumstances beyond his control' (UN General Assembly, 1948: art. 25).

What is an adequate standard of living in each country? This cannot be answered by a universal declaration, but, arguably, it can be answered by public reason in each country. If public reason is capable of determining *which* capabilities deserve social protection, as Martha Nussbaum holds (Nussbaum, 2006: 70), then, arguably, it must be capable of determining *at which levels* they must be protected. Nussbaum has often described this level as an 'ample minimum' (Nussbaum, 2000: 86; 2006: 70, 178, 427 n34; 2011: 32, 40).

My contention is that 'ample' and 'minimum' refer to two different thresholds, one being optimally high and the other being more urgently low. If public reasoning functions as it should, it will endorse both thresholds, giving some priority to the second. We could test this contention inductively by studying cases of deliberation about adequate standards of living to see which standards of living the deliberation endorses and whether the deliberation functions as it should. Case studies such as this would be valuable, yet a more analytical approach is also valuable, partly to hedge against the risk of studying deliberations that are hidebound by custom, ideology, fatalism or adaptive preference. Thus, in lieu of case studies, I will make two simplifying assumptions about public reason.

Public reason: simplifying assumptions

Inclusive impartiality: to function as it should, public reasoning must give due consideration to each person's good.

Equal dignity: to give due consideration to each person's good, public reasoning must be consistent with equal human dignity.

Although the concept of impartiality has come under criticism (Young, 1990: 96–121), the ideas of inclusiveness and due consideration are meant to accommodate this criticism. Amartya Sen's conception of open impartiality (Sen, 2009: 44–6, 124ff.) could be interpreted in this way by thinking of the impartial spectator not only as having no interests at stake but as being ideally compassionate (see Crisp, 2003). What this involves bears much further discussion. For instance, the impartial spectator should not give equal weight to each party's interests in cases when the parties are unequally advantaged in power, opportunity, resources or well-being. The main idea should be, rather, that an ideally compassionate person cares equally about each person's good and does not unduly weight anyone's particular aims and circumstances. Whether this move can succeed would need to be discussed at length, separately. That being said, this first assumption would seem open to interpretation in a virtuous way, insofar as objections can be accommodated by appropriate interpretations of 'due consideration'.

The second assumption is open to interpretation in a more worrisome way. Numerous conceptions of dignity have been used over many centuries. 'Dignity' has many connotations, yet, as a ground of human rights and a simplifying assumption for public reason, the relevant concept is something like this: when we talk about 'human dignity', we mean that there is something about human beings that calls for respect, care and concern towards them. Because there are many different ideas about what this 'something about us' is, there are many different conceptions of human dignity. According to the religions of the book, it is that we are made in the image of God; according to utilitarians and other sentientists, it is because we can suffer. Alternatively, it may be that we can rise above suffering; rationality and autonomy are Enlightenment favourites. Can public reason favour any one of these over the others? If not, it is reasonable to wonder how they could lead to agreement on an adequate standard of living.

However, remembering that this is only a simplifying assumption, not a full ethical theory, I employ a conception of equal human dignity that adds little beyond the idea that each person's good deserves due consideration. Essentially, it treats persons as good-seekers, and it is open but not committed to any of the various conceptions about how human good-seeking is special (e.g. rationality, autonomy, sentience, relation to God, or whatever).

If we follow Sen rather than Rawls in wishing to keep public reason open to any and all relevant ideas, even comprehensive doctrines (Sen, 2009: 124ff.), we will want to consider all of these and their particular implications for what an adequate standard of living is. Even so, there is a conception of equal human dignity that might be attractive to many if not all of these views. This conception was suggested to me by a passage in Nussbaum's *Women and Human Development*:

This idea of human dignity has broad cross-cultural resonance and intuitive power. We can think of it as the idea that lies at the heart of tragic artworks, in whatever culture. Think of a tragic character, assailed by fortune. We react to the spectacle of humanity so assailed in a way very different from the way we react to a storm blowing grains of sand in the wind. For we see a human being as having worth as an end, a kind of awe-inspiring something that makes it horrible to see this person beaten down by the currents of chance – and wonderful, at the same time, to witness the way in which chance has not completely eclipsed the humanity of the person. As Aristotle puts it, 'the noble shines through.' (Nussbaum, 2000: 72–3)

What do we see 'shining through' in this scene? What I see is a human being striving, vulnerably, to live well. I am not so much claiming this as an interpretation of Nussbaum as I am extracting what I think is a powerful conception of human dignity. What is it, about us, that calls for respect, care and concern? It is that we are all striving, vulnerably, to live well.

There are three underlying ideas: striving; living well; and vulnerability. By *striving*, I mean activity that is purposive, teleological. Nussbaum clarifies 'the noble [that] shines through' immediately as 'having activity, goals, and projects – as somehow awe-inspiringly above the mechanical workings of nature'. By 'striving' I mean this kind of activity, not the degree of energy or effort it involves. One possible objection to basing dignity on striving is the fact that some people are less capable of striving than others, such as newborns, or people who are extremely frail or cognitively disabled. Striving is not always self-sufficient; assisted striving is still purposive or teleological. A granddaughter in a family I know cannot speak and requires assistance in nearly everything she does; nevertheless, she is highly responsive to the personal interactions that she experiences between family members. So, perhaps oddly, 'striving' can be passively responsive rather than energetically active. Dignity, as I understand it, is based on striving *to live well*, conceiving of this as broader than any particular conception or doctrine of a good life: we can recognize someone as striving to live well even if we reject their particular conception of a good life. Indeed, it is possible to think of evil-doers as striving in their own twisted ways to live well. If, as the capability approach proposes, there are ways of functioning that we all have reason to value as elements of a good life, then these functionings will be realizable in multiple ways. Or, to put this in another way, we can understand these valuable functionings by abstracting from particular ways of realizing them, discerning each general functioning as what the particular realizations have in common; for example, some people love eating rice, others wheat breads, but we all value eating well. Although the thought of eating flesh may be disgusting to vegetarians, surely they can recognize that flesh eaters too are striving to live well. By saying that we strive *vulnerably* to live well, I mean that we encounter obstacles as well as opportunities. Following common usage (see the OED Online definition of 'opportunity, n.': www.oed.com/view/Entry/131973?redirectedFrom=opportunity&), we can say that opportunities and obstacles are favourable and unfavourable circumstances, respectively, and, in this context, favourable and unfavourable *to living well*. Finally, if someone's striving to live well matters to us, this implies that we are not indifferent to their success. Therefore, whether they overcome the obstacles facing them must also matter to us.

If this constitutes human dignity, then *equal human dignity* calls upon us not to privilege some people's vulnerable striving to live well over others'. To formulate this as a principle: each person's vulnerable striving to live well matters, and matters equally.

This evidently powerful principle has implications not only for sufficiency and insufficiency but throughout the spectrum of advantage and disadvantage. I have suggested that it represents more concretely and substantively the procedural principle of inclusive impartiality.

If this is right, then this pedigree gives its support for sufficiency considerable weight against other values that may compete in particular cases; at the same time, it may also call for accommodation and compromise with those values. For example, it may support the call for giving priority to those who do not have enough over those who have more than enough, but it may also provide grounds for exceptions on such grounds as talent or security. I return to this briefly at the end of the chapter.

Sufficiency: the argument

Nevertheless, the topic at hand is sufficiency, and so I focus down on the question of what guidance this principle of equal dignity provides concerning sufficiency. The principle supports four conclusions. First: it matters very much to assist people who are struggling with what I call 'existential' hardships. Second: there are hardships above this threshold that matter. Third: it also matters to assist people struggling to reach capability levels that could be generally available within a society, given its productive capacity. Fourth: it matters much less to assist people striving to expand their capabilities beyond these optimal levels, apart from some specific exceptions.

Conceptually, the idea of equal dignity seems not to fit well with levels of living or well-being. The principle of equal dignity tells us that John's striving to live well is no more or less important than Jane's, but how does it tell us whether either of them is living well or badly, much less where to 'draw the line'? Only in a richer informational space can equal dignity have any bearing on line-drawing questions.

Can the well-being space provide any traction? If there is a level of well-being below which life is bad, then leaving people below this level as if it did not matter would be wrong, because each person's striving to live well matters, and matters equally. Yet it is more than a little mysterious how such a level could be a feature of the human well-being space itself, in the way that every liquid has its own freezing point. In 2003 Roger Crisp wrote, 'It is hard to know how to answer such questions, but, on reflection, my own intuition is that, say, eighty years of high-quality life on this planet is enough, and plausibly more than enough, for any being' (Crisp, 2003: 762). Yet history confounds this kind of intuition. By the time Crisp wrote of his intuition, average life expectancy at birth had not quite reached 80 in England, and before 1750 it had not reached 40 (Roser, 2013). Yet English aristo-crats reaching the age of 21 between 1700 and 1745 could expect to live on average a further 43 years, to 64 (Lancaster, 1990: 8). Which life expectancy is or was enough? Clearly, the length of a good enough life is not a fixed feature of well-being per se. Philosophical argument supports the same conclusion: that levels at which life is bad or ade-quate are not features inherent in the well-being space (Segall, 2016).

Some traction could be provided by information about subsistence, basic needs and the correlative capabilities. Subsistence standards are set more or less by requirements for good health, whereas the concept of basic needs is broader, including requirements for participation in social activity (Doyal and Gough, 1991; Gutwald, 2018). Understood in terms of striving to live well, the concept of human dignity makes some decisive additions. While striving to live well aims for subsis-tence and basic needs, it also aims considerably beyond them. The difference allows us to capture the nature of a bad life in different ways. Intuitively, striving to live well but failing to meet basic needs is bad. Yet it is also a bad life in which all effort must focus on meeting subsistence needs – that is, in which all of one's striving to live well is consumed by tasks of meeting basic needs while unsurmountable obstacles stand in the way of living any better. The principle of equal dignity explains and supports these intuitions. According to the prin-ciple, it matters if some people cannot meet their basic needs while others can, as one could hold that this does not matter only if one could also assume that some people's striving to live well matters more than others', and the principle of equal dignity rules this out. Yet it also matters, by the same line of thinking, if some people's striving to live well is confined to meeting basic needs and blocked by obstacles to living any better. Karl Marx captured this in his 1844 manuscripts when he wrote that capitalism confines workers to meeting subsis-tence needs, subordinating all their distinctively human capacities (such as intelligence, creativity and self-consciousness) to maintaining their 'animal existence'. Thus, the worker 'makes his life activity, his *essential being*, a mere means to his *existence*' (Marx, 1975 [1844]: 276, emphasis in original). Life does not cease to be bad just when basic needs are met (or when we are capable of meeting them); it is still bad when all our efforts are required in order to meet these needs and we have little capability beyond this for living better. Again, leaving people in such a state could be condoned only if their striving to live well matters less than others', and the principle of equal dignity rules this out. Subsistence and basic needs alone are not enough for human dignity, and so they are not good criteria for sufficiency.

This claim, that subsistence and basic needs alone are not enough for human dignity, could meet with several objections. (1) Other conceptions of dignity might not support this, such as conceptions in which dignity delimits an undignified life – that is, there is a threshold below which life is undignified, and any level of living above this would count as a life of human dignity. Not all conceptions of dignity deflate the threshold in this way. For example, if 'dignity' means having autonomy or reason, or being made in the image of God, we are not warranted in lowering the limits of a dignified life to subsistence or basic needs: there is no reason why rational or autonomous or God-like beings should be satisfied with mere subsistence or meeting basic needs. Moreover, the principle of equal human dignity that I am applying here will not acquiesce in inequalities between levels of living that are at a level of subsistence or basic needs and levels that are higher. (2) This of course assumes that we live in societies in which resources and productive capacity are ample enough that living at or beyond subsistence levels is feasible. As Mulgan (2014) points out, in a 'broken world' where this is not feasible, everyone's social and political philosophy would need to change. This problem deserves further thought; I set it aside because it requires a longer discussion than I can give it here and because broken world problems affect all distributive theorizing, not just sufficiency approaches.

The reader may have noticed that the principle of equal dignity, as I have formulated it, has a relentless disposition to equalize. It cannot merely require subsistence for everyone, as long as *more than* subsistence is achievable by anyone; otherwise, some people would be confined to subsistence while others are not, and this is not acceptable if each person's striving to live well matters equally. This raises two questions. (1) Is there any ceiling? (2) Do the lower thresholds still somehow matter more?

Perhaps the productive capacity of a society has something to do with the ceiling. For example, we might ask ourselves what the highest health capabilities are that could be provided by our society, with its current productive capacity, *for each person*. Or what are the highest educational capabilities that this society, with its current productive capacity, could ensure for all its members? Of course, the comparative value of health and education may be weighted somewhat differently in different societies, or at different times. Nevertheless, we can think about what levels could be achieved for some of the valuable capabilities, consistent with reasonable support for the other valuable capabilities, within the productive capacity of our society. I am not claiming that we can calculate such levels, merely that we can think consistently about them. The aim of this thinking would be to roughly identify zones for each of the most valuable capabilities (or, anyway, of a chosen subset), specifically the *highest* zones that could be ensured generally throughout a society, within its present productive capacity. Such a set of capability zones, for a given society, comprise what I will call the *optimum social capability* for that society, or, in fewer words the *social optimum*.

It can be argued that nothing short of this social optimum is enough or sufficient for equal human dignity. Suppose that Z is the social optimum for society S. In other words, Z is a set comprising the highest capability zones that can be ensured for each member of this society by its productive capacity. So S could raise each person's capabilities to Z. Instead, S allows N per cent of the population to remain below Z. Does this matter much? It would *not* matter much – which is to say, it would be more or less all right, a matter of little concern – only if their striving to live well matters less than others' striving to live well. However, that would be inconsistent with equal human dignity, according to which each person's striving to live well matters equally. Therefore, leaving any group below the social optimum is of great concern, and, in this sense, nothing short of the social optimum is sufficient for equal human dignity.

In this argument, the concept of capability plays an essential role: the valuable capabilities are capabilities to live well, and striving to live well is the ground of human dignity. Some capabilities are not especially valuable, such as one's capability to use a favourite laundry detergent (Sen, 1992: 44) or to sing Yankee Doodle Dandy while standing on one's head (Nussbaum, 2011: 32). Much more valuable are capabilities to function in ways that people have reason to value as elements of living well. Living well is the middle term linking dignity with capability levels, allowing us to argue for optimizing capability levels in order to respect equal human dignity.

It could be objected that this conclusion is impractical because calculating such a social optimum is not feasible. I do not know whether the infeasibility premise of this objection is true, but, even if it is, the impracticality objection does not follow. The reason is that in many cases we can infer that one group's capability levels are insufficient even if the precise social optimum capability is unclear. We can draw this kind of inference when group disparities are especially great, since, the further that one group's capability levels fall below the social average, the more likely it is that they also fall below the social optimum. For example, there is little doubt that the health and longevity capabilities of the indigenous peoples of Canada are below what Canada could produce for all its people, when we read statistics such as these:

In 2017 the life expectancy for the total Canadian population is projected to be 79 years for men and 83 years for women. Among the Aboriginal population the Inuit have the lowest projected life expectancy in 2017, of 64 years for men and 73 years for women. The Métis and First Nations populations have similar life expectancies, at 73–74 years for men and 78–80 years for women. (Statistics Canada, 2015)

I conclude that nothing short of the social optimum is sufficient for equal human dignity. This conclusion should not be interpreted too rigidly, in the way that Richard Arneson has interpreted Nussbaum's sufficiency claims. According to Arneson (2006), saying that nothing short of a threshold T is sufficient for a life of human dignity means that we must give lexical priority to raising people to level T. Suppose that A is a person with capabilities slightly below the optimum and person B is a person with much more diminished capabilities, barely above the level of meeting basic needs. If sufficiency means lexical priority, then we must help A rather than B. Three replies come to mind. First, this is an uncharitable interpretation of Nussbaum (Kaufman, 2006). Second, the idea of lexical priority may be more useful for structuring dictionaries than for structuring societies.

Third, there is nothing in my argument that supports lexical priority. What it shows is that leaving people below the social optimum is of great concern; this is consistent with giving greater priority to those who are worse off. Rescuing people from disaster and helping them to overcome hardships are *first steps* towards reaching social optimum capability zones. Failing to do so is a disservice to the ultimate goal of bringing everyone to the optimum. There are also reasons for giving priority to these first steps. If it matters that people strive to live well in this world, not only in the hereafter, then survival is crucial. Priority also goes to people trapped in existential hardships, whose striving to live well is confined to being 'a mere means to his existence' (Marx, 1975 [1844]: 276). Hardships also matter because of the suffering they cause. Below the social optimum it may still be the case that 'benefiting people matters more the worse off those people are, the more of those people there are, and the greater the benefits in question' (Crisp, 2003: 752). The concern that no one should be left behind the social optimum is consistent with prioritarian concerns towards everyone who is striving to reach that level, from below. What the argument from human dignity will not permit is abandoning the goal of optimizing capabilities for the sake of poverty reduction; a just society, just social movements and just political actors will find a way to do both. I doubt there is any algorithm for how to do so. At the end of the day (and from the beginning) justice is a virtue (Drydyk, 2012, 2016).

Before leaving this topic, I would note that, besides the existential hardships captured by Marx, there are other hardships to which we must give some priority. As Iris Marion Young famously observed, oppression has many faces. One feature common to all forms and faces of oppression is that oppressed people encounter disproportionate incidence of obstacles to living well. David Axelsen and Lasse Nielsen conceptualize the same relationship (disproportionate obstacles to living well) in a different way, as 'pressures' constraining central capabilities (see Axelsen and Nielsen, 2015 and 2016, and Nielsen and Axelsen, 2017). The concept of an obstacle to living well is amenable to some straightforward conceptual analysis based on its common meaning (at least in English, and possibly in other languages as well). It is useful to conceive of 'obstacle' and 'opportunity' as opposites. 'Opportunity' can refer to any circumstance favourable to a purpose (see 'opportunity, n.', OED Online); in the context of striving to live well, we are interested in opportunities as circumstances favourable to living well. Then 'obstacles' can refer circumstances that are unfavourable to living well and 'hardship' can refer to disproportionate exposure to obstacles. 'Disproportionate' can be interpreted in different ways. The existential hardships identified by Marx compel people to devote their striving disproportionately to survival. Patriarchy and racism target women and racialized groups for disadvantage by exposing them to greater concentrations of obstacles than other groups encounter; these acts may include acts of discrimination, but also social actions and relations that are not enacted with conscious discriminatory motives. Either way, the obstacles are disproportionate in comparison with other groups. If each person's striving to live well matters equally, then it matters (with high priority) to assist people to overcome hardships of both kinds.

When the threshold for sufficiency is set at a high level, it seems plausible to think that 'enough is enough' – that it either matters not at all to raise anyone above that level, or that it matters much less. Roger Crisp conceives of the sufficiency threshold in this way, as a level at which compassion – even the compassion of an ideal spectator – runs out (Crisp, 2003: 757–8). Liam Shields advocates two more moderate versions. According to the 'diminution thesis', 'once people have secured enough our reasons to benefit them further are weaker' (Shields, 2012: 107). According to another version, which he calls the 'shift thesis', 'once people have secured enough there is a discontinuity in the rate of change of the marginal weight of our reasons to benefit them further' (Shields, 2012: 108).

If we set the sufficiency threshold at social optimum capability levels, the diminution thesis applies, for the simple reason that claims for any higher capability levels will not be supported by the principle of equal human dignity. To see this, once again consider society S with social optimum Z. Suppose now that N per cent of the population demands higher capability zones at Z', which can be provided only if the rest of the population are lowered to Z". Does this matter much? Other things being equal, it would *not* matter much – which is to say, it would be more or less all right, a matter of little concern – only if the rest of the population's striving to live well matters less than that of the N per cent. However, that would be inconsistent with equal human dignity. Thus, support for claims to capability levels higher than the social optimum is significantly diminished.

There are a few specific reasons for ensuring higher capabilities in specific contexts. (1) Some of these reasons may be instrumental: a new medical cure or treatment may bring some people above what passes at the time for the social optimum, yet in a robust social health system this will be a first step to bringing others (and eventually everyone) to a new higher optimum. (2) Yet, in other cases, allowing and even promoting optimum breakers may be valued intrinsically as well as instrumentally. Some talents are recognized as especially worthy of support. Great artists develop and exercise their capabilities for senses, imagination and thought (listed by Nussbaum as a central capability) to zones much higher than the social optimum, and, if they could not, their audiences would be worse off. (3) Arguably, capability *security* should be protected universally: if each person's striving to live well matters, and matters equally, then it matters to secure (against downside risks) the valuable capabilities that everyone has managed to develop, whether these are above the sufficiency threshold or below. Apart from exceptional cases such as these, the rationale for raising more people above the social optimum will lack the support of equal human dignity, so it will be weaker, and thus the diminution thesis prevails.

Conclusions and further questions

'Enough for all' seems a powerful and attractive slogan. On closer examination, this apparently straightforward slogan calls for a very complex programme of social and global change. Some parts of this complex programme have been discussed in this chapter, but other parts remain to be discussed.

There is no 'line' that defines 'enough' in the space of human well-being, like the freezing point in the temperature space for a liquid (see the OED Online definition of 'enough, adj. (and n.) and adv.': www.oed.com/view/Entry/62546?redirectedFrom=enough). Nor is 'enough for human dignity' a single line in the capability space. The principle of equal human dignity pushes upwards from any proposed threshold, and this pressure gives out only at the social optimum – the set of the highest capability zones that can be supported generally throughout a society by its existing productive capacity. The principle of equal dignity is not satisfied by a social safety net catching people before they fall below a poverty line. Rather, it demands raising everyone's capabilities to the social optimum. And this is not its only demand; in the process of bringing everyone to this level, it gives priority to overcoming hardships. These include existential hardships, whereby striving to live well is reduced to striving for subsistence. They also include oppressive hardships targeting particular groups with disproportionate obstacles to living well.

This new approach does not entirely abandon Nussbaum's conception of an 'ample minimum' as the threshold for sufficiency. The modifier 'ample' raises the threshold above the idea of a human minimum that she drew from Marx: the level at which all one's striving to live is reduced to striving for survival, or, in Marx's terms, meeting our 'animal' needs (Nussbaum, 2000: 72). This is what I have called 'existential hardship'. Not so clear in Nussbaum's formulation is how much higher than this a person's capabilities must rise to count as 'ample'. I have attempted to remedy this lack of clarity by suggesting higher thresholds that (1) overcome hardships of oppression and (2), as the final goal, reach the social optimum.

Thus, 'enough' should refer not to a single line but to multiple thresholds. Overcoming the lower thresholds is valuable both intrinsically and as a means to reaching the upper threshold: the social optimum. It is valuable capabilities (i.e. capabilities for living well) that these thresholds are levels *of*, and the importance of reaching them is underwritten by the principle that everyone's striving to live well matters equally.

I regret that I do not have space in this chapter to compare these conclusions thoroughly with those reached much earlier by Len Doyal and Ian Gough in *A Theory of Human Need* (Doyal and Gough, 1991) and subsequent work (Gough, 2014 and 2015). Arguably the entire stream of philosophical discussion of sufficiency, starting with Harry Frankfurt in 1987, has also paid inadequate attention to the discussion of needs. Doyal and Gough identify cultural pluralism as a challenge to identifying levels of need satisfaction that are adequate for everyone, and their solution is to conceive of adequacy in terms of social participation. Thus they grant (perhaps too readily) that 'there is little problem about identifying the most minimal levels of need satisfaction … But once we ask how much more than the minimum counts as an adequate level of basic need-satisfaction, the consensus begins to evaporate' (Doyal and Gough, 1991: 69), partly because 'the level of what is perceived as an acceptable level of need-satisfaction seems also to be culturally specific' (70). It is interesting that they conceive of this 'adequate' level as 'optimal' (73). Identifying health as one of two basic needs, they set the optimum here at 'as high a life expectancy and as little disability through disease as is possible in light of a person's genetic potential' (73). This move – setting the optimum in terms of genetic potential – may be somewhat ill considered. It is unabashedly ahistorical, and, as a result, unexpectedly elitist: in a society that cannot productively support anywhere near such high life expectancy and low morbidity for the entire population, elites would still be warranted in claiming that nothing short of 80 or more years of healthy living is adequate *for them*. (In my approach, by contrast, it is only in exceptional circumstances that people could claim more than the social optimum as enough for them.) The other basic need according to Doyal and Gough is autonomy. Here they identify two optimal thresholds. 'The lower optimum entails the minimisation of social constraints on a person's participation in socially significant activities coupled with access to as much cognitive understanding as is necessary successfully to pursue their chosen form of life' (73). Beyond this, a higher optimum also includes 'access to other cultures coupled with the critical skills and the political freedoms to evaluate their own and to struggle for change if they choose' (73). Setting a threshold at what is needed for social participation might seem to be warranted in view of what social creatures we humans are – considering how much of what we value as living well involves living well with other people. And yet, participating in social relationships is only as valuable as those relationships are: slavery and patriarchy too are social relations (see Sen, 2000). My prima facie conclusion is that, although sufficiency thinkers still have much to gain by thinking more about needs, needs theorists would also do well to consider setting adequacy thresholds (1) in terms of overcoming concentrations of hardships and (2) in terms of the highest levels that could be supported for everyone by this society's productive capacity.

In addition, several contributors to philosophical discussion have proposed sufficiency thresholds conceived as levels of subjective satisfaction (Frankfurt, 1987 and 2015; Huseby, 2010; Freiman, 2012; for an overview, see Casal, 2007). Elsewhere I would like to respond to these proposals in detail. In this chapter all I can do is refer to the general line of response; evaluating any aspect of advantage and disadvantage (including sufficiency) in terms of subjective satisfaction is skewed by the problem of adaptive preference (Sen, 1992, 53–5; 1999, 62–3; Khader, 2011). In other words, one response to poverty is to reduce one's expectations, becoming satisfied with a lower standard of living. If we take satisfaction as our criterion for sufficiency, we buy into the idea that what is enough for poor people can be less than what is enough for the better off. Acquiescing in this not only contravenes the principle of equal consideration but contributes ideologically to excusing structural injustice – despite the best intentions of authors who propose this view.

These are my conclusions concerning the *social* programme implicit in 'enough for all'. There must also be a *global* programme, which I have not mentioned so far. A global programme is required for the following reason. If we conceive of 'enough' simply in relation to the productive capacity of a society, then the capability level that is 'enough' in one society may be lower than the level in a society with greater productive capacity. The social optimum in a country such as Mali will be more restricted than it is in Brazil, and in Brazil the social optimum will be lower than it is in Germany. So the target for what is 'enough' in Mali will be lower than the target in Brazil, where the target in turn is lower than it is in Germany. Can these unequal standards be condoned? This would seem inconsistent with the principle of equal dignity.

Two possible solutions should be explored. One would be to conceive of the relevant optimum not as a social optimum but as a global optimum. Thus, the threshold could be set at the highest capability zones that could be ensured generally throughout the world, based on worldwide productive capacity. Alternatively, we could continue to regard the social optima as standards for each society, while demanding that inequalities of social productive capacity be reduced. In this case we accept differential social standards provisionally, aiming for the upward harmonization over time of social standards everywhere towards the highest social standards anywhere. In addition, it may be possible to achieve international agreement on steps to reach along the way, in the way that the Sustainable Development Goals have been set as first steps in reducing global inequality.

The other dimension of a global sufficiency programme is environmental. One virtue of the capability approach is that it conceptually separates living well from consumption, inviting discussion as to how we can live equally well or better with the same or fewer resources. Nevertheless, a political programme calling for 'enough for all', especially on the global scale, is likely to be a pro-growth programme. This raises the spectre of human dignity driving monstrous growth that is devastating environmentally. Again, two alternative solutions should be discussed. One would be to move towards a conception of sufficiency that is deflationary rather than expansionary. This would draw upon the connotation of 'enough' as 'just enough, and no more' (Spengler, 2016; Kanschik, 2016; Princen, 2005, 2003), as implied, for example, by the saying 'Enough is as good as a feast'. Alternatively, we could base the social optimum on a standard of *sustainable* productive capacity. Conceived in this way, the social optimum would comprise the highest capability zones that can be ensured sustainably for future generations by the productive capacity of the society, and, likewise, for future generations in other societies.

Finally, I have barely touched upon the philosophical issues surrounding the arguments I have discussed in this chapter. Sufficiency ideas have been debated vigorously since Harry Frankfurt's 1987 article 'Equality as a moral ideal'. Although I believe that the ideas and arguments presented in this chapter stand up well within those debates, this remains to be shown.

References

Arneson, R. (2006) Distributive justice and basic capability equality: 'good enough' is not good enough. In *Capabilities Equality: Basic Issues and Problems*, Kaufman, A. (ed.): 17–43. New York: Routledge.

Axelsen, D. V., and Nielsen, L. (2015) Sufficiency as freedom from duress. *Journal of Political Philosophy*, 23 (4): 406–26.

(2016) Essentially enough. In *What Is Enough? Sufficiency, Justice, and Health*, Fourie, C., and Rid, A. (eds.): 101–18. Oxford: Oxford University Press.

Casal, P. (2007) Why sufficiency is not enough. *Ethics*, 117 (2): 296–326.

Crisp, R. (2003) Equality, priority, and compassion. *Ethics*, 113 (4): 745–63.

Doyal, L., and Gough, I. 1991. *A Theory of Human Need*. London: Palgrave Macmillan.

Drydyk, J. (2012) A capability approach to justice as a virtue. *Ethical Theory and Moral Practice*, 15 (1): 23–38.

(2016) Justice as a virtue: what can we expect of our allies? In *Theorizing Justice: Critical Insights and Future Directions*, edited by Watene, K., and Drydyk, J. (eds.): 95–114. London: Rowman & Littlefield International.

Frankfurt, H. (1987) Equality as a moral ideal. *Ethics*, 98 (1): 21–43.

(2015) *On Inequality*. Princeton, NJ: Princeton University Press.

Freiman, C. (2012) Why poverty matters most: towards a humanitarian theory of social justice. *Utilitas*, 24 (1): 26–40.

Gough, I. (2014) Lists and thresholds: comparing the Doyal–Gough theory of human need with Nussbaum's capabilities approach. In *Capabilities, Gender, Equality: Towards Fundamental Entitlements*, Comim, F., and Nussbaum, M. C. (eds.): 357–81. Cambridge: Cambridge University Press.

(2015) Climate change and sustainable welfare: the centrality of human needs. *Cambridge Journal of Economics*, 39 (5): 1191–214.

Gutwald, R. (2018) Well-being: happiness, desires, goods, and needs. In *Routledge Handbook of Development Ethics*, Drydyk, J., and Keleher, J. (eds.): 55–67. Abingdon: Routledge.

Huseby, R. (2010) Sufficiency: restated and defended. *Journal of Political Philosophy*, 18 (2): 178–97.

Kanschik, P. (2016) Eco-sufficiency and distributive sufficientarianism – friends or foes? *Environmental Values*, 25 (5): 553–71.

Kaufman, A. (2006) A sufficientarian approach? A note. In *Capabilities Equality: Basic Issues and Problems*, Kaufman, A. (ed.): 71–6. New York: Routledge.

Khader, S. J. (2011) *Adaptive Preferences and Women's Empowerment*. Oxford: Oxford University Press.

Lancaster, H. O. 1990. *Expectations of Life: A Study in the Demography, Statistics, and History of World Mortality*. New York: Springer.

Marx, K. (1975 [1844]) Economic and philosophical manuscripts of 1844. In *Karl Marx, Frederick Engels: Collected Works*, vol. 3, *Marx and Engels 1843–1844*: 229–346. New York: International Publishers.

Mulgan, T. (2014) *Ethics for a Broken World: Imagining Philosophy after Catastrophe*. Abingdon: Routledge.

Nielsen, L., and Axelsen, D. V. (2017) Capabilitarian sufficiency: capabilities and social justice. *Journal of Human Development and Capabilities*, 18 (1): 46–59.

Nussbaum, M. C. (2000) *Women and Human Development: The Capabilities Approach*. Cambridge: Cambridge University Press.

(2006) *Frontiers of Justice: Disability, Nationality, Species Membership*. Cambridge, MA: Belknap Press.

(2011) *Creating Capabilities: The Human Development Approach*. Cambridge, MA: Belknap Press.

Princen, T. (2003) Principles for sustainability: from cooperation and efficiency to sufficiency. *Global Environmental Politics*, 3 (1): 33–50.

(2005) *The Logic of Sufficiency*. Cambridge, MA: MIT Press.

Roser, M. (2013) Life expectancy by age in England and Wales, 1700–2013. Our World in Data, May. https://ourworldindata.org/uploads/2013/05/Life-expectancy-by-age-in-the-UK-1700-to-2013.png [accessed 26 April 2019].

Segall, S. (2016) What is the point of sufficiency? *Journal of Applied Philosophy*, 33 (1): 36–52.

Sen, A. K. (1992) *Inequality Reexamined*. Oxford: Oxford University Press.

(1993) Capability and well-being. In *The Quality of Life*, Nussbaum, M. C., and Sen, A. K. (eds.): 30–53. Oxford: Clarendon Press.

(1999) *Development as Freedom*. Oxford: Oxford University Press.

(2000) Social exclusion: concept, application, and scrutiny, Social Development Paper 1. Manila: Office of Environment and Social Development, Asian Development Bank. www.adb.org/sites/default/files/publication/29778/social-exclusion.pdf.

(2009) *The Idea of Justice*. London: Penguin.

Shields, L. (2012) The prospects for sufficientarianism. *Utilitas*, 24 (1): 101–17.

Spengler, L. (2016) Two types of 'enough': sufficiency as minimum and maximum. *Environmental Politics*, 25 (5): 921–40.

Statistics Canada (2015) Life expectancy. 30 November. www150.statcan.gc .ca/n1/pub/89-645-x/2010001/life-expectancy-esperance-vie-eng.htm.

UN General Assembly (1948) Universal Declaration of Human Rights. UNHCR Refworld. www.refworld.org/docid/3ae6b3712c.html.

Young, I. M. (1990) *Justice and the Politics of Difference*. Princeton, NJ: Princeton University Press.

11 Adaptive preferences versus internalization in deprivation
A conceptual comparison between the capability approach and self-determination theory

TADASHI HIRAI

Introduction

There is a growing acceptance of subjective well-being for the assessment of quality of life in the international arena. The *World Happiness Report* has been published annually since 2011 under the auspices of the United Nations, while the International Day of Happiness was established in 2012 in the UN General Assembly. Nonetheless, it has been still viewed with scepticism to the point of alleging no use of it for policy making (see, for example, Stewart, 2014). A major reason for such a negative impression seems to be a belief that personal evaluation of one's own well-being is whimsical, and thus that there is no reliable metrics of this kind.

The assumed lack of reliability of subjective well-being relates to the interpretation of adaptive preferences and internalization processes, which varies widely between disciplines. On the one hand, development theorists regard both as problematic in view of justice, on the assumption that they equally do not reflect the distributive conditions of external goods such as basic material needs; subjective well-being could go up even without satisfying external goods (e.g. Sen, 1987; Nussbaum, 1995). On the other hand, some psychologists distinguish internalization from adaptation and regard only the latter as problematic, on the assumption that internalization cannot be made without external goods while adaptation can be made without them (e.g. Deci and Ryan, 2000). Facing the disparity, this chapter intends to examine conceptually whether adaptive preferences and internalization can be made indistinguishably in deprived conditions, as assumed by development theorists, or whether adaptive preferences can be made while internalization cannot in such conditions, as assumed by some psychologists. This is a fundamental question for the validity of people's subjectivity in policy making. For this examination, this chapter features two approaches: the capability approach (hereafter CA) in development and self-determination theory (hereafter SDT) in psychology.

The CA aims at overcoming injustice in society with a special focus on the capabilities and functionings each person holds. Although it has two versions (a comparative one, by Amartya Sen, and a constitutional one, by Martha Nussbaum), Nussbaum's version has been featured, given that it has a potential to measure subjective well-being more relevant to policy making by specifying some human conditions required for proper valuation (Nussbaum, 1987, 1990, 1992, 1995), unlike Sen's version, which does not specify an objective normative account and consequently views subjective well-being as evidential at best (Sen, 1985a, 1985b, 2008, 2009). In contrast, SDT is an approach to human motivation and personality developed by Edward Deci and Richard Ryan since the late 1970s, and well known in the field of positive psychology. Unlike the conventional psychological approaches, which see motivation as a unitary concept, it makes distinctions between different types of motivation and the consequences of them. Based on numerous empirical studies, it advocates, rather than the satisfaction of simple pleasures or the achievement of any life goals, the satisfaction of basic psychological needs for proper motivation, and thus for policy making when using subjective well-being (Deci and Ryan 2000; Ryan and Deci 2001).

Whereas SDT potentially contributes to the CA in terms of measurement, as argued in the past (Alkire, 2005; Klein, 2014; Vansteenkiste, Ryan and Deci, 2008; Hirai, 2018, 2021), the CA could in turn contribute to SDT in terms of justice if the inseparability is verified between adaptive preferences and internalization in relation to external goods. For this investigation, this chapter starts with a comparative analysis between SDT's basic psychological needs and Nussbaum's central capabilities to confirm the similarity in needs requirement. The next part examines the type of goods required for the need satisfaction and the way of assessing them in both approaches, respectively, and then moves on to the feasibility of justice in internalization vis-à-vis adaptive preferences.

SDT's basic psychological needs and Nussbaum's central capabilities for proper valuation

Both SDT and Nussbaum's theories are normative (see, for example, Ryan and Deci, 2001, and Nussbaum, 2000). They reject the pursuit of simple pleasures and define a good life as the satisfaction of objective needs, which results in a series of more positive outcomes. This should not come as a surprise, given that both follow the Aristotelian conception about the way of living (Ryan, Curren and Deci, 2013; Nussbaum, 1990). Their claim is grounded on the necessity of adjusting the skewed values that prevail in the world and are taken for granted.

Proposal for adjusting skewed values

SDT criticizes the cognitive theories that focus on the achievement of goals regardless of the content of the goals (e.g. Emmons, 1986; Bandura, 1977; Scheier and Carver, 1985). Based on the empirical finding that those who aspire to financial success more than other life goals hold negative well-being in the long run, Kasser and Ryan (1993) demonstrate that certain goals may have harmful consequences for well-being even if they are successfully achieved. More generally, SDT classifies goals into two types in relation to need satisfaction: intrinsic goals (such as affiliation, personal growth and community contribution), which harmonize with growth tendencies natural to humans and thus are closely associated with need satisfaction and enhance well-being; and extrinsic goals (such as wealth, fame and image), which depend on the approval of others or external signs of worth and thus are less likely to satisfy needs and do not enhance well-being (Kasser and Ryan, 1996; Deci and Ryan, 2000). The former correspond to eudaimonia while the latter correspond to hedonia (not the one as a by-product of eudaimonia). In this respect, it is need satisfaction that mediates the relation between the type of goals and the level of well-being (Vansteenkiste, Ryan and Deci, 2008). Although the causal relation here is from goals to need satisfaction, the opposite causal relation, namely from need satisfaction to goals, is also valid. On the one hand, the satisfaction of needs promotes intrinsic goals through proper motivation and valuation cultivated by need satisfaction, leading to more well-being; on the other hand, the frustration of needs is associated with stronger extrinsic goals through skewed motivation and valuation, leading to less well-being (Deci and Ryan, 2000). Therefore, the motivation and valuation that underlie goals ought to be accompanied by need satisfaction, and vice versa, to pursue eudaimonia.

Similarly, Nussbaum claims the satisfaction of human conditions is necessary to adjust skewed values ('false beliefs', in her words: Nussbaum, 2001) for proper valuation. In this regard, she accuses the liberals of laissez-faire policies that guarantee freedom of choice but not its quality. What is required, she argues, is a governmental intervention 'to make people really capable of choosing' (Nussbaum, 1990: 240). This can be directly related to the quality of democratic procedures, to the extent that the concept of reasonableness is decided by majority vote, namely the aggregation of subjective preferences. For her, reasonableness should be grounded by the human good or human needs to function well (Nussbaum, 1992, 1995). For this reason, she criticizes not only liberals, such as Immanuel Kant and John Rawls, but also Sen, for prioritizing the moral realm over the natural realm and thus not specifying an objective normative account based on needs, even though she shares many parts with him otherwise in the CA:

[I]t seems to me that the capability approach will exhibit similar deficiencies, unless we can specify an objective valuational procedure that will have the power to criticize the evaluations of functionings that are actually made by people whose upbringing has been hedged round with discrimination and inequity. Sen seems on the whole to think that we remove the problem by moving from the utilitarian emphasis on desire to his own approach's emphasis on the valuation of capabilities. But the valuational procedure that is involved in capability selection seems to me, at least without further description, to be no more uncorruptible than desire itself is. (Nussbaum, 1987: 39)

Valuation is, for her, much more intertwined with desires than Sen supposes. Indeed, she stresses the unavoidable link between the two, insofar as valuation cannot dispense with desires. Referring to Aristotle, she points out that many people are badly educated and want the wrong things and the wrong amount, but that it is also true of a good lawgiver who is not totally independent of human desire (Nussbaum, 1987). What is important is to make desires and valuation work naturally/properly and to see 'what people *would* desire if their education and knowledge of alternatives were above the threshold of what is required for practical reason and choice' (Nussbaum, 1990: 245, emphasis in original) or 'what the people involved are actually able ... to desire' (213). Hence desires as well as valuation need to be adjusted by the satisfaction of central capabilities, on the grounds that they are often not qualified for eudaimonia.

Both SDT and Nussbaum's CA do not accept all types of valuation, precisely because they are subject to individual upbringing, present circumstances and future perspective. In many cases people are unaware of injustice in their valuation. Whereas one might take it for granted that being battered is a precondition for being a reasonable wife, another might take it for granted that having champagne is a precondition for a reasonable dinner. Indeed it is skewed values that form unjustifiable adaptive preferences. To tackle them, SDT and Nussbaum's CA propose a list of human needs, which comes next.

Basic psychological needs and central capabilities

Both SDT and Nussbaum's CA require the concept of human needs (i.e. the objective criteria most relevant to good human life) to adjust skewed values. The next argument is about the coverage of needs. Considering that they pursue the same goal, namely Aristotle's eudaimonia, the needs they demand should be equivalent.

On the one hand, SDT specifies three psychological needs intrinsically worthwhile to all humans: autonomy, competence and relatedness. The need for autonomy is to feel volitional and fully endorse one's actions (Deci and Ryan, 1985); the need for competence is to feel effective in one's interactions with the social and physical environments (Deci, 1975); and the need for relatedness is to care for and feel cared for by others (Ryan, 1995). The theory claims that people thrive only if these needs are fulfilled. To put it another way, regardless of individual explicit values for these needs, the satisfaction or frustration of them predicts one's well-being (Ryan, Curren and Deci, 2013). It implies that need satisfaction should come prior to valuation to lead it towards eudaimonia. Given the universality of the basic psychological needs, it advocates that various goals and values in diverse societies be justified only if their aspirations and achievements accompany the satisfaction of these needs (Deci and Ryan, 2000).

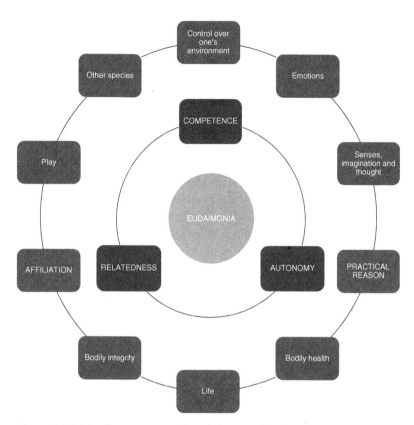

Figure 11.1 Nussbaum's central capabilities and SDT's basic psychological needs

On the other hand, Nussbaum specifies central capabilities for individuals to flourish. More faithful to the demarcation of virtues by Aristotle, she lists ten spheres of human experience (i.e. capabilities) as the most important in terms of which human life is defined (Nussbaum, 1993, 1995). They are represented in Figure 11.1, together with the correspondence with SDT's basic psychological needs.

At the first glance, Nussbaum's central capabilities seem not closely connected to SDT's basic psychological needs. But now it is important to remember that she gives a special role to practical reason and affiliation in their architectonic feature so as to make the other capabilities truly human. While the other capabilities can be shared by all animals, it is practical reason and affiliation that make us do everything in a human way, such that everything is planned and organized by practical reason as well as done with and to others (Nussbaum, 1990, 1992). More concretely, practical reason is defined as 'being able to form a conception of the good and to engage in critical reflection about the planning of one's life' and affiliation as 'being able to live with and toward others' and 'having the social bases of self-respect and nonhumiliation' (2011: 34). They correspond closely to autonomy (i.e. to feel volitional and fully endorse one's action) and relatedness (to care for and feel cared for by others) in SDT, respectively. Moreover, competence in SDT (to feel effective in one's interactions with the social and physical environments) corresponds closely to control over environments, defined as 'being able to participate effectively in political choices that govern one's life' and 'being able to hold property ... and having property rights on an equal basis with others' (34), but it is also relevant to all the capabilities, to the extent that capabilities – not only combined ones but also internal ones – demand how one interacts with the social and physical environments rather than the conditions of these environments per se (i.e. what one is actually able to do and to be).

Necessity of external goods

As shown so far, both SDT and Nussbaum's CA claim the necessity of adjusting values towards eudaimonia by satisfying human needs. SDT's autonomy and relatedness correspond closely to Nussbaum's practical reason and affiliation (which are regarded as architectonic), and SDT's competence corresponds closely to Nussbaum's control over environment but also relates to the other capabilities. Both SDT's basic psychological needs and Nussbaum's central capabilities are specified *objectively* for their universal applicability to all humans.

How about their way of assessment? On the one hand, SDT makes a *subjective* assessment, in that the needs it specifies are psychological. On the other hand, CA makes not only a *subjective* assessment, in that it takes seriously individual values on their own living, but also an *objective* assessment, in that it cares about their actual beings and doings precisely to tackle adaptive preferences formed in unjustified circumstances. Simply put, the basic psychological needs in SDT are identified objectively and assessed subjectively; the central capabilities in the CA are identified objectively and assessed objectively as well as subjectively. The difference in assessment becomes salient in the case of external goods (social and material conditions).

The importance of external goods is acknowledged by Aristotle, which is obvious from the following line: '[H]e (one) is happy who is active in accordance with complete virtue and is sufficiently equipped with external goods' (Aristotle, 1101a13–15, brackets added). He further explains the reason: '[T]he happy man needs (in addition to the goods of the soul) the goods of the body and external goods, i.e. those of fortune, namely, in order that he may not be impeded' (Aristotle, 1153b16–18, brackets added). In other words, external goods are required to make us engage in activity without hindrance, which leads to his concept of eudaimonia.

Indeed, the very requirement of external goods differentiates Aristotle from the Stoics. On the one hand, the Stoics insist that only virtue is to be good, while other things are to be indifferent, and thus focus on the goods of the soul only (Annas, 1996). On the other hand, Aristotle regards eudaimonia as distinct from virtue, to the extent that eudaimonia requires freedom from impediment due to the lack of external goods while virtue does not (Engstrom, 1996). The concept of eudaimonia is therefore more comprehensive than that of virtue by including not only the goods of soul but also external goods, including the goods of the body. Given its comprehensiveness, eudaimonia is seen as the end of virtue: '[V]irtue itself has eudaimonia as its end' (Engstrom, 1996: 132). This also leads to the difference in the quality of the goods of the soul between the Stoics and Aristotle: while the Stoics demand the goods of the soul regardless of the type of motivation, Aristotle demands them to be accompanied by intrinsic motivation (proper motivation for eudaimonia). Indeed, they can be called 'internal goods', to differentiate from the goods of the soul. Internal goods can be satisfied together with the satisfaction of external goods, whereas the goods of the soul do not necessarily require them. The distinction between Aristotle and the Stoics on external goods and their relation to SDT and Nussbaum's CA is summarized in Figure 11.2.

The conventional psychological approaches, such as the cognitive theories, follow the Stoics, because they aim at the realization of the inner self by focusing on the goods of the soul without caring about external goods. In contrast, Nussbaum follows Aristotle faithfully by acknowledging the significance of external goods, together with the goods of the soul, in the process of valuation; as she states: '[W]e need

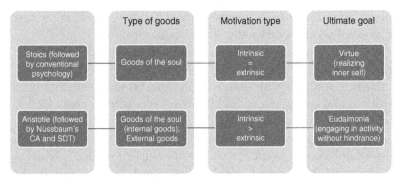

Figure 11.2 Aristotle and the Stoics on external goods

to worry, as well, about the external conditions in which people live' (Nussbaum, 1987: 23). Only by securing external goods can the goods of the soul turn into internal goods for eudaimonia. This is why she attacks the liberals, who simply support choice and autonomy without any such specific criteria. For her, autonomous action is achieved in a proper manner only if it is grounded by the conditions required to be human. In her words, 'If one cares about autonomy, then one must care about the rest of the form of life that supports it and the material conditions that enable one to live that form of life' (1995: 95). Human conditions, including external goods, thus need to be secured to make choice and autonomy right.

How are external goods treated in SDT? It would plainly be a mistake to jump to the conclusion that it ignores them, on the grounds that it focuses on the psychological aspect of human needs. SDT does surely care about external goods, to the extent that those who experience impediment in action caused by the lack of external goods would have difficulty in satisfying their psychological needs. In other words, by differentiating the type of motivation by the degree of the psychological need satisfaction, SDT takes it for granted that external goods are satisfied when the psychological needs are satisfied. In this view, SDT differs from the Stoics (followed typically by the conventional psychological approaches) and, rather, follows Aristotle.

Both Nussbaum's CA and SDT give importance to external goods. A possible coverage of external goods within the goods of the soul in SDT comes from its specification of psychological needs as a universal norm for a good living, unlike the conventional psychological approaches, whose norm is based on individuals. By satisfying the basic psychological needs, it assumes that external goods are also satisfied because the latter are required for the former. In this sense, SDT demands not the goods of the soul per se but internal goods (the goods of the soul equipped with external goods) for eudaimonia. However, sharing a universal norm, Nussbaum's CA recognizes the importance of external goods independently from internal goods, on the assumption that external conditions could not be reflected simply by the satisfaction of psychological needs even if they are specified by a universal norm. This leads to the difference in their way of assessment: SDT lets individuals make the decision regardless of the type of goods; the CA lets policy makers or the public make the decision on the satisfaction of external goods in view of justice prior to letting individuals make the decision on the goods of the soul.

Internalization and justice

Internalization is a core concept of SDT. It is defined as 'an active, natural process in which individuals attempt to transform socially sanctioned mores or requests into personally endorsed values and self-regulations' (Deci and Ryan, 2000: 235–6). Simply put, it is a process of taking in a value or regulation that has been socially formed. As shown in the previous section, SDT, unlike the cognitive theories (which see motivation as a unitary concept), distinguishes motivation behind life goals between intrinsic and extrinsic. By employing the concept of internalization, SDT goes further to examine the causality of extrinsic motivation in order to reflect the reality that we often need to follow extrinsic motivation to live as social agents. For example, Ryan and Deci (2000) provide an example as an illustration in terms of students' learning: on the one hand, there are the students who do their homework because they personally grasp its value for their chosen career, while, on the other, there are the students who do the work only because they are adhering to what their parents tell them to do. Both cases involve extrinsic motivation rather than intrinsic motivation, yet the former case of extrinsic motivation entails personal endorsement and a feeling of choice, whereas the latter involves compliance with external regulation. Both represent intentional behaviour, but they vary in the level of autonomy, or so-called 'relative autonomy' (Ryan and Connell, 1989).

In order to reflect the different level of autonomy, SDT formulates a more differentiated conception of extrinsic motivation by reclassifying it into autonomous vis-à-vis controlled depending on the perceived locus of causality (Deci and Ryan, 2000; Ryan and Deci, 2000). In this view, internalization is seen as a process that allows us to change the perceived locus of causality from external (i.e. more controlled) to internal (i.e. more autonomous). It is a positive thing for psychological need satisfaction and eudaimonia. This point is summarized in the following lines:

[T]o the extent that adopting values and behaviors that are manifest in the social world garners acceptance by the social world and permits efficacious functioning in it, people will be inclined to *internalize* the values and behavioral regulations. To the extent that they are able to experience supports for autonomy, they will be more likely to actively integrate the values and regulations, and thus to volitionally or authentically carry out the behaviors they inspire. (Deci and Ryan, 2000: 239, emphasis added)

In contrast, taking seriously the conditions of the deprived of any kind, the CA does not see internalization as necessarily positive, because it pays attention solely to individual perceptions and thus does not reflect the public reason required to tackle social injustice. This concern is expressed in the following lines by both Sen and Nussbaum:

A person who has had a life of misfortune, with very little opportunities, and rather little hope, may be more easily reconciled to deprivations than others reared in more fortunate and affluent circumstances. The metric of happiness may, therefore, distort the extent of deprivation, in a specific and biased way. (Sen, 1987: 45–6)

As Sen argues, they [deprived women in India] may have *fully internalized* the ideas behind the traditional system of discrimination, and may view their deprivation as 'natural'. (Nussbaum, 1995: 91, emphasis added)

Hence, they argue that internalization cannot be justified at face value, to the extent that it is based on values or regulations forged socially regardless of the justice and fairness underlying their circumstances. This phenomenon of internalization with negative implication is regarded in the CA as equivalent to 'adaptive preferences', which represent 'the adjustment of wants to possibilities – not the deliberate adaptation favoured by character planners, but a causal process occurring non-consciously ... to reduce the tension or frustration that one feels in having wants that one cannot possibly satisfy' (Elster, 1983: 25).

The crux of the matter is whether full internalization can be really made *in externally deprived conditions*, as Sen and Nussbaum describe. SDT assumes that adaptive preferences can but full internalization cannot, because psychological needs will not be fulfilled in such conditions, which in turn will not allow extrinsic motivation to be internalized. Indeed, it clearly distinguishes internalization from adaptation, which is self-defeating and associated with needs being thwarted and ill-being, although it helps protect people from the inner hurts in hostile circumstances (Deci and Ryan, 2000). By reclassifying the extrinsic motivation behind valuation and regulation socially formed depending on the perceived locus of causality, SDT assumes internalization (accompanied with autonomous causality) to lead to positive outcomes and adaptation (accompanied with controlled causality) to negative outcomes; in contrast, the CA regards internalization as not necessarily positive precisely because a judgement on the distributive conditions of external goods can be affected by valuation and regulation socially formed regardless of justice and fairness, and so cannot be separated from adaptation, and consequently proposes the necessity of making a different assessment depending on the type of goods.

However, it remains uncertain whether those who are externally deprived cannot satisfy all the psychological needs for internalization. The reasons for the uncertainty are twofold. First, it is because no empirical study has been carried out in SDT specifically for those who are in externally deprived conditions. Although a number of empirical studies around the world have been carried out, typically they target the externally non-deprived, such as college students and business people. A possible exception would be research into the intervention for motivating a cessation of smoking in a sample with lower incomes in the United States (William et al., 2006). Even so, the sample could not be regarded as impoverished, given that the average income was just about $10,000 below the national average. More importantly, many non-whites in the sample dropped out through the course of the research, even though they are likely to be more impoverished in American societies.

Another reason for the possibility of internalization in external deprivation is, as implied at the end of the previous section, that

SDT assesses people's living solely through the lens of perceived individual psychological needs. But cannot competence of any kind be satisfied by limiting the values and behaviours within their capacity? Cannot relatedness be satisfied by their following someone they trust or respect (e.g. parents, teachers, patriarchs) who would accept unfair customs embedded in their society? Cannot autonomy be satisfied by forming (internalizing) their values and behaviours so as to harmonize their traditions and customs? All the possibilities would be valid, to the extent that each psychological need could transform the perceived locus of causality from external to internal, which results, through personal endorsement and a feeling of choice rather than through compliance with external regulation, in internalizing the values and regulations formed in circumstances in which external goods are distributed unfairly. If so, this would leave open the possibility of not only adapting but also internalizing such an unfortunate status quo as a norm for the formulation of one's own values and regulations. Indeed, *The Voices of the Poor* (World Bank, 2000) reports revealing evidence about the poor, who happily sacrifice what few external goods they have to maintain social solidarity, on the one hand, and to avoid humiliation, loss of honour and psychological distress, on the other. The possibility would be even higher if they did not acknowledge conditions other than their own.

Going back to the requirement of external goods, a fundamental question is: isn't it possible that people's values are formed depending on the availability of external goods, which could be distributed unfairly? This point is strongly related to justice, which matters for Aristotle in view of eudaimonia: 'Those who say that the victim on the rack or the man who falls into great misfortunes is happy if he is good are … talking non-sense' (Aristotle, 1153b19–21). This sounds like a direct attack against the Stoics, as Engstrom (1996) points out. SDT would not judge such a person as good, on the assumption that one should not satisfy psychological needs in such conditions. This means that it can detect the lack of external goods only if one suffers from impediment in action. To put it another way, unless one is conscious of being impeded, internalization could be possible even in deprivation. Then, to what extent can injustice be reflected by failing in internalization? In this view, it is worthwhile to investigate the extent to which the externally deprived could satisfy their psychological needs and internalize their values formed in such circumstances.

If SDT can detect such conditions as adaptive and distinguish them from being internalized, it would be self-sufficient; otherwise, external goods should be included as an independent requirement and assessed objectively from the perspective of justice in addition to being assessed subjectively, as justice is an indispensable part of eudaimonia. This would become a possible contribution of the CA to SDT.

Conclusions

Following Aristotle, both SDT and Nussbaum's CA leave room for the possibility of revision in their exploration of the assessment of the quality of life in the pursuit of eudaimonia. This seems like an invitation to this research. Whereas Nussbaum's CA would benefit from SDT in the reflection of relative autonomy, SDT would benefit from the CA in the expansion of the sample coverage from the non-deprived to the deprived in terms of external goods. To delve into the latter, it would be meaningful to reconsider the way of assessing goods in search for an outline sketch more relevant to eudaimonia, particularly for the externally deprived sample, who would be at risk of internalizing their values and regulations in unjustified circumstances.

This chapter started with a common claim between SDT and Nussbaum's CA on the necessity of adjusting skewed values by a universal norm required for eudaimonia (i.e. basic psychological needs and central capabilities, respectively). After examining the goods required for eudaimonia and the way of assessing them, a fundamental question was proposed: whether full internalization can be made in externally deprived conditions, as the CA assumes, or whether it cannot be made in such conditions because the lack of external goods can be detected through the lens of the psychological needs dissatisfaction, as SDT assumes? The CA's assumption derives from the understanding that internalization is subject to values forged socially and is identified with adaptive preferences, while SDT's assumption derives from the understanding that psychological needs should not be fulfilled in such conditions, and so are distinct from adaptation. Now, the SDT's assumption about the impossibility of internalization in external deprivation remains uncertain, not only because no empirical research has been made for the corresponding sample but also because people's living has been assessed subjectively regardless of the type of goods, which would leave open the possibility of internalizing the values and practices formed in unjustified conditions. In turn, the CA's assumption about the possibility of internalization in such conditions can be applied typically to the conventional psychological approaches but not directly to SDT, to the extent that SDT has – unlike any other theories and approaches, including the CA – provided a more differentiated approach to motivation (extrinsic motivation in particular), among which internalization has been defined in a more specific and nuanced manner. With these points in mind, there is a need to examine the degree to which the externally deprived could satisfy psychological needs and internalize their values formed in unjustified circumstances. After all, the deprived conditions would be better evaluated both internally and externally, not only because both are required in pursuit of eudaimonia but also because external goods could be sacrificed even if deprived in exchange for psychological need satisfaction (as in the case of *The Voices of the Poor* presented at the end of the section 'Internalization and justice', who happily sacrifice what few external goods they have so as to maintain community relations), at least until the relation between them is clarified enough to rely on one of them.

References

Alkire, S. (2005) Subjective quantitative studies of human agency. *Social Indicators Research*, 74 (1): 217–60.

Annas, J. (1996) Aristotle and Kant on morality and practical reasoning. In *Aristotle, Kant, and the Stoics: Rethinking Happiness and Duty*, Engstrom, S. P., and Whiting, J. (eds.): 237–58. Cambridge: Cambridge University Press.

Aristotle (2009 [*c*. 340 BC]) *The Nicomachean Ethics*, Ross, D. (trans.). Oxford: Oxford University Press.

Bandura, A. (1977) Self-efficacy: toward a unifying theory of behavioral change. *Psychological Review*, 84 (2): 191–215.

Deci, E. L. (1975) *Intrinsic Motivation*. New York: Plenum Publishing.

Deci, E. L., and Ryan, R. M. (1985) *Intrinsic Motivation and Self-Determination in Human Behavior*. New York: Plenum Publishing.

(2000) The 'what' and 'why' of goal pursuits: human needs and the self-determination of behavior. *Psychological Inquiry*, 11 (4): 227–68.

Elster, J. (1983) *Sour Grapes: Studies in the Subversion of Rationality*. Cambridge: Cambridge University Press.

Emmons, R. A. (1986) Personal strivings: an approach to personality and subjective well-being. *Journal of Personality and Social Psychology*, 51 (5): 1058–68.

Engstrom, S. P. (1996) Happiness and the highest good in Aristotle and Kant. In *Aristotle, Kant, and the Stoics: Rethinking Happiness and Duty*, Engstrom, S. P., and Whiting, J. (eds.): 102–38. Cambridge: Cambridge University Press.

Hirai, T. (2018) For a happy human development. In *New Frontiers of the Capability Approach*, Comim, F., Fennell, S., and Anand, P. B. (eds.): 384–410. Cambridge: Cambridge University Press.

(2021) Measuring capabilities: taking people's values seriously. *World Development*, 148. DOI: 10.1016/j.worlddev.2021.105657.

Kasser, T., and Ryan, R. M. (1993) A dark side of the American dream: correlates of financial success as a central life aspiration. *Journal of Personality and Social Psychology*, 65 (2): 410–22.

(1996) Further examining the American dream: differential correlates of intrinsic and extrinsic goals. *Personality and Social Psychology Bulletin*, 22 (3): 280–7.

Klein, E. (2014) Psychological agency: evidence from urban fringe of Bamako. *World Development*, 64: 642–53.

Nussbaum, M. C. (1987) Nature, function and capability: Aristotle on political distribution, Working Paper 31. Tokyo: World Institute for Development Economics Research, United Nations University.

(1990) Aristotelian social democracy. In *Liberalism and the Good*, Douglass, R. B., Mara, G. M., and Richardson, H. S. (eds.): 203–52. New York: Routledge.

(1992) Human functioning and social justice. *Political Theory*, 20 (2): 202–46.

(1993) Non-relative virtues: an Aristotelian approach. In *The Quality of Life*, Nussbaum, M. C., and Sen, A. K. (eds.): 242–69. Oxford: Clarendon Press.

(1995) Human capabilities, female human beings. In *Women, Culture, and Development: A Study of Human Capabilities*, Nussbaum, M. C., and Glover, J. (eds.): 61–104. Oxford: Oxford University Press.

(2000) *Women and Human Development: The Capabilities Approach*. Cambridge: Cambridge University Press.

(2001) *Upheavals of Thought: The Intelligence of Emotions*. Cambridge: Cambridge University Press.

(2011) *Creating Capabilities: The Human Development Approach*. Cambridge, MA: Belknap Press.

Ryan, R. M. (1995) Psychological needs and the facilitation of integrative processes. *Journal of Personality*, 63 (3): 397–427.

Ryan, R. M., and Connell, J. P. (1989) Perceived locus of causality and internalization: examining reasons for acting in two domains. *Journal of Personality and Social Psychology*, 57 (5): 749–61.

Ryan, R. M., and Deci, E. L. (2000) Self-determination theory and the facilitation of intrinsic motivation, social development, and well-being. *American Psychologist*, 55 (1): 68–78.

(2001) On happiness and human potentials: a review of research on hedonic and eudaimonic well-being. *Annual Review of Psychology*, 52: 141–66.

Ryan, R. M., Curren, R. R., and Deci, E. L. (2013) What humans need: flourishing in Aristotelian philosophy and self-determination theory. In *The Best within Us: Positive Psychology Perspectives on Eudaimonic Functioning*, Waterman, A. A. (ed.): 57–75. Washington, DC: American Psychological Association.

Scheier, M., and Carver, C. (1985) Optimism, coping and health: assessment and implications of generalized outcome expectancies. *Health Psychology*, 4 (3): 219–47.

Sen, A. K. (1985a) *Commodities and Capabilities*. Amsterdam: North-Holland.

(1985b) Well-being, agency and freedom: the Dewey lectures 1984. *Journal of Philosophy*, 82 (4): 169–221.

(1987) *On Ethics and Economics*. Oxford: Blackwell.

(2008) The economics of happiness and capability. In *Capabilities and Happiness*, Bruni, L., Comim, F., and Pugno, M. (eds.): 16–27. Oxford: Oxford University Press.

(2009) *The Idea of Justice*. London: Penguin.

Stewart, F. (2014) Against happiness: a critical appraisal of the use of measures of happiness for evaluating progress in development. *Journal of Human Development and Capabilities*, 15 (4): 293–307.

Vansteenkiste, M., Ryan, R. M., and Deci, E. L. (2008) Self-determination theory and the explanatory role of psychological needs in human well-being. In *Capabilities and Happiness*, Bruni, L., Comim, F., and Pugno, M. (eds.): 187–223. Oxford: Oxford University Press.

William, G. C., McGregor, H. A., Sharp, D., Levesque, C., Kouides, R. W., Ryan, R. M., and Deci, E. L. (2006) Testing a self-determination theory intervention for motivating tobacco cessation: supporting autonomy and competence in a clinical trial. *Health Psychology*, 25 (1): 91–101.

World Bank (2000) *The Voices of the Poor: Can Anyone Hear Us?* New York: Oxford University Press.

12 | Enriching agency in the capability approach through social theory contributions

INA CONRADIE

Introduction

In this chapter I propose that there are many points of conceptual convergence between the capability approach and social theory debates, and that the capability approach could be significantly enriched by this knowledge, particularly concerning agency. It covers a vast range of scholars and ideas, of course, and this proposal could only be a very brief and very partial introduction to the subject. With reference to the capability approach, I shall concentrate on the work of Amartya Sen, and will also briefly discuss the views of Martha Nussbaum on capabilities and agency.

Although Sen did not theorize agency in the same extensive way he conceptualized other aspects of the capability approach, he emphasized it in many of his writings. He states: 'There is a deep complementarity between individual agency and social arrangements. It is important to give simultaneous recognition to the centrality of individual freedom and to the force of social influences on the extent and reach of individual freedom' (Sen, 1999: xii). This complementarity in particular is the conceptual area where social theory could make a contribution to the capability approach. From the outset the discipline of sociology developed around this exact question: how does social action – that is, individual action in a social context – take place? Based on his investigations into this question, Talcott Parsons developed a conceptual frame he called the 'unit act' (Parsons, 1937). Although Parsons was widely critiqued for various aspects of his own theoretical positions, this framework became the subject of one of the central debates within the discipline, and the work of Anthony Giddens, Margaret Archer and Jürgen Habermas (as well as that of many other social theorists) on agency and social structure can be seen as direct or indirect dialogues with the Parsonian framework (Joas and Knöbl, 2009).

It is generally accepted that the capability approach is a multidisciplinary approach that brings together many different theoretical traditions, although it originated in the disciplines of economics and philosophy. A number of scholars have commented on the possibility of a more substantial link between social theory and the capability approach, particularly on the theorization of structure and agency (Zimmerman, 2006; Gangas, 2016; see also Joas, 1996).[1] An 'enriched' view of agency might be best suited to qualitative capability studies with the potential to undertake a rich agency analysis, but this knowledge could possibly also be applicable to other capability analyses. Shaffer (2013) points out that some excellent studies do quantitative research to obtain an overview of a situation, and then qualitative research with a small and representative sample from the first cohort, to understand the trends better.

I start by introducing a research programme I was involved in, which illustrates some of the problems and considerations associated with how to interpret an investigation into agency and capabilities. Then I summarize the main positions on agency in the capability approach, without undertaking a comprehensive review of the topic. The contributions of a number of prominent social theorists on agency and structure are discussed, followed by suggestions of how some of these concepts can be integrated into a capability theory of agency. I then return to the case study and attempt to use some of the conceptual constructs in an agency analysis.

An empirical question

Between 2006 and 2013 I was involved in a research programme in Khayelitsha, near Cape Town, where about 50 women were assisted in achieving one central aspiration that they could choose to realize for themselves (Conradie, 2013; Conradie and Robeyns, 2013). In the course of this qualitative action research process I was compelled to examine my own assumptions on what agency is and on what agency freedom means in a severely constrained social context. Although the women's initial formulation of a key aspiration involved different

---

[1] A special edition of the journal *Critical Sociology* (2018, volume 44, number 6) was dedicated to examining different ways in which the capability approach could enrich and extend aspects of critical theory (Bonvin, De Munck and Zimmerman, 2018).

personal goals, such as furthering their studies, erecting a gravestone for a relative, going to the rural area to enact a traditional ceremony or buying new furniture, when they had to finally make a choice they all chose to start a small business. The area in which they live, Site C in Khayelitsha, is deeply impoverished. The vast majority of the women in this group were born in the rural Eastern Cape, were isiXhosa-speaking and came to Cape Town as the first generation of their families to search for better opportunities. They were all finding it hard to secure a point of entry into the modern economy of Cape Town, and, on reflection, they realized that a regular income would be instrumental in achieving their other aspirations.

It is important to know something about the nature of life in a 'township' such as Khayelitsha, in order to be able to get a basic understanding of the nature of the socio-economic exclusion that is prevalent in South Africa. About one-quarter of the South African population lives in such corridor cities, designed under apartheid to bring workers close to industrial complexes, while not allowing them to live in the towns or cities (Penneger and Godehart, 2007). Even after apartheid most of the urban poor still live in townships, some in brick houses and many in tin shacks. Not all homes have toilets or running water, electricity is often bought from one's neighbour, transport is expensive and crime is ever-present. Services are very basic and service delivery is unreliable, and the extensive networks that characterize the rest of the country's economy are usually absent in the township, although a rich variety of other kinds of networks exist. Many South Africans lack the skills to work in the sophisticated modern economy, and are caught in a poverty trap characterized by socio-economic exclusion (Adato, Carter and May, 2006).[2] The formal employment rates in townships are therefore often very low.

The women in our research project selected the type of businesses they wanted to have, and each woman selected to do either cooking, sewing, hairdressing or health care work for a living. They all participated in the training we organized, and gradually started to set up collective and individual businesses. When they reflected on their progress in 2010, there were 25 active members. Of this group, 23 had gained new functionings that they considered significant, such as

---

[2] The socio-economic exclusion of a large part of society is arguably the largest and most serious socio-political problem facing South Africa.

new skills, understanding and financial gain. Some of the group members exhibited a slow upward mobility, and four of the women were able to send some of their children to a tertiary institution for a post-school qualification.[3] Four women got and then again lost a job, due to circumstances beyond their control, but on the whole the group was better off than before. Nevertheless, none of them had permanently gained a sustainable income for their households, which was the goal they had in mind in starting their businesses. This led me back to the question as to why economic improvement was difficult under the conditions the women face. Are the reasons located in the social and institutional realm, in the women's agency or in the ways these two dimensions work together? I return to these questions later.

Agency and social arrangements in the capability approach

There have been a number of efforts to conceptualize agency in the capability approach. In this section I attempt to show how Sen and Nussbaum developed the concept, and how a number of other scholars extended this.

When a number of 'new disciplines' emerged from philosophy in the late nineteenth century, some argue that economics became increasingly utilitarian while sociology took on aspects of social and individual voluntarism (Wallerstein, 2004). The entrenchment of utilitarianism was partly facilitated by means of the theory of *marginal utility*, which was formulated simultaneously by William Jevons in England and by Carl Menger and Léon Walras on the continent. Value would now be assessed by analysing individual preferences and resources, and there would be fewer grounds for a social critique and for state intervention in the market (Joas, 1996: 36–7). Subsequently Paul Samuelson proposed the theory of *revealed preferences* in 1938, which strengthened the prominence of rational choice theory, in which agency is even further excluded (Alkire and Deneulin, 2000). This is the background against which Sen formulated the capability approach, which includes a prominent role for agency (Sen, 2002: 123–4).

From Sen's first formulation of the capability approach, agency was part of the theory he developed. In a 1977 paper, as he was

---

[3] There is considerable financial support from the South African national government for tertiary education for disadvantaged students.

conceptualizing the approach,[4] he set out to find a solution to the problems of self-interest and utility that would fit into the terms of the traditional debate, and therefore the discipline of economics, and yet break new ground. To achieve this purpose he introduced the notion of non-self-interested agency into the discussion in two different forms: *sympathy*, in which the concern for others directly affects one's own welfare, as in the case of feeling deeply upset by torture; and *commitment*, when one is not personally affected by the problem, but feels strongly enough to take action to put a stop to it. Sympathy would be more self-interested, as a change in the situation would immediately affect the person's own welfare. In the case of a commitment, the person could experience a lower level of anticipated personal welfare than would have been the case if he or she had decided not to act from a sense of commitment, due to the demands of the commitment (Sen, 1977: 326–30; 1987). Sen's introduction of the terms *sympathy* and *commitment* therefore introduce a first breach in the wall of traditional arguments in economics about agency being self-interested only.

The next phase in the evolution of the concept of agency in the capability approach came with the introduction of the distinction between well-being and agency (Sen, 1985; Crocker and Robeyns, 2010). Not all human activities are aimed at maximizing well-being, and agency is an important second consideration, expressing notions of 'autonomy' and 'personal liberty' (Sen, 1985: 186). This use of both the terms 'well-being' and 'agency' as informational sources does not imply that they are unrelated; they are almost inevitably deeply related: 'The person's actual *use* of her well-being freedom will depend *inter alia* on her agency objectives (since these will influence her actual choices)' (Sen, 1992: 72, emphasis in original). However, well-being and agency need to be distinguished (1985: 187). Agency manifests as the ability and autonomy to select those capabilities that one values, and to perform the activities required to turn those valued goals into actual beings and doings. Well-being freedom would then be the opportunity for beings and doings, and agency freedom would be the opportunity for autonomy, connected to values and goals: 'A person's "agency freedom" refers to what the person is free to do and achieve in pursuit of whatever goals or values he or she regards as important. A person's agency

---

[4] Meeks (2018) points out that Sen's conceptualization of the capability approach matured over a long period, dating from the mid-1950s to the 1970s.

aspect cannot be understood without taking note of his or her aims, objectives, allegiances, obligations, and – in a broad sense – the person's conception of the good' (Sen, 1985: 203). Agency freedom is less specific than well-being freedom, as it is generally not associated with one specific type of goal. It relies instead on the judgement of a responsible agent, in a well-considered, reflective assessment of the situation, which also includes the element of responsibility (203–4). If the assessment of the individual therefore shifts from checking the 'well-ness' of the person to checking *how well* he or she had pursued the objectives he or she had previously decided on in a reasoned, evaluative process, the evaluation is an assessment of *agency achievement* rather than of well-being achievement (Sen, 1984: 276). The 'How well?' question contains sub-components of motivation and ability or skill, which should therefore be considered in the assessment of agency. In summary: 'The well-being aspect of a person is important in assessing a person's *advantage*, whereas the agency aspect is important in assessing what a person can do in line with his or her conception of *the good*. The ability to do more good need not be to the person's advantage' (Sen, 1985: 206, emphasis in original). Sen therefore emphasizes a normative account of agency.

Another important dynamic in this regard is the question as to whether freedom relates to power or to control, which are two constituting elements of the idea of freedom. The element of power, or *effective power*, indicates whether a person is free to exercise a choice: whether his or her choices will be respected and whether the related things will happen. Whether he or she has *procedural control* asks whether he or she is actively engaged in choosing and executing the decision. For this consideration, it does not matter whether the goal is achieved or not. Procedural control is often seen as the main consideration in relation to autonomy of choice, but effective power can be seen as equally important (Sen, 1985: 208–11). By including the notion of power in the definition of agency, Sen ensures a layered and critical analysis of agency and action.

Importantly, in Sen's version of the approach, the opportunity aspect and the process aspect of freedom together constitute capability or freedom (Sen, 1999: 17). The opportunity aspect refers to real opportunities, our actual capability to achieve new functionings. The process aspect deals with the person's autonomy, the procedure of making a free choice, therefore with engaging one's agency without interference.[5] Sen refers to this freedom from interference as a *negative freedom* – 'the absence of encroaching activities' (508). He consequently links opportunities and agency conceptually.

Sen's view on agency is, therefore, that it refers to the individual who 'acts and brings about change, and whose achievements can be judged in terms of her own values and objectives, whether or not we assess them in terms of some external criteria as well' (1999: 19). This stands central, but '[i]t is important to give simultaneous recognition to the centrality of individual freedom *and* to the force of social influences on the extent and reach of individual freedom' (xii, emphasis in original). What Sen does not explore, beyond the above, is *how* that interconnectedness can be conceptualized. This is what we are exploring here.

Martha Nussbaum's ideas on agency differ from those of Sen. She states that it is difficult to compare her framework with that of Sen, 'since mine is a political conception and not a comprehensive conception of both well-being and agency' (Nussbaum, 2011: 200). She distinguishes between *basic capabilities*, 'the innate equipment of individuals that is the necessary basis for developing the more advanced capabilities, and a ground for moral concern' (2000: 84), and *internal capabilities*, which are also innate but, in contrast to the basic capabilities, are 'mature conditions of readiness' (84). Seeing and hearing can be seen as basic capabilities, which a newborn may have, while the developed capacity to see more complex things would be an internal capability. *Combined capabilities* are, then, the combination of internal capabilities with external conditions that will enable functionings to occur (84, 85). Agency is not specifically mentioned and is seen as part of the whole.

From the perspective of the kind of agency assessment I am proposing, which would primarily take place in qualitative assessments of how individuals (or groups) are able to make choices and decisions from a set of opportunities regarding possible valued outcomes, there are a number of potential problems in using Nussbaum's formulation. First, her conceptual framework was designed for a different purpose – that of guaranteeing political and constitutional rights – and has not been crafted for the purpose of qualitative individual assessments of the achievement of new functionings or of opportunities. Nussbaum's framework acknowledges both personal and social elements in the ways in which people pursue their rights and their capabilities, but

---

[5] See the point above on Sen linking autonomy with agency.

mainly from a political perspective (2000: 33).[6] Second, she does not distinguish between agency and capabilities, and her definition of an internal capability does not correspond with *opportunities* to be or to do but, rather, with innate *abilities*. In view of the fact that this is different from the way in which Sen and many other capability scholars use the term, it could, and does, lead to conceptual confusion (see also Robeyns, 2017: 93–4). I therefore prefer Sen's agency theory over Nussbaum's for qualitative agency assessments. Furthermore, Sen's conceptual frame of capabilities as opportunities for well-being, and of agency freedom, seems closely aligned to the ways in which social theorists conceptualize the interaction of individual agency with social arrangements, as is discussed below.

A recent theorization of agency by Rutger Claassen should also be considered. He proposes that the concept of *individual agency* be used as 'the underlying normative ideal to select basic capabilities' (Claassen, 2017: 1280), rather than well-being. With this proposal he intends to present a possible third way to the conflict presented by Sen's position on selecting well-being dimensions by means of public deliberation and Nussbaum's proposed list of dimensions. Claassen uses Nussbaum's notion of internal and external capabilities as a frame, and both these elements are reviewed in terms of autonomy/rational deliberation, and freedom/free action. He therefore includes both the individual and the social aspects, as Nussbaum does, and emphasizes the importance of social conditions. External capabilities consist of autonomy (non-manipulation by others) and freedom (non-interference by others), and individuals engage in both participatory and navigational agency in order to access social situations. He therefore makes use of Nussbaum's conceptual frame and of Sen's notion of negative freedom. However, it is not clear whether Claassen's frame would provide for existing and non-existing social opportunities. Is the only possible problem regarding external capabilities that others might interfere with one's access to these social capabilities? Or does that interference include the possibility that they might not exist? From the perspective of the theorization of agency within social arrangements that I am discussing here,

---

[6] For a clear exposition of Nussbaum's position on the differences between her and Sen's conceptualization of agency and capabilities, see Nussbaum (2011: 197–201).

Claassen's proposal might not work. Moreover, he devised it for a different purpose from that of assessing individual agency and social opportunities.

There is one more point to mention, and that is the important role of conversion factors in representing the social and institutional arrangements of society in a capability assessment. Bonvin, De Munck and Zimmerman (2018) refer to the usefulness of the concept of conversion factors as one of the reasons why they think social theory can benefit from insights in the capability approach. In particular, social and environmental conversion factors are additional tools to indicate how a person can convert resources into functionings, or what it is that prevents the person from doing so. The exercise of agency is therefore reliant on conversion factors, which will show how real and achievable the person's capabilities are (Sen, 1999: 74).[7]

Enriching the capability approach with social theory contributions

As Sen created the foundational ideas of the capability approach partly from his critique of utilitarianism, so the founders of social theory also created a discipline that studies social life, partly from their critique of utilitarianism. Talcott Parsons studied the work of a number of early economists, as well as that of Karl Marx, and concluded that by the early twentieth century there had been a synchronistic response to the capitalist consensus, especially in the work of Max Weber in Germany, Émile Durkheim in France, Alfred Marshall in Britain and Vilfredo Pareto in Italy. In 1937 Parsons published a classical synthesis of the work of these scholars, which he called *The Structure of Social Action*. In this work he attempts to show how these leading social theorists (who were also all prominent economists) independently and without mutual influence came up with both a critique of utilitarianism and with a voluntarist theory of action (Joas and Knöbl, 2009: 23).

---

[7] There are numerous other inputs on agency in the capability approach, but there is no space here for a comprehensive overview, and neither would it address the theme under discussion. Some contributions are as follows: Alkire and Deneulin (2000) make a significant contribution to the subject of agency dimensions; Ibrahim and Alkire (2007) write on agency indicators; Cleaver (2007) writes on collective agency; Drydyk (2008, 2013) writes on agency and empowerment; and Hart and Brando (2018) write on children's agency.

From this consensus in the work of the classical scholars, Parsons then formulates what he calls the 'action frame of reference', and its 'unit act' consists of the following elements: (1) an actor; (2) the end or goal of the action; (3) the action situation, which consists of the conditions of the action, or elements beyond the control of the actor, and the means of the action, or the elements at the disposal of the actor; and (4) the norms and values of action (Parsons, 1937; Joas and Knöbl, 2009: 38). As Parsons was accused of being excessively functionalist, and of explaining social phenomena in terms of their functions in a tautological way (Giddens, 1984), his own work did not immediately become part of the central debates in social theory. However, the above frame of action became one of the central ideas in much of social theory in the twentieth and twenty-first centuries, and large parts of the discipline developed in response to these ideas (Joas and Knöbl, 2009).

It will be clear to a capability scholar that there is some resonance between the ideas contained in the frame of action discussed above and in Sen's work, although there are obviously large differences as well. Sen declared from the start that agency is an important part of the theory he was developing. In the same way, Max Weber and others saw the task of social theory as partly to resurrect the idea that human beings have active agency (after the notion of *Homo oeconomicus* had gained ascendency) and the ability to act on that which they value. In social theory, the end of action is part of the frame, in that action is seen as deliberate, while the capability approach is normative and human beings are both actors and the end of action (Nussbaum, 2000: 56). The action situation, which consists firstly of elements beyond the control of the actor, is similar to conversion factors, over which the acting person also has little or no control. Elements that are 'at the disposal of the subject' or subjected to the practical consciousness of the actor could include processes such as adaptive preferences, habitus, and other conditions that might shape one's choices. Lastly, the norms and values that Parsons saw as the reason or the constraining factor that determined how people behaved as they did are seen completely differently by Sen. Parsons' normative theory is based on the notion that people conform to social order on the basis of values and norms, and if they do not conform they face social exclusion – an idea that possibly reflected Western society in the pre-war period of the 1930s. Sen, on the other hand, sees values in a positive sense, as the normative foundation for a life based on valued activities.

Joas (1996: 1) comments: '"Action" is a key concept in philosophy and almost all the social and cultural sciences today; efforts to construct a "theory of action" meet with especial interest in all these fields.' This is possibly because social change can be understood only in terms of human action, and the ways in which agency is exercised help us to understand not only how individual lives are lived but also how the whole of society transforms all the time. Paying more focused attention to agency and capabilities could therefore enrich the way in which we understand individual choices and decisions, as well as the dynamic social context within which those choices are made and exercised. Let us now see how the debates on these elements of the action frame might be of use to capability scholars who study agency. The first social theory contribution that I review is that of Anthony Giddens (1984, 1985).

Anthony Giddens and structuration theory

Structuration theory has been largely superseded in social theory debates, but Giddens' contribution can still be seen in current theories.[8] It is useful to understand how he theorized the conditions under which any action is undertaken, and his insight that structure is not a concrete, permanent phenomenon but something created by human thought is an important conceptual contribution.

Giddens (1984, 1985) attempts to resolve the problems associated with agency and structure. His main original contribution is that of structuration, which explains and explores the ways in which *agency and structure* operate. He sees these two dynamics radically differently from any of his predecessors, in that he does not see them as two separate dynamics that influence each other, as if they are two parts of a system. Rather, agency is central to his theory, and structures are in fact formed by acting agents, and not separable from agency. His startling new insight is to see structure as *a virtual reality only*, as 'memory traces' in the mind of the acting person, and not as somehow permanent or concrete. Giddens (1984: 25) puts it as follows: 'Structure, as recursively organised sets of rules and resources, is out of time and space, save in its instantiation and co-ordination as memory traces,

---

[8] Rob Stones (2005) argues for a 'strong' structuration theory, focused on the interpretation of empirical data.

and is marked by an "absence of the subject".' He takes trouble to introduce structure by emphasizing how he uses structure differently from what went beforehand:

But there can be no doubt about how 'structure' is usually understood ... as some kind of 'patterning' of social relations or social phenomena. This is often naively conceived of in terms of visual imagery, akin to the skeleton or morphology of an organism or to the girders of a building. Such conceptions are closely connected to the dualism of subject and social object: 'structure' here appears as external to human action, as a source of constraint on the free initiative of the independently constituted subject. (Giddens, 1984: 16)

He therefore prefers to talk about 'structural properties' rather than about structures – and he sees these as 'structured features of social systems, especially institutionalised features, stretching across time and space' (377). Structures are seen as consisting of rules and resources: 'Rules may be explicit or tacit, intensive or shallow, formal or informal, strongly or weakly sanctioned, but should generally be understood, in Wittgenstein's sense, as practical forms of knowledge that "allow us to go on" in novel circumstances' (cited in Loyal, 2007: 104). Agents can thus follow rules or norms, which exist as 'memory traces', to replicate structures or they can change these rules and norms and create new structures. 'Chronically reproduced rules' are *institutions* – instances when rituals, customs and norms have been reshaped by agents into more fixed social patterns, but patterns that can be changed again (Giddens, 1984: 375). The *duality of structure* is, then, 'structure as the medium and outcome of the conduct it recursively organises; the structural properties of social systems do not exist outside of social action but are chronically implicated in its production and reproduction' (374).

Giddens further distinguishes between three levels of consciousness: discursive, practical and unconscious (Giddens, 1984, 1979). For Giddens, the vast majority of our actions are based on our 'practical consciousness,' whereby we, the knowledgeable agents, draw on the 'stocks of knowledge' or 'mutual knowledge' that we have in common with others. This reservoir of common knowledge offers us routine ways of conducting the activities of every day. These three levels of consciousness are, moreover, linked to our *motivation for action*. We can be motivated by rational arguments that are raised in discursive conversations, by socialized stocks of common knowledge that exists within a specific cultural context, or by unconscious issues in our own lives of which we are not aware. In the theorization of agency in the capability approach, one could possibly incorporate some Giddensian material into the conceptualization of how agency contributes to the exercise of choice and decision making, and to subsequent action. I follow up on this idea in the next section.

Giddens (1979: 56; 1984: 5) sees the enactment of agency as organized around the 'reflexive monitoring of action'. This is associated with both the rationality of action, which expresses intentional action, and the motivation of the agent, as discussed above. Based on received cultural ideas, or on a combination of these and of discursive and unconscious ideas, on reflection, and on a rational expression of intention, agency takes place. It takes place freely, within these processes, but with two conditions attached: the agent will not have complete understanding of the context (unacknowledged conditions of action), and will also not know exactly what consequences might follow on his or her action (unintended consequences of action).

There are a number of useful concepts that Giddens could contribute to an enrichment of the theory of agency in the capability approach. His view of structure as ideas that people can continuously transform is a powerful conceptual tool, although Archer's corrective on this is helpful, as will be seen below. The three levels of consciousness that form Giddens' theory of motivation is a rich integration of insights from interpretative social theory and psychology, and allows one to analyse agency hermeneutically in terms of levels of motivation, levels of action and the impact of time and space on the conditions and consequences of such action.

Margaret Archer: morphogenesis

Margaret Archer's (1988, 1995, 1996, 2000, 2003, 2015) work is a synthesis of what other social theorists have proposed: a response to older theorization and a proposal for the future. She presents her theory, called morphogenesis, as a paradigm for thinking about social change, in which structure, agency and culture are seen as relationally connected components of how change occurs at present. She also uses critical realism as a neo-Marxist approach to integrate an analysis based on unequal power relations into her theory, with a detailed and articulated analysis of how power and dependence can operate in social relations (Porpora, 2013).

Her work is, especially initially, a response to Giddens and structuration theory (King, 2010), although she does depart from his theoretical scheme in significant ways. She emphasizes the need for analytical dualism, which contends that both Bourdieu and Giddens are wrong to conflate structure and agency, and that these concepts should be conceptually separated for the purpose of a clearer analysis. Agency and structure are therefore interdependent, but should be seen as different spaces for the purpose of analysis. Within morphogenesis, structures are principally viewed as relations, in contrast to Giddens, who sees them principally as memory traces of earlier forms of agency. Morphogenesis is indeed based on a relational ontology, with the insight that change occurs in interaction with and in relation to others (Porpora, 2013). Archer furthermore emphasizes praxis and the ways in which active agents establish their personal and social identity through both reflexive deliberation and through praxis (Archer, 2003). This can be followed by a researcher or observer by monitoring, with the person, the content of his or her internal conversations – one of the main ways in which Archer says we conduct our reflexive deliberation. Because of the conceptual separation of structure and agency, the emphasis on a relational ontology, the introduction of power analysis, the emphasis on the interrelatedness of structure, culture and agency and the use of praxis as a research tool, Archer's work is particularly suited to the interpretation of qualitative fieldwork, and therefore to the amplification of a capability theory of agency.

Pierre Bourdieu: habitus

French sociologist Pierre Bourdieu wrote most of his theoretical work in relation to the fieldwork he had done among the Kabyle people in Algeria. His interest is particularly in the structures that determine class mobility and immobility in the modern world. In the course of investigating social structures, Bourdieu distinguishes different key concepts. A *field* is a broad historical category that can be seen as a structural space in which power and conflict are enacted (Bourdieu, 1977; Schwartz, 2007). Within this structural space, agency engages.

Habitus is a term used by Bourdieu to denote the social framework or system that functions as an interpretative space for an individual, partly consciously and partly unknown to him or her; it is partly cognitive but also often non-rational. The habitus therefore acts as a set of internalized social constructs or socializations; as collective data about social histories that are used by individual agents for the interpretation of life experiences, and for the formulation of their own action (Bourdieu, 1977, 1990; Bourdieu and Passeron, 1990; Bourdieu and Wacquant, 1992). Action is often not rationally calculated but occurs as a kind of 'structured improvisation', and takes place in the space between the field and habitus (Schwartz, 2007). Bourdieu (1990: 54) captures it in the following way: 'The habitus, a product of history, produces individual and collective practices – more history – in accordance with the schemes generated by history. It ensures the active presence of past experiences, which, deposited in each organism in the form of schemes of perception, thought and action, tend to guarantee the 'correctness' of practices and their constancy over time, more reliably than all formal rules and explicit norms.' An obvious problem with the habitus concept described here is the impression of determinism it creates – as if it would be an inevitable process. Schatzki (1997) and King (2009: 264) also see this aspect of Bourdieu's work as deterministic. Porpora (2013) maintains that Bourdieu's field conflates agency and structure, in that structure becomes internalized through habitus.

Jürgen Habermas: communicative action

Habermas (1984, 1987, 1991) is a contemporary of Giddens and Bourdieu, an erstwhile member of the Frankfurt School and one of the foremost sociologists/philosophers in Europe. He works within the neo-Marxist tradition, and has done a broad integration of theoretical ideas, which also contributed significantly to critical theory. His work has been encyclopaedic, but there are two broad interrelated strains: one deals with a macro-theory on the political integration of modern society based on market forces, and the second is a micro-theory that deals with issues of rationality, communication and knowledge (Bohman and Rehg, 2014).[9] I concentrate on the second strain, and particularly on those aspects of his theory that contribute to a theory

---

[9] The revised review by Bohman and Rehg (2014) of the work of Habermas offers an insightful and in-depth overview of a complex theory.

of social action. Interestingly, Joas, an ex-student of Habermas, tells us that Habermas admits that *The Theory of Communicative Action* is directly structured along the lines of Parsons' *The Structure of Social Action* (Joas, 1996: 7).

In constructing his theory of action, Habermas (1984) borrows from Marx. He uses the forces of production and the relations of production to inform instrumental and communicative agency in a modern theory of social action (Honneth and Joas, 1988: 154). He also assigns types of rationality to types of action.[10] He distinguishes *teleological* or purposeful action, which is intended to manipulate the external world, *normatively regulated* action, based on social relations and their appropriateness, and *dramaturgical* action, which deals with self-representation. However, the typology he ultimately uses is based on his original focus, namely on the comprehensive rationality of action. With this in mind, he subdivides action into 'purposive-rational action' and 'strategic action' on the one side, and communicative action on the other. Purposive-rational action, or instrumental action, refers to action that deals with material objects or personal goals; the acting person is not in a social interaction, and acts in order to achieve success. Strategic action does not relate to material objects but to other subjects in the means–ends schema, such as action situations in game theory. Strategic action therefore involves social interaction, but the action is *goal-directed* rather than aimed at understanding. Communicative action is different from all other forms of action, in that it is predicated on *understanding*. Only in communicative action do the actors question all prerequisites and other characteristics of action situations, until they reach some form of consensus and understanding. This form of action is based on 'cooperative achievement of understanding among participants' (Roderick, 1986: 109). It does not attempt to achieve a specific goal, or specific ends, and is more open-ended (Joas and Knöbl, 2009: 228–35). 'Communicative action is thus an inherently consensual form of social coordination in which actors mobilize the potential for rationality' (Bohman and Rehg, 2014). Habermas then integrates both *Erklärung* and *Verstehen*; both positivism and the hermeneutic tradition of mainly Hans-Georg Gadamer (Bohman and Rehg,

---

[10] For the problems associated with this procedure, see Joas and Knöbl (2009: 232–3).

2014). Giddens (1985: 126) says in this regard: 'One of Habermas's most interesting contributions to philosophy is his attempt to reconcile hermeneutics and positivism and thereby overcome the division between them.'

I observed above that Habermas's work deals with a micro and macro aspect. From the early 1980s onwards he analyses political processes as a system, and personal interactions as communication within a *lifeworld* (Habermas, 1987: 153). The lifeworld encompasses the total social and cultural background that enables different individuals to achieve mutual understanding based on similar systems of meaning. Into the lifeworld of these knowledgeable and competent yet fallible agents enter complex and difficult decisions on the genetic engineering and modification of human beings and other animals, on new forms of democracy and legitimization and on why we should have values in a postmodern world. In this world, holds Habermas, social science and philosophy should be normative and play a role in the hermeneutic interpretation of our world and its complexities (Habermas, 1991, 2003).

When we consider the ways in which the work of Habermas could contribute to the theory of agency in the capability approach, one is struck by a number of ways in which Sen and Habermas have considered the same problems. Like Sen, Habermas values the insights of Rawls as central to current philosophy (Habermas, 2003). This refers to the fact that the individual is the originator of decisions about his or her own life, rather than that group norms or institutions should determine how people live. It does not imply that collective decisions cannot be made but that reflexivity and reason should steer the making of important decisions, rather than habituation or habitus. It also refers to the fact that the individual is responsible for normative and ethical reflection and action in both sets of theories. Both, then, also emphasize the importance of individual decision making and choice in the modern world, rather than pre-existing formulations of universal human needs. Furthermore, the agency description of both theories includes the reflective judgement of the agent, and a concept of the good. Both theorists also recognize and affirm the insights of Marx in their work, with Habermas basing the different aspects of agency respectively on the forces and relations of production. As Habermas partly built his theory on the concept of communicative action, his theory on agency is much more developed than that of Sen.

Integrating aspects of social theory into the capability approach

In considering how to integrate these two fields of knowledge, the first important consideration is whether capability scholars and practitioners and social theorists can talk to each other. I argue that they can, as both approaches deal with individuals in relation to society. The capability approach consists of a set of ideas dealing with how social arrangements can be evaluated, understood and changed, with a view to achieving better social justice for individual members of society. It is based on ethical or normative individualism, which claims that 'individuals, and only individuals, are the units of *ultimate* moral concern' (Robeyns, 2017: 184, emphasis in original). Within this framework, scholars such as Martins (2007), Smith and Seward (2009) and Owens et al. (2022) have argued for a relational ontology in the approach, whereby one recognizes that each individual act is set in a relational context. The capability approach therefore deals with individuals within social contexts.

The social theorists we are examining study the ways individuals act in social contexts, under what conditions and with what outcomes. They have influenced each other significantly and have been contributors to emerging insights into these complex realities. Although they have emphasized different ideas in developing their own positions, the knowledge about how social reproduction and social change take place can be understood, and applied, in coherent ways. The key insight gained from this body of knowledge is that, whether an individual act reproduces or changes the way things have been done beforehand, there are key components to agency that may be understood conceptually. These include the actor, the end of the action, the action situation and the norms and values associated with the action. Each of the four theorists we examine here has contributed significantly to theorizing these four components. This knowledge can be used in the capability approach at different levels – either by integrating the concepts to the already dense theoretical frame of the capability approach or by using the work of the different theorists at a deeper and more comprehensive level. Furthermore, the knowledge can be used to help us gain a deeper understanding either of one individual action or of how many actions contribute to social continuity or change.

I now proceed to suggest some potential links between social theory concepts and the capability approach. For the latter, I use Robeyns' well-known stylized visualization of the core concepts of the approach (Robeyns, 2017: 83). First I look at the core concepts that form part of a person gaining new functionings, and then at other components. One of the breakthroughs in Sen's theory is arguably the central position he gave to *individual choices made from opportunity sets of real, achievable opportunities.* This formulates development not as global plans of action but as individual achievements, accomplished on the basis of opportunities created – or not created – by socio-economic planners, and also by the person's own internal resources and previous agency. This interplay between personal choice and social conditions and opportunities or constraints forms the core conceptual unit in a capability assessment.

I would then argue that Sen's formulation of capabilities and agency is closely related conceptually to the theorization of agency and structure by the theorists I discussed here, in that agency and social opportunities reflect the same categories as agency and social structure. The actor makes what Robeyns (2017: 83) calls a 'constrained choice' – constrained by the ways in which personal, social and environmental conversion factors operate to shape the ways in which the person can convert resources into functionings. In addition, choices can also be constrained by unacknowledged conditions (Giddens, 1984). The person exercising the choice might be (vaguely) aware of these conditions, but might not fully understand the impact it has on his or her freedom of choice, as, for example, in the case of a woman choosing a simpler career than what she really wants, because of social pressure, and not understanding at the time how it could impact on her later life.

If we think of *reflection or practical reasoning* as a first step in making a choice, the work of Margaret Archer (1995) on reflexivity could be useful. She sees a rise in autonomous reflexivity in the era leading to the twenty-first century, and distinguishes between (1) conversational reflexivity in traditional settings, in which contextual continuities can be identified; (2) rational decision making, in which there might be contextual discontinuities; (3) meta reflexivity, when people critique and assess their own decision making in self-critical ways; and (4) fractured reflexes, when people are unable to respond to social challenges, and are largely shaped by forces external to themselves (Mutch, 2020). The first three modes correspond partly with Giddens' everyday reflexivity, rationalization and discursive consciousness (Giddens, 1985: 5, 6). Like the early Habermas, Giddens also adds unconscious influences, which are not easy to understand from an external position but which are undeniably important in decision making. Giddens' practical consciousness, seen by him as a form of internal motivation based on socialization and reflection, corresponds to some extent with Sen's practical reason, which consists of normative reasons and motivating reasons, as discussed by Austin (2017).

We therefore see that, in both sets of conceptual constructs, the capability approach and the social theorists under discussion, reflexivity is seen as central. Reflection can be the result either of a conditioned, socialized position or of a largely reasoned, conscious position – or, indeed, of a mixture of these. Sen argues that our views are influenced by our position in society, and this 'positional objectivity' has an influence on how we reflect on our choices (Austin, 2017). Archer (1995: 323) refers to the reflection that is strongly influenced by existing customs as *morphostasis*, and reflection that includes structural and cultural extension and 'elaboration' is called *morphogenesis*.[11] Bourdieu (1977) considers how our conditioned and socialized cultural habits can perpetuate our social and class position in society, and shows how difficult it may be to transcend or change these ways of behaving. Habermas shows how our 'practical knowledge' of how society works helps us to be a 'knowledgeable social actor among other knowledgeable social actors' (Bohman and Rehg, 2014).

When many actors reflexively change their behaviour in similar ways, social institutions and norms can change, and social transformation occurs. Giddens and Archer refer to this process as *praxis*; Giddens calls it 'the constitution of social life' (Cohen, 1989; Archer, 2003; Giddens, 1985). When Robeyns (2017: 83) indicates that a capability assessment includes the study of social and structural institutions and constraints, social theorists argue that these are not concrete structures but that they have been created by individual and collective agency, and are continuously being shaped and re-formed by these processes. Habermas then emphasizes that *deliberative democracy* is needed to infuse practical discourses with normative principles (Habermas, 1991).

Applying different theories in a capability analysis of agency

I now attempt to illustrate some of the ways in which these insights might be used to analyse agency in a hermeneutic report on qualitative research.

---

[11] One could possibly argue that there are similarities between Archer's morphostasis and Bourdieu's habitus.

I would like to emphasize that the frame introduced by Sen (Sen, 1985; Crocker and Robeyns, 2010: 85) is still the basis of such an analysis and that the material discussed here would be used as an amplification.

I attempt to do an agency analysis of some of the women from Khayelitsha by means of some of the theories mentioned above. I concentrate on three of the women who participated in the sewing group: Francis, Nondwe and Liziwe.[12] Francis and Nondwe were both older women and leaders in the group, as well as friends, but they did not always manage to work together. Liziwe was in her early thirties, was married to an abusive man and had three young children. She received no money from her husband and had a strong desire to have an independent income. All three were very active members of the sewing group and were highly motivated that the group should be successful. I mark conceptual terms in italics, to make them more recognizable, and where necessary I indicate the theoretical source of the term or tool.

The sewing group of about 12 women had been working together for about six months when the first difficulty arose. The women had by this time all received a sewing machine for their use in the group and some sewing training, and they had bought some materials collectively. The trainer had identified one of the members, Nomsa, a soft-spoken woman with a high level of sewing skill, as a potential quality controller. It quickly became clear that a quality controller was essential, but the group would not accept advice and leadership from one of their own members. The issue of *power* was a constant irritant in the group, and accepting leadership and authority from one of their own seemed really hard for the women. If we consider Archer's notion of structure as constituted of *human relations of power, competition, exploitation* and *dependence*, through *individual and collective agency*, we can apply that to the current example. The women told us, by sharing their thoughts and discussions (*internal conversations*), that they could not in their culture accept the authority of another woman who did not belong to their family. It is also quite possible that Francis and Nondwe, the two elected leaders of the group, felt in *competition* with Nomsa when she 'showed them what to do'. *Structure and culture thus interacted with agency* to cause this first big clash in the group.

---

[12] The three women were selected because their actions can be analysed in terms of capability selections. As the purpose of this analysis is to do a qualitative description, selection criteria were not applied in deciding on the three women. All names are fictitious.

Nondwe left, and very quickly got paid work in the clothing industry. This decision by the group limited their ability to compete on the open market, and, although they did not understand it at the time, they thus faced '*unacknowledged conditions*' (Giddens, 1984). It represented an *adaptive preference*, forcing them to work in the local market rather than in a more competitive open market in Cape Town. Their habitus could therefore be said to have shaped their decision making according to their socialized customs, without them realizing that they were acting within a narrow understanding of gender and racial equality. The decision-making process manifested as a *social conversion factor*, which *limited their functionings and also their capabilities*. Although they did *deliberate* on their collective decision, they did so without a critical understanding of the way in which their habitus operated.

Liziwe at this stage left the group with two other members, Patricia and Thembela, and joined a cousin of Patricia who had already established her own sewing business. For a while they did very well, and were even subcontracted by a prominent clothing group in South Africa. Liziwe found this very liberating, but her husband continued to challenge her on the grounds that she was working to meet other men. He initially often abused her quite violently, then stopped for a period, but eventually started again. She withdrew from the group after she had been injured in a bus accident, but also to mitigate the physical risk to herself and her children from constant violence and abuse. This decision was taken after careful *reflection* and use of *practical reason*, as she also understood that she might have to first leave her husband before she could build a new future for herself and her children. However, it was not easy with no income. Liziwe's husband had the cultural sanction of being permitted to 'discipline' her if she did not obey his authority, and her financial dependence on him created an unequal and dangerous relationship of *unequal power*. The interplay of *structure, culture* and *agency* (Archer, 1996), based on the habitus of her husband, reduced Liziwe's agency choices to being able to work while being abused or being without any financial support but not abused as often. It therefore also limited her *capabilities*.

The above short discussion attempts to show how many interrelated factors contribute to the capability constraints that limit the ways in which the women in Khayelitsha are able to make choices about the lives they would value. A more detailed hermeneutic description of their reflections, their decisions and their actions or praxis would enable the qualitative researcher to obtain a deeper understanding of how power relations and other social dynamics influence the daily course of their lives. Moreover, the researcher's position also contains elements of power, and there are elements of dependence in the action research relationship. These have to be examined and discussed honestly and transparently as well.

Conclusion

I have attempted to show that there is considerable synergy between the ideas of Amartya Sen and those of four prominent social theorists on the relationship between capabilities (seen as social opportunities) and agency. I have argued that Sen, in the conceptualization of the capability approach, points to the importance of the relationship between social opportunities and individual agency, but that his theorization on the subject is not sufficiently extensive. This can be considerably enriched by the work of the social theorists discussed here.

If capability scholars were to enrich their own work by cross-referencing some of the material discussed, it would have the potential to deepen and extend the theoretical reach and social depth of capability assessments. This chapter therefore serves as an initial proposal, which, if the idea is seen as useful, should be amended and elaborated in its turn by extensive further propositions and theorization.

References

Adato, M., Carter, M. R., and May, J. (2006) Exploring poverty traps and social exclusion in South Africa using qualitative and quantitative data. *Journal of Development Studies*, 42 (2): 226–47.

Alkire, S., and Deneulin, S. (2000) Individual motivation, its nature, determinants and consequences for within group behaviour, Working Paper 184. Tokyo: World Institute for Development Economics Research, United Nations University.

Archer, M. S. (1988) *Culture and Agency: The Place of Culture in Social Theory*. Cambridge: Cambridge University Press.

(1995) *Realist Social Theory: The Morphogenetic Approach*. Cambridge: Cambridge University Press.

(1996) *Culture and Agency: The Place of Culture in Social Theory*, rev. edn. Cambridge: Cambridge University Press.

(2000) *Being Human: The Problem of Agency*. Cambridge: Cambridge University Press.

(2003) *Structure, Agency and the Internal Conversation*. Cambridge: Cambridge University Press.

(ed.) (2015) *Generative Mechanisms Transforming the Social Order*. New York: Springer.

Austin, A. (2017) Turning capabilities into functionings: practical reason as an activation factor. *Journal of Human Development and Capabilities*, 19 (1): 24–37.

Bohman, J., and Rehg, W. (2014) Habermas, J. *Stanford Encyclopedia of Philosophy*. https://plato.stanford.edu/entries/habermas.

Bonvin, J.-M., De Munck, J., and Zimmerman, B. (2018) Introduction: the capability approach and critical sociology. *Critical Sociology*, 44 (6): 859–64.

Bourdieu, P. (1977) *Outline of a Theory of Practice*, Nice, R. (trans.). Cambridge: Cambridge University Press.

(1990) *The Logic of Practice*, Nice, R. (trans.). Cambridge: Polity Press.

Bourdieu, P., and Passeron, J.-C. (1990) *Reproduction in Education, Society and Culture*, Nice, R. (trans.). London: Sage.

Bourdieu, P., and Wacquant, L. J. D. (1992) *An Invitation to Reflexive Sociology*. Chicago: University of Chicago Press.

Claassen, R. (2017) An agency-based capability theory of justice. *European Journal of Philosophy*, 25 (4): 1279–304.

Cleaver, F. (2007) Understanding agency in collective action. *Journal of Human Development*, 8 (2): 223–44.

Cohen, I. J. (1989) *Structuration Theory: Anthony Giddens and the Constitution of Social Life*. London: Macmillan.

Conradie, I. (2013) Can deliberate efforts to realise aspirations increase capabilities: a South African case study. *Oxford Development Studies*, 14 (2): 189–219.

Conradie, I., and Robeyns, I. (2013) Aspirations and human development interventions. *Journal of Human Development and Capabilities*, 41 (4): 559–80.

Crocker, D., and Robeyns, I. (2010) Capability and agency. In *Philosophers in Focus: Amartya Sen*, Morris, C. (ed.): 60–90. Cambridge: Cambridge University Press.

Drydyk, J. (2008) Durable empowerment. *Journal of Global Ethics*, 4 (3): 231–45.

(2013) Empowerment, agency, and power. *Journal of Global Ethics*, 9 (3): 249–62.

Gangas, S. (2016) From agency to capabilities: Sen and sociological theory. *Current Sociology*, 64 (1): 22–40.

Giddens, A. (1979) *Central Problems in Social Theory: Action, Structure and Contradiction in Social Analysis*. London: Macmillan.

(1984) *The Constitution of Society: Outline of the Theory of Structuration*. Cambridge: Polity Press.

(1985) Jürgen Habermas. In *The Return of Grand Theory in the Human Sciences*, Skinner, Q. (ed.): 121–40. Cambridge: Cambridge University Press.

Habermas, J. (1984) *The Theory of Communicative Action*, vol. 1, *Reason and the Rationalization of Society*, McCarthy, T. (trans.). Boston: Beacon Press.

(1987) *The Theory of Communicative Action*, vol. 2, *Lifeworld and System: A Critique of Functionalist Reason*, McCarthy, T. (trans.). Boston: Beacon Press.

(1991) *Moral Consciousness and Communicative Action*, Lenhardt, C., and Nicholsen, S. W. (trans.). Cambridge, MA: MIT Press.

(2003) *The Future of Human Nature*, Rehg, W., Beister, H., and Pensky, M. (trans.). Cambridge: Polity Press.

Hart, C. S., and Brando, N. (2018) A capability approach to children's well-being, agency and participatory rights in education. *European Journal of Education*, 53 (3): 293–309.

Honneth, A., and Joas, H. (1988) *Social Action and Human Nature*, Myers, R. (trans.). Cambridge: Cambridge University Press.

Ibrahim, S., and Alkire, S. (2007) Agency and empowerment: a proposal for internationally comparable indicators. *Oxford Development Studies*, 35 (4): 397–416.

Joas, H. (1996) *The Creativity of Action*. Cambridge: Polity Press.

Joas, H., and Knöbl, W. (2009) *Social Theory: Twenty Introductory Lectures*. Cambridge: Cambridge University Press.

King, A. (2009) Overcoming structure and agency. *Journal of Classical Sociology*, 9 (2): 260–88.

(2010) The odd couple: Margaret Archer and Anthony Giddens and British social theory. *British Journal of Sociology*, 61 (Special 1): 253–60.

Loyal, S. (2007) Anthony Giddens. In *Fifty Key Sociologists: The Contemporary Theorists*, Scott, J. (ed.): 101–8. Abingdon: Routledge.

Martins, N. (2007) Ethics, ontology and capabilities. *Review of Political Economy*, 19 (1): 37–53.

Meeks, J. G. (2018) On Sen on the capability of capabilities: the story of a not-for-profit enterprise. In *New Frontiers of the Capability Approach*, Comim, F., Fennell, S., and Anand, P. B. (eds.): 12–50. Cambridge: Cambridge University Press.

Mutch, A. (2020) Margaret Archer and a morphogenetic take on strategy. *Critical Perspectives on Accounting*, 73: DOI 10.1016/j.cpa.2016.06.007.

Nussbaum, M. C. (2000) *Women and Human Development: The Capabilities Approach*. Cambridge: Cambridge University Press.

(2011) *Creating Capabilities: The Human Development Approach*. Cambridge, MA: Belknap Press.

Owens, J., Entwistle, V., Craven, L., & Conradie, I. (2022) Understanding and investigating relationality in the Capability Approach. *Journal of Social Behaviour*, 52 (1): 86–104.

Parsons, T. (1937) *The Structure of Social Action: A Study in Social Theory with Special Reference to a Group of Recent European Writers*. New York: Free Press.

Penneger, L., and Godehart, S. (2007) Townships in the South African geographical landscape: physical and social legacies and challenges. Pretoria: National Treasury.

Porpora, D. V. (2013) Morphogenesis and social change. In *Social Morphogenesis*, Archer, M. S. (ed.): 25–38. New York: Springer.

Robeyns, I. (2017) *Wellbeing, Freedom and Social Justice: The Capability Approach Re-Examined*. Cambridge: Open Book Publishers.

Roderick, R. (1986) *Habermas and the Foundations of Critical Theory*. London: Macmillan.

Schatzki, T. R. (1997) Practices and actions: a Wittgensteinian critique of Bourdieu and Giddens. *Philosophy of the Social Sciences*, 27 (3): 283–308.

Schwartz, D. (2007) Pierre Bourdieu. In *Fifty Key Sociologists: The Contemporary Theorists*, Scott, J. (ed.): 39–46. Abingdon: Routledge.

Sen, A. K. (1977) Rational fools: a critique of the behavioural foundations of economic theory. *Philosophy & Public Affairs*, 6 (4): 317–44.

(1984) Capability and well-being. In *The Philosophy of Economics: An Anthology*, Hausman, D. M. (ed.): 270–93. Cambridge: Cambridge University Press.

(1985) Well-being, agency and freedom: the Dewey lectures 1984. *Journal of Philosophy*, 82 (4): 169–221.

(1987) The standard of living. In *The Standard of Living*, Hawthorne, G. (ed.): 1–38. Cambridge: Cambridge University Press.

(1992) *Inequality Reexamined*. Oxford: Oxford University Press.

(1999) *Development as Freedom*. Oxford: Oxford University Press.

(2002) *Rationality and Freedom*. Cambridge, MA: Harvard University Press.

Shaffer, P. (2013) *Q-Squared: Combining Qualitative and Quantitative Approaches in Poverty Analysis*. Oxford: Oxford University Press.

Smith, M., and Seward, C. (2009) The relational ontology of Amartya Sen's capability approach: incorporating social and individual causes. *Journal of Human Development and Capabilities*, 10 (2): 213–35.

Stones, R. (2005) *Structuration Theory*. London: Red Globe Press.

Wallerstein, I. (2004) The actor in the social sciences: a reply to Hans Joas. *International Sociology*, 19 (3): 315–19.

Zimmerman, B. (2006) Pragmatism and the capability approach: challenges in social theory and empirical research. *European Journal of Social Theory*, 9 (4): 467–84.

13 Creativity and capabilities
A problem of change and uncertainty?

JONATHAN WARNER

Introduction

This chapter sketches the first part of an argument, more in the nature of an exploration than of a finished project. The topics it touches on – human creativity and economic growth; technology and capabilities; comparative statics and dynamic theories – all have significant literatures of their own. To attempt to combine them in one article is what Sir Humphrey Appleby (from the 1980s BBC comedy *Yes, Prime Minister*) would have called a 'courageous' decision. Nevertheless, I think that there are certain commonalities between the topics, ones that I intend to exploit in what follows.

Generally, an increase in income per capita is taken to be a good thing. Although there may be inequalities in its distribution (sometimes gross ones), a higher GDP per person gives the potential, at least, to broaden the feasible set of meaningful lives for (some) people. Given a means of conversion of income into functionings, richer individuals will have more options available to them: more meaningful choices available to live fulfilling lives. Alternatively, higher income per capita increases the scope for collective action to produce public goods that enhance capabilities and choice, either through voluntary means (via civil society organizations, for example) or through government's use of its ability to tax, spend or redistribute income. Thus, a rise in per capita GDP and economic growth, raising per capita incomes, tends to enhance capabilities.

But there is a second, albeit less certain, mechanism by which rises in GDP will affect capabilities. If the effect through incomes (and therefore expenditure) can be considered a demand-side effect, the route that I want to consider is a supply-side effect: the increase in potential output brought about by invention and innovation. The argument, in rough terms, is this.

Human creativity, grounded in the nature of human beings, will inevitably result in invention, innovation and change. Technological

284

changes, as well as producing real per capita growth in GDP, also change the way in which the economy functions. This might be directly as a result of the introduction of a new technology, increasing productivity in the industries affected, or indirectly, by releasing resources from those industries to productive uses elsewhere. These changes will, to a greater or lesser extent, affect the types of lives that we might have reason to value. Functionings can be enhanced; new ways of realizing capabilities become possible; and perhaps even new basic capabilities will emerge. Even if the broad contours of what constitute valuable lives remain the same, differences in external circumstances will make a difference to what this might look like. Amartya Sen engages with Adam Smith's claim that human dignity requires, of any valuable life, 'the ability to appear in public without shame' (Smith, 1776: bk 5, ch. 2; Sen, 1999: 73). What precisely this looks like varies by time and place. What kinds of lives we have reason to value also differ over time and place.

Changes external to our immediate environment, such as in institutions and the legal structure, and from globalization, automation and digitization, for example, also have the capacity to affect both economic growth and the lives we might have reason to value. For many people, the kind of work that they do is part of their identity. When being introduced, someone will almost certainly mention his or her occupation (or previous occupation if he or she has retired). Thus technological change, making some types of work obsolete (drivers of horse-drawn stage carriages, and then drivers of steam trains and their firemen), has the capacity to affect identity – to make some people feel useless and their lives of no value, because something that they took pride in doing has been taken from them. The deskilling of more skilled work, through its replacement by computer-generated algorithms, is also demeaning to those whose skills are no longer valuable. Lamp lighters a century ago and bank loan officers more recently provide examples. Other work is also threatened by computer data crunching: driverless cars are on the horizon, which will probably put taxi drivers out of work. One of the big challenges over the next few decades will be how to respond to the challenges of these changes.

The chapter proceeds as follows. The first section attempts to establish the connections between human creativity, innovation and various types of changes: economic growth and institutional development. To try to keep the chapter within reasonable bounds, I shall concentrate on how the other changes mentioned above are manifested in the type and quantity of output of the economy, rather than examining their effect on other aspects of society.

The link between changes in technology and valuable lives (capabilities) is discussed in the second section. As new technology has the potential to increase the feasible set of options on how we live, the set of possible valuable lives increases; but, just as technology destroys the economic value of some industries (Joseph Schumpeter's 'creative destruction': Schumpeter, 1942: 82–5), so certain previously valuable lives thereby become unvaluable – or, at least, have aspects that cease to be valuable.

The chapter concludes by briefly summarizing the proposed path forward: how change creates problems through uncertainty, both in economic theory and, more generally, in terms of the difficulty of knowing what society will look like in the future. For example, as Tim Harford (2017b) points out, the robot in *Blade Runner* is very similar to how we envisage robots today; but the portrayal of other 'futuristic' devices has not kept pace with actual developments. Regardless of what precisely the future holds, though, changes are occurring, and their effects on employment, the quality of life and identity will need to be addressed.

Creativity and innovation, growth and change

The benefits of economic growth are clear. Higher per capita incomes allow people more freedom on how to live their lives, and provide the resources to combat poverty, famines, plagues and pestilence; increase resilience to natural disasters, and provide for the public provision of such goods as education and health care. There are also potential negative effects: addiction to the trivia of social media (or TV, in a previous age: Postman, 1985); unemployment, and the stresses of learning new skills and coping with new things; facilitating ways of intentionally injuring people (more destructive weapons, online scams and blackmail); or unintentionally causing damage (to the environment, as climate change has been an unintended consequence of industrialization).

Other changes in society also have the ability to impact human welfare: institutional development and cultural changes (and changes in the prevailing worldview) provide examples. For instance, viewed through a Marxist lens, the dialectical interactions of thesis and antithesis lead to new structures and institutions. Karl Marx thought that, at a fundamental level, it was economic systems (the base) that determined the institutions, politics, culture and religion (the superstructure); the 'contradictions' inevitably present in the system would inevitably lead to revolutionary change – either gradually (such as the shift from feudalism to capitalism) or rapidly via a revolution, as the 'enlightenment' revealed by Marx's analyses meant that the historical process could be hurried along by a 'vanguard party' (at least, if Lenin, 1902, is to be believed). For a Marxist, a valuable life would be one on the 'right side' of history; those not realizing this are unaware of their true identity. In other words, they hold to (and suffer from) an 'ideology', a false consciousness, which leads them to live a life in opposition not only to the trajectory of history but also to their own best interests, if they would but realize it.

Technological innovation also has the capacity to produce change – most obviously in economic output, but also in the way that production is organized, and the types of lives people live. There has been much recent interest in the uses of blockchain technology (pioneered by Bitcoin and other digital currencies), with the potential to lead to new ways of doing things that open up new opportunities. The development of the digital gift economy, for example, changes the relationship between work and leisure (Elder-Vass, 2016), replacing any hard distinction between the two, and so opening up new opportunities for work–life integration, with 24/7 availability in danger of becoming the norm. In a previous age, the development of cheap artificial lighting meant that activities that required illumination could be decoupled from the diurnal day/night rhythm of life, allowing for shift work, which kept machinery running but had consequences for family and social life.

Theories of economic growth

Economists since at least Adam Smith (1776) have sought to discover the processes that would lead to increasing output and wealth, although the term we use for this – 'economic growth' – did not enter the literature until the 1930s (Flynn, 2018). The classical economists were certainly interested in how output might increase and what effects of this might be expected (Smith, 1776; Ricardo, 1817;

Marx, 1867; Kurz, 2010). David Ricardo's theory demonstrated that technological advances (more and better machinery) would lead to an increase in output, but his model assumed that the labouring classes would remain impoverished as any gains in output (food and nutrition were what Ricardo concentrated on) would be dissipated by increasing population. An improvement (better drainage or irrigation of arable land, for example, or an increase in the availability of land) would lead to an increase in food production. As a result, families would be able to support more children: either more children would be born or more would survive infancy. The population would grow until food per capita was just sufficient to survive. Hence, economics came to be dubbed the 'dismal science'. Thomas Malthus (1798) made it even more dismal, by setting the process to mathematics, suggesting that population would grow exponentially (one, two, four, eight, etc.), while food production would grow only arithmetically (one, two, three, four, etc.), resulting in less food per person. This was obviously unsustainable; the end result must be mass starvation.

Mass starvation has not occurred (FAO et al., 2017). World population is now seven to eight times what it was when Malthus and Ricardo were writing; life expectancy has increased massively, and fewer people are suffering from food shortages. So, it is legitimate to ask: why not? The answer usually given is that we have been saved from dismalness by technology and societal change. Even in Ricardo's day the size of upper-class families in Britain was falling; the aristocrats were not responding to increased food supplies by having bigger families. The middle class and 'lower orders' also switched to having smaller families over the course of the nineteenth century. Today in just under a half of the world's countries, including all those in Europe, the fertility rate (the average number of children born to each woman) is below 2.1, the minimum level necessary to keep the population from falling.

The standard model of economic growth (from authors such as Greg Mankiw, author of the best-selling introductory text in economics: Mankiw, 1997) is still the neoclassical-consensus Solow model, in which output (or GDP) depends on an exogenous state of technology and the available quantities of the input factors of production: land and natural resources, labour, human capital (which augments labour) and physical capital, machinery and buildings.

It is clear that the relationship between output and the factors of production is not a simple additive relationship. You cannot just add an extra unit of labour to get an extra unit of output. There are various degrees of substitutability and complementarity between the factors: you need all (or at least more than one of them) to produce anything; and, generally, the more you have of one of them, the smaller the increase in output from using more of it. (This is the law of diminishing marginal returns, which has been used to explain why human-resource-rich countries with little industrialization are poor.) On the other hand, you are, at the margin, able to substitute physical capital for labour (robotization, for example), giving a choice of combinations of the factors that will produce the same output.

The highly influential Cobb–Douglas production function, a two-factor version of the above model, specifies a determinate relationship between labour, capital and output, in the form of an exponential function that has proved to be remarkably good at predicting the observed changes in production. Increasing the stock of capital without increasing the number of workers will increase output, but at a declining rate. Therefore, in the model, increases in investment increase the capital stock as long as the investment rate exceeds the rate of depreciation of the capital – the rate at which it wears out. To increase investment, resources need to be diverted from consumption goods – that is, money needs to be saved. One can even calculate a unique 'golden rule' level of savings and investment – the amount necessary to maximize the level of per capita consumption over time (see Phelps, 1961). Unlike Ricardo's theory, the benefits of increased output are not dissipated by a rise in population. In fact, if the population is increasing, output can increase indefinitely if new capital equipment increases in proportion. In short, economic growth will occur if there is a change in technology or a change in the growth rate of population. But continual innovation (or population growth) will be necessary for growth to continue.

The standard neoclassical theory of economic growth, to which Robert Solow's (1956) contribution is foundational, is therefore an explanation of how changes in technology are transmitted into higher levels of output, and why, ultimately, that process comes to an end. But, as with the classical theorists, this begs the question of what causes the technological change in the first place.

Since the Industrial Revolution (and before) technological process has occurred, but it was caused by something not explicit in the model, or perhaps was just a random event. I try to explain this to students as rather like the popular mythology of invention went: someone would be tinkering around in his garden shed, and was suddenly struck by an inspiration. It is as if there are all kinds of ideas out there, and, every so often, one of them hits someone, and a new invention or innovation results. New investment then 'incarnates' or reifies the invention or innovation, and the economy grows. When the world has retooled, then growth will come to an end, and we will be back at a steady-state equilibrium of constant output (or output growth at the rate of growth of the labour force, if the amount of capital also increases in proportion).

Modern growth theories take a more optimistic view: perhaps we can fish for the ideas floating around, rather than waiting for them to strike us. The new, or endogenous, theory of growth stresses this. Usually, once a particular technological innovation has become diffused, ideas do not emerge from garden sheds but from research labs in businesses or academia. In the initial stages, though, the garden shed – or, today, the college dorm room or parents' garage – can still be important. The internet giant Facebook famously was birthed in this way; and innovative uses of the internet's ability to connect people continue to come from individual entrepreneurs. But, as technology matures, big players come to dominate. This suggests that it is possible to go fishing for ideas – for inventions, if 'outside the box' thinking is still the preserve of individuals. If we can continue to invent and innovate, we can continue to grow output per capita. Innovation is encouraged because, it is claimed, the rate of return on ideas exceeds the natural rate of interest. Policy can also affect innovation of at least some kinds. Offering patents that give the innovator monopoly rights over the production and sale of new things produced as the output of the innovation is one such policy. For example, producing and testing new drugs that are effective against some disease and have tolerable levels of side effects constitutes an expensive process with a high failure rate; the reward for success is the ability to sell the drug at a high price, which will, hopefully, cover those development costs. Policy issues remain. How long should the patent be for? Should it be extendable if the drug proves useful in combating some other ailment, or its use is extended to some other group?

The new theories suggest that growth can be targeted successfully by appropriate policy, and that material well-being can therefore continue to rise indefinitely. The doomsters who have suggested that there must be limits to growth – from Malthus through the US Patents Office to the Club of Rome (Meadows et al., 1972) and modern environmentalists – have, thus far, been wrong, although as evidence for human-caused climate change accumulates the reorientation of the current growth trajectory will doubtless need to be changed.

Growth in income per capita

Ancient societies probably had little experience of a growing standard of living. There were good days, good months, good years, when the crops flourished, the hunt went well and there were no marauders, earthquakes or other disasters to disrupt activity. But there were inevitably bad times, when the rains failed, the hunters came back empty-handed, enemies were at the door and plague stalked the land. As in Ricardo's model, populations fluctuated (although they generally got larger, as more land was used), but society was fairly static. Evidence of trade in the ancient world meant that at least some of the benefits of trade were captured, but, as transport was slow and expensive, it tended to be limited to luxury goods. When there was growth in per capita income before (say) 1600 AD, it was so slow as to be unnoticeable; perhaps lost amid the random variation in harvests. New technology might be developed, but perhaps forgotten.

However, Stephen Smith, in a recent presentation (Smith, 2017), suggests that growth is almost inevitable. As Adam Smith pointed out, greater population density means that members of the labour force can specialize, which will tend to increase labour productivity, and therefore output per worker. (Analysis by Robert Gilman's Context Institute, www.context.org, and others, has shown how the quantity of labour resources necessary to satisfy basic needs has declined, with big changes at the Neolithic and Industrial Revolutions.) So perhaps we might expect increasing returns to scale as output increases. But Stephen Smith goes further, saying that, as part of the image of God in humankind, how we mirror Him is in being creative. Human creativity will, every so often, other things being equal, produce ideas that make for more efficient production, and therefore higher productivity. Ideas produce inventions – new technologies that make things possible that were theretofore impossible. Dreams become reality; some of yesterday's science fiction becomes tomorrow's new product. A society that encourages this process will tend to be richer than one that doesn't. For example, government and civil society institutions, and legal structures within the society, will affect development (Heilbroner, 1953: ch. 1; Acemoglu and Robinson, 2012; Kuran, 2011).

Matt Ridley in *The Rational Optimist* (Ridley, 2010) suggests a reason why this might be the case: how human beings differ from other creatures is in their capacity not only to imitate but to combine ideas.

> Chimpanzees may teach each other how to spear bushbabies with sharpened sticks, and killer whales may teach each other how to snatch sea lions off beaches, but only human beings have the cumulative culture that goes into the design of a loaf of bread or a concerto. [...] Imitation and learning are not themselves enough... Something else is necessary; something that human beings have and killer whales do not. The answer, I believe, is that at some point in human history, ideas began to meet and mate, to have sex with each other. (Ridley, 2010: ch. 1)

For ideas to meet, people need to communicate. Recent research suggests that, other things being equal, higher populations are positively associated with higher rates of growth (Desmet, Kristian Nagy and Rossi-Hansberg, 2018). A greater number of people means more idea production capacity; proximity of neighbours (population density), and peaceful relations with them, means that the probability of successful idea mating increases. By contrast, a small population is likely to remain relatively underdeveloped.

Tim Harford (2017a) gives his readers a quick tour of what he sees as 50 of the greatest inventions that have shaped the world of today. Some of the usual suspects (such as the making of fire and the printing press) are missing. These are well known to be important, and Harford wants to major on some less obvious inventions; but also these ideas needed to mate with others to produce change. Thus, if the printing press could be used solely to print on vellum, then it would probably not have revolutionized the world, as books would have remained very expensive. It was the existence of a cheap alternative, paper (Kurlansky 2016), that led to mass printing at low cost – and so books became more widely available. Some of the inventions are tangible (barbed wire; the contraceptive pill; air conditioning); others are concepts (double-entry bookkeeping; seller feedback, as on eBay, Tripadvisor and Amazon; bar codes). Some are (intangible) innovations: ideas about how to combine ideas, such as public key cryptography and limited liability companies – to which one could add other recent developments based on digitization and connectivity, such as blockchain platforms for peer-to-peer sharing and service provision. Innovation appears to be happening at a faster rate; ideas are disseminated more rapidly, and so have more opportunity to meet and cross-breed with other ideas. But, for this to happen, there needs to be invention, to produce the designs and ideas that, later, can mate.

It would seem, then, that, once population had reached a sufficient size, and once famine, pestilence and plague had been largely tamed, and relatively peaceful coexistence within and between groups and tribes had been established, ideas could meet, mate and spread. Improvements in transport and (later) telecommunications bolstered and magnified this trend. As networking became easier, more ideas met, mated and produced inventions or innovative offspring. But quite what would emerge was almost impossible to predict.

Technology, change and valuable lives: towards the capability approach

Technological development, along with conceptual invention and innovation, changes the set of feasible valuable lives. Without invention and innovation, increases in GDP would be limited by the availability of inputs; otherwise, growth would peter out, as the neoclassical model suggests. The evidence of growth over the past 4,000 years could be read to suggest that they were also sufficient; the evidence is strong that societies that did not invent or innovate tended to stagnate, and were susceptible to decline and collapse when a new challenge arose.

Generally, since the eighteenth century, invention and innovation have been seen as a 'good thing'. New opportunities open up, unfreedoms are reduced or eliminated and the standard of living increases. But they are not unambiguously good. Conventional objections to economic growth concern the effects of an increased ecological footprint on the environment, leading to local problems of pollution, planetary issues from global climate change (Rockström et al., 2009) and a worry that human ingenuity will not be able to provide viable substitutes for exhaustible natural resources, such as metals and fossil fuels. There is no certainty that solutions to challenges (even anticipated ones) will emerge in time to prevent disaster, even in creative societies – but it will not be for the want of trying. The predictions of doom and collapse from Malthus onwards might have been premature. Jared Diamond (2005) argues that, to persist, all human civilizations need to succeed in meeting the challenges of environmental degradation, climate change and dealing with hostile neighbours (and cultivating friendly ones). In addition, they need creativity to be capable of developing responses to these and other threats that arise. Diamond can be read to mean that societies need to prove their viability over 400 years or so, before they can be seen as truly sustainable. He therefore thinks it is an open question whether Australian civilization will pass the test (Diamond, 2005: ch. 13).

Second, the benefits of growth are spread unevenly. Britain enjoyed a 'first mover' advantage; the United States and now China have successfully emulated Britain and achieved high rates of growth. But millions remain in poverty; and, in rich countries, income and wealth inequality have not declined. It is even possible that growth for some means impoverishment for others: if a new technique opens the way for mechanizing and deskilling a craft industry, then artisans will lose out, as home weavers discovered in the early years of England's industrial development.

Third, the new opportunities opened up by digitization, automation and globalization seem to be making the need for human labour obsolete. Although technological revolutions in the past have destroyed jobs (blacksmiths did badly out of the growth of mechanized transport; weavers lost out to Richard Arkwright's spinning machine), this time is thought to be different: Schumperian creative destruction (Schumpeter, 1942: 71ff.) in the past has moved labour from one sector to another, but has not destroyed the need for labour. The claim that human labour has now become obsolescent is controversial: automatic teller machines (ATMs) were supposed to replace bank employees; instead, employment in banks has increased, as tellers now spend more time dealing with clients (Harford, 2017c). Quite how further technological change will replace labour, or perhaps enhance it, is unclear, although most commentators think it will happen for more types of employment than to date – and soon (Lepore, 2019). The fear that it will, though, is inducing anxiety among those who believe that their lifestyle is under imminent threat. Like any good prophecy, the threat to the way we work is concentrating minds and fuelling calls for policy responses.

In his 1930 lecture 'Economic possibilities for our grandchildren', John Maynard Keynes (1930) sketched out what today's world might be like. Rather like Marx's utopian vision, Keynes' view was of a world without want, but also a world where there was ample time for leisure, as machines could do most of the work. Again, for overworked and tired labourers of the 1860s, or 1930s, this was a vision of a biblical *shalom* (the Sabbatical rest of the Promised Land: Numbers 14:30; Joshua 1:13, 15; Psalms 95:11; Hebrews 3:12–4:11). To have times of relaxation and refreshment, and to have varied, non-toilsome work and work-like activities (volunteering, hobbies), are part of that vision. Marx and Engels (1932: I-A) thought similarly, and saw striving after ever-increasing production through an increased division of labour as a road to alienation and revolution. The solution would be a diversity of activities in Utopia.

It is the diversity of activity that, for many, makes life interesting and valuable. Volvo, the Swedish car manufacturer, discovered that teams of workers building cars were more effective than production lines; one explanation of the Hawthorne effect (Mayo, 1949; Landsberger, 1958) is that offering variety – changing things around – increases productivity (Lohr, 1987 – the favoured explanation, that observation makes the observed work harder, is less attractive). A life of constant inactivity would not be desirable; activity becomes meaningless, and we would find it hard to argue that anyone (except perhaps Wally of Scott Adams' *Dilbert* cartoons) would have reason to value such a life.

Invention and innovation, born of human creativity, open up opportunities, and expand the feasible set of valuable lives. Although this probably affects more people in rich countries than in poor, as more countries develop and come to have access to technological advances, poor people are affected too. Let us take just two examples. Over 4.75 billion people in the world have access to a mobile phone – two-thirds of the total population, or nearly 90 per cent of the population aged 15 or above. Well over 2 billion people have active Facebook accounts (McRae, 2018). As mobile phones and internet access become cheaper, people in less wealthy countries are able to use them. As communication becomes easier, the ability to trade ideas, pictures, recipes and other intangibles increases. It is easier for ideas to have sex with each other, and produce new innovative possibilities. As internet connections improve, remote working becomes feasible in places that were until recently isolated, again expanding the opportunities (both in terms of employment and social life) for more people.

But there is a dark side to all this. The internet and mobile phones can be used for evil as well as good. Some of the innovative work might be in the sex trade; apparently, the services of prostitutes are becoming cheaper as the internet allows buyers and sellers to hook up more easily, and also because the growth of pornography means that there is now a cheaper substitute for their services. The 'dark web' facilitates trade in illicit drugs. The new professions of hacking and virus and malware writing have flourished. Leaking confidential information has become easier as more data are stored online.

For my purposes here, though, there is a more important potential negative effect that needs to be emphasized: that it is possible that innovation might render some valuable kinds of lives unfeasible, or might destroy their value as automation takes away the need for the services people living those lives would perform. If redundancy, deskilling and automation make many types of work superfluous, what will a valuable or meaningful life look like?

One could, of course, opt out of using new technology: one can live a life that one has reason to value regardless of innovations that render it anachronistic, hard or quaint. Many religious groups moved from Europe to the Americas mainly to avoid persecution for their beliefs, but also to live the way they wanted. For some, such as the Amish and some Mennonite groups, this meant the rejection of most modern technology. However, as the population grew, maintaining a distinctive and separatist lifestyle became harder. If there is enough land available, perhaps it can still be done, as some of the Old Order Mennonites in Belize have demonstrated, but it is becoming increasingly difficult (Roessingh and Plasil, 2010).

And one could, of course, commit to a life's work that has been rendered pointless because of technological change. Alexander Cruden is remembered today for his *magnum opus* – a complete concordance to the Bible. This took him more than two years to complete, working generally 16 hours a day. The first edition was published in 1737. There were errors; the last corrections were not made until the 1930s. No doubt this labour of love was valuable (the book has never been out of print) and helped give meaning to Cruden's life. Inspired by this, someone might wish to produce a concordance for a more modern version of the Bible (Cruden, of course, was working with the Authorized Version of 1611). But this would not be a meaningful experience: my primitive tablet has a Bible app; using the New

International Version, I can search for any word in the text and find all uses of it in less time that it takes to turn the pages of Cruden. And now Google and Amazon are, in effect, concordances of any book that is published in digital form.

Innovation has distributional effects, benefiting some, but depriving others of livelihoods, or taking the value from their lives. The early days of the Industrial Revolution saw the replacement of skilled jobs (weaving, for example) by machines tended by workers with lesser skills; it was this trend that the Privy Council had earlier sought to quash (Heilbroner, 1953: 28), and, after its prohibition had been lifted, the original Luddites tried to prevent through smashing machines. But the technological advances of the twentieth century went in the opposite direction: unskilled, mind-numbing jobs were automated. On the optimistic version of the narrative, this freed up people to do more creative things: Schumpeter's 'creative destruction' became the way towards more creativity. Toilsome labour was largely eliminated. There were, of course, transition costs (the unskilled unemployed; the miners' strikes in Britain in the 1970s and 1980s), but these costs were generally not passed on to the next generation. Education, and particularly flexible education (teaching people how to teach themselves the new skills they would need in a rapidly changing workplace), was highly valued – which, of course, was great news for academics.

Now, though, in the twenty-first century other jobs are encountering the effects of automation and digitization. Within academia, more and more courses are being recorded and made available to students online. So: why go to that 08:30 class, when you can watch a replay at a civilized time from the comfort of your own bedroom? In fact, why stay on campus at all – why not watch from home? The growth of MOOCs (massive online open courses) is beginning to produce another effect, rather akin to that of the advent of the gramophone on Iowa tenors 90 years ago. Why should I listen to a second-rate live performance when I can buy a recording of a superstar such as Caruso? Why should I go to a lecture at which a junior academic tries to explain what Greg Mankiw or Ha-Joon Chang are saying when I can watch the great teachers themselves explain it to me? I can even replay the bits I didn't understand the first time; my lecturer tends to get angry if I ask him to repeat himself multiple times. Furthermore, it would not seem to be an impediment for a superstar's career to have died. As long as the lecture videos are still available, the multiple-choice tests still graded by computer, and an expert system answers questions, using deceased personnel would be a great cost saving. This is all not such great news for most academics.

These changes, then, reduce the set of feasible valuable lives. If one really wants to be a professor, in this brave new world it might not be possible, just as fairly good tenors and artisan weavers discovered that their lives were undermined by technological change. Technology creates new opportunities; but destroys some others.

The argument above is predicated on the assumption that work that the worker knows is valuable can, and often does, form part of a life that someone has reason to value. This is not a necessary truth; but work is usually part of a person's identity (Steedman, 2013; Thompson, 1963). Unemployment is so debilitating not because of the waste of resources it involves, or the deterioration of skills not used, but because of the social and psychological costs it levies. For many people, most of their relationships are with work colleagues. In a sense, they form a second family: people we can argue with, fall out with, but who will (almost) always take us back. Shared experiences, discussion of both work and non-work topics, and so forth create the connections that we find most meaningful (even if we don't get on with our line managers). Not to have the opportunity to engage with this network leaves a person isolated, and, usually, unhappy.

Conclusion

Technology changes the way in which we produce things; but it also changes the feasible set of valuable lives. Thus, a life that someone has decided will be of value to him or her *ex ante* may turn out, in retrospect, to have been without value. As the rate of change increases, the chances of this happening become larger. Schools and universities cannot prepare their students directly for jobs that do not yet exist; the best approach is probably to teach students important transferable skills, and, importantly, how to teach themselves new things. Or, if machines will do much of the work, some consideration on how to use leisure time in valuable and meaningful ways will become important.

We have good reason to expect that disruptive change is likely to happen. Human ingenuity, increasing population and increasing networking possibilities allow for ideas to have sex more easily, producing more ideas. The family of ideas grows, increasing not only wealth but changing what is possible for us. But it is inherently unpredictable what, precisely, will change and what will not. (Watching old science fiction films brings this home: *Blade Runner* was referred to above; the various incarnations of *Flash Gordon* have other examples that are similar.)

For some, this 'brave new world' is exciting – a technical utopia; for others, though, it is deeply disturbing. Would decoupling work from income increase the feasibility set again? In other words, would something like a guaranteed basic income solve the problem, allowing people to live lives that they have reason to value without having to worry about their financial feasibility? Or, again, can we learn to live with uncertainty and unpredictability? Attempting to answer these big questions is work for another day.

References

Acemoglu, D., and Robinson, J. A. (2012) *Why Nations Fail: The Origins of Power, Prosperity and Poverty*. New York: Random House.

Desmet, K., Kristian Nagy, D., and Rossi-Hansberg, E. (2018) The geography of development. *Journal of Political Economy*, 126 (3): 903–83.

Diamond, J. (2005) *Collapse: How Societies Choose to Fail or Succeed*. New York: Viking.

Elder-Vass, D. (2016) *Profit and Gift in the Digital Economy*. Cambridge: Cambridge University Press.

FAO, International Fund for Agricultural Development, UNICEF, World Food Programme and WHO (2017) *The State of Food Security and Nutrition in the World 2017: Building Resilience for Peace and Food Security*. Rome: FAO.

Flynn, S. I. (2018) Economic growth. In *Principles of Business: Economics*: 87–93. Hackensack, NJ: Salem Press.

Harford, T. (2017a) *Fifty Inventions that Shaped the Modern Economy*. New York: Riverhead Books.

(2017b) What we get wrong about technology. *Financial Times*, 7 July: www.ft.com/content/32c31874-610b-11e7-8814-0ac7eb84e5f1.

(2017c). We are still waiting for the robot revolution. *Financial Times*, 30 June: www.ft.com/content/4423a404-5c0f-11e7-9bc8-8055f264aa8b.

Heilbroner, R. L. (1953) *The Worldly Philosophers: The Lives, Times, and Ideas of the Great Economic Thinkers*. New York: Touchstone.

Keynes, J. M. (1930) Economic possibilities for our grandchildren. Paper presented in Madrid, 29 June [also in his *Essays in Persuasion* (New York: Harcourt Brace, 1932): 358–73].

Kuran, T. (2011) *The Long Divergence: How Islamic Law Held Back the Middle East.* Princeton, NJ: Princeton University Press.

Kurlansky, M. (2016) *Paper: Paging through History.* New York: Norton.

Kurz, H. D. (2010) Technical progress, capital accumulation and income distribution in classical economics: Adam Smith, David Ricardo and Karl Marx. *European Journal of the History of Economic Thought,* 17 (5): 1183–222.

Landsberger, H. A. (1958) *Hawthorne Revisited: Management and the Worker: Its Critics, and Developments in Human Relations in Industry.* Ithaca, NY: Cornell University Press.

Lenin, V. I. (1902) *What Is to Be Done? Burning Questions of Our Movement.* Stuttgart: Dietz.

Lepore, J. (2019) Are robots competing for your job? *The New Yorker,* 4 March: www.newyorker.com/magazine/2019/03/04/are-robots-competing-for-your-job.

Lohr, S. (1987) Making cars the Volvo way. *New York Times,* 23 June: www.nytimes.com/1987/06/23/business/making-cars-the-volvo-way.html.

McRae, H. (2018) Five signs we have reached peak Facebook. *Independent,* 15 April: www.independent.co.uk/voices/social-media-facebook-fintech-alibaba-paypal-economy-a8305786.html.

Mankiw, N. G. (1997) *Principles of Economics.* New York: Harcourt College Publishers.

Malthus, T. (1798) *Essay on the Principle of Population.* London: J. Johnson.

Marx, K. (1867) *Das Kapital: Kritik der politischen Ökonomie,* vol. 1. Hamburg: Otto Meissner.

Marx, K., and Engels, F. (1932) *A Critique of the German Ideology.* Moscow: Marx–Engels Institute [written 1845–6].

Mayo, E. (1949) *The Social Problems of an Industrial Civilisation.* London: Routledge & Kegan Paul.

Meadows, D. H., Randers, J., Meadows, D. L., and Behrens, W. W. (1972) *The Limits to Growth: A Report for the Club of Rome's Project on the Predicament of Mankind.* New York: Universe Books.

Phelps, E. S. (1961) The golden rule of accumulation: a fable for growthmen. *American Economic Review,* 51 (4): 638–43.

Postman, N. (1985) *Amusing Ourselves to Death: Public Discourse in the Age of Show Business.* London: Viking Books.

Ricardo, D. (1817) *The Principles of Political Economy and Taxation.* London: John Murray.

Ridley, M. (2010) *The Rational Optimist: How Prosperity Evolves.* New York: HarperCollins.

Rockström, J., W. Steffen, K. Noone, A. Persson, F. S. Chapin III, E. F. Lambin, T. M. Lenton, M. Scheffer, C. Folke, H. J. Schellnhuber, B. Nykvist, C. A. de Wit, T. Hughes, S. van der Leeuw, H. Rodhe, S. Sörlin, P. K. Snyder, R. Costanza, U. Svedin, M. Falkenmark, L. Karlberg, R. W. Corell, V. J. Fabry, J. Hansen, B. Walker, D. Liverman, K. Richardson, P. Crutzen and J. A. Foley (2009) A safe operating space for humanity. *Nature*, 461: 472–5 [extended version published as Planetary boundaries: exploring the safe operating space for humanity. *Ecology and Society*, 14 (2). DOI: 10.5751/ES-03180-14023].

Roessingh, C., and T. Plasil (eds.) (2010) *Between Horse and Buggy and Four-Wheel Drive: Change and Diversity among Mennonite Settlements in Belize, Central America*. Amsterdam: VU University Press.

Schumpeter, J. A. (1942) *Capitalism, Socialism and Democracy*. New York: Harper & Brothers.

Sen, A. K. (1999) *Development as Freedom*. Oxford: Oxford University Press.

Smith, A. (1776) *An Inquiry into the Nature and Causes of the Wealth of Nations*. London: W. Strahan.

Smith, S. (2017) Is economic growth essential for human flourishing? A view from economics and Christian theology. Paper presented at a conference on human flourishing, LCC International University, Klaipėda, Lithuania, 24 March.

Solow, R. M. (1956) A contribution to the theory of economic growth. *Quarterly Journal of Economics*, 70 (1): 65–94.

Steedman, C. (2013) *An Everyday Life of the English Working Class: Work, Self and Sociability in the Early Nineteenth Century*. Cambridge: Cambridge University Press.

Thompson, E. P. (1963) *The Making of the English Working Class*. London: Victor Gollancz.

PART III

Social Choice and Capabilities in Action

14 Measuring the independence of 'dependent' persons based on the capability approach[*]

HIDEYUKI KOBAYASHI AND REIKO GOTOH

Introduction

This chapter is an attempt to formulate an individual capability to live 'independently', by shedding light on patients who live at home and use home caring services. Let us first briefly describe our research interest.

Elderly people living in a local community, and especially those discharged from hospital and receiving home-caring services, are often forced to live a 'dependent' life. They need public pensions, home caring services, moving support or neighborhood support. However, economic or social dependence does not necessarily imply individual existential dependence.

To understand individual independence as a whole, we need a broader perspective, which goes beyond economic and social independence. For example, the UN Convention on the Rights of Persons with Disabilities (United Nations, 2006), adopted in 2006, declares that all persons, however impaired physically or mentally, should have the right to maintain independence by using care services and the right to decision making with assistances. Economic or social dependence is not regarded as interfering with individual existential independence. Rather, such a dependence is considered an effective condition for the real 'independence' of a disabled person – that is, for living his or her own life and being respected as a unique individual.[1]

[*] We greatly thank the organizers and participants of the Cambridge Capability Conference from 22 to 23 June 2018 for their inspiring comments and discussions. We also heartily thank Flavio Comim and Hiroyuki Kuribayashi, who gave warm and useful advice for the revision of this chapter.
[1] Refer to article 19: 'Living independently and being included in the community. b) Persons with disabilities have access to a range of in-home, residential and other community support services, including personal assistance necessary to support living and inclusion in the community, and to prevent isolation or segregation from the community' (United Nations, 2006).

This chapter considers individual 'freedom', described in Sen's capability approach, an essential factor to understand individual independence as a whole (Sen and Williams, 1982; Sen, 2009). It involves the freedom to choose from an individual's 'capability' a style of living helped by others, according to his or her own aims and situations, while the decision to choose from his or her capability can be an assisted one if fully informed.

Suppose, for example, a visiting nurse helps her patient to 'bathe by himself' and to 'bathe assisted by a caregiver'. He might choose the former, which takes more time and energy, if he has no plan other than going to bed after bathing; or he might choose the latter, which takes less time and energy, if he wants to write a letter after bathing. Imagine, in contrast, the nurse sets a goal for the patient of escaping from economic or social dependence and concentrates only on improving his skill to 'bathe by himself'. Then he would be able to bathe but might have to give up many other activities on the day he bathes, as 'bathing by himself' takes time and tires him.

In Japan today, the costs of home-visit nursing services after a patient's discharge from hospital are covered by a universal social insurance system.[2] Behind this system there is an ideal of equality based on a deep recognition of human suffering, claiming that the enormous costs of diseases and disabilities should not be paid for by the patient alone but be shared by society. However, there is a growing demand to cut the increasing medical expenditures caused by a rapid ageing of the society. There is also a concern about the moral hazard of receiving benefits without paying the costs. In short, we still find a deep-rooted social norm to encourage 'self-support without social support'.

The purpose of this chapter is to consider the following questions. How much freedom do home care patients really have in terms of the capability to achieve independence by combining, for example, 'learning the art of living' and 'accessing social services'? How can we evaluate the effectiveness of the nursing care process through the capability approach?

Basic model for formulating the capability approach

To re-examine the inner relation between choice and opportunity, this chapter focuses on the 'fractal' structure of capability, as follows. An

---

[2] Home care nursing service is covered by universal long-term care or healthcare insurance. However, individuals are allowed to use their private assets and private care provided by family members, which are not examined in this study.

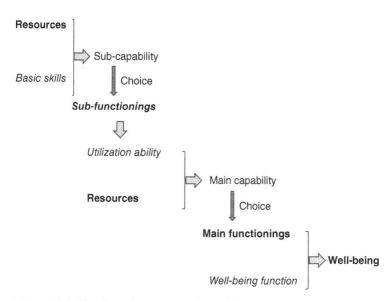

Figure 14.1 The 'fractal' structure of capability

Note: Well-being is produced by main functioning, which is produced by transforming resources with the individual's utilization ability, while his or her utilization ability is produced by transforming resources with sub-functionings, which are in turn produced by transforming resources with his or her basic skills

individual's well-being is generated by *main functionings*, which are produced by transforming resources with his or her *utilization ability* (Sen, 1980; Basu, 1987), while his or her *utilization ability* is produced by transfoming resources with *sub-functionings*, which are in turn produced by transforming resources with his or her *basic skills*.[3]

In sum, the level of an individual's *capability* (a set of *functionings*) is constrained by his or her total resources and *utilization ability*, as is usually understood in economic models (Sen, 1985; Basu and Lopez-Calva, 2011). Yet there are various intermediate factors between *capabilities* and *resource constraints*, as Figure 14.1 shows.

An individual's *sub-capability* is articulated in the following way (Gotoh, 2014a):[4] denote two kinds of commodities by z_1, z_2; the skill

[3] In this chapter, the distinction between '*functionings*' and '*sub-functionings*' is there only for analytical purposes. It does not mean that '*sub-functionings*' are in any way less important than '*main functionings*' in terms of morality or aesthetics, for example.

[4] The basic idea of the following model comes from Becker (1965, 1976) and Lancaster (1966).

to transform z_1 into sub-functionings x_1, x_2 by a_1, b_1; the skill to transform z_2 into sub-functionings x_1, x_2 by a_2, b_2; the prices of resources z_1, z_2 by p_1, p_2; and the total of resources (income, time, personal assets, social resources as nursing services, etc.) by Y, where a_j, b_j, z_j, p_j ($j = 1, 2$) are positive. Then we have the following formulation, which represents sub-capability:

$$p_1 z_1 + p_2 z_2 \leq Y, \text{ where } z_1 = a_1 x_1 + b_1 x_2, z_2 = a_2 x_1 + b_2 x_2.$$

That is, $(p_1 a_1 + p_2 a_2)x_1 + (p_1 b_1 + p_2 b_2)x_2 \leq Y$.

The equation part of this formulation expresses the *iso-cost curve*. It indicates the *absolute* ease or difficulty of an individual's realization of sub-functionings x_1, x_2, given his or her command over commodities represented by the resource constraint Y and given his or her ability to use them. It also indicates his or her marginal rate of technical substitution (MRTS) of two sub-functionings – that is, the *relative* ease or difficulty of an individual.

Given this curve as an upper boundary, an individual can achieve various combinations of sub-functionings by changing the way of using resources or his or her utilization abilities (Gotoh, 2014b). In the following analysis we assume that the resources z_1, z_2 are nursing services allocated to two sub-functionings z_{i1}, z_{i2}, and the prices p_1, p_2 represent the relative value of sub-functionings, which reflects a certain social norm. Figure 14.2 shows the iso-cost curve of a person in the space of two sub-functionings.

Note that, even with the same resources, two individuals with different utilization abilities may end up with different capability sets. In Figure 14.3, it is assumed that individual 2 is somewhat better in his or her utilization ability for functioning x_1, whereas his or her utilization ability for functioning x_2 is the same as that of individual 1. As a result, individual 1's capability is dominated by individual 2's capability.

Next, an individual's main capability is articulated in the following: denote the amount of an individual i's functioning of 'living in security' by t_i and the production function by f_i, which produces 'living in security' t_i using two sub-functionings x_{i1}, x_{i2} and the resources available for 'living in security' by r_i. That is: $t_i = f_i(x_{i1}, x_{i2}; r_i)$, where the partial derivatives of t_i with respect to both x_{i1} and x_{i2} are non-negative. We assume the strict quasi-concavity of function f_i.

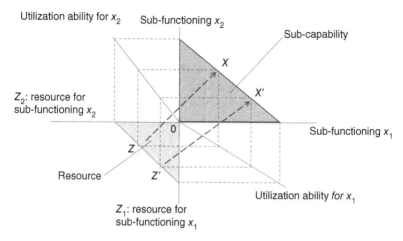

Figure 14.2 Iso-cost curves in the space of two sub-functionings
Note: The sub-functioning vectors **x**, **x'** are transformed from resources **z**, **z'**.

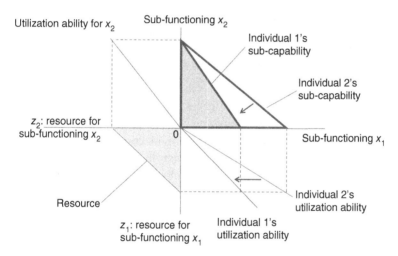

Figure 14.3 Domination in sub-capability by the differences in utilization ability
Note: Individual 1's capability is dominated by individual 2's capability, since individual 2 has a higher utilization ability for x_1, while his or her utilization ability for x_2 is the same as that of individual 1.

Similarly, denote the amount of an individual i's functioning of 'having enjoyment' by e_i and the production function by g_i, which produces 'having enjoyment' e_i using two sub-functionings x_{i1}, x_{i2} and resources available for 'having enjoyment' by m_i. That is: $e_i = g_i\,(x_{i1},$ $x_{i2}; m_i)$, where the partial derivatives of t_i with respect to both x_{i1} and x_{i2} are non-negative. We assume the strict quasi-concavity of function g_i. For simplicity, let us assume that the well-being function of individual i is represented by an additive form of those two main functionings. Then we can formulate the problem of choosing the optimal sub-functionings to maximize the sum of 'living in security' t_i *and* 'having enjoyment' e_i under the constraint of resources and utilization abilities as follows:

$$\text{Max.} \quad t_i + e_i = f_i\left(x_{i1}, x_{i2}; r_i\right) + g_i\left(x_{i1}, x_{i2}; m_i\right),$$
$$\text{s.t.} \quad P_Z\left(a_i x_{i1} + b_i x_{i2}\right) = Y.$$

Let us denote by x_i^{*} a sub-functioning vector that satisfies the first condition and denote by t_i^{*} and e_i^{*} the corresponding levels of 'living in security' and 'having enjoyment', where $p_z\left(a_i x_{i1}^{*} + b_i x_{i2}^{*}\right) = Y$ and $t_i^{*} = f_i\left(X_{i1}^{*}, X_{i2}^{*}; r_i^{*}\right)$ and $e_i^{*} = g_i\left(X_{i1}^{*}, X_{i2}^{*}; m_i^{*}\right)$ hold.

Setting up the space for measuring the achieved functioning vectors

Given a certain amount of resources and utilization ability, some functionings can be complementary to each other. For example, increasing functioning achievement in controlling pain leads to increasing functioning achievements in eating and bathing. However, other functionings substitute (trade off) each other. In order to grasp the frontier of an individual's capability – that is, the upper limit of his or her achievement in functionings – we focus on those functionings essential for individual 'independence' that substitute each other.

Figure 14.4 summarizes the structure of functionings identified in self-reported patients' experiences with nursing care services, which we gathered through this research. Enquiries as to patients' experiences have been carried out in order to overcome the problems of patient satisfaction questionnaires (Jenkinson, Coulter and Bruster, 2002; Coulter and Cleary, 2001). Individual functionings can be divided into basic functionings (eating, bathing, etc.), fundamental ones (getting relief from pain, knowing about one's own disease, etc.)

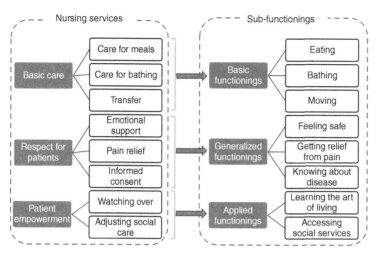

Figure 14.4 Individual functionings and sub-functionings identified in self-reported patients' experiences with nursing services

and applied ones (learning the art of living, accessing social services, etc.).[5] Note that 'learning the art of living' means coming up with or learning the small arts for managing one's daily living without help from anyone else. To help this (applied) functioning, the nursing service has to arrange things so that a patient can do things with minimal assistance. 'Accessing social services' means adjusting oneself to doing things with others' help, and the corresponding nursing service is to give a patient useful knowledge for activating social service usage.

We calculate correlations between functionings in order to examine their relationships. A strongly negative correlation between two functionings suggests a substitutional relationship (to be distributed downwards to the right). In contrast, a strongly positive correlation suggests a complementary relationship.

---

[5] It is assumed that a substitutional relationship can be inferred between basic functionings as well as between applied functionings, while a complementary relationship can be inferred between basic functionings and applied functionings. For example, individuals cannot eat while bathing, but improvements in 'eating' and 'bathing' will lead to improvements in 'learning the art of living' and 'accessing social services'. In addition, we can regard 'knowing about one's own diseases' and 'getting relief from pain' as more fundamental functionings.

Table 14.1 *Correlation between sub-functionings*

Variables	1	2	3	4	5	6
1 Eating	–					
2 Bathing	0.194	–				
3 Feeling	–0.071	0.082	–			
4 Getting relief from pain	0.092	0.150	0.050	–		
5 Knowing about disease	0.127	0.171	0.073	0.153	–	
6 Learning the art of living	0.044	–0.139	–0.190	–0.206	–0.229	–
7 Accessing social services	–0.038	–0.209	–0.334	–0.425*	–0.413*	–0.433*

Notes: Pearson product–moment correlation coefficients: $^*p < 0.05$, $^{**}p < 0.01$.

Pearson's correlation coefficients between two functionings are shown in Table 14.1. There is shown to be a mildly negative correlation ($p = -0.433$ with statistically significance) between 'learning the art of living' and 'accessing social services'. With this result, we select 'learning the art of living' and 'accessing social services' in setting up the space of individuals' capabilities.[6]

Collecting empirical data on functioning achievement and utilization ability

The enquiry was carried out for home care patients who utilized visiting nursing services at a visiting nursing station in 2012/13. Data analysis was carried out using responses to patients' self-administered questionnaires on their experiences with nursing services.[7] The respondents provided scores of five ('Always'), four ('Often'), three

[6] To measure achievements in functionings, we used a questionnaire of patients' experiences with nursing care, in which patients scored their sub-functionings achievement level from 1 to 5 (Kobayashi, Takemura and Kanda, 2011).

[7] We reworded the questionnaire for home care situations from the original version, which had been set up for hospitalized situations, since nursing services cover the reconstruction of daily life after discharge as well as treatment in the acute phases.

('Sometimes'), two ('Occasionally') and one ('Not') according to the frequency of patients' experiences with nursing service provision. The respondents who chose 'Does not apply' were excluded from the analysis.[8] In the enquiry 232 home care patients were invited to take part, and 192 valid responses were received (response rate: 83 per cent). Of the 192, 83 patients were excluded, who chose 'Does not apply' for at least one of the two items of 'learning the art of living' and 'accessing social services', so 109 home care patients were included for further analysis.[9]

The utilization ability itself is usually difficult to observe. We use a score based on the 'Usual activity' of the EuroQol indicator (EQ-5D-3L) in the Japanese version (Tsuchiya et al., 2002), which covers working, studying, family life, leisure activity, etc., to identify differences in utilization abilities (the ability to transform the nursing service provided to 'learning the art of living' and 'accessing social services'). With this indicator, we define the 'restricted group' as those home care patients who have severe problems in everyday activities, and the 'free group' as those with few problems in everyday activities.

Of the 48 respondents included in the analysis, 56 per cent of them are male, with a mean age of 75.2 years and an average length of visiting nursing usage of 3.4 years; 33 per cent are in the restricted group and 67 per cent in the free group. There is no statistically significant difference in the age and the length of visiting nursing usage between the two groups.

Table 14.2 shows the means of sub-functioning and main functioning achievements by the two groups. With this result, we can argue some interesting points, though there are statistically significant differences in all sub-functionings and main functionings between these two groups. First, with reference to the results for the sub-functioning achievement level, 'learning the art of living' and 'accessing social services' of the restricted group are not statistically different from those

---

[8] The category of 'Does not apply' was for respondents who felt they had not experienced any situation corresponding to an item (Labarere et al., 2001).
[9] It is worth noting that 61 of the 109 (56 per cent) chose the highest scores for both functionings (5, 5), presumably for the following three reasons. First, the respondents who wanted to give a score beyond 5 had to choose the vector (5, 5). Second, these two sub-functionings can be complementary for some individuals, depending on their attributes. Third, the respondents distributed in the upper right of (5, 5) in the functioning plane may have more resources (provided by family members) than others.

Table 14.2 *Difference in functioning achievement by activity restriction*

	The restricted	The free
	n = 16	n = 32
Sub-functioning achievement		
Learning the art of living	4.19	4.06
	(0.19)	(0.13)
Accessing social services	3.44	3.66
	(0.43)	(0.18)
Main functioning achievement		
Security	2.64	2.86
	(0.20)	(0.13)
Enjoyment	2.40	2.33
	(0.25)	(0.12)

Note: mean (SE).

of the free group. In addition, neither of the sub-functioning vectors of the two groups dominates the other. Why?

Second, comparing the two groups, we find several paradoxes, such as that the restricted group achieves somewhat higher in 'learning the art of living' than the free group, even though they have more severe problems with everyday activities than the free group. Moreover, comparing within the restricted group, its members achieve higher in 'learning the art of living' than 'accessing social services', even though, in terms of utilization ability, they are better at 'accessing social services'. To resolve these paradoxes, we need to know what their capability is behind their sub-functioning achievement. Next, therefore, we estimate their capability.

Estimation of an individual capability set

Theoretically, if all individuals have the same resources and the same utilization ability, then we can assume that they have the same capability sets, from which each individual can choose any functionings vector based on his or her diverse evaluation functions. Furthermore, if we can assume that each individual is rational enough to choose an optimal option, then he or she is expected to achieve a functioning vector on the frontier of his or her capability set. If this is the case, we can estimate the frontiers of capability sets of individuals with the same

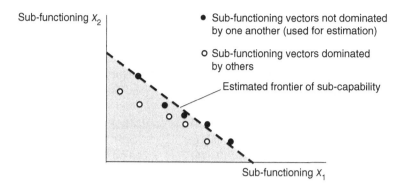

Figure 14.5 Estimating the frontier of capability using functioning vectors
Note: Functioning vectors, which are not dominated by one another, are assumed to be located on the frontier of capability, and are used for estimating the frontier.

resources and the same utilization ability by plotting and connecting their dispersed functioning vectors. Note that, if the utilization function is approximately linear, then the frontier of the capability sets is also approximately linear. This suggests that we might be able to use the ordinary least squares (OLS) method, which chooses parameters of a linear function of a set of explanatory variables by the principle of least squares, for estimating that frontier.[10] Figure 14.5 shows how to choose the sub-functioning vectors used for the estimation.

Then regression lines of their achievement points are derived by linear regression on the $x_1 x_2$ plane, as follows. First, x_2 is regressed only with x_1 (model 1). Next, a dummy variable r ($r = 1$ for the restricted group; $r = 0$ for the free group) is added to the regression in order to examine whether or not facing restriction influences the relation between the two functionings (model 2). Assuming that the degree of restriction influences the achievement level of x_1, a cross-term $x_1 * r$ is added (model 3). Finally, to control the effects of sex and age, dummy variables *male* (*male* = 1 for men) and *age80₊* (*age80₊* = 1 for respondents of 80 years of age or older) are added to the regression analysis (model 4).

---

[10] To obtain the frontier of the capability set, we may refer to the empirical estimation technique for the micro-production function of a firm with the maximum product obtainable from the input combination at the given state of the technical knowledge of the firm (Aigner and Chu, 1968).

Table 14.3 *Estimation of the frontier of sub-capability*

		Model 1	Model 2	Model 3	Model 4
β_0	Constant	11.584**	11.857**	8.250**	8.039**
		(1.427)	(1.438)	(1.596)	(1.615)
β_1	x_1	−1.794**	−1.820**	−1.000**	−0.894*
		(0.325)	(0.323)	(0.361)	(0.379)
β_2	R		−0.371	8.350**	8.256**
			(0.316)	(2.471)	(2.471)
β_3	$x_1 * r$			−2.000**	−1.977**
				(0.563)	(0.563)
β_4	Male				0.007
					(0.277)
β_5	age80$_+$				−0.435
					(0.283)
	R^2	0.465	0.471	0.612	0.617

Notes: Coefficients (standard errors) by multi-regression analysis objective variable: x_2, n = 48, * $p < 0.05$, ** $p < 0.001$.

The regression models are therefore as follows.

Model 1 $x_2{}^i = \beta_0 + \beta_1 x_1{}^i + \varepsilon.$

Model 2 $x_2{}^i = \beta_0 + \beta_1 x_1{}^i + \beta_2 r + \varepsilon.$

Model 3 $x_2{}^i = \beta_0 + \beta_1 x_1{}^i + \beta_2 r + \beta_3 x_1{}^i * r + \varepsilon.$

Model 4 $x_2{}^i = \beta_0 + \beta_1 x_1{}^i + \beta_2 r + \beta_3 x_1{}^i * r + \beta_4\, male + \beta_5\, age80_+ + \varepsilon.$

The result of regression analysis is shown in Table 14.3. Regression coefficients β_1 and β_3 in model 3 indicate statistically significant differences in the slopes of regressed lines between two groups. When adding controlling variables of sex and age (model 4), the fit of the model does not change. Model 3 is adopted for home care patients. Based on the assumption that individuals choose functionings to maximize their own aims, the areas surrounded by the regressed line and the two axes can approximate the capability set that they have in common (Figure 14.6). That is,

$$x_2^i + Bx_1^i \le Y, \text{ and } x_1 \ge 1, x_2 \ge 1.$$

Here, $B = -\left(\beta_1 + \beta_3 * r\right)$, $Y = \beta_0 + \beta_2 * r.$

Therefore, the capability set of each group is estimated as follows.

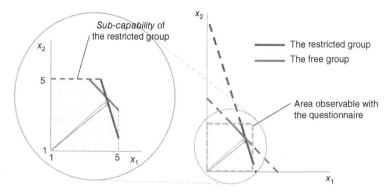

Figure 14.6 Sub-capabilities of the restricted and free groups
Notes: The right-hand panel is the estimated frontiers of two groups; the restricted group has a comparative advantage in 'accessing social services'; the left-hand panel focuses on the area observable by the questionnaire.

The free group of home care patients:

$x_1 + x_2 \leq 8.25$ and $x_1 \geq 1, x_2 \geq 1$.

The restricted group of home care patients:

$3x_1 + x_2 \leq 16.6$, and $x_1 \geq 1, x_2 \geq 1$.

The result of regression analysis shows statistically significant differences between the two groups in the slopes of the frontiers of their capability sets and in the x_2 intercepts. This suggests that different groups with different utilization abilities have different capability sets. The restricted group (with severe problems in everyday activity) has a steeper slope with a longer intercept for 'learning the art of living' and a shorter one for 'accessing social services' than the free group (patients with few problems in everyday activities). Given that the slope represents a marginal rate of technical substitution, the free group has a comparative advantage in 'learning the art of living', while the restricted group has one in 'accessing social services'. The results fit the features of comparative advantage.

Since scores for sub-functioning achievement are between one and five, the observable area of the two sub-functionings is $\{(x_1, x_2) \mid 1 \leq x_1 \leq 5, 1 \leq x_2 \leq 5\}$, shown in the left-hand panel of Figure 14.6. It shows that the frontier lines for the two groups cross in the observable area, and that the actual capability sets for the two groups do not dominate each other.

These results suggest the following. First, the difference in the shapes of the capability sets and intercepts can indicate that the capability sets are empirically different between groups with different utilization abilities, and the restricted group has a comparative advantage in 'accessing social services' and that the free group has one in 'learning the art of living'.[11] Second, the restricted group has a lower utilization ability, but their capabilities are not dominated by those of the free group. This indicates that more resources were distributed to the restricted group than to the free group, successfully improving the restricted group's capabilities to a level not inferior to those of the free group.

Production of main functionings by transforming sub-functionings

In this section we discuss how to capture the production of main functionings by transforming sub-functioning achievement. To specify main functionings, we use ICECAP-O, which was originally developed for the UK population (Grewal et al., 2006; Coast et al., 2008a, 2008b; Couzner et al., 2013). It is a measure of capability for the elderly and consists of five items: security, enjoyment, role, attachment and control. We choose security (an ability to think about the future without concern) and enjoyment (an ability to experience enjoyment and pleasure). We assume that the output (main functioning) is produced with the input (sub-functionings), where the input is combined with 'learning the art of living' and 'accessing social services', and the output is combined with 'living in security' (s_i) and 'having enjoyment' (e_i), without weighting, respectively. Thus we have definitions as follows.

Sub-functioning input　　　$X^i = x_{i1} + x_{i2}$.
Main functioning output　　$q_i = e_i + s_i$.

Under the assumption that the main functioning production function increases uniformly with inputs, its curve is estimated by regression. Uniformly increasing curves are obtained by linear regression, logarithmic regression and exponential regression without a constant term. Referring to coefficients of determination (R square), exponential

---

[11] Comparing the shapes (the slopes of the frontiers) of the capability sets for both groups, the x_1 intercept ('learning the art of living') is greater for the free group, while the x_2 intercept ('accessing social services') is greater for the restricted group.

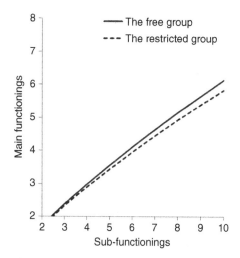

Figure 14.7 Main functioning production of the restricted and free groups
Note: The restricted group is less efficient than the free group in main functioning production even when inputs are similar.

regression fits the best among the estimated models. The result represents the main functionings production curve as follows.

The free group:

$$q_i = \left(x_{i1} + x_{i2}\right)^{0.788}, R^2 = 0.978.$$

The restricted group:

$$q_i = \left(x_{i1} + x_{i2}\right)^{0.766}, R^2 = 0.951.$$

Although the restricted group is not dominated in sub-functioning
achievement by the free group, this estimation suggests that the main
functioning achievement of the restricted group is lower than that of
the free group (Figure 14.7).

The result means that the restricted group is less effective than the
free group in producing main functionings, even though their sub-
functioning achievements are not dominated by that of the free group.
It is worth noting two points in the background. First, the production
function of the main functionings of the restricted group is less able
than that of the free group at any level of sub-functioning achievements. The disadvantageous condition for the restricted group fits
the actual situation. Second, there is a problem of freedom for the
restricted group in choosing a sub-functioning achievement vector.

Under the social norm of encouraging independent living without relying on others, the restricted group could not choose the optimum achievement vector but chose the vector 'learning the art of living' more than the optimal level, and thus they end up inferior to the free group in main functioning production. This is a loss in main functioning production, due to a social norm that restricts freedom of choice for sub-functioning achievement vectors.[12]

Conclusion

The capability approach gives us a conceptual framework for understanding what independence means in terms of freedom for an individual, as he or she can choose a particular style of independence from his or her capability set according to his or her own aims and situations. Our research question is how to formulate and measure an individual capability to live independently. To answer this question, we shed light on two types of home care patients, the restricted group and the free group, and investigate their capabilities to achieve independence by concentrating on their 'fractal structure', which consists of 'learning the art of living' and 'accessing social services' in a sub-functioning space and 'living in security' and 'having enjoyment' in a main functioning space.

Our conclusion can be summarized as follows. The empirical study shows that the restricted group receives more resources than the free group and that the sub-capability of the former is not dominated by the latter. However, the main functioning production of the restricted group is lower than that of the free group. Any judgement based on fairness would require us to take into account not only the richness of sub-capabilities but also social norms, as the latter can restrict the real freedom of choice of sub-functionings and expand the disadvantage of the restricted group in main functioning.

---

[12] Note that the free group chose an achievement vector in favour of 'accessing social services' against their comparative advantage, which causes a loss in main functioning production. We just mention two potential reasons for this. First, patients may mind the upper limit of social service provision and they might be apprehensive of a reduction in future service provision due to improvements in their daily living activities. Second, their care requirements are highly uncertain. There is a possibility that they will require a level of service at some point in the future that is not currently required. They are therefore liable to maintain their access to services by using them regularly even when they are not actually required at that time.

This chapter does not explicitly mention individual evaluation functions themselves but, interestingly, the 'fractal structure' of capabilities implicitly indicates individuals' own conceptions of independent lives. We hope that this research can help in a re-examination of how nursing care services can support the independence of people living at home in a community.

References

Aigner, D. J., and Chu, S. F. (1968) On estimating the industry production function. *American Economic Review*, 58 (4): 826–39.

Basu, K. (1987) Achievements, capabilities and the concept of well-being. *Social Choice and Welfare*, 4 (1): 69–76.

Basu, K., and Lopez-Calva, L. F. (2011) Functionings and capabilities. In *Handbook of Social Choice and Welfare*, vol. 2, Arrow, K. J., Sen, A. K., and Suzumura, K. (eds.): 153–87. Amsterdam: Elsevier.

Becker, G. (1965) A theory of the allocation of time. *Economic Journal*, 75: 493–517.

(1976) *The Economic Approach to Human Behavior*. Chicago: University of Chicago Press.

Coast, J., Flynn, T. N., Natarajan, L., Sproston, K., Lewis, J., Louviere, J. J., and Peters, T. J. (2008a) Valuing the ICECAP capability index for older people. *Social Science and Medicine*, 67 (5): 874–82.

Coast, J., Peters, T. J., Natarajan, L., Sproston, K., and Flynn, T. N. (2008b) An assessment of the construct validity of the descriptive system for the ICECAP capability measure for older people. *Quality of Life Research*, 17 (7): 967–76.

Coulter, A., and Cleary, P. (2001) Patients' experiences with hospital care in five countries. *Health Affairs*, 20 (3): 244–52.

Couzner, L., Crotty, M., Norman, R., and Ratcliffe, J. (2013) A comparison of the EQ-5D-3L and ICECAP-O in an older post-acute patient population relative to the general population. *Applied Economics & Health Policy*, 11 (4): 415–25.

Gotoh, R. (2014a) Equality of capabilities: how should we identify the boundary of an individual's capability? Paper presented at the 14th SAET conference on current trends in economics, Tokyo, Waseda University, 21 August.

(2014b) Reconceptualization of the capability approach: opportunity set/autonomy/identity. *Keizai Kenkyu*, 65 (4): 318–31 [in Japanese].

Grewal, I., Lewis, J., Flynn, T. N., Brown, J., Bond, J., and Coast, J. (2006) Developing attributes for a generic quality of life measure for older people: preferences or capabilities? *Social Science and Medicine*, 62 (8): 1891–901.

Jenkinson, C., Coulter, A., and Bruster, S. (2002) The Picker Patient Experience questionnaire: development and validation using data from inpatient surveys in five countries. *International Journal for Quality in Health Care*, 14 (5): 353–8.

Kobayashi, H., Takemura, Y., and Kanda, K. (2011) Patient perception of nursing service quality: an applied model of Donabedian's structure–process–outcome approach theory. *Scandinavian Journal of Caring Sciences*, 25 (3): 419–25.

Labarere, J., Francois, P., Auquier, P., Robert, C., and Fourny, M. (2001) Development of a French inpatient satisfaction questionnaire. *International Journal for Quality in Health Care*, 13 (2): 99–108.

Lancaster, K. J. (1966) A new approach to consumer theory. *Journal of Political Economy*, 74 (2): 132–57.

Sen, A. K. (1980) Equality of what? In *The Tanner Lectures in Human Values*, vol. 1, McMurrin, S. M. (ed.): 197–220. Cambridge: Cambridge University Press.

(1985) *Commodities and Capabilities*. Amsterdam: North-Holland.

(2009) *The Idea of Justice*. London: Penguin.

Sen, A. K., and Williams, B. (eds.) (1982) *Utilitarianism and Beyond*. Cambridge: Cambridge University Press.

Tsuchiya, A., Ikeda, S., Ikegami, N., Nishimura, S., Sakai, I., Fukuda, T., Hamashima, C., Hisashige, A., and Tamura, M. (2002) Estimating an EQ-5D population value set: the case of Japan. *Health Economics*, 11 (4): 341–53.

United Nations (2006) Convention on the Rights of Persons with Disabilities. New York: United Nations. www.un.org/disabilities/documents/convention/convention_accessible_pdf.pdf.

15 Indigenous challenges to the capability approach
A relational ontology of community and sustainability

ANA ESTEFANÍA CARBALLO

Introduction

The remarkable expansion of ethical considerations within development thinking is one of Amartya Sen's greatest legacies. For many, his work represents the fruition of Denis Goulet's call for reflection on the ethics of development.[1] Although he was not the first, Sen has perhaps been the most successful advocate of wedding these two enquiries. Framed within his criticism of neoclassical economics, he has attempted to integrate economics with normative considerations in the construction of his capability approach (CA). The latter reconstructs the concept of development in terms of and through examinations of individual freedom.

Sen's contributions to economics and development stem from his early work on social choice theory, growing from an early critique of the neoclassical definition of human being – challenging the narrow concept of the *Homo oeconomicus* – to the broader project of incorporating ethical considerations in mainstream economics and development thinking.[2] It was in this particular space that he included the possibility of making interpersonal comparisons between individual welfare and, at the same time, provided an analytical tool that portrayed individual agency as a fundamental element in development

---

[1] Among others, Goulet himself has highlighted the similarities between his project and Sen's actual work; see Goulet (1997), Crocker (1991) and Qizilbash (1996).

[2] See, for example, Sen (1977, 1984, 1987). The connection between Sen's work in social theory and the construction of the capability approach has been pointed out by many; see, for example, Agarwal, Humphries and Robeyns (2003), Alkire (2005), Evans (2002), Peter (2003) and Robeyns (2005).

strategy and economic growth. Sen shifted the concept of social choice, moving the 'focus from problems of aggregating individual preferences to participation and inclusion in democratic decision-making' (Agarwal, Humphries and Robeyns, 2003: 5). In this, he argued for considering broader sources of information for social choice, redirecting the focus towards fair procedures and democratic stances of participation. These, in turn, required more robust accounts of the agency and freedom of individuals in processes of choice. This way in which Sen articulated his concerns within social choice theory created a new space to reflect on considerations of individual freedom, and expanded beyond economics to become one of the pillars of mainstream development theory.[3] Development, in the words of Sen, should be seen as a process 'of expanding the real freedoms that people enjoy' (Sen, 1999: 36). The CA, therefore, analyses the different kinds of freedom that individuals enjoy 'in terms of the *capabilities* that a person has, that is, the substantive freedoms he or she enjoys to lead the kind of life he or she has reason to value' (Sen, 1999: 88, emphasis in original). However, beyond Sen's work critical engagement with the CA has expanded at a remarkable rate, both in academic and policy spheres in recent decades. In development policy, the clearest example is the human development (HD) approach, most notably articulated and employed by the United Nations, which is largely indebted to the work of Sen in particular, and the CA in general.[4] As a result of this success, there is a now a robust literature around the CA, both

[3] In fact, although Sen was generally concerned with the social evaluations of welfare, and incorporated moral principles into his studies of poverty and quality of life, it was not until the early 1980s, with the publication of his 'Development: which way now?' (Sen, 1983), that Sen started the discussions of the application of his theories of economics to a more systematic approach to development. And it was from here onwards that most of his works would address issues of development, leading him to engage in the construction of the human development approach, which would perhaps reach the highest systematization in his *Development as Freedom* (Sen, 1999).

[4] Sen was a key figure in the original team that developed the first *Human Development Report* (UNDP, 1990a), which developed the HD methodology, and has often contributed to the yearly background papers of the annual reports subsequently. See UNDP (1991), Anand and Sen (1994), (1995) and (1998) and UNDP (1999) and (2004). Further, the centrality of his role in the construction of the HD approach has been widely recognized, and Sen is credited with giving the theoretical framing to the policy project originally coordinated by Mahbub Ul Haq. See, for example, UNDP (1990b), Fukuda-Parr (2003a) and (2003b), McNeill (2007) and Ki-moon (2010).

challenging it theoretically and practically, and extending its insights to diverse contexts and areas of enquiry; clear examples of this are the edited collections of Comim, Qizilbash and Alkire (2008), Basu and Kanbur (2009) and Comim, Fennell and Anand (2018).

In recent years the CA's relations to non-Western, particularly indigenous, theories and peoples have become a growing area in the literature for the possibilities they offer to expand considerations of environmental justice, to frame intercultural public policies and considerations on issues of self-determination or valuations of the natural world and to contribute to a dialogue on the philosophical foundations of the approach.[5] This chapter contributes to this literature, by analysing the connections between the CA and contemporary trends in development discussions in Latin America stemming from indigenous views of development. In particular, the chapter explores the discussions of 'buen vivir' (Spanish for 'good living') emerging from the Andean region, and the contributions they can make to explore collective and environmental issues within the CA. 'Buen vivir' (BV), itself a translation into Spanish, refers to a notion emerging from the indigenous philosophies in the region, which focuses on a harmonic understanding of the life cycle.[6] In recent years policy documents and initiatives have linked the ideas of BV and HD, particularly to Sen's work.

This chapter explores these connections and offers a rereading of Sen's CA from the perspective of the Andean region, which highlights their differences. The aim of this chapter is to contribute to the engagement of the CA with indigenous philosophies, and to use the latter's insights to push the former's boundaries. In particular, I will discuss the differences between the relational ontology that underpins the BV

---

[5] See, for example, Schlosberg and Carruthers (2010), Panzironi (2012), Klein (2015) and (2016), Bockstael and Watene (2016), Watene and Yap (2015), Watene (2016), Merino (2016), Godfrey-Wood and Mamani-Vargas (2017), Yap and Yu (2016) and Sangha et al. (2015). In 2016 the *Oxford Development Studies* journal dedicated an entire issue to expanding these conversations.

[6] The translation of these terms is a hotly debated issue. 'Buen vivir' (in Spanish) is a translation of *sumak kawsay* (SK) in Quechua, both of which are only the most well-known terms that could be understood in English as 'good living', 'good life' or 'life in plenitude' and are commonly used to refer to these indigenous frameworks. In general, I use either BV or SK interchangeably to refer to these ideas. This by no means seeks to ignore the multiplicity of debates on the issue of translation (from the indigenous languages into Spanish or English) but, rather, is an attempt to direct our attention to the impact of these ideas on other frameworks. On this issue, see Gudynas (2014a).

framework and the dualistic ontology upon which Sen's CA is built. While Sen's ethical considerations in development remain of paramount importance for contemporary thinking and practice, the focus on individual freedom within the CA is embedded within a dualistic ontology that separates humans from nature and individuals from their societies. A consideration of the challenges associated with BV allows us to address some of the most contentious areas within the CA literature: those relating to collective capabilities and sustainability issues.

The discussion is articulated in two main sections. In the first section, discussions of BV are analysed in connection to contemporary policy and academic discussions of development. Here, the links with ideas of HD and to the work of Sen become explicit. In the second section, the chapter explores in more detail the ethical challenges that the ideas of BV make to Amartya Sen's CA. It does so by engaging two indigenous notions, *ayllu* (community) and *Pachamama* (Mother Earth). Exploring the tensions that stem from the relevance that these notions have for BV serves as an open invitation for capability theorists to engage with non-Western philosophical frameworks and a reminder of the importance of providing social and collective spaces to reflect on the ethical value that non-human others and nature have for discussions of development.

Contemporary trends of human development in Latin America: Sen and the policy understandings of 'buen vivir'

'El retorno del Indio': reframing the debate on development

In 1991 Xavier Albó published his famous essay entitled 'El retorno del Indio' ('The return of the Indian') in *Revista Andina,* a famous Peruvian journal (Albó, 1991). There he addresses the rise of indigenous social movements and political groups in South America in the 1970s and 1980s. His insightful survey of the events occurring across the region gave ample evidence of a phenomenon that, although it did not originally emerge in the 1980s, has experienced a significant expansion since then. The 'indigenous problematic' – that is, the articulation of issues and social movements around indigenous peoples, groups and movements – appeared to have recovered its strength after decades in which social and political resistance was articulated mainly around the constitution of trade unions, syndicates and peasant organizations (Albó, 1991: 299). From that period onwards the indigenous roots of social struggles have had a stronger presence in public spaces, confronting the exclusionary politics of modern democracies in Latin America. In the Andean countries in particular, this has been accompanied by a process of recovery of the indigenous past and customs as central categories for national politics (Rivera Cusicanqui, 1990, 2010; Choque and Mamani, 2001; Albro, 2006; de la Cadena, 2010; Fabricant, 2010).

The struggles of these social movements have not only focused on an expansion of democratic politics but have, more largely, included an attempt to recover indigenous philosophical traditions and knowledge, once seen as synonymous with barbarism and 'incompatible with civilization and development'.[7] This irruption of indigenous knowledge in national politics historically dominated by social segregation – particularly built on the exclusion of the indigenous heritage – has brought forward an agenda of political, social and economic demands largely neglected in political discussions. Indigenous epistemologies, institutions and traditions, historically relegated to an 'uncivilized' past, have made a fruitful and forceful irruption in contemporary politics. Transcending the boundaries that labelled them exclusively as remnants of the past, they have significantly altered the political universe of the Andean countries, opening up spaces for an intercultural and intertemporal dialogue of forms of knowledge that has profoundly shaped decision-making processes and policy plans (Albro, 2006: 395). Perhaps the most salient of these efforts to create a space for local traditions and indigenous philosophies in contemporary policy making has been that of the 'buen vivir' initiatives, which have spearheaded regional discussions of development. It is precisely the incorporation of indigenous philosophies and knowledges – historically displaced from the public sphere in the name of development – and their inclusion as providing an authoritative voice in recent debates that have become one of the most enriching paradoxes in contemporary critical thinking.[8]

---

[7] Sadly, these remnants of colonial politics are not buried in the annals of history but have very recent examples, these words being used by literature Nobel Prize winner Mario Vargas Llosa in 2003 in a workshop in Colombia: Albro (2006: 391); Vargas Llosa (2004).

[8] Indigenous philosophies in the region have been historically neglected, reaching what Boaventura de Sousa Santos calls 'epistemicide'. Sousa Santos refers to epistemicide as the 'murder of knowledge'; in other words, the suppression, marginalization or denaturalization of culture, forms of knowledge or symbolic universes that were distinct from the predominant ones – in these cases, those associated to the colonial, modern forms of knowledge. Sousa Santos (2003: ch. 3).

The roots of these policy initiatives can be found in the notion of 'buen vivir', which is, arguably, a Spanish translation of the term *sumak kawsay* (SK) in the Quechua language, and of similar ideas and terminology that can be found in various indigenous languages across the region.[9] We can understand BV/SK as an integral vision of life that is 'based on the communion of humans and nature and on the spatial-temporal-harmonious totality of existence' (Walsh 2010: 18). Fernando Huanacuni Mamani, an Aymara intellectual, has analysed the indigenous philosophical roots of these terms (Huanacuni Mamani, 2010a, 2010b), and translates the idea of *sumak* and *suma* as 'plenitude, sublime, excellent, beautiful', and *kawsay* and *qamaña*, respectively, as 'to live, or being, to coexist'. Cautioning against a literal translation, he indicates that both terms should be understood as the achievement of a 'life in plenitude' going beyond a consideration of humans at its centre (Huanacuni Mamani, 2010b: 7, own translation). In general terms, BV/SK ideas underline the connection and the interrelation of humans with the Earth, nature and each other, and the necessity to achieve a harmonious coexistence, at the core of the indigenous notion of a 'life in plenitude'. These ideas appear embedded in a cosmovision articulated around the principles of relationality, correspondence, complementarity and reciprocity that extend from the relational ontology that underpins the BV/SK (Walsh, 2011; see also Macas, 2014, and Yampara, 2004). The four principles point towards a holistic vision of the life cycle and the community, and an integral consideration of the multiple dimensions – material and spiritual – necessary for the achievement of a good life.

With these principles, the SK/BV has offered a framework from which to rethink contemporary efforts to pursue development plans and projects in the region, particularly in Ecuador and Bolivia. These ideas have been included, to varying degrees, into a myriad of policy and academic contexts reframing the debates on development in the last decades (Monni and Pallottino, 2015; Villalba, 2013). Even so, the implication of these ideas for discussions of development and their implementation in policy initiatives has been far from smooth. Critics

---

[9] 'Buen vivir' and 'vivir bien' are the Spanish translations of the ideas of *sumak kawsay* in Quechua, *suma qamaña* in Aymara, *ñandereko* in Guaraní, *shin pujut* in Awajún or the *kyme mogen* in Mapuche, among others: Hidalgo-Capitán and Cubillo-Guevara (2014: 26).

of this reframing of development within the SK/BV framework abound, in academic discussions as well as in evaluating government policies implemented under the broad 'buen vivir' banner. Many question the essentialization of the indigenous people and knowledge that often underpins the discussions of BV (Spedding Pallet, 2010; Mansilla, 2011; Viola Recasens, 2014; Grosfoguel, 2016). Others point out the clear contradictions existing between the rhetorical remarks on the importance of natural and ecological conservation that accompany BV-inspired policy initiatives and the consolidation of dynamics of development based on extractive industries that can be traced back to the colonial period in the region (see Radcliffe, 2012, Gudynas, 2014a, and Acosta, 2014, among others). However, while some see in it a project that is fundamentally distinct from that of 'development' and others merely a notion of 'alternative development', at the very least the SK/BV framework certainly has opened up a space to question the boundaries that the project of development – or the process to achieve a 'good life' – entails (for a clear overview of the different ways in which these ideas have been incorporated in development discussions, see Vanhulst and Beling, 2014, and Hidalgo-Capitán and Cubillo-Guevara, 2014).

Ideas of a 'good life' built upon the Andean cosmovision act as critical resources and invite us to reframe the current development debate so as to include new ethical considerations.[10] For example, rather than pursuing an endless quest for an improvement in life conditions, SK/BV seeks to attain a 'good living'; in other words, the quest is to 'live well' rather than to continuously strive for 'living better' (Huanacuni Mamani, 2010a). The focus is, thus, put on understanding the pursuit of the good life following an ethics of sufficiency, rather than the ethics of efficiency that pervades developmentalist attempts to achieve material affluence and high levels of productivity (Acosta, 2012). Further, the 'good life' that the SK/BV seeks necessitates a 'biocentric turn' that goes beyond mainstream sustainability concerns (see, for example,

---

[10] The engagement with notions of 'buen vivir'/*sumak kawsay* has expanded at a remarkable rate, not only in Latin America but outside the region as well. See, for example, Gudynas and Acosta (2011a) and (2011b), Acosta (2010) and (2012), Acosta and Martínez (2011), Gudynas (2011) and (2012), Walsh (2010) and (2011), Mignolo (2011), Escobar (2010b) and Radcliffe (2012). A more general overview of the different bibliography on the matter can be found in Vanhulst and Beling (2014) and Altmann (2013).

Escobar, 2010b, Gudynas and Acosta, 2011a, Gudynas, 2014b, and Escobar, 2011). The epistemological force of these ideas, institutions and forms of knowledge (and of knowing) has made them a critical resource to rethink contemporary efforts in development thinking and practice in general.

Yet, in spite of fundamental differences, SK/BV ideas have been widely associated with discussions of 'sustainable development' or human development (Vanhulst and Beling, 2014; Merino, 2016; Walsh, 2010). This has both contributed to expanding the scope of established narratives of development in the region and limited the critical potential of these ideas. Although there exists vast potential to explore the ways in which such narratives can strengthen one another, to enter into a productive dialogue it is necessary to clarify their differences and understand the challenges they may pose to each other (for a discussion of ways in which different transformation discourses – including HD, BV/SK and degrowth – can contribute to strengthening each other, see Beling et al., 2018). In the next section I review some of the connections that have been drawn between the HD and the SK/BV – particularly those that build onto Sen's CA – before exploring the ethical contributions and ontological challenges that these indigenous philosophies can offer to the HD paradigm, and the CA in particular.

Exploring the connections between indigenous philosophies and human development

The governments of Ecuador and Bolivia – particularly under the mandates of Rafael Correa and Evo Morales, respectively – have put forward initiatives that recover the indigenous past and knowledge in undertaking a strong transformation of the political landscape of their countries. From the constitutional reforms of Ecuador (in 2008) and Bolivia (in 2009) to creating national development plans in both countries, or launching the failed Yasuni-ITT international conservation project in Ecuador, as well as passing laws to protect the rights of nature, both countries have taken multiple steps to use the philosophical resources of the BV/SK framework in devising concrete policy measures (Merino, 2016). The move to link development policies with BV/SK has been a contentious one, and some have cautioned the terms of the incorporation of indigenous knowledge (Kowii, 2014; Huanacuni Mamani, 2010b; Oviedo Freire, 2012). However, while in academic contexts controversies around the definition of these terms remain far from settled, the use of these ideas in Andean national political discussions has brought them significantly closer to ideas of HD and the work of Amartya Sen than expected.

A very clear example comes from the publication of the national development plans of Ecuador, both of 2009 and of 2013. These plans emerged as a result of the process of 'strategic participative planning' envisaged in the Constitution of 2008 (articles 279 and 280) and were specifically designed to outline a roadmap for the achievement of the *sumak kawsay*. The plans draw clear connections with the HD approach and with Sen's work, especially in framing the achievement of a good life in terms of the expansion of individuals' freedoms and capabilities. Using Sen's work and the UNDP approach as a core point, the need for 'complying with universal rights and promoting human capabilities' is stated as one of the principles around which the SK is articulated (SENPLADES, 2009: 21; 2013).

At the same time that these government documents have drawn on the CA framework to design policies using the SK/BV framework, the UNDP regional offices have also incorporated elements of the SK/BV into their work (see UNDP, 2010a, 2012, and Programa de Pequeñas Donaciones, 2012). In a clear attempt to consolidate both these approaches, the *Bolivian National Human Development Report* for 2010 highlights the necessity to connect the 'normative horizons' of the HD – framed in Amartya Sen's CA – and the BV/SK ideas. For the report, both 'frameworks converge in an ideal of development that transcends the material scope, and above all coincide in the principles of equality, respect and social recognition' overcoming differences in the consideration of welfare (UNDP, 2010b: 49–51). In Ecuador, the BV/SK framework has been used by the UNDP in the implementation of new projects and initiatives. However, even when some of them have effectively expanded the focus of the work of the UNDP in the region to include new topics, strategies and practices of development, others simply incorporate the new terminology while continuing with previous practices.[11] The latter case can clearly be seen in the efforts

---

[11] For example, the UNDP regional office in Ecuador has included new areas of work, such as the promotion of ideas of intercultural citizenship or the creation of 'Biocorridors for Living Well'. See UNDP (2013) and Programa de Pequeñas Donaciones (2012).

to combine ideas of solidarity economics – present in the BV/SK framework – with the implementation of micro-entrepreneurial practices of development, such as microfinance projects (UNDP, 2012). Other policy initiatives that trace the connections between these two frameworks are directed to assess the achievements of BV/SK policies. Frequently, these attempts to conceptualize and operationalize BV advance together with those already established measurements related to the HD. Here we can see, for example, the 'Programa SIIDERECHOS' in Ecuador, an initiative to build human rights indicators (HRIs) that attempted to measure 'buen vivir' policies, or the collaboration between the Oxford Poverty and Human Development Initiative and the Bolivian government to implement new measurement tools to incorporate the BV/SK framework in their analyses (Waldmüller, 2014, 2018).

These are just a few examples illustrating the ways in which SK and HD have been connected in policy discussions, specifically to Sen's CA. While the framing of these policies has often been presented as a break with mainstream development approaches, efforts to translate the indigenous mandate for a good life into concrete policies have allowed for the continuation of seemingly incompatible visions of development. In general in the region, the progressive, radical rhetoric from governments to recover the indigenous heritage so long neglected has coexisted with a continuation of 'business as usual' in promoting development policies that continue the extractivist focus of the past (Radcliffe, 2012). Exploring these trends in the development policies of Ecuador, Catherine Walsh speaks of a co-optation of the indigenous notion of SK in the establishment of what she notes as a '*paradogma*' of HD, which withers away its conceptual rupture and loses part of its radical force (Walsh, 2010: 17). This selective use of the SK/BV framework has allowed for the paradoxical increase of environmental and sustainability concerns in discussions of development together with an unparalleled rise in environmental conflicts, fuelled in large part by the deployment of new extractive projects in the name of development (on the increase in environmental conflicts in the last decade, see Escobar, 2010a, Gudynas, 2014c, and Petras and Veltmeyer, 2011). However, despite the limitations on their implementation, the insights that these indigenous philosophies bring to debates on development offer a rare opportunity to rethink the implications of existing approaches. In particular, the connections between the SK/BV framework and the HD that have been identified serve as an invitation to open a dialogue exploring their implications for the CA. While it is clear that the policy initiatives developed under the HD paradigm should not be considered as a direct interpretation of Sen's work or of the CA more generally, the unmistakable connections that exist between these frameworks offer a unique opportunity to explore the foundational issues present in Sen's CA. In the next sections, then, I take this opportunity to look in more detail at the ontological challenges that ideas of BV/SK bring to the CA.

Human development and indigenous philosophies: ontological challenges to the capabilities approach

The ayllu *in the Andes: recovering the communal dimension of development discussions*

One of the strongest elements that indigenous frameworks bring to development discussions is the centrality of the communal dimensions in their analysis of what a 'life in plenitude' should entail. Importantly, the communal analysis here is connected to discussions of nature and sustainability.[12] Understanding the centrality of the community for the SK/BV framework becomes then an essential step to engage in the discussions of nature and the environment – a step that has not been taken in many of its policy interpretations, including those that connect it with HD. The notion of community within SK is rooted in a territory. This notion of territory, rather than being one of a limited spatial understanding, is built upon the idea that a spiritual connection between the human being, the territory and nature is intrinsic to the notion of a good life. The community, thus, becomes a multidimensional entity, whose different aspects are deeply interrelated, in what is termed the *ayllu*. Understanding this notion and its implications can contribute to strengthening the capacity of the CA to acknowledge indigenous philosophical values and expand on the space for collective considerations.

The *ayllu* plays a central role in the history of the Andean peoples. Pre-dating the colonial period, it is a social institution that has been

---

[12] This connection is similar with other indigenous peoples in the world; see Bockstael and Watene (2016).

maintained (albeit with significant changes) throughout centuries and remains a key notion to understanding the multiple dimensions that the SK/BV entails. It is the basic form of communal social organization that can be found in the majority of the indigenous groups present in the Andes, and it has been referred to by indigenous intellectuals as the 'seed of the Andean political institutions and civilization' (Choque and Mamani, 2001: 202; Yampara, 2004: 74: Rivera Cusicanqui, 2010: 100). It is within the *ayllu* that the 'good life' – the SK/BV – can be achieved, and it is its multiple, interrelated dimensions that should be included in the consideration of well-being.[13] Within the SK framework, both the human and extra-human elements included in the *ayllu* are essential to pursuing the good life, which is considered a communal endeavour. The notion thus prompts a different economic and political understanding of community, allowing us to envisage and discuss ideas of well-being beyond the individual so as to include not only social but territorial and environmental concerns. As we have seen, the notion of SK has been incorporated into policy and academic discussions, associated in general to the ideas of sustainability and the furthering of ideas of development exceeding a pure economic focus (in line with Sen's work). However, in general, the community concept of *ayllu* has remained largely neglected. Beyond a simple essentialization of the concept, it is necessary to understand the paramount importance of the role that the *ayllu* plays within the indigenous philosophies of the Andes in order to create fruitful connections with the HD and the CA.

*Ayllu*s have been mostly studied for their novel articulation of territoriality and spiritual life, as well as for their administrative and political forms of organization (Harris, 2000; Weismantel, 2006; Godoy, 1986; Rivera Cusicanqui, 1990). Their different organizational, territorial, legal, political and spiritual dimensions play a central role in these indigenous philosophies as a principle of organizing social and economic life, both in the Quechua and Aymara traditions (see Choque and Mamani, 2001, Choque, 2000, and Untoja Choque, 2001). To some Aymara intellectuals, its principles of service, property and communal participation have served to maintain political institutions that

---

[13] Many have highlighted the centrality of the *ayllu* for the achievement of the *sumak kawsay*; see, for example, Yampara (2004), Uzeda (2009), Altmann (2013) and Gudynas and Acosta (2011a).

differ from those enshrined in liberal democracies (Rivera Cusicanqui, 1990; Choque and Mamani, 2001). Despite the meaning of the term shifting throughout its history, examples of the communal ethos that underpins the formation of *ayllu*s remain. Here, for example, we can see the construction of a system of exchange upon the *ayni*, or principle of reciprocity, which has been described as a Maussian gift rather than a capitalist exchange (Weismantel, 2006: 94). Institutions such as the *minga* – a form of collective work that is not remunerated but allows for cooperation around specific initiatives – put forward an economic principle centred in the pursuit of welfare for the community, rather than the increase of productivity.[14] A second example, which has evolved considerably to become of paramount importance in contemporary processes of land titling, can be found in the existing forms of collective ownership. Property rights within the *ayllu* are conceived of in a communal dimension, often involving distinctive systems of ecological management.[15]

At the same time, the notion of *ayllu* has a phenomenal evocative power, given its subsistence beyond the different historical periods, particularly colonial domination and its subsequent legacies in the consolidation of modern states in the region (Albro, 2006; Weismantel, 2006; Rivera Cusicanqui, 1990). The transformation and resilient persistence of this indigenous institution throughout the centuries has much more than the anecdotal value of the reproduction of a peculiar cultural pattern; it serves as a locus of geographic and imaginary resistance, as the collective space from which to rethink alternative processes of development. In national or regional politics, to speak of the *ayllu* goes beyond speaking of a communal property or a principle of political organization: it refers to a communal ethos that is transversal to the indigenous cosmologies of the SK. This communal ethos can contribute to two important, and interrelated, conversations within the CA. First, the notion of *ayllu* is intrinsically tied to the role of the Earth and Mother Nature in conceptions of the good life, thus offering a communal insight into environmental and sustainability debates.

---

[14] This is connected to the ethics of sufficiency versus ethics of efficiency dilemma discussed above; see Hidalgo-Capitán (2012: 19) and Altmann (2013: 294).

[15] John Murra made an extensive analysis of the singularity of the Andean *ayllu*'s ecological management and collective ownership, in what he terms the 'vertical archipelago'; see Murra (2002: ch. 3). On the use of *ayllu* traditions for processes of land titling, see Crabtree and Chaplin (2013: chs. 2–3).

As discussed in the following section, in the SK/BV framework the community cannot be dissociated from the natural world (or, in other words, Nature is an intrinsic part of the *ayllu*), and, as such, environmental issues take a different stance, embedded in communal considerations. Second, focusing on the importance of the notion of *ayllu* contributes to the conversation on collective capabilities within the CA, and it does so by highlighting the need to understand the role of relational ontologies in considerations of community issues.

As we have seen, the notion of *ayllu* emphasizes the consideration of the well-being of the community as a whole, rather than a perspective of atomized individualities whose well-being may or may not be achieved together with that of their societies. To Raul Llasag Fernández, a Kichwa researcher at the University of Coimbra, this implies a primacy of the community above the individual, as he states, that 'in the Andean world, the human being as an individual does not exist, because (s)he exists integrated to the community, outside of it there is non-existence or an incomplete one'.[16] This is, naturally, a contentious point, and some argue that *ayllu*s do not eradicate individual considerations but that these are conceived 'through complementarity with other beings of the group' (Villalba, 2013: 1430). Others highlight the problems that these strong communal ties can create. Godfrey-Wood and Mamani-Vargas (2017), for example, argue that, although these collective institutions are highly successful in contributing to collective well-being, they often do so at the cost of constraining individual freedom (such as enforcing the participation of members in collective *sindicatos*). Further, often the contemporary real-life subsistence of these communities is even farther from idyllic. Nicole Fabricant's (2010) analysis is enlightening here. Beyond a simple 'romanticisation' of the concept, she reminds us that the contemporary daily functioning of these *ayllu*s is often prey to petty

---

[16] Llasag Fernandez (2009). This is echoed by one of the interviews conducted by Marisol de la Cadena, in her analysis of Andean politics, when citing an indigenous teacher, who argues: 'The community, the *ayllu*, is not only a territory where a group of people live; it is more than that. It is a dynamic space where the whole community of beings that exist in the world lives; this includes humans, plants, animals, the mountains, the rivers, the rain, etc. All are related like a family. It is important to remember that this place [the community] is not where we are from, it is who we are. For example, I am not from Huantura, I am Huantura' (de la Cadena, 2010). A similar point can be found in Fernández Osco (2005).

discussions of domestic politics, in which individual interests take a stronger stance than the philosophical principles of the indigenous cosmovision would indicate. However, she argues that it is precisely this tension between the 'romanticised vision' of the community and the individualistic desires of its members that pushes the transformative political agenda of the region (Fabricant, 2010). And it is what reminds us of the necessity to further reflect on the consequences of these strong communal insights, with their emphasis on the spiritual interconnection of all beings, in discussions of development. The point is not to disregard the individuality of human existence but, rather, to emphasize the relational ontology that underpins this indigenous cosmovision and focus on the complementarity and reciprocity principles beyond the human that are intrinsic to the SK/BV. Arguably, it is this interconnectedness between all beings that has been brought into considerations of sustainability such as those of the rights of the Earth, as I discuss in the next section. The understanding of *ayllu* goes beyond that, though, merging the necessity of understanding the lives and well-being of individuals within those of their communities to consider the spiritual, environmental and extra-human ties of human existence. It brings, then, a novel articulation of collective and social concerns that can expand this conversation with the CA beyond aspects of collective capabilities.

The communal ethos enshrined in the *ayllu* is part and parcel of a relational ontology in which the separation between human and nature and between individuals and their communities becomes much more diffused (Villalba, 2013; Costoya, 2012). In the words of Arturo Escobar (2010b: 38), 'Relational ontologies are those which eschew the divisions between nature and culture, individual and community, us and them that are central to the modern ontology (that of liberal modernity).' Recognizing the importance of this relational ontology within the SK/BV, then, becomes central to exploring its connections with the CA. Within the CA, the argument that Sen's framework appears embedded in a relational ontology has been made in the past (Longshore Smith and Seward, 2009; Oosterlaken, 2011). However, the *relationality* of the CA appears defined in different terms from those of the SK/BV. The *relational* ontology, as discussed in the literature of the CA here, puts a stronger emphasis on the social considerations of the CA, as part and parcel of individual capabilities. As Matthew Longshore Smith and Carolina Seward (2009: 214) note, 'Sen's notion of capabilities and freedoms implies an ontology of a relational society. Within a relational conception of society, a particular capability is the outcome of the interaction of an individual's capacities and the individual's position relative to others in society.' The *relational* ontology referred to here calls for a stronger appreciation of the fundamental role that society plays in the attainment and configuration of capabilities. However, the dualist ontology upon which liberal modernity is structured, in which individuals appear as separate from society, and the Earth, remains a cornerstone element of the CA. The discussions and complex operationalizations[17] that have followed these discussions within the CA ideas emphasize the intrinsic and constitutive role of social relationships for processes of individual freedom offerings. They offer a stronger argument to consider social aspects, yet they remain embedded in the *ethical* or *normative* individualism that characterizes the CA (Robeyns, 2005, 2008, 2017). This *ethical* or *normative* individualism, as Ingrid Robeyns notes, 'postulates that individuals, and only individuals, are the units of moral concern' (Robeyns, 2005: 107) and remains firmly framed within a dualist ontology that clashes with the *relational ontology* that pervades the SK/BV.[18]

In this sense, while the contentious issue of collective capabilities has expanded significantly the space for social and collective considerations within the CA, the focus on the promotion of individual capabilities as an expansion of freedom that the HD and Amartya Sen espouse falls short of the ideas of the 'good life' for the SK framework. In the latter, community is understood as more than the communion of human beings, and ideas of well-being are necessarily expanded beyond the capabilities of individuals, even if these are based on sustainable

---

[17] See Giraud et al. (2013) for an impressive exercise in terms of operationalizing the relational aspects of capabilities.

[18] Importantly, this *ethical* or *normative* individualism is not to be confused with other forms of individualism. In a similar perspective to Sen's, Robeyns argues that *methodological* individualism assumes that 'all social phenomena can be explained in terms of individuals and their properties' while *ontological* individualism assumes that 'society is built up from only individuals and nothing other than individuals, and hence is nothing more than the sum of individuals and their properties'. Hence, according to Robeyns, the CA does not fall into either category (Robeyns, 2008, 90). Although this chapter is focused on Sen's version of the CA, it is worth noting that Nussbaum's perspective shares this commitment to *normative* individualism: Robeyns (2017: 58).

practices. The principles that guide the SK cannot be separated from the community, cannot be achieved at a purely individual level. The goal of a good life, the *suma qamaña* or the *sumak kawsay*, cannot be understood outside the *ayllu*. It is, fundamentally, a social goal.

It can surely be argued that Sen's project of 'development as freedom' and the HD paradigm are not purely individualistic, and it is not my intention to suggest that this is the case. Sen builds his theory of the development of human capabilities (and, thus, of the enlargement of freedom) upon a critique of the idea of *Homo oeconomicus*, which considers only individualistic behaviour as rational. Furthermore, Sen's CA recognizes how fundamental social reasoning is in the path to achieving justice, and endorses even more strongly ideas of social participation, embedded in participatory democracy, and has recently advocated for considerations of sustainability insofar as they affect the capabilities of future generations (Sen, 2009, 2013, 2002). However, although Sen's CA certainly includes social considerations, this is only insofar they contribute 'to enhancing and guaranteeing the substantive freedoms of individuals, seen as active agents of change, rather than as passive recipients of dispensed benefits' (Sen, 1999: xiii). Although society's influence on the individual (and, conversely, of the individual in their societies) is taken into consideration, the analysis of institutions or 'societal arrangements' is relevant only as an instrument for the pursuit of the expansion of individuals' freedoms. This instrumentalist vision of the relevance of society and collective aspects of development reduces the space that might be given to more communal concerns in discussions of development.

Furthermore, it confines society's intrinsic relevance for development to the valuation that its individual members may have of social life: aside from their instrumental value, societal or collective capabilities have an intrinsic value only when it is given by its members. As Sen (2009: 246) states,

Ultimately, it is individual valuation on which we would have to draw, while recognizing the profound interdependence of the valuations of individuals who interact with each other. The valuation involved would tend to be based on the importance that people attach to being able to do certain things in collaboration with others. In valuing a person's ability to take part in the life of the society, there is an implicit valuation of the life of the society itself, and that is an important enough aspect of the capability perspective.

Sen thus recognizes the 'implicit valuation of the life of the society itself', but its value is determined by the preferences of the individuals, again, becoming instrumental to fulfilling the 'lives that people value and have reason to value'.[19] Social life, and, in general, a more structural macro-analysis of the process of development and the conditions for achieving individual empowerment, are not of central concern for the CA. Their role is a subsidiary one insofar as they affect individuals' well-being. The ultimate moral foundation of the value of society is the value that individuals can give to social life, not social life in and of itself, as a requisite for freedom. Aside from precluding any larger criticism of social life, Sen's perspective makes the individual the only determining force of whether the social is a necessary part of the process of development as capabilities expansion.

Of course, HD is a social project in itself. It happens only within a society, and participation in the society is an intrinsic part of the process. And, importantly, Sen's CA's strong emphasis on the importance of individual agency and local decision making may grant larger considerations of communal/collective issues than those normally considered in Western democracies. As Krushil Watene (2016) highlights in her analysis of the valuation of the natural world within the CA and Māori philosophies, this opens up a possibility of valuing communal issues in two different ways. Issues of communal/collective concern can be considered valuable within the CA instrumentally because they contribute to the well-being and agency of people, or, when they are an expression of such agency.[20] Yet, ultimately, in Sen's CA the achievement of 'development as freedom', or human development, occurs at the individual level and does not necessarily include a transformation of the communities to the same extent; nor does it open up a sufficient space for ethical considerations of the Earth and nature as part of this

---

[19] Sen uses the expression 'to live the life they value and have reason to value' as one of his main recurring arguments for the superiority of the capability approach in relation to other conceptions of development. The expression is included in several of his works; see, for example, Sen (1999: 18), (2009: 231) and (2013: 10).

[20] As Watene indicates, this is an important distinction, which differentiates Sen's CA from Nussbaum's quite starkly. In Watene's view, Sen's refusal of a universal list of capabilities has left the possibility of a strong valuation of communal issues open (subject to local democratic deliberation) – in her case study, particularly in the valuation of nature – in a way compatible with these relational ontologies, while Nussbaum's dignity-based list of capabilities precludes it. Watene (2016: 295).

communal perspective in the process and achievement of well-being. While social and communal considerations are by no means absent from CA discussions (nor from HD ones), granting a certain weight to Longshore Smith and Seward's (2009) argument of the relational ontology of capabilities, they remain embedded in the dualist onto-logical separation between the individual and society and between the individual and the Earth, which is challenged by the SK/BV commu-nal ethos. This becomes particularly clear when analysing sustainabil-ity and environmental concerns, opening up a unique opportunity to expand the scope of the CA in incorporating these discussions.

Beyond sustainability concerns: the Pachamama *and the biocentric turn*

In policy discussions of the SK/BV – including those connecting this framework to the HD and Sen's work, as we have seen – the notion of *Pachamama*, an indigenous term common to many Andean indig-enous languages and referring to Mother Nature, is quite common, in contrast to the notion of *ayllu*. The main contribution and impact that these indigenous philosophical frameworks have had may be seen in terms of the inclusion of concerns for 'nature's rights'. For example, these were included in the preamble of the constitutional reform of Ecuador in 2008 as follows:

We women and men, the sovereign people of Ecuador; *Recognizing* our age-old roots; wrought by women and men from various peoples; *Celebrating* nature, the Pacha Mama (Mother Earth), of which we are a part and which is vital to our existence ... ; *Hereby decide to build*: a new form of public coexistence, in diversity and in harmony with nature, to achieve the good way of living, the sumak kawsay.[21]

Further, the constitution included a whole chapter that spelled out the rights of nature, starting with article 71, which recognized nature's 'right to integral respect for its existence and for the maintenance and regeneration of its life cycles, structure, functions and evolution-ary processes' (República del Ecuador, 2008: art. 71). Even though environmental concerns in discussions of development are, of course, not exclusive to the SK/BV framework, it is the centrality that these

---

[21] República del Ecuador (2008: 15). I have selected the relevant excerpt from the preamble and reformatted it. Highlights are from the original.

play in the achievement of a 'life in plenitude' that has caught the attention of academics and policy practitioners of development. These ideas, so widely incorporated into the Ecuadorian constitution and in other policy initiatives in Bolivia, have filtered down to academic discussions and policy implementation in terms of development in the region, where concerns for the environment appear to have taken a stronger stance. However, for the most part, these ideas have not yet come to radically challenge mainstream notions but, rather, have become associated with the existing literature on sustainable development. Environmental considerations have thus been framed within discussions of sustainability that argue we must ensure that future generations will be able to enjoy and reap the same level of welfare that current development patterns allow us (Vanhulst and Beling, 2014; Merino, 2016; Beling et al., 2018).

The welfare of future generations is clearly included within the SK/BV framework. The relational ontology that underpins this framework is built upon a cyclical vision of life, which connects past, future and present generations, with the past, present and future of nature, in establishing a communal vision that transcends unilinear visions of progress (Thomson, 2011).[22] These interrelated perspectives, then, offer a comprehensive approach to consider issues of sustainability in development discussions. It might, therefore, be useful to explore in which ways SK/BV's relational ontology offers a distinct possibility to attend to these sustainability concerns and contribute to the way in which the CA in general, and Sen's work in particular, approach these issues.

Amartya Sen has addressed the issue of sustainability, including environmental concerns, as a matter of inter- and intragenerational justice and argued for framing these issues in terms of freedom and capabilities (Anand and Sen, 1994; Sen and Anand, 2000). In one of his first interventions on the topic, Sen argues that among the most important reasons for the protection of the environment is 'the ethical need for guaranteeing that future generations would continue to enjoy similar opportunities of leading worthwhile lives that are enjoyed by generations that precede them' (Anand and Sen, 1994: 2030). The necessity of ensuring distributive equity between human beings of different

---

[22] In general, in the indigenous communities of the Andes, social, agricultural and political institutions are often connected to a cyclical vision of life, which connects past, present and future. See Harris (2000).

generations is, accordingly, a main driver of the quest for environmental sustainability. Importantly, this quest for distributive justice is of central importance not only for future generations (intergenerational justice) but also among the individuals of the current generation (intragenerational justice). This point is made to highlight that the level of development to be 'sustained' ought to also be equitably distributed among the people of current generations, as we should not 'deny the less privileged today, the attention that we bestow on generations in the future' (Anand and Sen, 1994: 2031).

In his *The Idea of Justice,* published in 2009, Sen argues for the necessity of reconceptualizing discussions of sustainability as expanding the freedoms that people enjoy (of generations today and in the future) rather than focusing on needs or living standards (Sen, 2009; see also Sen, 2013). 'There is cogency in thinking not just about sustaining the fulfilment of our needs, but more broadly about sustaining – or extending – our freedom (including the freedom to meet our needs)' (Sen, 2009: 252). Sen advocates for defining sustainability in terms of respecting the 'capabilities and freedoms' of future generations, to overcome the more restricted ideas of 'needs' or 'living conditions' that other approaches sustain. The crucial importance of this distinction lies, for Sen, in the possibility of highlighting, within the concept of sustainable development, the central role of individuals as agents, as intrinsically able to make reasoned social choices within the realm of environmental sustainability. In other words, reframing the idea of sustainable development in terms of capabilities and freedoms, rather than needs and/or living standards, would open the necessary space to include considerations of the expansion of individual freedom, of individual empowerment (both of current as well as future generations), as a central feature of sustainability.

In general, seeing development in terms of increasing the effective freedom of human beings brings the constructive agency of people engaged in environment-friendly activities directly within the domain of developmental achievements. Development is fundamentally an empowering process, and this power can be used to preserve and enrich the environment, and not only to decimate it. (Sen, 2009: 248)

According to his perspective, the protection of the environment in relation to issues of sustainable development would respond, on the

one hand, to the necessity of ensuring that future and current generations enjoy a sustained level of freedom to choose and make reasoned
social choices and, on the other hand, to the moral responsibility
attached to the possibility of making reasoned social choices. To Sen,
'[s]ince we are enormously more powerful than other species, we have
some responsibility towards them that links with this asymmetry of
power' (Sen, 2009: 251). The inclusion of specific arguments addressing the necessity of ensuring *intra-* and *inter*generational equity illustrates Sen's more egalitarian inclinations and reminds us to ensure that
we address current development challenges together with more long-
term concerns. However, what is perhaps more remarkable is the clear
articulation of these sustainability considerations within his concerns
for the expansion of individual agency.

Development should be achieved in a sustainable manner, so as not
to trump future generations' possibilities of expanding their freedoms
and capabilities. Rather than intrinsically assigning a valuation to sustainability considerations, these become relevant insofar as they may
become a source of unfreedom for future and present human beings.
This particular aspect has been praised as a possible way out from the
imposition of our normative valuations of the consideration of nature
that we bestow upon future generations, which has been defined as
'environmental domination'.[23] To Scholtes, 'in so far as it program-
matically locates the processes of valuing nature and the formulation of
environmental problems in the space of public deliberation and social
value formation', Sen's capability approach offers a promising base for
considering sustainability issues (Scholtes, 2010: 303). The space for
social reasoning (and, inherent to it, for individual agency and empowerment processes) that the capability approach gives to considerations
of sustainability becomes, then, a fundamental element to clarify its
relation with the SK/BV framework. Seen from this perspective, Sen
undoubtedly gives a compelling view on considerations of sustainable development, which have echoed discussions of HD across the
years (see, for example, Anand and Sen, 1994, UNDP, 2011, and Kaul,
2014). Yet, at the same time, it strongly illustrates the anthropocentric

---

[23] Fabian Scholtes defines environmental domination as the process through
which, 'by making decisions regarding nature that have inescapable
consequences for others, we exert our ideas of the good upon others and shape
their options in a definitive way' (Scholtes, 2010: 292).

and instrumentalist view of the environment and of the consideration of nature of Sen's version of the CA, which once again clashes with the relational ontology of the SK/BV.[24] The relevance of ensuring environmental sustainability, in Sen's perspective, appears linked only to its instrumental value in ensuring and maintaining an equitable enjoyment level of the individual's freedom. Even when nature may receive an intrinsic valuation when it becomes an expression of individual agency in social deliberations, its valuation is still instrumentally linked to the expression of such agency (Watene, 2016).

In the indigenous cosmologies, environmental considerations are not only framed in terms of sustainability concerns, but are intrinsic to the achievement of a 'life in plenitude' on a material and spiritual level. The achievement of the *sumak kawsay* is envisaged within the *Pachamama*, or Mother Nature, to which all natural beings belong and in which they are connected (Vanhulst and Beling, 2014: 58). It thus appears as ontologically indivisible from human beings, and, as a result, environmental and sustainability concerns cannot be understood in or argued for in an instrumental manner: they are inherent to the idea of *sumak kawsay*, or of a good life. The SK/BV pushes the boundaries of Sen's CA to expand beyond its anthropocentric concerns. In fact, Eduardo Gudynas and others have termed the considerations of nature and environmental issues within the SK/BV framework a 'biocentric turn', whereby 'the good life of humans is only possible if the survival and integrity of the web of life of nature can be guaranteed' (Gudynas, 2009a: 52; see also Gudynas, 2009b, Gudynas and Acosta, 2011a, Acosta, 2010, and Escobar, 2011). It is the same *relational ontology* of the SK/BV framework upon which the ideas of *ayllu* are built, which advocates for a more holistic consideration of nature as having intrinsic value, and not only in relation to the fulfilment of the needs of present and future human beings (Villalba, 2013; Costoya, 2012). The biocentric turn that the indigenous cosmologies advocate cannot be simply subsumed within a discourse of

---

[24] It is important to note here that, once again, Nussbaum's version of the CA differs from Sen's on this point. As Nussbaum's list of capabilities includes a valuation of 'other species', the consideration of non-human beings and nature occupies a larger space in this version of the CA than in Sen's (Nussbaum, 2003). Yet, as Watene (2016) demonstrates, Nussbaum's considerations of the relevance of nature and of environmental issues remain instrumentally tied to the fulfilment of human capabilities.

sustainability that simply instrumentalizes nature. Rather, environmental concerns appear embedded in the communal vision of life that also pervades the notion of *ayllu*.

Although this is certainly not meant to indicate that nature's resources cannot or should not be used for the reproduction of human life, it does certainly indicate the need to revise the priorities of development, and the value assigned to the valuation of nature and of environmental concerns more generally. The SK/BV's notion of *Pachamama* should not be understood as an advocate for a return of a Stone Age engagement with nature, but it should remind us of the centrality that environmental concerns have for the achievement of a 'life in plenitude', beyond anthropocentric considerations that continue to instrumentalize nature. Beyond the connections that have already been made between the SK/BV and the CA, the insights that these indigenous philosophies bring stem from the relational ontology that underpins this cosmovision. If these are to become meaningful in advancing the conversation on sustainable development within and beyond the CA, then the conceptualization of environmental and sustainability concerns should be explored within the cyclical and communal understanding of well-being inherent to the SK/BV.

Conclusion

This chapter has sought to contribute to the growing literature connecting indigenous philosophies and the capability approach. It has done so by exploring the connections that have been made between the work of Amartya Sen and HD, on the one hand, and the SK/BV framework emerging from the indigenous philosophies of the Andean region in Latin America, on the other. These links have been developed in the last decade upon the identification of broad coincidences and general affinities between the perspectives. While these have resulted in the achievement of significant transformations in the conceptualization of development policy in the region, they importantly offer an opportunity to expand the boundaries of the CA, particularly by bringing new insights to discussions of collective and environmental issues.

This chapter has sought to advance in this direction. To do this, the chapter has explored the ethical dilemmas and challenges that emerge from the relational ontology that underpins the SK/BV framework and weighed its implications in understanding the communal and collective dimensions of development, and the anthropocentric versus biocentric consideration of sustainability issues. Exploring the notion of *ayllu* has given us the possibility to further recover the communal dimension of the development endeavour and to connect this to discussions of environmental issues. In exploring the implications of this notion, I have sought to identify both contradictions and potential avenues that could and should be further considered if we are to achieve a fruitful engagement between the ideas of HD derived from Amartya Sen's work and those of BV/SK emerging from the indigenous philosophies of the Andes.

In Bolivia, the *ayllu*s have a growing space within policy initiatives (mostly as a result of the work of the National Council of Ayllus and Markas of Qullasuyu, founded in 1997). The *ayllu* has also been officially incorporated as a form of landownership, and it has played a significant role in the process of land titling in Bolivia in the last two decades. Often *ayllu*s have been given prerogatives at the local level of government, and have played an important role in processes of justice administration (Crabtree and Chaplin, 2013: ch. 3). At the same time, celebrations and references of the *Pachamama* abound in Bolivian and Ecuadorean contemporary life and policy discussions (Rivera Cusicanqui, 2010). From national laws to development programmes and international projects, these have sparked the most varied initiatives across the Andes, where the revivals of nature considerations appear to have reached new heights. Nevertheless, it remains necessary to move beyond a romanticized vision of these concepts and engage the ethical challenges that they offer through a view of the development process beyond the human.

This chapter has argued that considering the challenges that these ideas present may give us new theoretical resources to analyse two of the most contentious issues within the CA: issues of collective capabilities and of sustainability. However, beyond the specific contributions to the CA literature, they should remind us of the importance of considering social and collective spaces of reflection in discussions of development, and the connections with the central role that nature plays in the development process. In revisiting the indigenous philosophies as a framework to advance our ethical considerations of development, they should help us reframe the debate in a more holistic manner, understanding that the 'whole' extends beyond its human ties.

References

Acosta, A. (2010) El buen vivir en el camino del post-desarrollo: una lectura desde la constitución de Montecristi, Policy Paper 9. Quito: Fundación Friedrich Ebert.

(2012) *Buen Vivir – Sumak Kawsay: Una oportunidad para imaginar otros mundos*. Quito: Abya Yala.

(2014) Poscrecimiento y posextractivismo: dos caras de una misma transformación cultural. In *Pos-crecimiento y Buen Vivir: Propuestas globales para la construcción de sociedades equitativas y sustentables*, Endara, G. (ed.): 93–122. Quito: FES-ILDIS.

Acosta, A., and Martínez, E. (eds.) (2011) *La naturaleza con derechos: De la filosofía a la política*. Quito: Abya Yala.

Agarwal, B., Humphries, J., and Robeyns, I. (2003) Exploring the challenges of Amartya Sen's work and ideas: an introduction. *Feminist Economics*, 9 (2/3): 3–12.

Albó, X. (1991) El retorno del Indio. *Revista Andina*, 9 (2): 299–346.

Albro, R. (2006) The culture of democracy and Bolivia's Indigenous movements. *Critique of Anthropology*, 26 (4): 387–410.

Alkire, S. (2005) Why the capability approach? *Journal of Human Development*, 6 (1): 115–35.

Altmann, P. (2013) El Sumak Kawsay en el discurso del movimiento indígena ecuatoriano. *Indiana*, 30: 283–99.

Anand, S., and Sen, A. K. (1994) Sustainable human development: concepts and priorities, Occasional Paper 1. New York: United Nations Development Programme.

(1995) Gender inequality in human development: theories and measurement, Occasional Paper 19. New York: United Nations Development Programme.

(1998) Consumption and human development: concepts and issues, occasional paper. New York: United Nations Development Programme.

Basu, K., and Kanbur, R. (eds.) (2009) *Arguments for a Better World: Essays in Honor of Amartya Sen*, vol. 1, *Ethics, Welfare, and Measurement*. Oxford: Oxford University Press.

Beling, A. E., Vanhulst, J., Demaria, F., Rabi, V., Carballo, A. E., and Pelenc, J. (2018) Discursive synergies for a 'great transformation' towards sustainability: pragmatic contributions to a necessary dialogue between human development, degrowth, and buen vivir. *Ecological Economics*, 144: 304–13.

Bockstael, E., and Watene, K. (2016) Indigenous peoples and the capability approach: taking stock. *Oxford Development Studies*, 44 (3): 265–70.

Choque, M. E. (2000) *La reconstitución del ayllu y los derechos de los pueblos indígenas*. Quito: FLACSO.

Choque, M. E., and Mamani, C. (2001) Reconstitución del ayllu y derechos de los pueblos indígenas: el movimiento indio en los Andes de Bolivia. *Journal of Latin American Anthropology*, 6 (1): 202–24.

Comim, F., Fennell, S., and Anand, P. B. (eds.) (2018) *New Frontiers of the Capability Approach*. Cambridge: Cambridge University Press.

Comim, F., Qizilbash, M., and Alkire, S. (eds.) (2008) *The Capability Approach: Concepts, Measures and Applications*. Cambridge: Cambridge University Press.

Costoya, M. M. (2012) Latin American post-neoliberal development thinking: the Bolivian 'turn' toward suma qamaña. *European Journal of Development Research*, 25 (2): 213–29.

Crabtree, J., and Chaplin, A. (2013) *Bolivia: Processes of Change*. London: Zed Books.

Crocker, D. (1991) Toward development ethics. *World Development*, 19 (5): 457–83.

De la Cadena, M. (2010) Indigenous cosmopolitics in the Andes: conceptual reflections beyond 'politics'. *Cultural Anthropology*, 25 (2): 334–70.

Escobar, A. (2010a) *Una minga para el postdesarrollo: Lugar, medio ambiente y movimientos sociales en las transformaciones globales*. Lima: Programa Democracia y Transformación Global.

(2010b) Latin America at a crossroads: alternative modernizations, post-liberalism, or post-development? *Cultural Studies*, 24 (1): 1–65.

(2011) Sustainability: design for the pluriverse. *Development*, 54 (2): 137–40.

Evans, P. (2002) Collective capabilities, culture, and Amartya Sen's *Development as Freedom*. *Studies in Comparative International Development*, 37 (2): 54–60.

Fabricant, N. (2010) Between the romance of collectivism and the reality of individualism: ayllu rhetoric in Bolivia's landless peasant movement. *Latin American Perspectives*, 37 (4): 88–107.

Fernández Osco, M. (2005) Ayllu: decolonial critical thinking and an (other) autonomy. In *Globalization and Autonomy Online Compendium*, 1–2. www.globalautonomy.ca/global1/article.jsp?index=RS_FernandezOsco_Ayllu.xml.

Fukuda-Parr, S. (2003a) Rescuing human development concept from the Human Development Index. In *Readings in Human Development: Concepts, Measures and Policies for a Development Paradigm*, Fukuda-Parr, S., and Shiva Kumar, A. K. (eds.): 117–24. New Delhi: Oxford University Press.

(2003b) The human development paradigm: operationalizing Sen's ideas on capabilities. *Feminist Economics*, 9 (2/3): 301–17.

Giraud, G., Renouard, C., L'Huillier, H., and De La Martinière, R. (2013) Relational capability: a multidimensional approach, working paper 1306. Paris: ESSEC.

Godfrey-Wood, R., and Mamani-Vargas, R. (2017) The coercive side of collective capabilities: evidence from the Bolivian Altiplano. *Journal of Human Development and Capabilities*, 18 (1): 75–88.

Godoy, R. A. (1986) The fiscal role of the Andean ayllu. *Man: Journal of the Royal Anthropological Society*, 21 (4): 723–41.

Goulet, D. (1997) Development ethics: a new discipline. *International Journal of Social Economics*, 24 (11): 1160–71.

Grosfoguel, R. (2016) Del 'extractivismo económico' al 'extractivismo epistémico' y al 'extractivismo ontológico': una forma destructiva de conocer, ser y estar en el mundo. *Tabula Rasa*, 24: 123–43.

Gudynas, E. (2009a) La dimensión ecológica del buen vivir: entre el fantasma de la modernidad y el desafío biocéntrico. *Revista Obets*. 4: 49–53.

(2009b) *El mandato ecológico: Derechos de la naturaleza y políticas ambientales en la nueva constitución*. Quito: Abya Yala.

(2011) Buen vivir: today's tomorrow. *Development*, 54 (4): 441–7.

(2012) *Transiciones Para Salir del Viejo Desarrollo*. Lima: Centro Peruano de Estudios Sociales.

(2014a) Buen vivir: sobre secuestros, domesticaciones rescates y alternativas. In *Bifurcación del Buen Vivir y el Sumak Kawsay*, Oviedo, A. F. (ed.): 23–45. Quito: Ediciones Yachay.

(2014b) El postdesarrollo como crítica y el buen vivir como alternativa. In *Buena vida, buen vivir: Imaginarios alternativos para el bien común de la humanidad*, Delgado Ramos, G. C. (ed.): 61–95. Mexico City: Universidad Nacional Autónoma de México.

(2014c) Conflictos y extractivismos: conceptos, contenidos y dinamicas. *DECURSOS: Revista en ciencias sociales*, 27: 79–115.

Gudynas, E., and Acosta, A. (2011a) El buen vivir mas allá del desarrollo. *Qué hacer*, 181: 70–81.

(2011b) La renovación de la crítica al desarrollo y el buen vivir como alternativa. *Utopía y praxis Latinoamericana*, 53: 71–83.

Harris, O. (2000) *To Make the Earth Bear Fruit: Essays on Fertility, Work and Gender in Highland Bolivia*. London: Institute of Latin American Studies.

Hidalgo-Capitán, A. L. (2012) *El buen vivir: La (re)creación del pensamiento del PYDLOS*. Huelva y Cuenca: PYDLOS Ediciones.

Hidalgo-Capitán, A. L., and Cubillo-Guevara, A. P. (2014) Seis debates abiertos sobre el sumak kawsay. *Iconos. Revista de Ciencias Sociales*, 48: 25–40.

Huanacuni Mamani, F. (2010a) Paradigma occidental y paradigma indígena originario. *America latina en movimiento*, 452: 17–23.

(2010b) *Buen vivir/vivir bien: Filosofía, políticas, estrategias y experiencias regionales andinas.* Lima: Coordinadora Andina de Organizaciones Indígenas.

Kaul, I. (2014) Fostering sustainable human development: managing the macro-risks of vulnerability, occasional paper. New York: United Nations Development Programme.

Ki-moon, B. (2010) Remarks at launch of 20th Human Development Report. United Nations, 4 November. www.un.org/sg/en/content/sg/speeches/2010-11-04/remarks-launch-20th-human-development-report.

Klein, E. (2015) A critical review of the capability approach in Australian Indigenous policy, Working Paper 102/2015. Canberra: Centre for Aboriginal Economic Policy Research, Australian National University.

(2016) The curious case of using the capability approach in Australian Indigenous policy. *Journal of Human Development and Capabilities*, 17 (2): 245–59.

Kowii, A. (2014) Sumak kawsay. In *Antología del pensamiento indigenista ecuatoriano sobre sumak kawsay*, Hidalgo-Capitán, A. L., García, A. G., and Guazha, N. D. (eds.): 161–8. Huelva y Cuenca: Universidad de Huelva.

Llasag Fernandez, R. (2009) El sumak kawsay y sus restricciones constitucionales. *Foro: revista de derecho*, 12: 113–25.

Longshore Smith, M., and Seward, C. (2009) The relational ontology of Amartya Sen's capability approach: incorporating social and individual causes. *Journal of Human Development and Capabilities*, 10 (2): 213–35.

Macas, L. (2014) El sumak kawsay. In *Antología del pensamiento indigenista ecuatoriano sobre sumak kawsay*, Hidalgo-Capitán, A. L., Guillén García, A., and Deleg Guazha, N. (eds.): 169–77. Huelva y Cuenca: PYDLOS Ediciones.

Mansilla, H. C. F. (2011) Ideologías oficiales sobre el medio ambiente en Bolivia y sus aspectos problemáticos. *Ecuador Debate*, 84: 89–106.

McNeill, D. (2007) 'Human development': the power of the idea. *Journal of Human Development*, 8 (1): 5–22.

Merino, R. (2016) An alternative to 'alternative development'? Buen Vivir and human development in Andean countries. *Oxford Development Studies*, 44 (3): 271–86.

Mignolo, W. (2011) *The Darker Side of Western Modernity: Global Futures, Decolonial Options.* Durham, NC: Duke University Press.

Monni, S., and Pallottino, M. (2015) A new agenda for international development cooperation: lessons learnt from the Buen Vivir experience. *Development*, 58 (1): 49–57.

Murra, J. (2002) *El mundo andino: Población, medio ambiente y economía.* Lima: Pontificia Universidad Católica del Perú.

Nussbaum, M. (2003) Capabilities as fundamental entitlements: Sen and social justice. *Feminist Economics*, 9 (2/3): 33–59.

Oosterlaken, I. (2011) Inserting technology in the relational ontology of Sen's capability approach. *Journal of Human Development and Capabilities*, 12 (3): 425–32.

Oviedo Freire, A. (2012) El posmoderno buen vivir y el ancestral sumakawsay. In *Construyendo el buen vivir*, Guillén García, A., and Phelan Casanova, M. (eds.): 49–84. Huelva y Cuenca: PYDLOS Ediciones.

Panzironi, F. (2012) The 'Indigenous Capability – Right to Health' and Australia's 'Close the Gap' Indigenous health policy. In *The Capability Approach: Development Practice and Public Policy in the Asia-Pacific Region*, Panzironi, F., and Gelber, K. (eds.): 68–83. New York: Routledge.

Peter, F. (2003) Gender and the foundations of social choice: the role of situated agency. *Feminist Economics*, 9 (2/3): 13–32.

Petras, J., and Veltmeyer, H. (2011) *Social Movements in Latin America: Neoliberalism and Popular Resistance*. Basingstoke: Palgrave Macmillan.

Programa de Pequeñas Donaciones (2012) *Nuestro biocorredores para el buen vivir*. Quito: United Nations Development Programme.

Qizilbash, M. (1996) Ethical development. *World Development*, 24 (I): 1209–21.

Radcliffe, S. (2012) Development for a postneoliberal era? Sumak kawsay, living well and the limits to decolonisation in Ecuador. *Geoforum*, 43 (2): 240–9.

República del Ecuador (2008) Constitución de la República del Ecuador. www.gob.ec/sites/default/files/regulations/2020-06/CONSTITUCION% 202008.pdf.

Rivera Cusicanqui, S. (1990) Liberal democracy and ayllu democracy in Bolivia: the case of northern Potosí. *Journal of Development Studies*, 26 (4): 97–121.

(2010) *Oprimidos pero no vencidos*, 4th edn. La Paz: WA-GUI.

Robeyns, I. (2005) The capability approach: a theoretical survey. *Journal of Human Development*, 6 (1): 93–117.

(2008) Sen's capability approach and feminist concerns. In *The Capability Approach: Concepts, Measures and Applications*, Comim, F., Qizilbash, M., and Alkire, S. (eds.): 82–104. Cambridge: Cambridge University Press.

(2017) *Wellbeing, Freedom and Social Justice: The Capability Approach Re-Examined*. Cambridge: Open Book Publishers.

Sangha, K. K., Le Brocque, A., Costanza, R., and Cadet-James, Y. (2015) Application of capability approach to assess the role of ecosystem services in the well-being of Indigenous Australians. *Global Ecology and Conservation*, 4: 445–58.

Schlosberg, D., and Carruthers, D. (2010) Indigenous struggles, environmental justice, and community capabilities. *Global Environmental Politics*, 10 (4): 12–35.

Scholtes, F. (2010) Whose sustainability? Environmental domination and Sen's capability approach. *Oxford Development Studies*, 38 (3): 289–307.

Sen, A. K. (1977) Rational fools: a critique of the behavioural foundations of economic theory. *Philosophy & Public Affairs*, 6 (4): 317–44.

(1983) Development: which way now? *Economic Journal*, 93: 745–62.

(1984) *Resources, Values and Development*. Oxford: Blackwell.

(1987) *On Ethics and Economics*. Oxford: Blackwell.

(1999) *Development as Freedom*. Oxford: Oxford University Press.

(2002) Response to commentaries. *Studies in Comparative International Development*, 37 (2): 78–86.

(2008) The idea of justice. *Journal of Human Development*, 9 (3): 331–42.

(2009) *The Idea of Justice*. London: Penguin.

(2013) The ends and means of sustainability. *Journal of Human Development and Capabilities*, 14 (1): 6–20.

(2014) Global warming is just one of many environmental threats that demand our attention. *The New Republic*, 23 August.

Sen, A. K., and Anand, S. (2000) The income component of the Human Development Index. *Journal of Human Development*, 1 (1): 83–106.

SENPLADES (2009) *Plan Nacional para el buen vivir 2009–2013: Construyendo un estado plurinacional e intercultural – versión resumida*. Quito: Secretaría Nacional de Planificación y Desarrollo de la República del Ecuador.

(2013) *Buen vivir: Plan Nacional 2013–2017*. Quito: Secretaría Nacional de Planificación y Desarrollo de la República del Ecuador.

Sousa Santos, B. de (2003) *La caída del Angelus Novus: ensayos para una nueva teoría social y una nueva práctica política*, vol. 1. Bogotá: ILSA.

Spedding Pallet, A. (2010) 'Suma qamaña' ¿kamsañ muni? (¿Qué quiere decir 'vivir bien'?). *Fe y pueblo*, 17: 4–39.

Thomson, B. (2011) Pachakuti: indigenous perspectives, buen vivir, sumaq kawsay and degrowth. *Development*, 54 (4): 448–54.

UNDP (1990a) *Human Development Report 1990*. New York: Oxford University Press.

(1990b) Defining and measuring human development. In *Human Development Report 1990*, 9–16. New York: Oxford University Press.

(1991) *Human Development Report 1991*. New York: Oxford University Press.

(1999) *Human Development Report 1999*. New York: Oxford University Press.

(2004) *Human Development Report 2004: Cultural Liberty in Today's Diverse World*. New York: Oxford University Press.

(2010a) *Informe regional sobre desarrollo humano para América latina y el Caribe 2010*. San José de Costa Rica: United Nations Development Programme.

(2010b) *Informe nacional sobre desarrollo humano en Bolivia 2010: Los cambios detrás del cambio*. La Paz: United Nations Development Programme.

(2011) *Human Development Report 2011: Sustainability and Equity: A Better Future for All*. New York: Palgrave Macmillan.

(2012) *Ecuador: Economía y finanzas populares y solidarias para el buen vivir*. Quito: United Nations Development Programme.

(2013) *Ciudadanía intercultural: Aportes desde la participación política de los pueblos indígenas en Latinoamérica*. New York: United Nations Development Programme.

Untoja Choque, F. (2001) *Retorno al ayllu: Una mirada aymara a la globalización*. La Paz: Fondo Editorial de los Diputados.

Uzeda, A. (2009) Suma qamaña, visiones indígenas y desarrollo. *Traspatios*, 1: 33–51.

Vanhulst, J., and Beling, A. E. (2014) Buen Vivir: emergent discourse within or beyond sustainable development? *Ecological Economics*, 101: 54–63.

Vargas Llosa, M. (2004) Palabras de clausura. In *Las amenazas a la democracia en América Latina: Terrorismo, neopopulismo y debilidad del estado de derecho*, 123–30. Rosario: Editorial Amalevi.

Villalba, U. (2013) Buen Vivir vs development: a paradigm shift in the Andes? *Third World Quarterly*, 34 (8): 1427–42.

Viola Recasens, A. (2014) Discursos 'pachamamistas' versus políticas desarrollistas: el debate sobre el sumak kawsay en los Andes. *Íconos*, 48: 55–72.

Waldmüller, J. M. (2014) Human rights indicators as 'Development 2.0'? *Alternautas*, 1 (1): 76–88.

(2018) Lost through translation: political dialectics of eco-social and collective rights in Ecuador. In *Human Rights Transformations in an Unequal World*, Merry, S. E., and Destrooper, T. (eds.): 101–27. Philadelphia: University of Pennsylvania Press.

Walsh, C. (2010) Development as buen vivir: institutional arrangements and (de)colonial entanglements. *Development*, 53 (1): 15–21.

(2011) Afro and Indigenous life-visions in/and politics: (de)colonial perspectives in Bolivia and Ecuador. *Revista de Estudios Bolivianos*, 18: 49–69.

Watene, K. (2016) Valuing nature: Māori philosophy and the capability approach. *Oxford Development Studies*, 44 (3): 287–96.

Watene, K., and Yap, M. (2015) Culture and sustainable development: Indigenous contributions. *Journal of Global Ethics*, 11 (1): 51–5.

Weismantel, M. (2006) Ayllu: real and imagined communities in the Andes. In *The Seductions of Community: Emancipations, Oppressions, Quandaries*, Creed, G. (ed.): 77–99. Santa Fe: School of American Research Press.

Yampara, S. (2004) ¿Desarrollo/progreso o summa qamaña de los ayllus andinos? In *Memoria del foro: ¿A dónde vamos? Progreso en diferentes culturas*, 81–102. La Paz: Fundación PIEB – GTZ.

Yap, M., and Yu, E. (2016) Operationalising the capability approach: developing culturally relevant indicators of Indigenous wellbeing – an Australian example operationalising the capability approach: developing culturally. *Oxford Development Studies*, 44 (3): 315–31.

16 | Situating the family within the capabilities framework: a collective conversion factor
The role of the household configuration in the quality of life in Mali

CLAUDINE SAUVAIN-DUGERDIL AND
SIAKA CISSÉ*

Introduction

At present family studies make little use of the capability approach (CA), and, as underlined by Hall (2017), the family is an intermediary level between the individual and society that is rarely considered in the capabilities framework. In a few cases, the family has been conceived as a collective capability. For instance, Hall (2017) describes the collective activities of the Garifuna in Honduras as a 'joint capability'. More globally, Dubois and Rousseau (2001) consider the household in terms of collective capabilities that need to be reinforced in order to avoid the risk of poverty.

Sen and Nussbaum account for family mainly through the impact of family life on the well-being of its members. Nussbaum (2000) refers to the family as the fundamental sphere for affiliation. She considers family structure not as an organic unit but in terms of what Brighouse and Swift (2016) call 'relationship goods'. In line with Becker's 'negotiation unit', it is the locus of human development, education, association and expression. The same is true for Sen, who emphasizes the problem of unequal income distribution among family members through rules stemming from 'established conventions'. Norms and values relating to gender and generation relationships shape the

* This research project is part of the European programme DEMOSTAF, i.e. Demography Statistics for Africa (grant agreement no. 690984, https:// demostaf.site.ined.fr/en), which has made it possible to develop an intensive North–South partnership.

perception of individual needs, contributions and entitlements (see, in particular, Sen, 1999: 71, 88, ch. 8). Family thus expresses what Sen (2017) refers to as the 'challenges of group choice', due to the 'divergent interests and concerns of its members'.[1] Most of all, as Nussbaum (2000) stresses, problems arise when some family members – especially women and children – are not considered as an end but as an instrument for others' achievements. Public policies would have to protect and enhance all capabilities of the members of the family; it is thus not the family itself, except some vulnerable groups, that should be targeted by public policies but the norms and values to which it refers, especially in terms of gender inequality.

We postulate that the family, especially in sub-Saharan Africa, is also a decision unit in the sense that different types of families develop different subsistence strategies. More than a resource shared (unequally) by its members, it influences individual means to access and to convert resources, as well as life choices. Therefore, it has to be seen instead as a collective conversion factor. It affects individual capabilities in two ways that Robeyns (2016) includes within the core of the CA. On the one hand, it regulates the different abilities of people to convert resources and, on the other, it imposes structural constraints through social norms. Subsistence strategies differ according to family composition and, in turn, affect the individual's capacity to convert the resources of the context into capabilities. But the family is also the place where social values are translated into practical norms that will influence individual preferences and behaviour. Family is thus central in the ability to access resources and use them to 'live the life one has reason to value' (Sen, 1999: 14–15) by influencing, positively or negatively, a person's quality of life. Opportunities and achievements are therefore the result of the interaction between conversion factors and resources, which Chiappero, Salardi and Scervini (2018) formalize in terms of conversion rate.

In this regard, family studies and the capabilities framework can mutually enrich each other's approaches. Family studies focus on the diversity of family configurations and strategies and how this influences individual behaviour and quality of life, and it can thus enrich the capabilities debate about means. On the other side, the CA shines

---

[1] First sentence of the new introduction in *Collective Choice and Social Welfare* (Sen, 2017).

new light on how the family, as a conversion factor, influences a person's opportunities. These cross-enrichments can be seen, in particular, around three notions that are central to understanding the role of the family and that are discussed as transversal dimensions in this chapter. First, family plays a role of *social reserve*, in a way similar to cognitive reserve, described in psychology as an aid to coping with life's uncertainties (Stern, 2002). But the CA goes further, distinguishing between the availability of resources and the ability to access and use them. Second, as emphasized in recent research in family sociology, family values themselves – positive or negative ('misleading norms': Widmer and Spini, 2017) – reflect meta-values and shape *identity and preference*. This is an important issue in the CA, especially in social choice theory, revisited by Sen (2017) or with regard to the construction of a multiple identity (Sen, 2006). Last but not least, the CA shines new light also on family changes at the centre of the theory of demographic transition – i.e. the *paradigm of modernity* as the nuclearization of the family and the transformation of the role of children (Caldwell, 1982).

We illustrate here the role of the family as a collective conversion factor influencing the quality of life through an analysis of the Mali census. The 'household' is used as a proxy for the family decision unit. In the first step, the aim is thus to identify household characteristics and configurations that best express the diversity of family forms in Mali. Then we analyse the association between these household configurations and the quality of life to the extent that it is possible to express with census data. We first recall the results of our former analyses that consider the quality of life at the household level through three dimensions: the household's standard of living as information about its material wealth and access to modern commodities; and two measures of the opportunities enjoyed by household members: children's schooling and women's autonomy. We then present new analyses focusing on individual achievement through access to education. In the CA, Sen has long highlighted that education is important as both an end and a means to facilitate social change, political development and economic progress, which have a pivotal role in women's empowerment. It is an end in opening up the child's opportunities, but it is also instrumental – that is, an investment for the society and the family. As underlined by Walker and Unterhalter (2007), Sen (1999) emphasizes the importance of schooling to nurture future capabilities.

In other words, education 'influences the world' by enhancing the capacity for freedom, agency and well-being. In capability terms, education is a key factor for functioning in society, thanks to increased individual and collective agency. Education is a central capability in Nussbaum's list of major functions for human flourishing and dignity; it is not limited to basic knowledge and literacy but accounts for the broader ability to use the senses and to imagine, think and reason (see, for example, Nussbaum, 2011: 33). As stressed by Sen (1999), the benefit of education exceeds its effect of increased agency in production, such as one finds in the notion of 'human capital'.

The family as a collective conversion factor

Considering the role of the family in the capabilities framework is part of a broader questioning about how the CA takes into account the influence of an individual's social network. This social insertion factor is implicit in the definition of 'capabilities' as the 'freedom to live the life one has reason to value' (Sen, 1999: 14–15), itself implying that capabilities refer to what Bassand and Kellerhals (1975) call a 'situated project'. From this viewpoint, capabilities are contingent on the specific context and life circumstances, but are also anchored in social interactions and cultural norms. The person is embedded in a network of social relationships that are shaped by social institutions and their norms and values. The capabilities framework is therefore not purely individualistic – a frequent criticism – but focuses on the person's agency. Yet, as underlined by Ballet, Dubois and Mahieu (2007), the CA explicitly refers more especially to 'weak agency', centred on individual action, rather than on the 'strong agency' that links individuals to others through a set of responsibilities and commitments – what these authors refer to as 'collective capabilities'. The individual freedoms are also modulated by social norms and values, especially relating to gender (see Robeyns, 2005). For instance, many examples highlight women's strategies for using norms to their own benefit, or, at least, to adjust to them. This is especially the case with the ability of African women to manage their own economic activities but without jeopardizing their husband's role and privilege. Publicly, a wife does not question his decision-making power and ensures that he benefits somewhat from her gains, but without losing control of her income. This is clearly highlighted, for instance, in polygynous societies in which women give their husbands some money but not enough for him to use it to take a new wife.[2]

We consider here 'family' as a decision-making unit that develops subsistence strategies affecting the quality of life of its members. However, each person's life trajectory is unique even while interacting with others', a notion well expressed as 'linked lives' (Elder, 1995; Levy et al., 2005) – i.e. interdependence with the trajectories of parents, partner, children and other close persons. Even in traditional societies, where collective organization plays an important role, one's life course is individual. The collective dimension applies to specific functions or activities, such as political activism, the management of pastures and water in traditional Swiss Alpine societies or the example given by Hall (2017) concerning the preparation of cassava bread among the Garifuna in Honduras. Therefore, although we agree with Hall about the importance of taking into account the role of the family, we do not interpret it in terms of family joint capabilities. The freedoms remain individual, but the family shapes the person's ability to access and use the resources for him- or herself, especially in the case of children; rather, it is to be seen as a collective conversion factor. Considering family as a conversion factor implies highlighting its instrumental role: family is not the cause but a means.

The family has to date remained a central though complex entity. Contrary to what had been predicted in the 1970s and 1980s, the process of modernization has neither erased its role nor led to a unique model. The 'convergence towards diversity' (Billari and Wilson, 2001) is a worldwide reality. In Western societies, the complexification of life trajectories has increased the diversity of family forms. Many studies highlight that it remains a shelter at times of stress and a source of help. In Switzerland, the results of Coenen-Huther, Kellerhals and von Allmen (1994) about solidarity among family members certainly remains a reality, as shown, for instance, by different kinds of ongoing support – material, financial and emotional – that parents provide adult children. Our recent analysis of the quality of life of childless persons, based on the 2013 Swiss family survey (Sauvain-Dugerdil, 2018), stresses the role of children

---

[2] These women's strategies for managing their incomes are often mentioned in reports of projects to promote the economic activities of women, which came out recurrently in our field research in rural Mali (not published).

as a social reserve for old age. Compared with people having adult children, childless women and men aged 50 and over are worse off regarding mental health (negative feelings and loneliness) and have a smaller network of close persons, but also are less invested socially (they offer less help to others and are less active in voluntary activities). Children, although they are no longer a pillar for the material well-being of older parents, thus appear to play a role of reserve in the sense shown in social psychology – i.e. as human resources that help to cope with ageing. Children contribute to the social integration of parents, and childless people apparently do not compensate for this by developing other long-term social links. Children secure better access to, and use of, social resources and therefore can be considered as a collective conversion factor.

In non-Western societies, the paradigm of the nuclearization of households, seen as a necessary dimension for demographic transition, has not been verified. Historical demography[3] has highlighted that the nuclear family was never the only family configuration in the Western world and that it therefore cannot be taken as an essential feature of modernity. Moreover, urbanization does not lead to the universality of nuclear households. Many studies, especially in Africa, show that nuclear households have spread somewhat, but are not becoming the only family model. Many examples show that household size is larger in urban areas and has been increasing. In times of uncertainty the sheltering role of families is important. The need to cope with multidimensional change leads families to diversify their sources of income. What Batterbury (2007) has called the 'adaptive bricolage' of the Sahelian populations relies much on the ability of families to cope with uncertainties by adapting their subsistence strategies. In the present context of increasing uncertainties, Toulmin's (1992) observation of the advantage of large families in rural Mali is becoming even more pertinent in urban areas. Large, extended households appear to be better able to diversify their strategies. Nuclear families may express more modern values, but, as shown by Pilon and Vimard (1998) in Côte d'Ivoire, Senegal and Cameroon, they are also often the outcome of precariousness. Toulmin's comment about the increased fragility of large families, as a result of the authority of elders being questioned, is

---

[3] In particular, the Cambridge group; see Laslett and Wall (1972) and Wall, Robin and Laslett (1983).

certainly correct, but this has not led to generalized conflicts between generations. Modernity is bringing with it new expectations among young generations, leading to this 'Afrique des individus', as described in the volume edited by Alain Marie (1997), but in Africa, as highlighted by Calvès and Marcoux (2007), individualization means higher personal autonomy (individuation), but not the collapse of family ties. The person is endowed with more agency, but in the form of what Ballet, Dubois and Mahieu (2007) refer to as strong agency – that is to say, agency embedded in social interactions.

It is often difficult to determine family membership. The 'family' can refer to a nucleus of close relatives or to a more extended group, an economic or decision-making unit, people with special affective ties or those who share a place of residence (household). The increasing diversity of family forms, the complexity of customary living arrangements and the individuation of decisions make it more and more difficult to find a way to measure it. Family studies have developed new tools based on the notion of 'entourage' – in which Bonvalet and Lelièvre (1995, 2012) include close relatives, plus persons with whom one has cohabitated. The new field of network studies includes close persons, such as those self-defined as 'meaningful', or those who give/receive help (Widmer, 2010). This broadly fits with Nussbaum and Sen's family notion, recalled above, which considers the nature of the family living rather than its exact composition. These various approaches highlight the varying confines of the family circle depending on its definition. For instance, close relatives – i.e. the partner and the children – are not always living in the same household, designated as important persons and/or part of the exchange group. In addition, the intensity and strength of links can vary. However, more refined analyses of the family require ad hoc surveys that it is not always possible to carry out. In most large-scale surveys – such as a census – the listing of household members and their link to the household head remain the basic information available. Clearly, this does not document the real social, affective or economic links. Moreover, the contours of the household will depend on the definition adopted by the initiators of the surveys. In a census, it is usually the sharing of a common residence or meals – in other words, the people with whom someone shares an important part of his or her daily life. Reference is also often made to the recognition of a common head. In this case, especially in patriarchal/matriarchal societies, the household can be accepted as a proxy for a decision-making unit. This is why we consider it reliable to use the association between household configuration and quality of life in order to examine the ability of different types of households – depending on their composition and values – to develop subsistence strategies that will diversely affect individual fates and well-being.

We test this assumption here through a study of the association of household configuration with the quality of life in Mali, using census data. The first set of analyses has examined the association between household configuration and the overall quality of life of its members. In the present chapter, we also consider the role of household configuration as a mediator for individual access to school.

Quality of life in different types of households: in Mali, is it an advantage to live in a large, complex household?

Census data provide only limited information on life circumstances but highlight the nationwide diversity in the composition of the population and of households.[4] Considering the household as a proxy for the family decision-making unit, we have used Mali's most recent census to construct a typology reflecting the diversity of household composition, and examined whether different compositions are associated with variations in quality of life.

Beyond its mere size and the specificities of its head, which are often the bases for describing households, we take into account a series of characteristics chosen in light of the quality of information: size and type of household (nuclear, extended to other relatives and/or extended to non-relatives); its age structure, described by the number of children, young people and adults; and some characteristics of the head of the household (sex, age and education level). Their discrimination power – that is to say, their variability across households – was identified through a multiple correspondence analysis, the results of which were used to build a typology of so-called household configurations, through a cluster analysis. All analyses have been carried

---

[4] In line with the global aims of the European program DEMOSTAF, one objective of this research is to contribute to an effort to exploit existing data better, especially censuses, in a context of an inflation of surveys, designed to measure just one often underutilized achievement of the Millennium Development Goals/Sustainable Development Goals.

out separately for urban and rural settings, as their situations differ widely. For both cases, the best model is that with five clusters. In each setting, the reference is the most prevalent type, accounting for some 40 per cent (Tables 16.1 and 16.2).

In each setting, three groups of households differ mainly by their size and type, and the two others by the characteristics of the household head. In urban settings, the reference profile is a nuclear household of a varying size, but rarely with more than eight persons; the head is always a man, aged between 25 and 60 years, and with diverse education levels (urban 1 – U1 – representing 36.5 per cent of urban households). Two types are rather large, and extended to other relatives (U2, 26 per cent) and/or non-relatives (U3, 19 per cent). The latter is often very large, with many children and young adults. The two remaining types are characterized by their small size and the characteristics of their head: a small, atypical group of households (U5, 6 per cent), usually of very small size and often nuclear, has no children in eight out of ten cases and, in half of them, no young or adult persons; the second atypical group is a little more frequent (U4, 12 per cent) and differs by the fact that it is headed by a woman.

In rural settings, the reference profile (R1, 43 per cent) is middle-sized, often nuclear, with at least one young or adult member, but in one-third of cases there are no children; the head is a man, not educated. Two small atypical groups (R5, 9 per cent, and R4, 11 per cent) often have a limited number of members, in R5 often with no young persons/adults, and in R4 with no children; their head is either older (R5) or younger (R4) than average. The two other profiles differ either by their size or the characteristics of their head: in nine cases out of ten, the R2 type (21 per cent) has more than eight persons, including numerous children and young persons; while R3 (17 per cent) is the rural profile that more often has a head who has been at school, even beyond primary level. In turn, female-headed households in rural settings do not have a specific profile but are to be found in a similar proportion – about one-third – in the households with educated (R3), younger (R4) or older (R5) heads.

The quality of life was considered on the basis of three indicators available in the 2009 census:[5]

---

[5] Child survival, a very sensitive indicator of the quality of the context, could not be taken into account because of problems with the quality of the information.

Table 16.1 *Configuration of urban households: results of multiple correspondence and cluster analysis*

		Urban clusters					
		U1	U2	U3	U4	U5	
Variables	Values	Urban reference type	Extended to other relatives	Very large, extended to non-relatives	Household head female	Very small, head younger or older	Total
Household size	Very small (1–2)	21.3	3.2	0.4	16.8	81.6	15.7
	Small (3–5)	54.8	28.4	9.5	42.1	13.7	35.1
	Large (6–8)	23.6	42.4	18.8	24.9	4.2	26.5
	Very large (9+)	0.3	26.1	71.3	16.1	0.5	22.7
Household type	Nuclear	97.3	4.6	20.3	37.3	81.4	50.2
	Extended other relatives	0.1	94.0	26.1	45.4	15.8	35.8
	Extended other or non-relatives	2.6	1.4	53.6	17.3	2.8	14.0
Number of children (6–14 years)	0	53.7	29.3	14.2	37.4	83.8	39.6
	1–2	37.0	54.7	26.5	45.1	13.0	39.0
	3+	9.4	16.0	59.3	17.4	3.1	21.4
Number of young or adults (15–44years)	0	0.0	0.1	0.0	2.4	3.6	3.6
	1–2	91.9	32.7	10.1	55.2	44.7	53.4
	3+	8.1	67.3	89.9	42.4	1.1	43.0
Sex Household head	Man	100.0	100.0	100.0	0.0	85.6	87.0
	Woman	0.0	0.0	0.0	100.0	14.4	13.0
	None	54.4	47.4	39.7	61.7	58.2	50.8

Table 16.1 (*cont.*)

		Urban clusters					
		U1	U2	U3	U4	U5	Total
Variables	Values	Urban reference type	Extended to other relatives	Very large, extended to non-relatives	Household head female	Very small, head younger or older	Total
Education level Household head	Primary	16.9	22.5	6.6	13.7	11.2	15.6
	Secondary and above	28.8	30.1	53.7	24.6	30.6	33.6
Age Household head	< 25 years	1.1	2.6	0.7	9.0	34.3	4.4
	25–44 years	76.2	51.5	36.8	42.2	0.0	53.4
	45–59 years	17.8	24.9	48.7	29.9	35.5	28.2
	60+	4.9	21.0	13.8	18.9	30.2	14.0
Total		100.0	100.0	100.0	100.0	100.0	100.0
Number of observations		184,974	130,871	98,290	61,463	30,961	506,559
Percentage		36.5	25.8	19.4	12.1	6.1	100.0
Highest values				Lowest values			

Notes: The results show that, for example, more than 80 per cent of U5 households are very small, nuclear and with no children, and about a half of them have no young adults, whereas U3 households are usually very large, with more than two young adults, half of the time more than two children or extended to other persons (relatives and non-relatives), but very rarely with a head younger than 26 years; U4 distinguishes itself mainly by the fact that it is always headed by a woman, and U1 mainly by being nuclear and middle-sized.

Source: Mali population census, 2009: https://ghdx.healthdata.org/record/mali-population-and-housing-census-2009.

| | | Rural clusters | | | | | |
| | | R1 | R2 | R3 | R4 | R5 | |
Variables	Values	Rural reference type	Very large	HH head educated	Very small, head younger	Head older	Total
Household size	Very small (1–2)	0.3	0.0	0.9	87.3	46.7	13.5
	Small (3–5)	56.2	1.5	58.2	4.0	34.1	37.5
	Large (6–8)	42,5	7.2	31,4	8.7	18,2	27,6
	Very large (9+)	0.9	91.3	9.6	0.1	1.0	21.4
Household type	Nuclear	72.1	43.6	59.3	87.6	74.6	65.8
	Extended, other relatives	27.0	49.7	34.9	11.8	23.9	31.2
	Extended, other or non-relatives	0.9	6.7	5.8	0.6	1.5	3.0
Number of children (6–14 years)	0	37.3	3.3	28.2	89.8	56.4	35.8
	1–2	50.4	16.9	57.7	3.4	35.5	38.3
	3+	12.3	79.8	14.1	6.9	8.0	25.9
Number of young or adults (15–44 years)	0	0.0	0.3	0.9	0.0	84.2	7,4
	1–2	81.8	14.1	72.8	98.6	0.8	60.8
	3+	18.2	85.6	26.3	1.4	15.0	31.8
Sex HH head	Man	100.0	96.6	63.3	67.1	68.5	87.0
	Woman	0.0	3.4	36.7	32.9	31.5	13.0
Education level HH head	None	100.0	89.5	31.1	80.2	94.9	83.9
	Primary	0.0	5.8	39.5	7.5	2.5	8.8
	Secondary and above	0.0	4.6	29.3	12.2	2.6	7.3

Table 16.2 (*cont.*)

Variables	Values	Rural clusters					
		R1	R2	R3	R4	R5	Total
		Rural reference type	Very large	HH head educated	Very small, head younger	Head older	Total
Age HH head	< 25 years	4.0	0.6	5.1	30.6	0.0	5.9
	25–44 years	58.7	37.9	60.7	57.4	0.0	49.5
	45–59 years	22.4	43.3	26.0	7.1	26.0	26.1
	60+	14.9	18.3	8.1	4.9	74.0	18.5
Total		100.0	100.0	100.0	100.0	100.0	100.0
Number of observations		771,313	377,702	295,163	188,780	152,512	1,785,470
Percentage		43.2	21.2	16.5	10.6	8.5	100.0
Highest values			Lowest values				

Notes: The results show that R2 is in most cases very large, with more than two young adults and two children; it is the configuration more often extended to relatives other than direct ones, and, like R1, is headed by a man with no schooling. R4 is in most cases very small, nuclear, with no children and one to two young adults, and it is the configuration that more frequently has a young head. R3 is the configuration in which the head has more often been at school, while R5 often has no young adults and a head aged 60 or more.

Source: Mali population census, 2009: https://ghdx.healthdata.org/record/mali-population-and-housing-census-2009.

- the standard of living, measured through assets, materials used for housing construction, and types of water access and sanitation facilities;[6]
- an index of average schooling of the children (the proportion of children accessing school for each education level relative to that among households with the same number of children in that school age group); and
- women's autonomy (the proportion who are literate and with their own occupation).

The results of regression analyses, not shown here (INSTAT, 2016; Nouhou et al., 2016; Sauvain-Dugerdil et al., 2018),[7] confirm inequalities in the quality of life between household types that express different opportunities by household configuration.

➢ Large, complex households are better off in the different dimensions considered. The very large urban households (U3 type), and to a lesser extent the large ones extended to relatives only (U2) and the large rural ones (R2), appear to have a higher standard of living, their children have better access to school, and women's autonomy is higher (women are more often literate and have their own occupation). The diversity of their members enables them to exploit existing opportunities better and have the means to put and maintain their children in school. However, more often in these large households only some of the children and women are accessing, respectively, education and an occupation. Therefore, their abilities to diversify their strategies may also imply inequalities between individuals.

➢ In general, nuclear-type households appear to be less well off but more equal. This is the case for the reference type in both urban and rural settings, which are, respectively, 97 per cent and 72 per cent nuclear. In urban settings they are the worst in terms of quality of dwellings, second to last as to children's schooling and women's

---

[6] This widely used type of index is often considered as a proxy for wealth but, especially in a context such as that of Mali, is, rather, an indication of access to modern amenities.

[7] The results were set out in a publication of the Mali National Institute of Statistics (INSTAT, 2016) and in two scientific papers, one focusing on the standard of living and average schooling of children (Nouhou et al., 2016) and the other on the situation of women (Sauvain-Dugerdil et al., 2018).

autonomy and in an intermediate position in rural settings. There is a diversity of nuclear households: the very small rural ones headed by an old person are the worst off, and children in all very small ones are less educated.

➤ But size and type of household are not the only characteristics that account for their unequal well-being. In both settings, one of the household types distinguishes itself by the specificity of its head: in rural populations, those with an educated head; and, in urban ones, those that are female-headed. In rural settings, where access to education is still very limited, especially among older generations, heads who have been to school appear to improve household well-being. They are more often among those with a better dwelling, and have more children at school and more women who are literate. Access to education is also more equal. Regarding the quality of the dwellings, the schooling of children and women's autonomy in urban setting, female-headed households feature second, after the very large ones. Thus, contrary to what the literature often reports, female-headed households are not systematically disadvantaged or more vulnerable. However, female-headed household are also to be found in some cases among the very small households, which are the most vulnerable ones, illustrating the varied situations of female-headed households. This variety of situations is even more obvious in rural settings, where female headed households do not characterize one specific cluster but are mainly found among the best off – households with an educated head – and the worst off – small households with an older head.

In conclusion, these results show that the composition of the household, not just its size, influences its ability to be part of the modernization process of society, as measured by the amenities of their residences, the investment in children's education and women's autonomy. Nuclear households appear less able to take up opportunities than more complex households. Furthermore, the latter may have more lasting well-being: because they are better off, they can receive newcomers, who will, in turn, contribute to their wealth, and better-educated children will enhance the family's agency. In rural settings, the level of education of the head is an important advantage. In urban ones, female-headed households form a specific group, but not one that is systematically more vulnerable. This reflects the diversity of situations that lead a woman to become the family head. It is not the fact of living in a female-headed household that is crucial, therefore, but the reasons why the woman ended up in this situation. Very small, atypical households appear most vulnerable. These outcomes are coherent in the three dimensions of the quality of life considered here, and they are in line with previous studies in west Africa that highlighted the capacity of extended households to diversify their subsistence strategies and their refuge roles in harsh times (Toulmin, 1992; Pilon and Vimard, 1998; Locoh and Mouvagha-Sow, 2005). However, census data preclude going beyond analyses of associations. In-depth studies would be necessary to interpret these results, especially as to the exact reasons for the advantaged position of larger households. In addition, of course, factors other than household configuration impact the quality of life of its members, as reflected in the large unexplained variance. These unobserved factors are in part taken into account in the multi-level analysis presented in the next section.

Household configuration as a mediator for differences in access to education: a multi-level analysis[8]

We now consider the impact of household configurations, as defined and constructed above, on individual opportunities to access education in Mali. In a context of a very low level of education, does access to school differ by household configuration? Moreover, does this effect remain when controlling for a household's standard of living? In other terms, is it more than just the consequence of wealth differences? Finally, do these differences contribute to explaining inequalities in education between places of residence?

Education has been recognized as a central dimension of human development per se, but also as a means for social and economic progress. For households, putting children in school is an investment for the future that nonetheless has immediate costs, both direct (even though there are no fees, parents often have to bear the costs of supplies, food and transport) and indirect (loss of children's contributions to family activities). In our former analyses, we observed that child labour was much more frequent in poorer households (Nouhou et al., 2016). As noted by Hart (2018: 636), child education is 'a balancing act between an individual's capabilities and functionings and those of others': the contributions that the parents make imply 'trade-offs

---

[8] Multi-level logistic regression made with the Stata 12 software.

between present and future well-being, freedoms and achievements' for themselves and their children.

Education is more than school attendance, but, as underlined by Walker and Unterhalter (2007), Sen recalls the importance of literacy for enhancing agency and social participation. In spite of frequent poor school infrastructure and quality of learning in countries such as Mali, schooling makes a difference by opening new opportunities. However, Lange and Pilon (2000) have shown that poor infrastructure can be an obstacle to school attendance, especially for girls, and that poor quality is a disadvantage that can persist throughout a lifetime (see also Walker and Unterhalter, 2007); more globally, as recalled by Hart (2018), a series of studies show the potentially negative impact of schools, through the types of values that they transmit – especially gender stereotypes – or by restricting or orienting children's aspirations (see Vos and Ballet, 2018, about the French case).

In Mali, progress in education has been slow (Sauvain-Dugerdil and Thiriat, 2009). Education has improved, but it is still far from universal, especially in rural areas and for girls. It even declined during the last decade, due to the security problems in the northern and central parts of the country. The net, primary enrolment rate in 2009 was 58.1 per cent for girls and 68.9 per cent for boys, yet only 57.7 per cent and 64.6 per cent, respectively, in 2017.[9] We consider here access to education, measured by children's present or past school attendance ('Are they at school or have they been to school?') as declared in the 2009 census. By this definition, 75 per cent of the boys and 59 per cent of the girls aged 15 to 29 years were educated; these figures reach 80 and 73 per cent among those aged ten to 14 years in urban areas, but only 39 and 25 per cent and 48 and 39 per cent, respectively, in rural areas. In a context such as Mali, where a significant share of the population is not literate and many children do not go to school, school attendance represents a proxy for education: going to school means, especially for rural girls, an opportunity to experience the outside world. It also expresses the priority given by parents to an investment for the future of their children and of the family.

We apply a multi-level logistic regression to analyse the role of household configuration in the capacity to access school. The multi-level analysis enables us to examine the embeddedness of people's opportunities in different levels of their context, the first being the household,

[9] See http://uis.unesco.org/fr/country/ml#slideoutmenu.

then the geographical location (region of residence) and the characteristics of the municipality (density of schools, households' average wealth, population age structure and level of education). The results show that household configuration is an important mediator that has a net effect on all models, even when controlling for household standard of living and the characteristics of the context (Tables 16.3 and 16.4). In both settings, school attendance is lower for those living in nuclear households (reference types), consistent with the above observations about global quality of life in these households. The globally worst situation in very small households with a young head, reported in the last section, is reflected here by the worst access to education. In both settings, children living in this atypical household are those less able to attend school. In rural areas, this disadvantage is higher among girls, which is in line with the fact reported above: that they are more affected by poorer infrastructure, particularly distance to school.

In rural settings, access to education is highest among those living in a household headed by an educated person, the type of household seen globally as having a better quality of life. Large households come next. In urban settings, access to education is higher in a female-headed household and, to a slightly less extent, in a very large extended one. This confirms the overall quality of life in large households. The fact that the advantage of a female-headed household is independent of the overall situation of the household may reflect the higher importance given to education by women than by men, as reported in west Africa[10] (Cosio et al., 2003; Kobiane, 2006; Wayack Pambè and Pilon, 2011). The results also highlight different treatments of boys and girls: boys have better access to school when living in households that are female-headed and, to a lesser extent, in very large extended ones; in turn, for girls, schooling is not highest among female-headed households but among large households with relatives only. This may indicate gender inequalities, in terms of a somewhat higher importance that lone women give to investment in their sons (who remain more important than girls for support in old age), and highlights the fact that, for a girl, most important is the possibility of sharing domestic tasks with other female members of the household (for Mali, see, for instance, Marcoux, 1994). This advantage is lower in households extended to non-relatives, where in fact the girl can be the maid, who, in most cases, does not attend school.

---

[10] Kobiane (2003) shows that, in Ouagadougou, this is even more the case among poorer households.

Table 16.3 *School attendance, urban settings, children aged ten to 19 years: multi-level logistic regression analysis*

	Boys								Girls							
	Model nul		Mod1		Mod2		Mod3		Model nul		Mod1		Mod2		Mod3	
Urban settings	Exp (B)	Sig.	Exp	Sig.	Exp (B)	Sig.	Exp	Sig.	Exp (B)	Sig.	Exp	Sig.	Exp	Sig.	Exp (B)	Sig.
Fixed effects																
Household configuration (reference: urban type)																
U2 Extended other relatives			1.11	***	1.02		1.02	***			1.70	***	1.68	***	1.68	***
U4 Female-headed			1.40	***	1.27	***	1.27	***			1.35	***	1.36	***	1.36	***
U5 Very small, head younger or older			0.43	***	0.41	***	0.41	***			0.82	***	0.85	***	0.85	***
U3 Very large, extended to (non-) relatives			1.28	***	1.15	***	1.15	***			1.16	***	1.19	***	1.19	***
HH standard of living (reference: poor)																
Medium					3.46	***	3.46	***					2.51	***	2.51	***
High					4.66	***	4.66	***					1.84	***	1.84	***
Region (reference:: Bamako)																
Kayes							0.50	***							0.74	*
Koulikoro							2.51	***							3.56	***
Sikasso							1.15								2.34	***
Ségou							1.03								2.16	***
Mopti							0.73								1.90	***

Gao				0.56 *				1.70
Kidal				0.36 ***				1.06
Municipality, density schools/10,000 habitats (reference: low)								
Medium				0.90				1.11
High				1.28 **				1.28 **
Municipality, proportion HH head educated (reference: low)								
Medium				0.74 **				1.07
High				1.08				1.27 **
Constant	3.71 ***	3.16 ***	1.57 ***	1.27 **	1.60 ***	1.25 ***	0.71 ***	0.30 ***
Random effects								
Variance (SE)	0.90 ***	0.90 ***	0.54 ***	0.14 ***	0.69 ***	0.69 ***	0.51 ***	0.11 ***
(VPC) = ICC (%)	21.53	21.57	13.99	4.14	17.42	17.35	13.35	3.20
Number observations	256,317				296,097			

Notes: Statistical significance: * $p < 0.1$; ** $p < 0.05$; *** $p < 0.01$. VPC = variance partition coefficient; ICC = intraclass correlation coefficient. Controlled for municipality age structure and average household assets. This table shows that in urban settings, for example, girls living in a household extended to other relatives have an almost twofold higher probability (1.68 times) of attending school than do girls living in the reference type. This result is not modified when controlling for the effects of standard of living, region of residence and characteristics of the municipality. The so-called random effects highlight that differences between municipalities account for 21 per cent of the inequalities in boys' schooling and a little less (17 per cent) for girls. Household configuration does not modify these differences between municipalities by one-third for boys and one-quarter for girls. Above all, we see that most of these inequalities are explained by the characteristics of the context (region of residence, availability of schools and proportion of household heads who have themselves been to school): when taking them into account, the variance between municipalities falls to 4 per cent.

Source: Mali general census of population and habitats, 2009, total population ten to 19 years: https://ghdx.healthdata.org/record/mali-population-and-housing-census-2009.

Table 16.4 School attendance, rural settings, children aged ten to 19 years: multi-level logistic regression analysis

	Boys								Girls							
	Model nul		Mod1		Mod2		Mod3		Model nul		Mod1		Mod2		Mod3	
Rural settings	Exp (B)	Sig.	Exp (B)	Sig.	Exp (B)	Sig.	Exp (B)	Sig.	Exp (B)	Sig.	Exp (B)	Sig.	Exp (B)	Sig.	Exp (B)	Sig.
Fix effects																
Household configuration (reference: rural type)																
R3 HH head educated			2.72	***	2.43	***	2.43	***			3.17	***	2.97	***	2.79	***
R2 Very large			1.32	***	1.23	***	1.23	***			1.92	***	1.81	***	1.81	***
RS HH head older			1.16	***	1.13	***	1.13	***			1.79	***	1.74	***	1.74	***
R4 Very small, head younger			1.00		0.97		0.97	*			0.75	***	0.74	***	0.74	***
Quality of lodging (reference: poor)																
Medium					2.43	***	2.43	***					2.36	***	2.35	***
High					5.88	***	5.85	***					5.09	***	5.06	***
Region (reference: Koulikoro)																
Kayes							1.00								0.95	
Sikasso							0.82	***							0.99	
Segou							0.70	***							0.91	
Mopti							0.54	***							1.14	
Tombouctou							0.46	***							0.87	
Gao							0.69	***							1.10	
Kidal							0.28	***							0.42	***

	(1)	(2)	(3)	(4)	(5)	(6)	(7)	(8)
Municipality, density schools/10,000 habitats (reference: low)								
Medium			1.54 ***					1.52 ***
High			1.71 ***					1.77 ***
Municipality, proportion HH head educated (reference: low)								
Medium			1.57 ***					1.52 ***
High			2.49 ***					2.51 ***
Constant	0.80 ***	0.60 ***	1.58 ***	0.67 ***	1.07 ***	0.45 ***	0.70 ***	0.36 ***
Random effects								
Variance (SE)	0.86 ***	0.83 ***	0.67 ***	0.37 ***	0.67 ***	0.62 ***	0.48 ***	0.26 ***
(VPC) = ICC (%)	20.72	20.22	16.96	8.82	17.01	15.80	12.76	7.30
Number observations	815,409				796,755			

Notes: Statistical significance: * $p < 0.1$; ** $p < 0.05$; *** $p < 0.01$. VPC = variance partition coefficient; ICC = intraclass correlation coefficient. Controlled for municipality age structure and average household assets. The results for the rural settings are similar to those for the urban settings. However, we see that households play a more important role in rural than in urban settings. The differences between households are greater: a household with an educated head has a 2.5 times higher probability (nearly three times higher for girls) of attending school than those in the reference type; the effect of household standard of living is also stronger (for those living in a wealthier household, school attendance is five times higher than among the poorer). Furthermore, among girls, the differences between households play a clear role in the overall variance between municipalities. Moreover, we see that, for both sexes, the remaining unexplained variance between municipalities is somewhat higher in rural than in urban settings.

Source: Mali general census of population and habitats, 2009, total population ten to 19 years: https://ghdx.healthdata.org/record/mali-population-and-housing-census-2009.

Although household configuration appears to mediate a person's access to education, in turn differences in household configuration do not explain unequal access between municipalities: the geographic variance in school attendance is not reduced when introducing the household configuration. Household amenities and, above all, the characteristics of the context are the keys to interpreting inequalities of education between municipalities. The density of schools plays an important role in the countryside but not in urban settings; in both settings, an influential factor is the overall level of education, as measured by the average proportion of literate household heads in the municipality. The effect of the geographical location, as measured by the differences between regions of residence, is not homogeneous. While in the region of Koulikoro, surrounding the capital city, access to education is 2.5 times higher than in the capital city for boys and 3.6 times for girls, and in Kidal, in the north-eastern region, school attendance is the lowest, there is no clear trend in regional differences and in gender differential: among girls, geographic location appears more important in urban settings, while, for boys, it is the case in rural areas. The results show that most of the variance in individual access to education between municipalities is explained by these different characteristics: the main causes of low schooling are poor supply, problems of access and, more broadly, environments that are not propitious.[11] However, these specificities of context do not erase the net mediating role played by household configuration. In all contexts, children's access to schooling differs by household configuration. Different households develop different schooling strategies that influence their children's access to education. The role of household configuration therefore has to be seen as a collective factor of conversion.

Concluding remarks

The aim of this chapter is to consider the role of the family in people's quality of life, a level in between the person and society that has been barely considered in the capabilities approach. Capabilities are

---

[11] However, in rural settings for girls, there is a little more unexplained variation (see Table 16.2), which is in line with the comments above noting the fact that a longer journey to school or poorer quality in terms of the infrastructure affects girls more than boys (Lange and Pilon, 2000).

individual, but a person's opportunities and agency are embedded into his or her surroundings, including his or her family. We postulate, therefore, that family configuration works as a collective conversion factor; that is to say, it affects individual freedom to 'live the life one has reason to value'. The role of the family takes particular meanings in the present context of the worldwide diversification and complexification of families. This is especially the case in sub-Saharan Africa, where multiple types of crises increase the role of shelter played by the family, which is, at the same time, destabilized by exposure to new values from a globalizing world.

This chapter is part of a research programme that considers the associations between the configurations of households and their quality of life in Mali through census data. The results show statistically significant differences between household configurations that express the instrumental role that the composition of the household plays in unequal access to goods and opportunities. However, the large non-explained variance confirms that other factors affect the quality of life, in particular characteristics of the context such as those shown in the multi-level analysis.

Our analyses provide three lines of evidence. First, the comprehensiveness of the census data makes it possible to build a refined typology of household configurations that accounts for the varying discrimination power of household characteristics. We thus consider household configurations reflecting a series of characteristics (size, type and age structure, but also specificities of the household head in rural and urban settings) and not, as is usually done, just one trait – i.e. size or type. In both settings, the statistical procedures led to the construction of five configurations. The main one is a middle-sized, nuclear household headed by a man, distinct from larger ones in the urban context, with a further distinction between those comprising only relatives and very large ones, extended to non-relatives. In both settings, one type is also defined by the specificity of the household head: women in towns and an educated person in the countryside.

Second, a clear association has been shown between the household configuration and the overall quality of life of its members, both with regard to goods (standard of living) and opportunities (such as children's schooling and women's autonomy). In the Mali context, large households, especially extended ones in urban settings, are better off than the dominant middle-sized, nuclear ones. The larger number of their members constitutes a social reserve, and their individual agency increases the household's capacity to diversify its subsistence strategies. These households thus appear to cope better with uncertainties than do nuclear households, despite their supposedly being more modern in their lifestyles; the so-called 'nuclearization paradigm' is not therefore verified. Although larger households appear to be characterized by more inequality between members, the risk of becoming more fragile, as the result of the weaker cohesion mentioned by Toulmin (1992), apparently does not affect their quality of life. The characteristics of the household head, usually examined in diagnostics of vulnerable households, do not appear to be the main factor of well-being. However, in rural settings, households headed by an educated person are the best off, confirming Sen's view that education enables other capabilities. Moreover, urban households headed by a woman form a specific type, rating rather well. These two last points illustrate an intermingling of material and cultural factors that shape household strategies: educated heads have better means to access and transform resources into well-being, but they are certainly also vehicles of more progressive values, whereas women heads are known to give a higher priority to family well-being than men, but their economic situations are quite diverse, depending on the reasons that led them to become heads of the households.

Last but not least, household configuration appears to mediate individual capabilities, such as those examined here, with respect to children's ability to access school and future opportunities opened by schooling. Our postulate – that family is a collective conversion factor – is therefore verified. Belonging to a specific family configuration is an important dimension for explaining unequal access to education, independently from household standard of living, geographic location and the characteristics of the municipality of residence.

A challenge for this research has also been to exploit better the existing large-scale survey data, which are most often underused. In a context in which security issues prevent international and national researchers from carrying out fieldwork, they take on a new importance. In spite of the obvious limitations of the very simple, factual information collected by the national census, we show here its usefulness for analysing the diversity of household configurations. Clearly, as is well known in family studies, the household does not reflect the complexity of family and social networks. However, at least in a patriarchal society such as

Mali, our results make sense and therefore show that the household can be taken as a proxy for a decision-making unit.

Of course, only in-depth studies would be able to go beyond these broad accounts. The typology offers a picture of the varying characteristics that best describe the diversity of households. However, the data available in the census do not provide information about their history. In particular, it would be necessary to explore in more detail the situation of atypical, very small households and of female-headed ones. We question here the widely spread notion of the vulnerability of the latter, a key issue that needs to be further considered. In a context in which a woman can be a household head only in the absence of an eligible man, it would be necessary to investigate what leads a woman to take on this function. Moreover, more information would be needed about large households' well-being: are they better off because they are larger, or were they able to take in newcomers because they already had more resources?

Above all, it should be remembered that these results are specific to a patriarchal context in which the household can be considered a decision-making unit for subsistence strategies and solidarities. Our Swiss study into the role of children as a social reserve for coping with ageing (Sauvain-Dugerdil, 2018), and studies about the role of the stability of parental couples in children's well-being (Härkönen, Bernardi and Boertien, 2017), are examples highlighting the fact that, in present day Western societies, family configuration also matters. Family works as a collective conversion factor, but in different ways, depending on the meanings and roles of the family in each context.

References

Ballet, J., Dubois, J.-L., and Mahieu, F.-R. (2007) Responsibility for each other's freedom: agency as the source of collective capability. *Journal of Human Development*, 8 (2): 185–201.

Bassand, M., and Kellerhals, J. (1975) *Familles urbaines et fécondité*. Geneva: Librairie de l'Université Georg.

Batterbury, S. (2007) Monde rural et transformations agraires au Sud: débat et défis. In *Actes du Colloque International PRIPODE*, 177–184. Paris: CICRED.

Billari, F., and Wilson, C. (2001) Convergence towards diversity? Cohort dynamics in the transition to adulthood in contemporary western

Europe, Working Paper 2001–039. Rostock: Max Planck Institute for Demographic Research.

Bonvalet, C., and Lelièvre, E. (1995) Du concept de ménage à celui d'entourage: une redéfinition de l'espace familial. *Sociologie et Sociétés*, 27 (2): 177–90.

(eds.) (2012) *De la famille à l'entourage: L'enquête biographies et entourage*. Paris: INED.

Brighouse, H., and Swift, A. (2016) *Family Values: The Ethics of Parent–Child Relationships*. Princeton, NJ: Princeton University Press.

Caldwell, J. C. (1982) *Theory of Fertility Decline*. London: Academic Press.

Calvès, E. A., and Marcoux, R. (2007) Les processus d'individualisation 'à l'africaine'. *Sociologie et sociétés*, 39 (2): 5–18.

Chiappero, E., Salardi, P., and Scervini, F. (2018) From resources to functioning: rethinking and measuring conversion rates. In *New Frontiers of the Capability Approach*, Comim, F., Fennell, S., and Anand, P. B. (eds.): 232–45. Cambridge: Cambridge University Press.

Coenen-Huther, J., Kellerhals, J., and von Allmen, M. (1994) *Les réseaux de solidarités dans la famille*. Lausanne: Réalités sociales.

Cosio, M., Marcoux, R., Pilon, M., and Quesnel, A. (eds.) (2003) *Éducation, famille et dynamiques démographiques*. Paris: CICRED.

Dubois, J.-L., and Rousseau, S. (2001) Reinforcing household's capabilities as a way to reduce vulnerability and prevent poverty in equitable terms. Paper presented at the conference 'Justice and poverty: examining Sen's capability approach', University of Cambridge, 6 June.

Elder Jr, G. H. (1995) The life course paradigm: social change and individual development. In *Examining Lives in Context: Perspectives on the Ecology of Human Development*, Elder Jr, G. H., and Lüscher, K. (eds.): 101–36. Washington, DC: American Psychological Association.

Hall, K. M. Q. (2017) Introducing joint capabilities: findings from a study of development in Honduras' Garifuna ancestral villages. *Journal of Human Development and Capabilities*, 18 (1): 60–74.

Härkönen, J., Bernardi, F., and Boertien, D. (2017) Family dynamics and child outcomes: key findings and unresolved questions. *European Journal of Population*, 33 (2): 163–84.

Hart, C. S. (2018) Education, capabilities and sustainable development. In *New Frontiers of the Capability Approach*, Comim, F., Fennell, S., and Anand, P. B. (eds.): 617–40. Cambridge: Cambridge University Press.

INSTAT (2016) *Configuration des ménages et qualité de vie: Les avantages et désavantages des grands ménages au Mali*. Bamako: Institut National de la Statistique.

Kobiane, J.-F. (2003) Pauvreté, structures familiales et stratégies éducatives à Ouagadougou. In *Éducation, famille et dynamiques démographiques*,

Cosio, M., Marcoux, R., Pilon, M., and Quesnel, A. (eds.): 153–82. Paris: CICRED.

(2006) *Ménages et scolarisation des enfants au Burkina Faso: À la recherche des déterminants de la demande scolaire*. Louvain-la-Neuve, Belgium: Academia-Bruylant.

Lange, M.-F., and Pilon, M. (2000) La persistance des inégalités d'accès à l'instruction. In *Rapport de genre et questions de population*, vol. 2, *Genre, population et développement*, Bozon, M. (ed.): 69–80. Paris: INED.

Laslett, P., and Wall, R. (eds.) (1972) *Household and Family in Past Time*. Cambridge: Cambridge University Press.

Levy, R., Deschamps, J.-C., Elcheroth, G., Forney, Y., Gauthier, J.-A., Ghisletta, P., Kellerhals, J., Lalive d'Épinay, C., Le Goff, J.-M., de Ribaupierre, A., Sauvain-Dugerdil, C., Spini, D., Tettamanti, M., and Widmer, E. (2005) Why look at life courses in an interdisciplinary perspective? In *Towards an Interdisciplinary Perspective on the Life Course*, Levy, R., Ghisletta, P., Le Goff, J.-M., Spini, D., and Widmer, E. (eds.): 3–32. Oxford: Elsevier.

Locoh, T., and Mouvagha-Sow, M. (2005) Vers de nouveaux modèles familiaux en Afrique de l'Ouest? Paper presented at the 25th congress of the Union International pour l'Étude Scientifique de la Population, Tours, 20 July.

Marcoux, R. (1994) *Le travail ou l'école: L'activité des enfants et les caractéristiques des ménages en milieu urbain au Mali*. Bamako: Éditions du CERPOD.

Marie, A. (ed.) (1997) *L'Afrique des individus: Itinéraires citadins dans l'Afrique contemporaine*. Paris: Karthala.

Nouhou, A. M., Cissé, S., Fané, A. D., Doumbia, A. G., and Sauvain-Dugerdil, C. (2016) Stratégies familiales et qualité de vie au Mali à travers les données du recensement. *African Population Studies*, 30 (2 Suppl.): http://aps.journals.ac.za/pub/article/view/895.

Nussbaum, M. C. (2000) *Women and Human Development: The Capabilities Approach*. Cambridge: Cambridge University Press.

(2011) *Creating Capabilities: The Human Development Approach*. Cambridge, MA: Belknap Press.

Pilon, M., and Vimard, P. (1998) Structures et dynamiques familiales à l'épreuve de la crise en Afrique subsaharienne. Paper presented at the Chaire Quetelet 'Ménages et familles face à la crise', Louvain-la-Neuve, Belgium, 27 November.

Robeyns, I. (2005) The capability approach: a theoretical survey. *Journal of Human Development*, 6 (1): 93–114.

(2016) Capabilitarianism. *Journal of Human Development and Capabilities*, 17 (3): 397–414.

Sauvain-Dugerdil, C. (2018) Une vie florissante sans enfant? Infécondité et qualité de vie en Suisse, Working Paper 2018/72. Lausanne: Swiss National Centre of Competence in Research LIVES.

Sauvain-Dugerdil, C., Nouhou, A. M., Cissé, S., Diawara, A. k., and Doumbia, A. G. (2018) Configurations familiales et situation des femmes: le cas du Mali à travers les données du recensement. In *Observer, décrire et analyser les structures familiales*, Cauchi-Duval, N. (ed.): 5–24. Paris: AIDELF.

Sauvain-Dugerdil, C., and Thiriat, M. P. (2009) *Développer le genre en démographie: De la naissance à l'âge adulte*. Paris: CEPED.

Sen, A. K. (1999) *Development as Freedom*. Oxford: Oxford University Press.

(2006) *Identity and Violence: The Illusion of Destiny*. New York: W. W. Norton.

(2017) *Collective Choice and Social Welfare*, expanded edn. London: Penguin.

Stern, Y. (2002) What is cognitive reserve? Theory and research application of the reserve concept. *Journal of the International Neuropsychological Society*, 8 (3): 448–60.

Toulmin, C. (1992) *Cattle, Women and Wells: Managing Household Survival in the Sahel*. Oxford: Clarendon Press.

Vos, F. R., and Ballet, J. (2018) Final education, well-being and aspirations: a capability-based analysis on high school pupils in France. In *New Frontiers of the Capability Approach*, Comim, F., Fennell, S., and Anand, P. B. (eds.): 549–70. Cambridge: Cambridge University Press.

Walker, M., and Unterhalter, E. (2007) The capability approach: its potential for work in education. In *Amartya Sen's Capability Approach and Social Justice in Education*, Walker, M., and Unterhalter, E. (eds.): 1–18. New York: Palgrave Macmillan.

Wall, R., Robin, J., and Laslett, P. (eds.) (1983) *Family Forms in Historic Europe*. Cambridge: Cambridge University Press.

Wayack Pambè, M., and Pilon, M. (2011) Sexe du chef de ménage et inégalités scolaires à Ouagadougou (Burkina Faso). *Autrepart*, 59 (3): 125–44.

Widmer, E. (2010) *Family Configurations: A Structural Approach to Family Diversity*. Farnham: Ashgate Publishing.

Widmer, E., and Spini, D. (2017) Misleading norms and vulnerability in the life course: definition and illustration. *Research in Human Development*, 14 (1): 52–67.

17 | An ethical perspective on the United Kingdom's Improving Lives: The Future of Work, Health and Disability

JACQUES TAMIN

Introduction

The UK government has published its ten-year strategy for work, health and disability (Department for Work & Pensions [DWP] and Department of Health [DH], 2017), called *Improving Lives* (IL). Its headline aim is to have '1 million more disabled people in work' by 2027 (DWP and DH, 2017: 3). There are two main drivers for this aim. The first is that '[g]ood work supports our good health' (3). However, although the overall UK employment rate is 75 per cent, that of disabled individuals is only around 50 per cent. In IL, this disability employment inequality is said to have a negative impact on the good health and social opportunities of the disabled. The second driver is that ill health that prevents people from working (which includes the disabled) is estimated to cost the UK economy some £100 billion a year.

IL uses the Equality Act 2010 definition of disability. The Act defines a disabled person as 'someone who has a physical or mental impairment which has a substantial and long-term adverse effect on their ability to carry out normal day-to-day activities. "Long-term" is defined as lasting or expecting to last for at least 12 months.' This is a somewhat limited definition of disability, as it does not adequately take account of the effect of resources or structural (including environmental) factors in alleviating or accentuating (and, indeed, causing!) any functional limitation that arises from the personal factors. I suggest that a more fully developed account of disability can be found in the human development model of disability, health and well-being (Mitra, 2017). I will come back to this later.

In this chapter, I explore some of the ethical issues that IL raises through a capability lens. In particular, I am concerned that the IL

385

headline aim, as it currently stands, can have a negative rather than positive effect on the health of some of the disabled. I therefore propose an amendment to, and justify my iteration of, IL's headline aim, supported by arguments from the health capability literature (Ruger, 2010; Venkatapuram, 2013).

Health and work

There is evidence that 'good' work can be health[1]-enhancing (Waddell and Burton, 2006), so there could be a prima facie case for encouraging those with chronic health conditions and disabilities to work. However, not all disabled individuals would consider themselves as having a health problem. Indeed, some are high-performance athletes, as in the case of Paralympians. Nonetheless, for many other disabled people, their long-term health or physical impairment is not sufficiently compensated for by their environment to allow them full access to all aspects of a life that they might value, including the ability to work. Work can be considered an intrinsically valuable activity in itself (for example, in providing income), but in this chapter I wish to focus on the value of work as a means of achieving health (which is also IL's stated interest). IL does recognize that 'the wrong kind of work can be damaging' (DWP and DH, 2017: 11, para. 11), so, for work to be health-enhancing, it must be 'good work'. Examples of 'good work' are to be found in workplaces that give workers the feeling that they are valued, promote their self-esteem and self-worth and encourage their personal development; examples of 'bad work' will be found in workplaces where workers feel undervalued, devalued or bullied, lack control over their work and feel unfairly treated. In the latter situations, not only would such work not improve health, it could lead to a worsening of many health conditions, especially in relation to mental health and well-being, and could even cause new health problems (such as work-related stress). Psychosocial stress at work is a major cause of ill health in the United Kingdom (Marmot, 2010) and in Europe (WHO, 1998).

'Health' has previously been considered in the capability literature (Ruger, 2010; Venkatapuram, 2013). From that perspective, health

---

[1] In this chapter, I use a conception of health previously elaborated in the capability literature, especially by Ruger (see below).

is 'a person's ability to achieve or exercise a cluster of basic human activities' (Venkatapuram, 2013: 271), and a 'prerequisite for other types of functioning, including one's agency, or the ability to lead a life one has reason to value' (Ruger, 2010: 3). Health improvements then lead to an improvement of an individual's capabilities (such as Nussbaum, 2011: 32–4) and functionings. In this chapter, I mainly use the conception of health articulated by Ruger, which emphasizes the individual's agency. I question whether IL's approach to getting the disabled to work will bring about the desired health improvement, at least with the current formulation of its headline aim. I describe the issues that underlie my concerns about IL's approach in the next two sections, when I consider the disadvantages the disabled can face, and then the role work could play in alleviating these.

Disability and disadvantage

Disability is associated with multidimensional poverty, lower educational attainment, higher morbidity and lower employment rates (Mitra, 2017). Moreover, the 'earning handicap' of individuals with disabilities 'tends to be reinforced and much magnified' by the 'conversion handicap' – 'the difficulty in converting incomes and resources into good living, precisely because of disability' (Sen, 2009: 258–60). In her study of UK disabled households, Kuklys (2005) notes in her conclusion that 'a disabled individual has a consumption opportunity set which is significantly reduced compared to a non-disabled individual. Our point estimates indicate that this reduction is of the order of 40%. It is important to reiterate that this reduction occurs despite the fact that many disabled individuals already receive compensation benefits and other allowances to help them with the additional cost' (99).

Although not all disabled individuals have poor health, low education and low income (I return to this point in the next section), there are many who are severely disadvantaged in terms of health, education and income. Not only are these disadvantages multidimensional, they can also compound each other. For example, health and education can impact on the ability to work, which in turn affects income. If in addition we consider the potential effect of work on health, it is possible that those who suffer chronic ill health and disability are at least doubly disadvantaged by the barriers to improving their health and accessing paid employment. So, we can see how the disadvantaged can find themselves in a vicious circle, which may be extremely difficult to get out of.

Disability, health and work

The human development (HD) model of disability defines disability as 'a deprivation in terms of functioning(s) and/or capability(s) among persons with health deprivations. Disability results from the interaction between resources, personal and structural factors, and health deprivations' (Mitra, 2017: 13). However, as noted above, there are some individuals with disabilities who would not consider themselves as having a health problem, as long as structural factors were adequately addressed. In the informational space of health and work, I suggest the following groupings of disabled individuals.

(1) Group 1 would consist of those disabled individuals who do not regard themselves as having a health problem, or whose health problem is fully controlled. They are fully able to participate in activities they value, such as sports and work.

(2) Group 2 would consist of those with health problems that currently limit their activities, including work. Improving their ability to work could also ameliorate their health.

(3) Group 3 would consist of those with severely limiting health problems, and for whom work would be unlikely to improve their health.

I recognize that this is an oversimplification. Individuals can vary greatly between each other, and over time. Conditions can be complex and multifactorial. Social support can improve or deteriorate over one's life course. For all these reasons, individuals may move from one group to the next at different times of their life. Therefore, this grouping reflects only a snapshot of anyone's situation at a given time, to help with this analysis of interactions between disability, health and work. I illustrate what I mean by the following examples and narratives of individuals I have known in my capacity as an occupational physician.

Group 1: Anji is an insulin-dependent diabetic and her diabetes is well controlled. She works full-time as a personal trainer, and she goes skiing and snowboarding at least once a year.

Dan is a double amputee. He works in IT and plays wheelchair basketball twice a week.

Group 2: Karl suffers from chronic depression and social anxiety. He has not worked for five years. He is now starting to improve with medication and engages well with counselling. He could benefit from working in a supportive environment.

Sonia is visually impaired and lost her job as an administrative assistant two years ago, when her eyesight deteriorated further. She has lost her confidence and rarely leaves home. Her mental and emotional health could improve from working, with the appropriate assistive technology (AT) and in a supportive work environment (and possibly with psychological support).

Pearl has suffered from rheumatoid arthritis for the last 15 years. It can affect most joints at various times, but especially her hands, feet and knees. The disease activity is reasonably well controlled on very potent medication. She can experience extreme fatigue at times. Her joints are stiffer in the mornings, lasting between one and four hours. She lost her job as a typist five years ago when her function was less good and she had more frequent flare-ups, necessitating considerable time off work. Her employer had applied their sickness absence policy and procedures quite rigidly (although probably still within the scope of the Equality Act), and she had been dismissed for poor attendance. Her mental and emotional health would probably improve if she were at work, with the provision of appropriate AT and some adjustments and flexibility in her working hours. However, this would also depend on whether she was working in a supportive work environment (see later, when I return to Pearl's case to discuss the medical assessment).

Group 3: Tom suffers from severe chronic obstructive pulmonary disease (COPD) and heart failure. His conditions have deteriorated in the last year despite intensive treatment. He has frequent 'blackouts' and needs constant supervision. He is very short of breath, and this is exacerbated by the slightest effort, including talking for less than a minute. In his case, unfortunately, his health is unlikely to improve by his trying to work.

Kim had a severe stroke six years ago. This has left her with severe weakness of her right arm and leg, poor memory and concentration, difficulty in speaking and some visual impairment. She completed her rehabilitation programme four years ago. She still experiences severe dizziness at various times, especially if she is in a car. She has had frequent falls and needs constant care. It is also likely that Kim's health will not improve with work.

I recognize that using narratives in this way does not reflect the whole range of possibilities, but my intention here is to clarify, by means of examples, how the health of some disabled individuals might improve with work, whereas others might not. I argue later that it is the medical assessment that needs to be sensitive to the individual's personal and structural factors (from the HD model), as well as the individual's agency. In general, I would expect those in group 1 not to concern us here, as they would already be in work, and not relevant to IL's aim. However, there could be some whose health or social circumstances deteriorate so much that they move to groups 2 or 3 at some point in the future. For those in group 3, I would expect most to be found unfit for work when they are medically assessed for this purpose.[2] There again, there may be a few exceptions, in that some individuals in group 3 might benefit from being in work, but the work environments would need to be exceptionally supportive, and the work organization would have to be tailored to their needs, with appropriate provisions such as being able to attend their hospital appointments and working shorter hours flexibly.

Most of those disabled individuals who would be of concern to IL, and therefore to this analysis, are in group 2. The use of assistive technology, such as IT hardware and software, and other adjustments, such as help with transportation, could make work more accessible for those in this group, which is what IL aims to achieve. IL promotes the use of AT, which could be good news for those disabled individuals who would be able to work with such help (that is, potentially those in group 2, although I argue below that just because AT might technically help an individual does not mean it would necessarily improve their health). However, what about those who do not achieve 'the Holy Grail' of being able to work, even with AT? Would they be seen as failures? Freeloaders? Could there be additional pressures on them if the government targets were not achieved?

However, just providing AT will not necessarily improve the health of all those even in group 2. To explain this further, let us consider two related issues: the medical assessment and responsibilization. I will use the cases of Pearl and Karl, described above, to illustrate my concerns.

---

[2] In progressing the IL agenda, policy makers met with disability groups to develop the criteria and guidance for ending the assessments for those with the most severe conditions (DPW and DH, 2017: 47, para. 185). I believe this should be applauded.

For the first example, let us look at Pearl's situation. She does want to work. However, her joints can still flare up from time to time, and she can experience very debilitating fatigue for a day or two at a time. She would have to wake up at 4:00 a.m. to take her first medication, to be able to start moving at 6:00 a.m. to slowly get herself ready for work. The medical assessment of disability would take account of her personal factors, but it would not usually take account of all the relevant societal and environmental factors, including the actual level of support and inclusiveness that Pearl would experience at work. The assessment usually gives a binary outcome in terms of ability to work – that is, either fit or unfit to work – whereas the reality of most situations is much more nuanced. The AT requirements (including IT adaptations) that may help her mobility, manual dexterity and grip strength might be reasonably straightforward. But how does one ensure that her employer will be supportive and understanding (see later for actual disabled employees' experiences at work)? Therefore, the medical assessment might conclude that she is fit for work, with specified AT and support, but whether Pearl could successfully remain at work in practice will depend more on her employer's attitude. So, if Pearl failed in her attempt to work, should she be blamed?

For our second example, let us consider Karl's situation. He is less depressed now and feels ready to work. Previously he could not leave the house without feeling anxious, could not think clearly and felt tired all the time. He was offered medication and counselling by his primary care team, who also advised him to exercise more, eat healthily and reduce his alcohol intake. To his dismay, he could not afford the healthier foods, or a gym membership or the bus fares to attend the group counselling sessions. Karl did eventually manage to turn his life around with the help of family and friends. Lifestyle factors can contribute to some health conditions (such as obesity, cardiac disease and mental health) that affect the ability to work. However, addressing these lifestyle factors can be harder for disadvantaged individuals, such as Karl. In the context of work and health, it has been said that 'individuals have a fundamental personal responsibility to maintain their own health' (Black, 2008: 99). Here, responsibilization (which is a familiar concept in public health ethics) appears to go beyond expecting individuals to pursue healthy lifestyles, to expecting the individual to improve his or her health sufficiently to be able to work. However, I would suggest that there is not equal opportunity for all individuals to improve and maintain their health through their lifestyle choices, especially when we consider the multidimensional disadvantages faced by those who are both disabled and poor. Instead, we should aim to have social arrangements that give better opportunity to the disadvantaged, including the disabled, to make these healthier choices (rather than blaming them for not pursuing healthier lifestyles). In turn, this could improve their ability to work, should this be their wish. If they manage to access good work, then their health could improve further.

Therefore, although the medical assessment is a crucial step in the IL process, it is necessarily limited because other factors (such as the structural ones in the HD model) should also be taken into account to reflect the reality of that disabled person's circumstances. I also argue later that the assessment needs to be individualized, so as, for example, to take account of the individual's agency. Furthermore, one should resist 'victim blaming' (in the form of responsibilization) when individuals do not succeed in improving their health because of the additional (and sometimes unsurmountable) barriers they may face in trying to achieve this (as in Karl's case).

Nonetheless, proponents of IL may argue that, once a disabled person is in work, then that person's health will improve. Unfortunately, empirical research into what disabled employees can experience in the workplace makes for uncomfortable reading (Fevre et al., 2016). For example, a nurse of 24 years' service who became a wheelchair user reports: My manager thought it was a huge joke to put his metal briefcase under the fax machine so I couldn't get my feet under. I couldn't see the buttons on it because it was at my eye level and I couldn't actually manage to do any faxing until I'd moved his briefcase out of the way' (Fevre et al., 2016: 35). Disabled employees are more likely to be in part-time jobs, to be paid less and to have fewer opportunities for training and development (Fevre, 2017). They are more likely to have their employment rights infringed, despite legislation intended to prevent this. They also experience difficulties during employment that 'are not caused by their impairments or long-term health problems but can be traced to the behaviour of employers, managers and other employees' (Fevre, 2017: 593).

Therefore, although good work should potentially improve the health of disabled workers, the negative experiences described above could have the opposite effect, and cause deterioration of their health. Accordingly it seems that the disabled can have greater difficulties both in accessing good work and in having the opportunities to improve their health through their lifestyle choices.

How IL could further improve the health of the disabled

I suggest that, if the UK government's headline aim were modified thus: 'to give 1 million more disabled people the opportunity to work by 2027', it would achieve better health for more disabled individuals. The main difference between the existing strategic aim (the 'IL aim') and my modified one ('modified aim') is the choice that the disabled individual can make as to whether to work or not – that is, recognizing his or her agency. In other words, the opportunity freedom provided by the IL aim would become a process freedom if the modified aim replaced it. 'Process freedoms are related to persons' ability to exert agency in ways that further their conception of the good' (Alkire et al., 2019: 3). It could also be said that the IL aim provides the disabled with a negative freedom (by providing the absence of a restraint on their ability to work), whereas the modified aim provides them with a positive freedom (by concentrating on what the individual chooses to do or achieve) (Sen, 1988). I believe that this modification would lead to the following:

(1) disabled individuals would be less likely to be pressurized into work when they do not feel able to work; and (2) the assessment process for work disability would be more likely to be fair and supportive.

Although it can be argued that IL itself does not intend to either pressurize individuals, as in (1), or cause unfair assessments, as (2) would imply, I believe that the target as it is currently expressed ('1 million more disabled people in work by 2027') could influence the implementation[3] of this policy. I suggest that this target may lead to situations in which some disabled individuals feel they have been wrongly assessed or have felt pressurized into work they feel is not suited to them. Both the IL aim and the modified aim have health as their end: work is a means to achieve health. However, my claim is that the modified aim will achieve greater overall health for disabled individuals. I now

---

[3] Although this is a UK policy document, much of the implementation will be devolved regionally. For example, Scotland, Wales and Northern Ireland could implement parts of this policy differently from each other, and from England.

demonstrate this by comparing the effect of work on the health of disabled individuals, when either the IL aim or the modified aim is used as the policy strategic aim. Let us consider their health in relation to or as a result of work, in the following examples of individuals deemed to be 'fit for work' following their medical assessment.

(1) Alison, a disabled individual, has been given the necessary support to be in good work. She now has a sense of purpose, and her self-esteem and overall health have improved. There is a positive health outcome for disabled individuals in such a scenario, whether the IL aim or the modified aim is used as the strategic goal. (2) Beth, a disabled individual, feels that she has been coerced into bad work. Her health deteriorates as a result of being in work. This is a possible negative outcome of the IL aim, but would not occur with the modified aim. (3) Lisa, a disabled individual, is assessed as being fit for work with suitable support and AT. She chooses not to work and, instead, uses the improved functioning that this support and AT give her to write and perform songs about her experience of disability. This improves her social life, and her mental health and well-being are greatly enhanced. This is a possible outcome with the modified aim, but not with the IL aim.

In example 1, although Alison could achieve improved health whether the IL or the modified aim is used, there are possible resource implications. In other words, we could envisage that, given the choice, fewer disabled individuals might opt to work. UK policy makers could then argue that the government funding would produce a lower return on investment if the modified aim were used. I accept that this could be true. However, in this chapter I am making the case for the modified aim based on health arguments. I have made the case on economic grounds elsewhere (Tamin, 2018). I think it suffices to say here that I believe the difference in funding requirements is not as great as might initially be thought. Furthermore, if all work offered to the disabled were good work, then the likelihood of their opting to work would be much greater. This is the ideal solution in the longer term, but the culture change required to make all workplaces inclusive, supportive and fair is a challenging one. In the meantime, it would be safer to allow the disabled a choice of whether to work or not, if we are concerned about their health.

Example 2 illustrates the possible negative impact of the IL aim on the health of disabled individuals. Given the existing empirical evidence as previously described, this type of situation in the workplace is, unfortunately, not rare (Fevre et al., 2016). However, IL aim supporters could argue that, even with the existing IL approach, there is no coercion to work involved at the assessment stage. I would refute this by pointing out that, once targets are specified, there will be inevitable pressures (real or perceived) for these targets to be operationalized, whether explicitly or implicitly.[4] Medical assessments are not an exact science, and do not take all social and environmental factors into account. There is room for subjective opinions as to the level of function that could be achieved given a certain level of support. I believe that the assessors could be influenced, consciously or subconsciously, if they knew that they had to achieve certain targets (that is, numbers of disabled in work), dictated by an IL aim approach. My concerns in this example also go beyond the initial assessment. Once the disabled individual is in a job that is unsuitable (for example, because of bullying – that is, bad work), if he or she continues in that job his or her health could inexorably deteriorate. If Beth decides to leave this job, she may become further stigmatized as a freeloader, not 'willing to pay own her way'. She would be in a no-win situation, with either course of action having negative consequences for her health. This would not arise if a modified aim approach were taken at a strategic level: there would not be such targets, and therefore not the same pressure to 'get more disabled individuals into work'. Instead, the medical assessment would focus on optimizing the possible support and AT for that individual and the job, and allowing him or her to make the final choice, without fear of stigmatization if he or she decided not to work. An alternative proposal to reduce the negative impact of bad work could be that the assessment include reviews to reassess those who were at work, to ensure that the AT had in fact been provided (at the right time), whether any additional adjustments might be required and – even more importantly – whether the work environment was, and continued to be, supportive and inclusive. I agree that this would reduce the risk of health deterioration from bad work, but it would not reduce the possibility of coercion from the assessment process itself.

---

[4] There is already a negative perception of the UK DWP's Work Capability Assessment; see, for example, Litchfield (2014). Policies that have the effect of setting targets that could be perceived as requiring more disabled persons to be fit for work will probably augment distrust in the impartiality of the assessments.

Example 3 illustrates the fact that the modified aim strategy can do more than just prevent the negative health consequences of the IL aim. The modified aim approach allows Lisa's agency to be recognized, and her ability to make her choices allows her to flourish. Ruger (2010: 62) states that 'human flourishing provides the justification for taking health capabilities as the objective of health policy'. IL would currently only count Lisa being in work as success, and her choosing not to work as being failure. However, if IL is a policy that has health as its primary focus, then it should take account of the agency, and value the flourishing, of disabled individuals. This would require a modified aim approach, rather than the current IL aim stance, as Lisa's example demonstrates.

In summary, those individuals as in example 1 would have health improvements whether the IL's stated aim remains the same or is modified. However, those in the example 2 situation could experience negative health outcomes with the IL aim, but not with the modified aim. And the modified aim would also allow greater health improvements for those individuals as in example 3, as it would recognize their agency and value their flourishing, which are aspects of health that the IL aim currently appears to ignore. The net effect is, therefore, greater positive health improvement if the modified aim were adopted.

However, proponents of the IL aim could raise three types of objections to my arguments in support of a modified-aim-based IL strategy. The first objection is that the illustrations I have used do not adequately represent all disabled individuals. The second is that I have described only positive outcomes in these scenarios, and not considered negative consequences, especially of the modified aim. The third type of objection is that I have not addressed the possible resource implications of the modified aim and the trade-offs there may need to be in choosing health over, say, human capital formation or other ends. I now therefore discuss these objections in turn.

With regard to the first objection, it is true that a few examples cannot reflect all the possible disabled individuals' situations. However, this was not the objective of presenting these examples. This group consists of those who are found to be 'fit for work' – that is, the group of relevance to the IL strategy. The aim of the examples was to distinguish between the IL aim and the modified aim approaches. Although I accept that more examples would have illustrated more nuanced differences in outcomes, I believe that the three outcomes I have described are sufficient in the context of explaining the consequential differences between the IL aim and modified aim approaches. This leads us to the second objection. In fact, Alison represents a positive outcome for IL, regardless of whether the IL or the modified aim were used. On the other hand, Beth's health deteriorates as a result of work, so this is a negative outcome. I maintain that this is a possible consequence of the IL aim, but not the modified aim, as Beth would have the choice not to work in a job that was deleterious to her health with the modified aim. Thus, Alison and Beth represent maybe the most obvious outcomes of being found 'fit for work'. However, I also suggest a third outcome, represented by Lisa, whereby she is found fit for work, but chooses to make use of available AT to live a life that she values. This is, arguably, more contentious. I have described only the case in which Lisa flourishes from her choice and her health greatly improves. However, there are at least another two possible outcomes: Lisa could either have refused the work on offer (this is possible with the modified aim) and not pursued any activity that she particularly valued; or she could have attempted her singing/songwriting, but 'failed' in this endeavour. It could be debated whether such a 'failure' should count as human flourishing, but space does not allow a full discussion on this subject here. I would argue that, as she has had the positive freedom to decide in this matter, her experience is nonetheless health-enhancing. As to the possibility of her deciding not to pursue any valuable (to herself) activity, at least her health would not be damaged by 'bad work' that she wanted to avoid (such as Beth's situation). Insofar as Lisa's example represents the different choices of a large heterogeneous group of people, there may be further subtle differences in choices and outcome not adequately reflected here. However, I have used Beth and Lisa to illustrate how the modified aim, by recognizing their agency, would offer the possibility of more disabled individuals in similar situations to have better health. This brings us to the third type of objections: can we afford a modified aim approach? Should health be prioritized over other ends? In terms of financing the IL strategy, I would argue that the UK government has already committed to the funding requirements of the necessary AT and support to help the disabled get into work, and using a modified aim approach would not cost more than the IL aim one. However, if a return-on-investment view were taken, then it could be argued that fewer of the disabled individuals would contribute to the economy if they decided to opt not to work. But the main objective of IL is supposed to be to improve the health of disabled individuals, and I have posited that this can be better achieved through the modified aim. As to whether we ought to prioritize health over other ends, to paraphrase Ruger, health is a precondition to achieving many other capabilities. For instance, if one is healthy, one can benefit more effectively from education and training, and other means of human capital formation.

Conclusions

Disabled individuals who remain unable to work in spite of the offer of AT and other support may find themselves further stigmatized (as 'freeloaders'), even though their inability to work may be due to their greater difficulty in achieving sufficient health (as a more socially deprived group), or the medical assessment process, or both. In other words, the barriers are multidimensional, and these should be reflected in the implementation of the IL strategy. Moreover, I have argued that valuing the agency of disabled individuals – that is, respecting their choices in relation to working or not (and not blaming them if they choose not to work): positive freedom – would in fact increase the health of this disadvantaged group when compared to what would be achieved with the current IL strategy, which offers only negative freedom.

I have suggested that IL's use of a legal definition of disability may also be limiting, by focusing only on impairments, and not on the environmental and structural factors that are also key to what, and how much, disability is experienced. In contrast, see the approach taken in Mitra's human development model (of disability, health and wellbeing): 'The end of research or policy initiatives guided by this model is thus to enhance human development, i.e., to expand the functionings/capabilities of individuals with health deprivations or to expand functionings/capabilities by preventing health deprivations. It affirms flourishing as the end of human development. Resources or structural factors (e.g., health care services, assistive devices) and other means may be used to achieve this end but are not ends per se' (Mitra, 2017: 14–15). It is possible that a richer and more comprehensive understanding of disability, such as Mitra's, would have widened IL's scope, and, rather than concentrate too much on what can be done for the disabled (such as AT), it would also have reflected on the important roles that their agency and flourishing play in achieving health.

However, there is much in IL that is very positive. For example, there is a commitment to 'personalised employment support' and 'improving assessments' (DWP and DH, 2017: 16, para. 40). It also states: 'Our work goes beyond providing a safety net: it is about offering the choices and support to help individuals realise their potential and ambitions, in a tailored and accessible way' (16, para. 41). This seems to imply that IL might recognize individual agency and offer process freedom to the disabled (though I have argued that it does not). I maintain that IL, with its headline aim as currently phrased, will only partially achieve its laudable intentions. Greater health improvements would result by changing its headline strategic aim to '1 million more disabled people' having the opportunity to work, rather than being in work, as IL's end goal.

Acknowledgements

I would like to thank the staff and students of the Hoover Chair in Economic and Social Ethics, Université Catholique de Louvain, for their most helpful advice on the original idea for this chapter (which I developed during my time with them at Louvain-la-Neuve as an Honorary Fellow), especially when I presented it to them in April 2018; the attendees of my poster presentation at the Cambridge Capability Conference 2018 for their encouraging feedback; and the referees for their insightful comments on the previous draft of this chapter.

References

Alkire, S., Chiappero-Martinetti, E., Deneulin, S., Ryan, R., and Silva, S. (2019) Measuring the freedom aspects of capabilities. www.researchgate .net/publication/228355513_Measuring_the_Freedom_Aspects_of_ Capabilities%27.
Black, C. (2008) *Working for a Healthier Tomorrow: Dame Carol Black's Review of the Health of Britain's Working Age Population*. London: TSO.
DWP and DH (2017) *Improving Lives: The Future of Work, Health and Disability*, Cm 9526. London: HMSO.
Fevre, R. (2017) Why work is so problematic for people with disabilities and long-term health problems. *Occupational Medicine*, 67 (8): 593–5.
Fevre, R., Foster, D., Jones, M., and Wass, V. (2016) Closing disability gaps at work: deficits in evidence and variations in experience. Cardiff: Cardiff University.

Kuklys, W. (2005) *Amartya Sen's Capability Approach: Theoretical insights and Empirical Applications*. Dordrecht: Springer.

Litchfield, P. (2014) *An Independent Review of the Work Capability Assessment: Year Five*. London: HMSO.

Marmot, M. (2010) *Fair Society, Healthy Lives: The Marmot Review*. London: Institute of Health Equity, University College London.

Mitra, S. (2017) *Disability, Health and Human Development*. New York: Palgrave Macmillan.

Nussbaum, M. C. (2011) *Creating Capabilities: The Human Development Approach*. Cambridge, MA: Belknap Press.

Ruger, J. P. (2010) *Health and Social Justice*. Oxford: Oxford University Press.

Sen, A. K. (1988) Freedom of choice: concept and content. *European Economic Review*, 32 (2/3): 269–94.

(2009) *The Idea of Justice*. London: Penguin.

Tamin, J. (2018) Should we give preference to Rogini? An ethical perspective on disability, health inequalities and work. Paper presented at the Human Development & Capability Association conference 'Human development and social inclusion in an urbanizing world', Buenos Aires, 1 September.

UK government (2010) Equality Act.

Venkatapuram, S. (2013) Health, vital goals and capabilities. *Bioethics*, 27 (5): 271–9.

Waddell, G., and Burton, A. K. (2006) *Is Work Good for Your Health and Well-Being?* London: TSO.

WHO (1998) *The Solid Facts: Social Determinants of Health*. Copenhagen: WHO Regional Office for Europe.

18 | Public services as conversion factors
Exploring the theory and practice

RICHARD BRUNNER AND NICK WATSON

Introduction

There is now a substantial body of research examining the utility of the capabilities approach (CA) and the opportunities it affords for framing how we understand human well-being, development and social justice. CA is an exceptional philosophy, in that it has actually been applied and has led to policy development and implementation at local, national and supranational levels. It is also exceptional in that it is an idea first applied in the Global South that is now starting to influence policy in the Global North, reversing traditional assumptions about the migration of ideas. In this chapter we focus on its application in the Global North and its potential to achieve a more effective model for conceptualizing, driving and evaluating public services and how they are designed and delivered.

One of the underexplored aspects of the CA is the role of conversion factors (CFs) and how they operate in the real world, to either enable or hinder the acquisition of capabilities. Here, we use empirical evidence drawn from two independent research projects to explore this gap. These projects aimed to evaluate the effectiveness of two relatively small public service interventions that sought to improve outcomes for people in areas of high social deprivation in Glasgow, Scotland. In our analysis, we draw on the CA and conceptualize these two projects – one an anti-gang initiative, the other a family meal and homework club – as conversion factors to explore the potential of CFs for conceptualizing and evaluating public services in Global North contexts. We argue that CFs offer a means of delineating and clarifying the impact of public service initiatives at the personal, social and structural levels. The delineation of structural CFs provides necessary clarity on the extent to which initiatives reach the underpinning social structure that, ultimately, shapes the health and well-being of local communities and individuals.

The chapter opens with a brief description of the role of public services before moving on to frame CA, followed by a justification of its use as a framework for analysing public service reform and delivery.

The changing role of public services

Public services are those services provided by governments. They may be delivered by agencies directly funded by the government or by those at arm's length. Examples include police, fire, education, social care, housing and health services. Public services play a key role in maintaining and improving quality of life, tackling social injustice and promoting well-being. In its review of public services conducted for the Scottish government, the Christie Commission argues that the chief purpose of such services is 'to combat the negative outcomes for individuals and communities arising from deep-rooted inequalities' (Christie Commission, 2011: 6). Although this challenge is not new – indeed, it could be argued that it has always been at the heart of public service delivery – there is now overriding evidence to suggest that, in many areas, public services have failed to deliver on these key challenges (Christie Commission, 2011). As a consequence, reform of public services is now high on the agenda of many countries. The drivers for reform are varied, as countries seek to change the way they deliver services to meet a range of different challenges. These include demographic changes (Appleby, 2013), emerging economic and fiscal challenges (Independent Budget Review Panel, 2010: 2.23), promoting and producing services that recognize the need for cross-boundary cooperation (Zeemering, 2008), maximizing transparency in decisions (Fung, 2013) and enabling citizen participation, accountability and empowerment (Meijer, 2011; Nalbandian, 2008; World Bank, 2003). Allied to these is the imperative for public services to tackle endemic long-term 'wicked problems' (Rittell and Webber, 1973), including persistent inequalities in terms of income, employment, health, learning and public safety (Lupton et al., 2013; Marmot, 2010; Christie Commission, 2011).

Although there are a diversity of frameworks for reform, the role of communities and calls for increased community participation are central (Sørensen and Torfing, 2016). There is a shift towards a collaborative governance model that rejects the traditional top-down model of service delivery in which decisions to design, deliver and evaluate services are made by professionals, managers and those who fund the services (Huxham et al., 2000; Newman et al., 2004; Le Grand, 2007). The aim is to develop services for which individuals, communities and service users are involved in their design and delivery, with citizens regarded as asset holders (Christie Commission, 2011: ch. 4). Instead of services that are provided *to* individuals they are 'designed *for* and *with* them' (Christie Commission, 2011: 21, emphasis in original). This reform agenda also maintains an emphasis on public services to focus towards those in greatest need, and increasingly on prevention. Governments 'must prioritise expenditure on public services which prevent negative outcomes from arising' (Christie Commission, 2011: vi).

This shift from government to governance (Newman, 2001) is also accompanied by an expectation of increased collaboration between public services. The model assumes that the twin processes of greater public involvement in the design and delivery of public services and stronger partnership working across public services will result in better outcomes.

Although this is laudable, these aims can appear 'naive' when faced with the vast array of social determinants experienced by those living in areas of multiple deprivation (Ennis and West, 2013). For Marmot (2010), policies seeking to tackle these issues through locally based initiatives are not sufficient to address the underlying causes. Marmot and Wilkinson (1999: 354) conclude that 'population health is sensitive to particular dimensions of the wider social structure and environment', and that the 'causes of the causes' of social gradients in health are what need to be addressed in order to sufficiently address inequalities of morbidity and mortality. In similar vein, the importance of partnership working to public service reform, and in particular its reliance on co-production and asset-based approaches, has been criticized for the danger that it fails to address the macro-level structures that impact on individuals and communities (Ennis and West, 2013; Friedli, 2012, 2013).

Having examined the concepts and ideas that underpin the reform of public services, this chapter now moves on to explore the potential CA offers in evaluating and exploring the workings of public services and their reform.

The capabilities approach and public services

The capabilities approach has been operationalized to engage 'abstract concepts of human well-being and development with the values and experiences of the poor' (Clark, 2005: 8). It is an analytical framework or partial theory of social justice that considers the state in which a person or group is actually living (functioning) and their practical opportunity (capability) to make alternative choices (Sen, 1992: 87; 2009: 296–8; Nussbaum, 2006: 75–6). There is no single CA; indeed, the two key proponents of the approach differ in the way they conceptualize it (Robeyns, 2017). However, these differences are not pertinent to the points we wish to make in this chapter. The CA provides a metric of quality of life and well-being, with an integrated notion of equity, coupled with a focus on agency. The CA is interested in evaluating the actual outcomes experienced by people, contrasting with other approaches that emphasize what people possess or do not possess, what they have done or how they feel. Moreover, unlike other dominant approaches to evaluating justice, the capabilities approach assumes that the social world is made up of heterogeneous people, with different interests, efficiencies and levels of power (Sen, 1999). The normative dimension of the CA is on the role of states, systems and societies in promoting the well-being and flourishing of communities and individuals, with a focus on those in greatest need. Participation, deliberation and public involvement are central (Nussbaum, 2006; Sen, 1999). Sen argues that '"choosing" itself can be seen as a valuable functioning' (1999: 76), implying that groups and individuals must be actively involved in judging which substantive and valued capabilities are most important to them.

Perhaps most importantly in the context of this chapter, the CA is politically practical (Sayer, 2011). It has been applied to a range of different public service activities, including education, equality, employment initiatives, economic development, child development and policy development (Deneulin, Nebel and Sagovsky, 2006; Kuklys, 2005; Robeyns, 2003).

This range of values, purposes and practicalities suggests compatibility with the plurality of principles and drivers that frame the public service reform agenda, its design and delivery. For example, for Orton (2011: 358, emphasis added), CA has the ability to offer 'an alternative conceptualization of the *very purpose of public policy* … [It] is best thought of not as offering a detailed road map for policy, but as providing fundamental principles that guide policy development.' The foundational work of Drèze and Sen (2002: 6) also highlights this role for CA:

The options that a person has depend greatly on relations with others and on what the state and other institutions do. We shall be particularly concerned with those opportunities that are strongly influenced by social circumstances and public policy, especially those relating to education, health, nutrition, social equity, civil liberties, and other basic aspects of the quality of life.

Robeyns (2005: 109–10) extends this to argue that, in order for the CA to fully engage in the analysis of institutions while incorporating social norms, social determinants and social structures, interdisciplinary work is required. Holmwood (2013: 1179) makes the point that the CA has been too focused on the economic and the philosophical and has failed to adequately engage with the sociological, resulting in analytical weaknesses, in particular its failure to adequately examine structural explanations for individual vulnerabilities. The CA takes a naive approach to the role of government and policy making in addressing social problems, sidelining structural questions of political and economic power (Sayer, 2012).

These points are reinforced by Venkatapuram (2011) in his work on the determinants of health. Venkatapuram shows how the CA has thus far taken an overly narrow, individualized and service-focused approach to the analysis of the economic, cultural and social conditions into which people are born. Similarly, Wolff and de-Shalit (2007), in an empirical-ethical exploration of the role of public services in the lives of vulnerable groups in global north contexts, find the CA wanting in terms of analysis of the social structures, social determinants and dominant cultural norms, as it is these that shape 'the rules of the game' (2007: 173), so dominating life chances, social hierarchies and the characteristics of good living. The CA addresses the impact of poverty and inequality, but has rarely examined or challenged the root causes of poverty and inequality, especially in the Global North. These structural conditions are significant and pervasive in their influence on social outcomes. The result is that the CA has an inadequate analysis of what it is that causes the social injustices at the heart of its concerns.

So, just as the public service reform agenda has been critiqued for contending that improved service delivery can improve social outcomes for those most impacted by structural determinants, the CA may also exaggerate the ability of public policy to achieve this.

Sen's argument has been that the structural drivers of inequality can be addressed through what he calls 'contingent circumstances' or 'circumstantial variations' (1999: chs. 3 & 4). These have become known as conversion factors, and it is to an exploration of these that we now turn.

Conversion factors and public services

Conversion factors (CFs) are a heuristic conceptualization of the mechanisms through which the present and future capabilities and functionings of individuals and groups are either constrained or enhanced. They are the mechanisms through which resources are converted into 'characteristics of good living and into the kind of freedom valued in human life' (Sen, 2009: 254), and they 'matter most for social justice' (Nussbaum, 2006: 75). CFs are both individual and contextualized, suggesting that they are a potential mechanism for bringing structure and agency together in a real-world analysis of opportunities and outcomes.

However, this is an area of the CA that has been, to date, conceptually and empirically underdeveloped. In the CA literature, conversion factors are typically assumed to operate at three levels (see, for example, Kuklys, 2005, and Robeyns, 2017). First, personal CFs are those micro-level features held within the individual (e.g. sex, age, physical condition, bodily prowess, intellectual abilities). Second, environmental CFs include elements such as climate, physical location and physical infrastructure. Third, social CFs are an unpacked repository for meso- and macro-level features, from everyday social practices to public services and policies through to societal hierarchies, social structures, social determinants and dominant cultural norms. Discussion focuses on how these three dimensions collectively expand or narrow the opportunities for individuals and social groups to convert resources into functionings and capabilities. However, in terms of social CFs in particular, the literature fails to allow an analytical distinction to be made between its sub-concepts, which encompass everything from the very local to the overarching structural 'causes of the causes' that set 'the rules of the game'. The local-social will have a very different impact on capability achievement and be far simpler to influence through policy and practice than will the deeper and wider social and cultural structures. For example, in the Global North, enabling children living in an area of multiple deprivation to access schools through adapting policy and practice is a far more straightforward social 'conversion' than transforming the social class structure shaping the educational and life opportunities that are ultimately available to those disadvantaged children. One approach to framing this distinction is to distinguish social CFs from structural CFs.

Chiappero, Salardi and Scervini (2018) identify three key ways CFs have been used to unpack the link between resources and capabilities. One strand has employed proxy indicators for capabilities, and, through applying factor analysis or similar econometric models, has explored the relationship between CFs and capabilities. In a second strand, focus is placed on socio-demographic variations and their role in accounting for heterogeneities in the conversion process. A third approach has looked at the actual conversion process itself as it has attempted to examine how individuals with different characteristics are able to convert resources into functionings. This body of work has provided a useful exploration of the factors that influence the ability of individuals or groups to convert resources to functionings, understood either through primary or, more usually, secondary data. However, it has failed to examine how conversion factors empirically operate. It has focused on the outcomes rather than the processes, and the complex relationship between the personal, social and structural is under-examined. Structural dimensions can best be incorporated through a sociological approach (Holmwood, 2013; Hvinden and Halvorsen, 2017), and we argue that the CA can empirically and analytically better engage with this sociological concern by analytically distinguishing social CFs from structural CFs.

Public services are an archetypal example of a social CF and therefore afford a prime opportunity to explore the theory and practice of conversion factors. Public services should help to support individuals, groups and communities to enhance their functionings and capabilities; and they should help to offset disadvantaging structural CFs – the broader social, cultural and economic structures that shape human well-being. If public services are to operate effectively, there is a need to explore the work that they do at personal, social and structural levels to assist in the conversion of resources to functionings and capabilities. In turn, this can allow an explanation of why social change may or may not happen in particular circumstances (Hvinden and Halvorsen, 2017: 15).

Undertaking a capabilities analysis in this way will allow us to understand how public services actually operate. Framing public services as an example of a social CF affords an opportunity to specifically understand whether CA can offer an effective means of analysing the way that public services operate. Fully grounded exploration and unpacking of how public services as a social CF empirically act at personal, social and structural levels will help the CA in meeting the challenges of specification of CFs, and the work that they allow the CA to do. To enable clarity of focus on the personal, social and structural layers of conversion, for the purposes of this analysis environmental CFs are left aside.

In the next section, we draw on data from two case studies of contemporary public service activities in Glasgow, Scotland. We unpack the way the services work as social CF, the levels at which they operate, the outcomes they achieve, the compatibility of these projects with CA principles and the logic of distinguishing personal, social and structural CFs to conceptualize their impacts. The discussion and conclusion set out what this tells us about the potential for the CA, and in particular for CFs, in framing and evaluating the work of public services. We also discuss wider implications for the practice and theory of the CA.

Empirical examples of public service reform analysed using conversion factors

The data we present in this section were developed as part of 'What Works Scotland', a research programme aimed at developing a better understanding of public service reform in Scotland. The two examples, both located in Glasgow, are Operation Modulus (OM), a youth crime prevention programme, and the Family Meal and Homework Club (FMHC). Both interventions are located in areas of high social deprivation, but focus on different population groups. Each intervention was implemented to meet a normatively defined need, and in both cases the services were designed with the communities. In developing this analysis, we have drawn strongly on three research reports: an evaluation of the FMHC (McLaren, 2016) and two evaluations of OM (Brunner and Watson, 2016; Cullingworth, Brunner and Watson, 2018).

Operation Modulus

Operation Modulus is an innovative, co-produced programme tackling violence and anti-social behaviour by young people in areas of multiple deprivation in Glasgow. Originally developed in the Gorbals locality, it has been adapted in other areas in the city (Cullingworth, Brunner and Watson, 2018). Led using a facilitative leadership model, it brings together multiple public services and third-sector organizations to collaborate and work in partnership, including housing, local authority, fire services, employment support services and community safety. OM targets specific young individuals who are persistently involved in criminal and anti-social behaviours, including gang crime. The young people are treated as asset holders, and their voluntary involvement in co-producing the programme is key.

At the outset of the Gorbals programme the young people were individually asked about their interests, what they wanted to do and what would make them desist from crime and anti-social behaviour. They were then asked to co-produce a tailored group programme based on their personal interests and assets. The aim was to help them each reach their desired goal, which for almost all the young people was gaining employment. They voluntarily committed to take part in the four- to six-week full-time co-produced programme. The programme drew on expertise from across the range of public services, including community safety, fire services, employment support services, housing associations and training bodies, which jointly co-delivered the programme. The results have been better outcomes for the young people, including gaining trades qualifications and employment. The community have also benefited, and there was an 80 per cent reduction in crime in Gorbals. There have also been better outcomes for society more widely, including cost savings for public services (Brunner and Watson, 2016).

Capability development in OM is about augmenting agency, or 'empowerment' (Hill, 2003: 117), and treating the young people as asset holders. This contrasts with more traditional approaches in the criminal justice system, in which the potential for decision making and participation is constrained, and young people are framed in terms of deficits (Brownlee, 1998). Traditional criminal justice approaches, from a CA perspective, act as a barrier to expanding functionings and capabilities.

OM operates as a public service collaboration, with the focus on supporting the attainment of outcomes defined by the young people rather than on narrow service-defined goals. Using a capabilities framework, it is possible to explore and unpack what it is about OM as a social CF that has made it a success. It aims to change the functionings and capabilities of the young people, supporting them to move away from crime and anti-social behaviour and towards a self-selected alternative. It treats the young people as heterogeneous agents who may each want to do and be different things, and focuses on their assets through offering a series of individualized, co-produced training and development activities. OM assumes that outcomes are emergent, processes are ongoing and outputs are relational, in an open system in which no trajectory is guaranteed. The evidence suggests that this is succeeding (Brunner and Watson, 2016; Cullingworth, Brunner and Watson, 2018).

In the next section we unpack OM as a social CF to examine how the programme impacted on personal, social and structural CFs shaping outcomes for the young people, followed by some reflections on impacts on the public services themselves.

Impact on participants

Personal CFs: through the use of co-production and by drawing on the young peoples' individual resources and assets, OM offers the potential for each participant to use, develop and achieve alternative functionings to his or her current capability set. They were offered help through mentoring, training, accreditation, soft skills development, CV and interview development and direct offers of employment. These all acted on the young people's personal CFs. The process helped to advance their agency, their education and skills and their personal interests. The new personal CFs engendered through the process included new practical skills and knowledge, better literacy and numeracy skills and qualifications. Although it was not a traditional diversion programme, OM afforded them the alternative agency not to participate in criminal or gang-related activities, and so to maintain freedom from the criminal justice system. OM therefore enhanced the personal CFs of the young people involved.

Social CFs: at the level of the social, for the young people one social CF has replaced another. Gang membership brings with it a range of social CFs, such as friendship, support and strong group bonding, but with poor health, well-being, social and economic prospects. By fostering new networks through participation, training and mentoring, and potential employers, and with the multiple individuals using or providing these services, OM offers the young people an alternative set of social CFs with better prospects in terms of health, well-being and life opportunities.

Structural CFs: OM is very limited in its capacity to challenge the historical and ongoing cultural, economic and social structures that create the high social deprivation of the area and curtail the opportunities available to its residents. Its work is primarily at the level of improving personal CFs for the participants and nurturing alternative social CFs. Although there have been improvements in the social environment, such as the 80 per cent reduction in crime associated with this programme in Gorbals, this impact is meso rather than macro. It does not address the socio-economic factors that structure disadvantages experienced by those who live in the community.

Impact on public services as social conversion factors

In OM, the public services collectively operate as a social CF seeking to change the functionings and capabilities of the young people. They do this both through collaborating with the young people to co-produce the programme and by collaborating together to design and deliver the tailored programme. This marks a change from the more traditional top-down, single-service, approach taken by public services, in which services are designed for rather than with citizens. All those working on this programme had to relinquish some power, both to each other and to the individuals they have worked with. The latter is a necessary step for the achievement of social justice (Bhaskar, 1993).

OM has also had wider impacts, both locally and city-wide. In Gorbals and Govan, two of Glasgow's most deprived neighbourhoods, community groups, statutory organizations and housing associations report that, as a direct result of working with OM, they are now more likely to work collaboratively and to co-produce services with local communities as they develop new initiatives (Brunner and Watson, 2016; Cullingworth, Brunner and Watson, 2018). For example, Govan Housing Association now actively seeks to employ local people in a community interest company, with all profits being ploughed back into the community – a move away from a marketized model of open competition for jobs and profits being dispersed out of local areas. New Gorbals Housing Association has taken a more preventative and collaborative approach to work with other public services to support local children at risk of criminal activity. Across Glasgow, the collaborative and co-productive principles of OM have been applied in other localities in which there is also a high prevalence of youth crime.

OM has helped to make local services more responsive to the needs of their communities, becoming more effective social CFs. By framing this public service reform project in terms of CFs, we have been able to explore how it has worked primarily on the personal and social levels of conversion. However, our analysis has been unable to demonstrate any significant impact at the structural level.

We now move on to examine our second case study, the Family Meal and Homework Club.

Family Meal and Homework Club

The Family Meal and Homework Club is based in a community centre in Glasgow's East End, another area of high social deprivation. It operates for one evening a week during term time and engages with parents and their children of primary school age (four to 11 years) from two local schools. In the first hour of the club the children receive support with their homework from teachers, followed by 30 minutes of play time. While the children are doing their homework and playing, their parents/guardians have the opportunity to be involved in a cooking group facilitated by community workers, in which they co-produce a nutritious and affordable meal. At the end of the club the children, parents and staff come together and share the food. Like OM, the club was developed through collaboration by several public services, including the local authority, housing associations, health and the two local schools, all of which provide support at the club.

Any parent/guardian from the two schools can attend, it is voluntary and no payment or accreditation is required. The main aim of the club is to create a space that the adults and children can enjoy in and of itself, one that they would choose to attend. Beyond this entry-level aim are a range of second-tier endeavours. These include the improvement of learning skills by involved children; providing a nourishing free hot meal to families in poverty; cultivating parents' cooking and nutrition skills; offering opportunities to parents to gain formal qualifications; offering opportunities to discuss parenting; providing space in which people from different cultural backgrounds can get to know each other; and improving connections between parents, between parents and schools and across the two schools.

The FMHC is founded on the basis of enjoyment and 'wants', not simply the provision of needs. At root, it seeks to foster an enjoyable place to attend, trying to make homework fun rather than a chore, and collective rather than individual. The meal element emerged as the project evolved, through engagement with the parents. In 2015/16 approximately 22, predominantly female, parents/guardians attended each week, of various age ranges and national, religious and ethnic backgrounds. The club aims to eventually become parent-led, and the model is being spread to other areas of multiple deprivation in Glasgow.

Both adults and children greatly enjoyed attending the club. It gave parents/guardians a sense of belonging, a break from the mundane duties of day-to-day life, a chance to enjoy some time away from their children and an opportunity to communicate with the other parents. It brought together parents from diverse backgrounds who had had little previous contact, so addressing social barriers. Parents shared responsibilities at the club and gained confidence in communicating. They were more able to discuss educational concerns about their children, and discuss their own needs and concerns. It broke through communication barriers that had previously existed between parents and teachers. Parents described how, because of their involvement in the club, they felt able to take on new challenges, such as re-entering further education and participating more fully in community activities, such as lobbying for environmental improvements and joining the school Parents Council (McLaren, 2016).

As with OM, the FMHC involves public services collaborating to create a space for improving outcomes in an area of multiple deprivation, rather than focusing on narrower, service-defined goals. The FMHC concept recognizes that traditional public services models were not adequately supporting families, and that alternative ways of working were required.

From a capabilities perspective, the FMHC seeks to change the functionings of the parents and the children, widen their capabilities and improve educational, health and well-being outcomes. It is about helping parents realize their assets and make the most of their resources, converting them into functionings and capabilities. As with OM, it assumes that outcomes are emergent, processes ongoing and outputs relational, in an open system in which no trajectory is guaranteed.

In the next section we unpack the FMHC as a social CF to examine how the programme impacted on personal, social and structural CFs shaping outcomes for the involved citizens, followed by some reflections on impacts on the public services themselves.

Impact on participants

Personal CFs: the aim of the club was to provide participants with the opportunity to develop and improve individual skills and connections.

Parents gained skills in cooking and budgeting, built new social relationships, learnt about their children's education and how best to support them and co-produced and ate a nutritive meal. All these changed their personal CFs. The children were supported in their homework, in learning how to learn, and ate a nutritious meal.

Social CFs: by building social relationships and engendering community participation for adults and children, the FMHC has helped to establish a network and build a sense of community and belonging. It has helped to build relationships across and between different social communities. The club has opened up the opportunity for continued connections beyond the club. Parents and guardians have become more confident in their ability to talk with professionals and to take on roles and responsibilities in other social settings.

The club helps to build community capacity and gives the community the opportunity to act collectively as an agent. It is a space in which people can turn personal problems into public issues. People came together through the club and lobbied the local authority for improved services. The FMHC is acting to change collective functionings by participants, and the aggregated nature of this change is a social CF for all involved. These have impacted on the capabilities and functions of the community. Participants have become active citizens and are taking decisions through the community, and as a community. There is a real emphasis on community capacity building in the FMHC – something that was missing from OM.

Structural CFs: the economic, social and cultural environment exists outside the club. The power dynamics that have structured the families into living in an area of multiple deprivation continue to exist. However, by spending time with others in similar circumstances, and with committed public service workers, new types of community solidarity may be starting to emerge. The emergent community have already come together to challenge the way services are delivered in their community. Yet, despite the collective nature and wider potential of this approach, it is hard to evidence anything but clues to conversion at the level of the structural.

Impact on public services as social conversion factors

The FMHC has changed the way the schools engage with the community, coming out of school buildings to meet parents in a community space. By doing this, teachers should become more attuned to the wants and needs of both pupils and parents/guardians. Public services are collectively operating as a social CF, seeking to change the functionings and capabilities of involved parents and children and collaborating with parents in the process. This is a change from the more traditional top-down, single-service, approach in which public services are designed for rather than with citizens. Public services have relinquished some power, both to each other and to the individuals they have worked with, the latter being a necessary step for the achievement of social justice (Bhaskar, 1993).

One of the headteachers, as a direct result of this programme, became involved in the development of a wider place-based approach that sought to promote collaborative and co-productive working by public services in other areas of multiple deprivation in Glasgow. However, it is difficult to determine whether the club has changed the way services operate in Glasgow, driving public service reform, or if the FMHC is a product of changes in the way services are delivered in the city, reflecting public service reform principles. What we can say is that lessons learnt from the FMHC are influencing how homework clubs operate across areas of multiple disadvantage in the city; the approach taken is spreading.

Discussion

This chapter set out to explore whether the capabilities approach, and in particular conversion factors, can provide an effective means for analysing public service delivery. We have done this through secondary analysis of two case studies in Glasgow. We have been able to demonstrate how CFs can be operationalized to show how public service interventions work. By reconceptualizing public services as social CFs, we have been able to unpack their impacts at personal, social and structural levels.

By employing CFs as a framework, we have been able to generate a stratified or layered analysis. We have shown how public services operate as a social CF and the way they impact on individuals and communities. By disaggregating and differentiating their effects at personal, social and structural levels, we are not suggesting that these are distinct kinds of events; rather, they are distinct mechanisms (Bhaskar, 1975). Interventions such as these have effects at all levels, and all operate with a contingent dynamism; they are separable only by abstraction (Collier, 1998).

This was apparent in both the case studies. The interventions were aimed at different sub-populations: one was targeted with the other open to all, and the focus on outcomes was looser and less instrumental in the FMHC than in OM. The intensity of the programmes was also different and each held different expectations with regard to participation. However, they did share some characteristics. Each was focused on populations in areas of multiple deprivation and worked with groups who are disadvantaged. They were founded on principles of collaboration and co-production, working with rather than on, or for, citizens. They sought to support people to do and be things in life that are important to them, taking account of their assets, agency and heterogeneity, thus cultivating capabilities. Dean et al. (2005) argue that, when evaluating programmes aimed at people with complex lives, the CA makes it possible to take account of individuals and the wider context of their lives. We would argue that our examples demonstrate that applying conversion factors provides an effective framework for this level of analysis.

CFs also enhance the potential for CA to be used in the planning of services. If it is taken at the outset that the aim of public services is to act as social CFs, working to expand the functionings and capabilities of individuals and/or groups by acting at personal, social or structural levels (or, indeed, all three), then that is what public services can plan for and, importantly, be evaluated against. Public service programmes that operate strongly on the personal, or individual, level but weakly on the structural level can be identified and the efficacy of their approach for tackling disadvantage can be determined in context.

We have also been able to highlight competing choices for citizens as a feature for capabilities analysis. People using services already have resources, and they also have competing CFs. For example, the participants in OM were not 'empty vessels' waiting for services to fill their lives. They had gang life as a social CF, competing with the OM programme, which offered an alternative social CF. Using CFs shows how public services should consider these trade-offs in order to devise services that are meaningful to how people actually live. As Wolff and de-Shalit (2013) argue, encouraging people to choose the 'right' functioning is key to any intervention. Using CFs, we have been able to examine the role of the intervention in guiding people to make that choice.

A major critique of the CA has been its perceived failure to account for change at the level of the structural (Venkatapuram, 2011; Sayer,

2012; Holmwood, 2013). We would argue that it is not that the CA does not allow this but, rather, it is the way that the CA has been applied. By 'bundling together', or collapsing, everything deemed 'social' into social CFs – from the very local to the highly macro, social structures, determinants and dominant cultural norms – CA analysis tends to lose sight of the less remediable, structural 'causes of the causes' that profoundly shape disadvantage. Distinguishing structural CFs from social CFs is a necessary analytical move to fill this lacuna. The distinction opens up conceptual space for empirical CA analyses to identify and so to 'challenge the reproduction of structural inequalities that cause capability deficits' (Sayer, 2012: 583).

However, there is a great deal of complexity here, and the operation of an intervention cannot easily be disaggregated into personal, social or structural impacts. They all operate at the same time, combining and reinforcing, or undermining, each other. CFs are contingent, their actions piecemeal and fragmented. Everything has the potential to act as a CF. However, part of the work of any capabilities analysis is to specify categorical limits. That notwithstanding, and recognizing that disaggregating to the personal, social or structural CFs can only ever be partial, the distinction provides a useful heuristic for CA analysis.

Also from our analysis, although Wolff and de-Shalit (2013) argue that many functionings can be capabilities, we would argue that functionings can also, in and of themselves, be conversion factors. Literacy, for example, enables reading, and this can in turn give an individual access to resources such as schools, libraries, and colleges, which in turn enable capabilities. The interplay of conversion factors, functionings and capabilities is dynamic. This dynamic, additive aspect has been demonstrated here. As participants became more confident in their own abilities and functionings, so they were able to employ those functionings as CFs to enable them to utilize other assets and resources, and thus further improve their capabilities and functionings. In OM, for example, the young people gained functionings in terms of employability and were able to use these skills to access jobs or further training. The parents in the school gained functionings in terms of their own perceived ability to participate in community activities, and this turn further enhanced their capability set.

Conversion factors, at the personal and social level, can, like functionings, be observed and their workings analysed. How they work, and who they work for, are key, and it is here that an approach that can distinguish between the structural and social is a necessary next step. Public services of the types analysed here have been criticized for their failure to challenge the macro-level structures that impact on individuals and communities and to combat the social determinants of health (Ennis and West, 2013; Friedli, 2012, 2013). Policies that attempt to tackle these issues at the scale of the local have also been claimed to be insufficient to address underlying causes (Marmot, 2010). There is, clearly, much evidence to support these claims; achieving change at the level of the structural is very difficult, as we show above. By breaking down the services into their effects at the personal, social and structural levels, we have been able to show not just how and where they are operating but also the potential pathways for them to effect change beyond the individual level. These debates reinforce arguments that drawing further on sociology would help to fully engage with these issues (Holmwood, 2013; Hvinden and Halvorsen, 2017).

Conclusion: the theory and practice of conversion factors

We have demonstrated how the concepts that underpin conversion factors can be employed as an analytical framework to conceptualize, drive and evaluate public services and the way they work as social CFs. We have shown that operationalizing CFs can both widen and focus the analytical lens, unpacking how real opportunities and substantive freedoms – or the capabilities and functionings – of individuals and communities can be enhanced or constrained by the choices made and work done by public services. The conceptual delineation we have made enables a focus on their work at personal, social and structural levels. Conversion factors are part of both process and outcome, just as Sen (1999) conceptualizes capabilities as both process and outcome in the wider CA literature. The analysis of empirical examples of public services using CFs has enabled the identification of the 'social institutions, processes and values' that Venkatapuram (2011: 152) argues are required to secure social justice for particular communities and groups. The analysis has also explicitly connected structures and agency, reinforcing the potential for stronger dialogue between the capabilities approach and sociology (Hvinden and Halvorsen, 2017).

Conversion factors offer a paradox: although they 'matter most to social justice' (Nussbaum, 2006: 75) they are among the least-explored concepts in the capabilities lexicon. Recently, Chiappero, Salardi and

Scervini (2018) and Krishnakumar and Nogales (2018) have worked on these, albeit from an econometric perspective. Hvinden and Halvorsen (2017) have taken a more sociological approach, and in this chapter we have built on and added to their work. This chapter has demonstrated why these conceptual advances are necessary, and how CFs can be empirically useful. It has demonstrated that, when public services are conceptualized using CFs, clarity of evidence about the role of those services and the way they work can emerge. It also, simultaneously, allows analysis of their impacts at personal, social and structural levels.

Using case studies, we have been able to excavate the processes of this under-explored CA concept to understand 'what makes' the conversion, how and for whom. Our methodology has allowed an evaluation to be made of whether changes engendered by public services as social CFs open up or constrain individual and collective functionings and capabilities. The incorporation of sociological reasoning into this public policy context has also allowed structural features to be made explicit, and so become more tangible within a capabilities analysis.

References

Appleby, J. (2013) *Spending on Health and Social Care over the Next 50 Years: Why Think Long Term?* London: King's Fund.

Bhaskar, R. (1975) *A Realist Theory of Science*. London: Verso.

(1993) *Dialectic: The Pulse of Freedom*. London: Verso.

Brownlee, I. (1998) New Labour – new penology? Punitive rhetoric and the limits of managerialism in criminal justice policy. *Journal of Law and Society*, 25 (3): 313–35.

Brunner, R. and Watson, N. (2016) Operation Modulus: putting Christie into practice in Gorbals, working paper. Glasgow: What Works Scotland.

Chiappero, E., Salardi, P., and Scervini, F. (2018) From resources to functioning: rethinking and measuring conversion rates. In *New Frontiers of the Capability Approach*, Comim, F., Fennell, S., and Anand, P. B. (eds.): 232–45. Cambridge: Cambridge University Press.

Christie Commission (2011) *Report of the Commission on the Future Delivery of Public Services*. Edinburgh: Scottish government.

Clark, D. A. (2005) The capability approach: its development, critiques and recent advances, Global Poverty Research Group Working Paper 32. Swindon: Economic and Social Research Council.

Collier, A. (1998) Stratified explanation and Marx's conception of history. In *Critical Realism: Essential Readings*, Archer, M. (ed.): 258–81. London: Routledge.

Cullingworth, J., Brunner, R., and Watson, N. (2018) The Operation Modulus approach: further lessons for public service reform, working paper. Glasgow: What Works Scotland.

Dean, H., Bonvin, J.-M., Vielle, P., and Farvaque, N. (2005) Developing capabilities and rights in welfare-to-work policies. *European Societies*, 7 (1): 3–26.

Deneulin, S., Nebel, M., and Sagovsky, N. (2006) *Transforming Unjust Structures: The Capability Approach*. Dordrecht: Springer.

Drèze, J., and Sen, A. K. (2002) *India: Development and Participation*. Oxford: Oxford University Press.

Ennis, G., and West, D. (2013) Community development and umbrella bodies: networking for neighbourhood change. *British Journal of Social Work*, 44 (6): 1582–601.

Friedli, L. (2012) CS06-03 – Mental health, resilience and inequalities: a social determinants perspective. *European Psychiatry*, 27 (1): DOI 10.1016/S0924-9338(12)74077-4.

(2013) 'What we've tried, hasn't worked': the politics of assets based public health. *Critical Public Health*, 23 (2): 131–45.

Fung, A. (2013) Infotopia: unleashing the democratic power of transparency. *Politics & Society*, 41 (2): 183–212.

Hill, M. (2003) Development as empowerment. *Feminist Economics*, 9 (2/3): 117–35.

Holmwood, J. (2013) Public reasoning without sociology: Amartya Sen's theory of justice. *Sociology*, 47 (6): 1171–86.

Huxham, C., Vangen, S., Huxham, C., and Eden, C. (2000) The challenge of collaborative governance. *Public Management: An International Journal of Research and Theory*, 2 (3): 337–58.

Hvinden, B., and Halvorsen, R. (2017) Mediating agency and structure in sociology: what role for conversion factors? *Critical Sociology*, 44 (6): 1–17.

Independent Budget Review Panel (2010) *Report of the Independent Budget Review Panel*. Edinburgh: Independent Budget Review Panel.

Krishnakumar, J., and Nogales, R. (2018) Demystifying the use of simultaneous equation models for operationalising the capability approach. In *New Frontiers of the Capability Approach*, Comim, F., Fennell, S., and Anand, P. B. (eds.): 246–70. Cambridge: Cambridge University Press.

Kuklys, W. (2005) *Amartya Sen's Capability Approach: Theoretical Insights and Empirical Applications*. Dordrecht: Springer.

Le Grand, J. (2007) *The Other Invisible Hand: Delivering Public Services through Choice and Competition*. Princeton, NJ: Princeton University Press.

Lupton, R., Hills, J., Stewart, K., and Vizard, P. (2013) Labour's social policy record: policy, spending and outcomes 1997–2010, Social Policy in Cold Climate Research Report 1. London: Centre for Analysis of Social Exclusion, London School of Economics.

McLaren, I. (2016) Thriving Places' Family Meal and Homework Club: parents' experiences of social capital, MSc dissertation. Glasgow: University of Glasgow.

Marmot, M. (2010) *Fair Society, Healthy Lives: The Marmot Review*. London: Institute of Health Equity, University College London.

Marmot, M., and Wilkinson, R. (1999) *Social Determinants of Health*. Oxford: Oxford University Press.

Meijer, A. (2011) Networked coproduction of public services in virtual communities: from a government-centric to a community approach to public service support. *Public Administration Review*, 71 (4): 598–607.

Nalbandian, J. (2008) Predicting the future: why citizen engagement no longer is optional. *Public Management*, 90 (11): 35–7.

Newman, J. (2001) *Modernising Governance: New Labour Policy and Society*. London: Sage.

Newman, J., Barnes, M., Sullivan, H., and Knops, A. (2004) Public participation and collaborative governance. *Journal of Social Policy*, 33 (2): 203–23.

Nussbaum, M. C. (2006) *Frontiers of Justice: Disability, Nationality, Species Membership*. Cambridge, MA: Belknap Press.

Orton, M. (2011) Flourishing lives: the capabilities approach as a framework for new thinking about employment, work and welfare in the 21st century. *Work, Employment and Society*, 25 (2): 352–60.

Rittell, H., and Webber, M. (1973) Dilemmas in a general theory of planning. *Policy Sciences*, 4 (2): 155–69.

Robeyns, I. (2003) Sen's capability approach and gender inequality: selecting relevant capabilities. *Feminist Economics*, 9 (2/3): 61–92.

(2005) The capability approach: a theoretical survey. *Journal of Human Development*, 6 (1): 93–114.

(2017) *Wellbeing, Freedom and Social Justice: The Capability Approach Re-Examined*. Cambridge: Open Book Publishers.

Sayer, A. (2011) *Why Things Matter to People: Social Science, Values and Ethical Life*. Cambridge: Cambridge University Press.

(2012) Capabilities, contributive injustice and unequal divisions of labour. *Journal of Human Development and Capabilities*, 13 (4): 580–96.

Sen, A. K. (1992) *Inequality Reexamined*. Oxford: Oxford University Press.

(1999) *Development as Freedom*. Oxford: Oxford University Press.

(2009) *The Idea of Justice*. London: Penguin.

Sørensen, E., and Torfing, J. (2016) Metagoverning collaborative innovation in governance networks. *American Review of Public Administration*, 47 (7): 826–39.

Venkatapuram, S. (2011) *Health Justice*. Cambridge: Polity Press.

Wolff, J., and de-Shalit, A. (2007) *Disadvantage*. Oxford: Oxford University Press.

   (2013) On fertile functionings: a response to Martha Nussbaum. *Journal of Human Development and Capabilities*, 14 (1): 161–5.

World Bank (2003) *World Development Report 2004: Making Services Work for Poor People*. Washington, DC: World Bank.

Zeemering, E. S. (2008) Governing interlocal cooperation: city council interests and the implications for public management. *Public Administration Review*, 68 (4): 731–41.

Index

b| in the United States
by| r & Taylor Publisher Services